Rediscovering the American Midwest

Series Editors: Jon K. Lauck and Patricia Oman

The Midwestern Moment The Forgotten World of Early Twentieth-Century Midwestern Regionalism, 1880–1940	Jon K. Lauck, ed.
A Scattering Time How Modernism Met Midwestern Culture	Sara Kosiba, ed.
Pieces of the Heartland Representing Midwestern Places	Andy Oler, ed.
The Making of the Midwest The Formation of Midwestern Identity, 1787–1900	Jon K. Lauck, ed.

The Making of the Midwest

The Making of the Midwest

Essays on the Formation of Midwestern Identity, 1787–1900

Edited by
Jon K. Lauck

Hastings College Press | Hastings, Nebraska

© 2020 by Hastings College Press

All rights reserved. No part of this book may be used or reproduced in any manner whatsoever without permission from the publisher, except in the case of brief quotations embodied in critical articles and reviews.

Copy Editors
Bruce Batterson
Patricia Oman
Eric Tucker

Editorial Assistants
Lillian Nelms
Kyler Samples
Jora Jackson-Brown

Book Design
Patricia Oman

Paperback   ISBN-13: 978-1-942885-75-7

Hardback   ISBN-13: 978-1-942885-76-4

For David L. Knudson

Litterateur
Historian
Bibliophile
Midwesterner

Contents

Jon K. Lauck	Introduction Making an American Region	xiii
Terry A. Barnhart	An Emerging Voice The Origins of Regional Identity and Mission in the Old Northwest	1
Jason S. Lantzer	Forging God's Country The Northwest Territorial Ordinance, the Second Great Awakening, and the Midwestern Vision for America	17
Marcia Noe	The Innocent Midwest and the New Midwestern Pastoral	37
Wayne Duerkes	Travel Literature and Midwestern Identity The Case of Illinois	53
Michael J. Sherfy	Place-Making in the Midwest Pioneer Memoirs in Early Illinois History	67
Barton E. Price	The Protestant Imagination and the Making of the Midwest as America's Heartland	85
Kenyon Gradert	Walt Whitman's Heartland Romance	101
Nicole Etcheson	The Making of Midwesterners The Fletcher Family in Indiana	115
A. James Fuller	A Copperhead Construction The Northwestern Confederacy and the Making of the Midwest during the War of the Rebellion	129

Contents

Edward O. Frantz	When the Midwest Controlled the Presidency, 1860–1930	143
Gregory S. Rose	On the Path Toward National Eminence Economic Development in the Old Northwest, 1850–1860	157
Jacob K. Friefeld	Homesteading and the Making of the Midwest	183
Sara Egge	The Emergence of Midwestern Political Culture in Northwest Iowa	199
Lisa Payne Ossian	The "I Too" Temperance Movement A Reevaluation of Midwestern Women's Political Action at the Turn of the Last Century	215
C.A. Norling	"To improve the musical taste, capacity and voices of our people" The Rise of Public Art-Music Interests Amidst the Rise and Fall of the Iowa State Normal Academy of Music, 1867–1871	231
Christa Adams	Creating a Site of Midwestern Cosmopolitanism Heterotopia, East Asian Art, and the Cleveland Museum of Art, 1914–1916	249
Joshua Jeffers	Colonizing the Indigenous Past Settler-Colonial Place Making and the Ancient Landscape of the Early Midwest, 1775–1840	265
Michael Leonard Cox	Isaac Walker and the Complexities of Midwestern Native American Identity	289

Eric Michael Rhodes	Midwestern "Mobocracy" The Emergence of Labor Politics and Racial Exclusion in Cincinnati and the Lower Old Northwest, 1829–1836	305
Brie Swenson Arnold	African American Migration to Cedar Rapids, Iowa, and the Making of the Midwest, 1860–1900	331
David C. Miller	"Blood and Iron" and the Formation of German American Identity in the Midwest Recollections of a Union Veteran	349
Jason Stacy	Popucrats Producerist Populism and the Formation of Midwestern Political Identity in the 1890s	379
	Contributors	395

Jon K. Lauck | Introduction

Making an
American Region

During the American colonial period, what would become the Midwest was the "backcountry," or the area behind the coastal population centers.[1] It was rural and rough, the sort of place that fueled populist resistance to the federal taxation of whiskey.[2] At the time of the Revolution, it was the West, often undifferentiated between north and south and largely associated with Kentucky. In the early years of the republic, however, the regional differentiation deepened and grew until the latter half of the nineteenth century, when the Midwest emerged as a fully formed region.[3] The Midwestern Moment had arrived.[4] It is the burden of the essays in this book to help explain this process of region-making.

The critical first step to the development of the Midwest was the passage of the Northwest Ordinance in 1787 by the Continental Congress. This legislation shaped the settlement of and institution building in the early Midwest and set the pattern for the broader region. The Ordinance ensured democratic governments in the Midwest, the creation of independent states instead of the emergence of colonial holdings by the original thirteen states, the entrenchment of civil rights, and the planting of schools, and, most importantly, it banned slavery, putting the region on a widely divergent track from the original southern states and their interior satellites such as Alabama and Mississippi. Ohio-bound Reverend Manasseh Cutler wrote to his fellow New Englander Nathan Dane in March 1787 and observed that northern settlers "are undoubtedly preferable to those from the southern states. They [Northerners] will be men of more robust constitutions, inured to labor, and free from the habits of idleness."[5] Most of these early northern settlers in the Midwest became small-scale yeoman farmers, just as Jefferson's Ordinance intended, and a distinctive form of "Midwestern pastoral" resulted.[6] Even Walt Whitman joined the chorus of boosters of midwestern prosperity. Word spread, letters from the Midwest were sent forth, memoirs of early life in the region circulated, and more and more prospective settlers heard the news and decided to move to the Midwest.

What emerged in the Midwest was a culture dense in Christianity, civic commitments, and attention to the arts. The Ordinance guaranteed the free exercise of religion in the Midwest and Christian settlers went to work, vigorously building thousands of churches and a hundred denominational colleges.[7] Early Protestants in the region "imagined that the Mississippi Valley was a future center of Christendom."[8] Midwesterners also devoted themselves to civic life, including the promotion of musical training for public enjoyment, the creation of midwestern symphonies, and the building of art museums that housed collections from around the globe to promote the appreciation of the fine arts.[9] The collective power of the civic groups active in the Midwest was tapped by women seeking the vote and the protection and promotion of a humane social order free from alcohol and its deleterious effects on family life.

During the Civil War era midwestern regional consciousness deepened. In the run-up to the war, during the crisis years, most Midwesterners were staunchly pro-Union. This included the prominent Yankee families who moved to the Midwest such as the Fletchers of Vermont who settled in Indiana. As the most southern of the midwestern states, or the state that had the highest number of southern migrants in its southern regions down along the Ohio river, Indiana saw some sharp civic conflicts. But the overall effect of the war was to intensify regional inclinations and solidify midwestern loyalties to their region and the Union.[10] Many midwestern soldiers were appalled by what they saw in the South.[11] When the Midwest began a pattern of winning the presidency in the decades after the war these Union veterans in the Midwest enthusiastically waved the bloody shirt. They were proud that their region supplied the men who won the war and the region's booming manufacturing sector provided the munitions that preserved the Union. The predominance of midwestern Republicans in Congress during the war and the absence of Southerners also allowed the midwestern-born GOP to pass the Homestead Act, which guided the settlement of the final agricultural territories of the Midwest.

Not everyone thrived in the Midwest, of course. Native Americans endured wars, violence, and dislocation and saw their way of life fade from prominence. Settlers often saw the earliest occupants of the region as ancient civilizations that had long passed and not the more recently present Native Americans. Some Native Americans such as the Wyandot Isaac Walker became tightly integrated into the dominant society. While African Americans eagerly moved into the region from the South and desperately wanted to escape slavery, they also encountered resistance in cities such as Cincinnati. In an indication of regional variation within the Midwest, African Americans fared much better in Cedar Rapids, Iowa, but they still encountered difficulties. Some immigrant groups such as the Germans, who became a large presence in the Midwest and sought to preserve much of their culture, were treated with much derision during the run-up to World War I but ultimately become highly integrated into midwestern life. Some emerging leaders of the American left also found themselves alienated from the market-oriented and Christian-dominated society.

All of these angles and perspectives on the emergence of the Midwest as a region are explored in this volume. Regional identities, Terry A. Barnhart explains, emerge from various sources. They coalesce incrementally, have distinct phases of development, and are subject to change over time. But at their most basic level regional identities arise from the aspirations, visions, and self-perceptions of those who create and monopolize the discourses about the localities and regions in which they occur. Barnhart shows how the process of identity formation originated in the first public addresses pertaining to the organization and settlement of the Old Northwest—the first national territory of the United States. It was an incomplete narrative—the story of the winners written by the winners—but one that long held an important place within the master narrative of region and nation. The Ohio Company settlers who founded what is today Marietta, Ohio, saw themselves as republican colonizers, as indeed they were, and the trusted agents of the federal government. The Ohio Company associates wedded their own self-interests as land speculators in a joint stock company to the desire of the federal government to promote the orderly settlement of the territory and realize much needed land-sale revenues from private interests like the Ohio Company. Those who settled at the Muskingum River characterized the western movement of which they were a self-conscious and significant part as the fulfillment of the American

Revolution—republicanism moving west. While Barnhart's essay is not compensatory history per se, it does aim at a wider vision than that found in the triumphalist Whig histories of the antebellum era, especially regarding the dispossession of Native American communities. The process of regional identity formation and an early sense of national mission in the region created an origin myth concerning the allegedly peaceful and humane possession of the land, the earliest expressions of which date to the nationalist rhetoric of its first spokespersons during the 1780s.

The creation of the Midwest as a region, explains Jason Lantzer, owes much to the Northwest Territorial Ordinance, the founding charter of the Midwest. The fusion of antislavery with religious liberty in that document, and the adherence to its principles by the states that emerged from the territory, resulted in a place radically different from the Northeast and South. Sure of their own exceptionalism and confident that they were the true heirs of the Founders, Midwesterners during the Civil War felt empowered to transform the nation in their image.

In keeping with Barnhart and Lantzer and the midwestern mission they outline, Marcia Noe argues that midwestern innocence has, over time, become a defining characteristic of the region. She locates the origin of this notion in the democratic and Christian ideologies that undergird our national culture and discusses four early American novels that construct the Midwest as an Edenic region that offers a fresh start for a virtuous and harmonious life to characters from locales constructed as decadent and superficial: the eastern seaboard, the South, and Europe.

Some early Midwesterners wrote down what they saw and their travel narratives played an important role in establishing a midwestern identity, as Wayne Duerkes explains. In the first thirty years after achieving statehood in 1818, for example, Illinois witnessed a surge of over 400 written accounts telling of emigration and settlement in the new frontier state. This body of work, meant to inform potential migrants of the challenges and opportunities in the West, displayed a continuity in its format and descriptiveness, despite the broad diversity of its contributors. The individual author's textual styles gave life to a genre of books that helped draw people of particular characteristics westward. Through the narratives, these like-minded migrants developed shared expectations of frontier Illinois. As a result of relocation and settlement, in a relatively short window of time, the entire shared experience of these newcomers contributed to regional identity that separated them from their counterparts back east.

The early Illinois settlers who wrote down what they saw when they first encountered the Midwest sometimes wrote memoirs later in life. These pioneer-authors created a set of tropes that allowed them a sense of primacy and placed them on a higher social and historical level than more recent arrivals, as Michael J. Sherfy explains in his chapter. American settlers of their generation had arrived in a country fraught with difficulties—both natural and man-made—and they had overcome them. Their shared experiences had instilled in them a particular identity and sense of values, but this identity—like their claims to the land and its history—was jeopardized by the rapid influx of migrants who flooded the region after the mid-1830s. From more long-established states in the East and from Europe, these newcomers transformed the region's culture and seemed little interested in those who had preceded them. The early settlers found themselves displaced—both culturally and physically—by the generation that built the Midwest as we think of it today. A few reacted by putting their lives on paper and preserved in words a world that was rapidly vanishing from the landscape and from living memory. They described a "wilderness" undisturbed by railroad or plow and nostalgically recounted anecdotes of men and women—both Native and white—who appear more vital and vibrant than the farmers and businessmen who came later. By the time their works were published, few traces remained on the landscape of the not-yet-midwestern region that these memoirists described. But, in their pages, that vanished history lived on.

Whether they arrived early or late, most settlers brought with them Christian beliefs. Barton E. Price's analysis of the religious rhetoric about the trans-Appalachian west explores the idea of the Midwest as the American heartland in the early decades of the nineteenth century. Throughout the nineteenth century, the Midwest emerged in the American consciousness as the center of the American physical and moral landscape. Missionaries and boosters conceived of the Midwest as the center of an American heartland and stressed that missionary endeavors were vital to preserving the moral character of the young nation. At the core of that conception were the religious and moral characteristics of the Midwest. These Protestant missionaries saw the region as at the heart of the country, but were concerned about the presence of Catholics and later Mormons in the region. Yet Mormons especially adapted the same notion of the importance of the Midwest and expanded it to place the region at the heart of a cosmic plan. Following the Civil War, Protestant groups within the region worked to attenuate the sectional tensions wrought by the middle decades of that century. In the process, they recast the heartland as a region that encompassed all regions by evincing none.

The grand imaginings of Price's settlers about the emerging Midwest would have resonated with Walt Whitman. Kenyon Gradert explores how Whitman laid the groundwork for the Heartland as a myth, idea, and feeling in poetry and prose that praised what he called America's "dominion-heart," a fecund prairie interior centered on the Mississippi Valley where Whitman imaginatively planted his desires for the nation. Enraptured by its growing agricultural, industrial, and political power, Whitman chronicled his hopes that the American interior would likewise produce an autocthonous national culture that would ease postbellum tensions and bind the country around this stable cultural core.

Overcoming the Civil War divisions that concerned Whitman and Price's Christian settlers was no small matter given the tensions between midwestern abolitionists and Unionists on the one hand and midwestern settlers from southern states who did not think slavery worth fighting over on the other. In the former camp was the Fletcher family of Indiana, the subject of Nicole Etcheson's chapter. Calvin Fletcher left Vermont as a poor youth and became one of the early settlers of Indianapolis, prospering as a lawyer and businessman. He and his Ohio-born wife, Sarah, raised a large family and maintained connections with family in New England and even a slave-owning brother in Virginia. The Fletcher children went east for schooling and to New England and Virginia to visit family. The story of the Fletcher family in Indiana from the 1820s through the Civil War is a story of shifting regional identities. The Fletchers retained a sense of themselves as New Englanders and therefore different, and often superior, in certain ways from their neighbors, but they increasingly accommodated themselves to the southern-influenced society in which they lived although they rejected the proslavery culture of the South itself. The Fletchers' transformation into Midwesterners is a microcosm of the region's formation of midwestern identity out of the diverse migrant groups that populated the Midwest.

In his contribution, A. James Fuller also connects midwestern regionalism to the Civil War. He argues that the idea of the Midwest as a separate regional identity emerged during the war as part of a plan concocted by the Copperheads, who opposed the war and resisted what they perceived to be the tyranny of the Republicans led by Abraham Lincoln. In Ohio, Indiana, and Illinois Democrats' opposition to the war led them to entertain disloyal ideas like withdrawing from the Union and creating their own Northwestern Confederacy. Men like Clement L. Vallandigham of Ohio, Thomas Hendricks and Daniel Voorhees of Indiana, and William Richardson of Illinois were alarmed by the expanding power of the national government. They feared tyranny, opposed conscription, hated higher taxes, and railed against emancipation. Hoping to capitalize on issues like taxes and the draft and playing to racism, they tried to defeat the Republicans in the Midwest politically. They also appealed to Copperheads who joined secret societies and planned to carry out acts of sabotage against the Union and, possibly, to overthrow their state governments. The political Copperheads offered the idea of what to do next: They would secede from the Union and create a Northwestern Confederacy made up of the states of Ohio, Indiana, Illinois, and maybe other parts of the old Northwest Territory. Their calls for a Northwestern Confederacy were made in opposition to both the South and the East. They used geographic, cultural, and economic arguments in support of their plan and, in so doing, constructed an idea of the region we now know as the Midwest.

The Copperheads failed, however, and the midwestern Republican Party held sway for many more decades. In his chapter, Edward O. Frantz analyzes the post–Civil War era, in which Republican Midwesterners had a virtual lock on the presidency. Although observers have made casual observations about the number of Midwesterners who occupied the presidency, few have ventured to describe how that came to be and what that says about midwestern identity during the nineteenth century. This chapter corrects this oversight by examining the importance of Midwesterners to the presidency between 1860 and 1930. Exploring functional as well as cultural explanations for the proliferation of midwestern Republican presidents, Frantz argues that as midwestern identity solidified during the late nineteenth century and early twentieth centuries, many of its residents became particularly preoccupied with their region's distinctiveness. At a time of national transition between agrarian and industrial, rural and urban, it is only fitting that the region that contained a balance of those elements became the center of American political life.

The impact of the Civil War on politics and regional identity generally was due, in part, to the growing economic strength of the Midwest. As Gregory S. Rose explains, the rise of the Old Northwest into a position of agricultural and industrial leadership within the United States was well underway by the time of the Civil War. That this was the case fails to align with the common perception that the Old Northwest's economic development did not occur until the last decades of the nineteenth century. Yet, despite the fact that settlement of the region by non–Native Americans began just over half a century previously, various indicators of development by 1860 clearly place the Old Northwest as the nation's third most economically advanced region, behind only the Middle Atlantic States and New England. The older South Atlantic and the contemporaneously settled Old Southwest regions were far behind in their economic development. The Old Northwest led the nation in corn, wheat, and livestock production and was a major or leading producer of flour, corn meal, wine, and distilled spirits. Its transportation and communication infrastructure rivaled that of any other region. Its population was large, rapidly growing, ethnically diverse, and urbanizing. The Midwest dominated the manufacture of agricultural implements and ranked third in overall manufacturing statistics. The base upon which the Old Northwest's economic development expanded after the Civil War was firmly in place by 1860.

The economic impact of the Civil War and the influence of the Midwest can also be seen in the Homestead Act, as Jacob K. Friefeld explains. The Homestead Act of 1862, passage of which was made possible by the war-time absence of southern Congressmen and the dominance of Congressional Republicans, created two midwestern settlement patterns. Euro-Americans settled the Old Midwest mostly through cash sales, but settlers claimed land in the New Midwest of

Kansas, Nebraska, and the Dakotas largely through the Homestead Act. The race and gender-neutral nature of the Homestead Act caused this settlement to include more women and Black landowners. While encouraging different settlement patterns, the Homestead Act also encouraged settlers from the Old Midwest to claim free land and replicate midwestern identity in these new midwestern states. The Homestead Act helped consolidate the Midwest from Ohio in the East to Kansas, Nebraska, and the Dakotas in the West.

The western sections of the Midwest, which were more heavily influenced by the homestead legislation, are examined by Sara Egge and Lisa Payne Ossian in their chapters on midwestern political and social movements. Egge explains how a distinct political culture developed in the late-nineteenth-century Midwest as the region forged its identity. Created out of the process of community-building, this political culture appeared as native-born Yankees and foreign-born individuals settled in scattered groups. At the heart of this settlement was civic responsibility, or a commitment to community uplift, which drove the construction of both infrastructure and social networks among residents. While Yankees most often took leadership roles in local governance, making most of the practical decisions like building roads, founding schools, and collecting taxes, immigrants also cared deeply about establishing institutions like churches and parochial schools to preserve specific ethnic or cultural values. Ethnicity, gender, and religion forged a distinctive nineteenth-century midwestern political culture that flourished among a mosaic of organizations and public institutions. Stories in local newspapers reveal this vibrant political culture, one in which politics and social ties were often indistinguishable. Finally, this community-building impulse also promoted gender inclusivity and women often played a highly visible and prominent role in forging midwestern political culture.

The role of women, Ossian explains, was particularly prominent in the temperance movement. Although the temperance movement at the turn of the last century has been typically viewed as a failed moralistic experiment, it must be remembered that midwestern women created the largest women's political movement and passed two Constitutional amendments aimed at increasing women's political representation and decreasing men's domestic violence. Midwestern women, in numbers too big to ignore, publicly announced accounts of male violence and neglect due to alcohol as they formed what Ossian calls the original "I Too" movement of the last century.

The focus on civic affairs and community uplift that Egge and Ossian emphasize was manifest in community activities and institution-building, as C.A. Norling and Christa Adams explain. While reconstructing the story of the five seasons of the Iowa State Normal Academy of Music in Iowa City, Norling's chapter chronicles a postbellum upsurge in the state's public musical interests and, in doing so, highlights the growing density of midwestern civic culture. Following the end of the Civil War, increased attention to music training resulted in the unprecedented success of local singing-school conventions and subsequently incited demand for a permanent music school in Iowa City. The Iowa State Music Academy, incorporated in 1866 by a committee of local musicians and community leaders, sought to provide year-round musical training to Iowa residents through a connection with the University of Iowa's teacher-training program and generous, statewide scholarship offerings. What is more, the academy's well-attended public concerts, which featured large European choral works such as Mendelssohn's "Elijah" and Haydn's "The Creation," were covered widely in the local press, who touted them as harbingers of Iowa's potential cultural achievements. Though its operations were cut short by curricular restructuring within the university, the academy serves as a case study for the establishment of public discourse surrounding civic musical organization and the region's burgeoning cultural self-awareness.

In her chapter Christa Adams discusses the early twentieth-century phenomenon of midwestern urban art museum construction through an examination of the collecting practices and methods of display developed by staff at the Cleveland Museum of Art in its formative period (1914–1916). The museum's first director, Frederic Allen Whiting, strove to promote the development of both edification and cultural refinement amongst visitors, who largely hailed from the city's working classes. To realize these goals, he endeavored to construct a museum collection composed of finely crafted art objects and antiquities from global points of origin. These objects would, in Whiting's mind, both educate and inspire members of Cleveland's working classes to embrace new designs and methods of production, expanding their collective "aesthetic consciousness."[12] Cleveland's museum moment occurred in tandem with the development and expansion of similarly sized entities in cities like Toledo, Indianapolis, Dayton, Youngstown, and Detroit, reflecting a broader midwestern movement toward the promotion of public education and practical inspiration via the medium of institutions like art museums. An analysis of the methods of acquisition and display developed by staff at the Cleveland Museum of Art during its inaugural period functions as an excellent lens for evaluating comparable practices enacted by museum employees in other similarly sized midwestern art museums in the early twentieth century.

The building of a new civic order in the emerging Midwest, it must be emphasized, came after earlier indigenous populations had been pushed aside and sometimes forgotten or misremembered. In his chapter, for example, Joshua Jeffers examines how early Midwesterners explained the existence of the extensive mound complexes that blanket the region. For many, investigating and interpreting these earthen remnants offered a way to connect with the land and its history, and it directly shaped the ideological development of American settler colonialism. In their efforts to explain the existence of this earthen architecture, Euro-American antiquarians and intellectuals produced an extensive literature that included everything from what might be called proto-archaeological analysis to works of poetry, fiction, and even political satire. Given their assumptions about Native American societies and the explanations of human history offered by Christianity, these efforts tell us almost nothing about pre-Columbian cultures in North America or the variety of North American societies that constructed earthen architecture, but it does offer compelling insight into the ways in which Americans generally and early Midwesterners in particular, intellectually transformed a recently conquered, supposedly wilderness landscape into a settler homeland. Living among, collecting and displaying, and theorizing about the Mounds and the "Moundbuilders" offered early Midwesterners a way to connect with the physical landscape, dissociate Native peoples from the history of the land, and intellectually colonize the past. This literature also lent a distinctiveness to the region and contributed to the development of a national narrative that many Americans found redeeming and satisfying. Through these "mythstories" Americans situated themselves as redeemers of an ancient landscape and the Midwest became the region where this ancient heritage resided. Thus the Midwest came to represent the heart of the new nation, where its glorious, ancient past met its providential future.

The complexity of Native American and midwestern identity is brought to life by Michael Leonard Cox in his chapter about the life of a Wyandot man at a transitional point in his peoples' history and the history of the early nineteenth-century Midwest. Isaac Walker rose to prominence among the Ohio Wyandots in the years after the War of 1812, a time of intensive American settlement and Native American marginalization in the Midwest. Walker and his family exemplify the changing economic lives and "racial" identities of some mixed ancestry Wyandots in the Midwest in the years before Indian Removal. Walker's personal life and economic livelihood existed both within and without the Wyandot community. When Walker died in the late 1820s, his story and identity took on new levels of meaning as his widow (a white woman) married a white settler. While the Wyandot Nation and the Walker family worked to protect Isaac's property for his young son, his widow's husband engaged in a lengthy process to press his rights to Walker's (Wyandot) land. Eventually, the Ohio State Supreme Court ruled on the case, in the process partially defining his complicated racial/ethnic identity. Isaac Walker's story serves as a case study of identity formation and expression at a liminal moment in American history. While stories of multicultural individuals such as Walker exist in other regions, the unique confluence of peoples, cultures, and historical moments that make up the early nineteenth-century Midwest provided the milieu to produce a story like Walker's at the very moment of American midwestern historical formation.

Similar to Walker and the Wyandots, African Americans faced challenges in the emerging Midwest. In his chapter, Eric Michael Rhodes explains how a leveling respect for humble hard work emerged in the Midwest during the early nineteenth-century and how a "Western" spirit of egalitarianism and free labor prevailed. By examining the growth of Cincinnati, however, Rhodes explains how the Midwest has also exhibited exclusionary tendencies. His chapter details the ways in which two cultural proclivities—egalitarianism and exclusion—changed and remained the same after some of the first urban race riots in the United

States. It also considers how they shaped midwestern culture for years to come.

In her chapter, Brie Swenson Arnold expands the story of the African American Midwest beyond the early nineteenth century and far from the Ohio River borderland of Cincinnati. Between the Civil War and the end of the nineteenth century, she explains, thousands of African Americans left the South and ventured to the Midwest, making it the region to which most postwar black migrants relocated. Given antebellum restrictions on black settlement, the late nineteenth-century migration was a significant development for the region. Focusing on Cedar Rapids, Iowa—a prototypical midwestern city whose African American community emerged during the same moment in which the city and the Midwest also came of age—Arnold's chapter uncovers the individual experiences of black migrants and points to ways in which migrants and migration shaped the emergent Midwest. The Civil War was a major factor in this migration, as in the region's overall development and importance. Migration increased the region's diversity, one of its distinguishing features in the late nineteenth and early twentieth centuries. Migrants contributed to the development of the region's communities and characteristics, especially through creating close-knit communities, challenging discrimination and white supremacy, and embracing the region's new postwar political influence, legal equity, and educational opportunities. In these ways and more, black Midwesterners fundamentally contributed to the late nineteenth-century making of the Midwest.

While the African Americans examined by Rhodes and Arnold faced varying challenges based upon time and place and Egge's Yankees tended to wield great civic influence, other social groups fell some place in the middle. David C. Miller's examination of the recollections of the immigrant Carl Humke offers insights into how he and other nineteenth-century German Americans gradually assimilated into the Heartland. Good fortune while serving in the Union Army during the Civil War and material success afterwards partly explain why Humke continually affirmed his bicultural identity—indeed, his earlier military service remained a lasting source of pride, as it did for many Union veterans in the Midwest. War experiences also gave depth and meaning to his life as family man, farmer, and "American by choice." Humke's selective integration into American society, moreover, reveals much about the composite character of his identity formation. His example reminds readers of the several adaptive channels open to central European immigrants who inhabited a dynamic polyglot Midwest that was already becoming "culturally pluralistic" many years before the concept was articulated.

The stories of African Americans and European immigrants in the Midwest highlight the at-times contested nature of midwestern political space. In his chapter Jason Stacy focuses, in particular, on analyzing the existence of and interaction between working-class and rural resentments. Stacy traces attempts by prominent midwestern Populists like Herman Taubeneck and reform-minded Democrats like Henry Demarest Lloyd, John Peter Altgeld, and Clarence Darrow to fuse midwestern agricultural and labor interests during the early 1890s and thereby remake political discourse into a fight between "producers" and "parasites." In this regard, the longstanding integration of agriculture and industry in the Midwest provided the economic foundation for what Stacy calls "producerist populism," a midwestern political identity from the 1890s that still has national resonance today.

All of these political and cultural dynamics help explain how the Midwest came to be seen as a distinct region and a source of identity and meaning for millions of Americans. This process of regional identity formation is complex and will take years to study and understand. We think this volume is a crucial step forward in this process.

Notes

1. Andrew R.L. Cayton and Frederika J. Teute, "On the Connection of Frontiers," in Andrew R.L. Cayton and Frederika J. Teute, eds., *Contact Points: American Frontiers from the Mohawk Valley to the Mississippi, 1750–1830* (Chapel Hill: University of North Carolina Press, 1998), 1.
2. Thomas P. Slaughter, *The Whiskey Rebellion: Frontier Epilogue to the American Revolution* (New York: Oxford University Press, 1988).
3. Michael C. Steiner, "The Birth of the Midwest and the Rise of Regional Theory," in Jon K. Lauck, Gleaves Whitney, and Joseph Hogan, eds., *Finding a New Midwestern History* (Lincoln: University of Nebraska Press, 2018), 3–24; James R. Shortridge, *The Middle West: Its Meaning in American Culture* (Lawrence: University Press of Kansas, 1989).
4. Jon K. Lauck, ed., *The Midwestern Moment: The Forgotten World of Early Twentieth-Century Midwestern Regionalism, 1880–1940* (Hastings, NE:

Hastings College Press, 2017). See, in particular, chapter 1 by Elizabeth Raymond, "Creating the Heartland: The Midwest Emerges in American Culture," 1–19.

5. Terry A. Barnhart, "An Emerging Voice: The Origins of Regional Identity in the Old Northwest," 1–16.

6. Marcia Noe, "The Innocent Midwest and the New Midwestern Pastoral," 37–52.

7. Kenneth H. Wheeler, *Cultivating Regionalism: Higher Education and the Making of the American Midwest* (DeKalb: Northern Illinois University Press, 2011); Russell M. Storey, "The Rise of the Denominational College," *Ohio History Journal* 25, no. 1 (January 1916): 52–58; Thomas N. Hoover, "The Beginnings of Higher Education in the Northwest Territory," *Ohio History Journal* 50, no. 3 (July–September 1941): 244–60; E. Kidd Lockard, "The Influence of New England in Denominational Colleges in the Northwest, 1830–1860," *Ohio History Journal* 53, no. 1 (January–March 1944): 1–13 (noting that the number of denominational colleges in the Midwest grew from 32 in 1840 to 102 by 1860); Daniel T. Johnson, "Financing Western Colleges, 1844–1862," *Journal of the Illinois State Historical Society* 65, no. 1 (Spring 1972): 43–53.

8. Barton E. Price, "The Protestant Imagination and the Making of the Midwest as America's Heartland," 85–100.

9. See Michael J. Pfeifer, "A Symphonic Midwest: The Minneapolis Symphony Orchestra and Regionalist Identity, 1903–1922" in Lauck, ed., *The Midwestern Moment*, 101–12.

10. Christopher Phillips, *The Rivers Ran Backward: The Civil War and the Remaking of the American Middle Border* (New York: Oxford University Press, 2016).

11. L. Bao Bui, "Letter Writing, Civilization, and Midwesterners," paper presented at the Organization of American Historians annual conference, April 2019.

12. Frederic Allen Whiting cited in Carl Wittke, *The First Fifty Years: The Cleveland Museum of Art 1916–1966* (Cleveland: Cleveland Museum of Art Press, 1966), 46.

Terry A. Barnhart | An Emerging Voice

The Origins of Regional Identity and Mission in the Old Northwest

The first stirrings of regional identity and mission in the Old Northwest emerged during the region's organization under the Northwest Ordinance of 1787 and initial settlement by the Ohio Company of Associates the following year. Passage of the Northwest Ordinance was the first act of self-definition; the writings and public addresses by members of the Ohio Company and government officials the second. The Ohio Company, a joint stock company composed of Revolutionary War veterans from New England, purchased 1.5 million acres of land from Congress in 1787 to begin a new American settlement at the mouth of the Muskingum River. The anonymously written promotional pamphlet published at Salem, Massachusetts, in November 1787, actually written by the Reverend Manasseh Cutler, expressed the colonizing mission of the Ohio Company. So, too, did the public addresses of James Mitchell Varnum, Arthur St. Clair, and Solomon Drowne. Those early texts—articulated at the beginning of the process of being and becoming "Westerners"—represent the first attempts at constructing a regional identity. They reflect ideas about the westward movement and American society as a whole that were already deeply embedded in American thought. Those assumptions traveled west in the cultural baggage of the region's emigrants and promoters and were prologue to themes that later emerged in the first historical narratives of the region.

Manasseh Cutler's account appeared under the cumbersome if exact title of *An Explanation of the Map Which Delineates that Part of the Federal Lands Comprehended Between [the] Pennsylvania West Line, The Rivers Ohio and Scioto, and Lake Erie, ...* The accompanying map appeared as "A map of the Federal Territory from the Western Boundary of Pennsylvania to the Scioto River" in the spring of 1788. Cutler's map shows the tract of land purchased by Ohio Company, the seven ranges of six-mile square townships surveyed under the Congressional Land Ordinance of 1785, and a conjectural plan of "the City to be built on the Muskingum River" in an orderly grid of streets in the form of a parallelogram.[1]

Cutler prepared his explanatory pamphlet for the benefit of those wishing to become adventurers in the Ohio Country. His description of the region is based on several sources: the Congressional reports submitted by Thomas Hutchins as the Geographer of the United States during the Seven Ranges Survey of 1785 to 1787, the first division of public lands under the American rectangular survey established by the Land Ordinance of 1785; the journal kept by Captain Harry Gordon during his surveying expedition down the Ohio River in 1766, which originally appeared as part of Thomas Pownall's *Topographical Description of Such Parts of North America As Are Contained in the (Annexed) Map of the Middle British Colonies, etc., in North America* published at London in 1776; and the firsthand knowledge of Benjamin Tupper, Winthrop Sargent, and Ebenezer Sproat, all of whom traversed the area as surveyors on the Seven Ranges and who were also directors and agents of the Ohio Company. Thomas Hutchins, the Geographer of the United States, certified the authenticity of Cutler's descriptions of the fertility of the soil and other natural advantages for agricultural production based on his own firsthand knowledge of the region.[2]

The Ohio Company settlement about to be established at the Muskingum, said Cutler, would shape the character of those that followed. It would serve as "a wise model for the future settlement of all the federal lands." The Ohio Country was *tabula rasa*—a clean slate upon which the social ideals, values, and aspirations of both the Ohio Company and the national government could be imprinted. The self-conscious mission of the Ohio Company was to transplant republican ideas, institutions, and "virtue" in the Northwest Territory, as well as to promote their own self-interest and prosperity as land speculators. Ohio Company settlers, said Cutler, had an opportunity to start society anew: "there will be one advantage which no other part of the earth can boast and which probably will never again occur—that, in order to begin *right*, there will no *wrong* habits to combat, and no inveterate systems to overturn—there is no rubbish to remove, before you lay the foundation." The very act of migrating to a new country was psychologically, socially, and culturally part of the equation. Adapting and accommodating themselves to the conditions of frontier society significantly changed emigrants and made the societies they founded something more than the sum of their parts. "We, indeed, bring our habits of thinking and acting in some degree with us, but a new state of things, new objects, new prospects, new connections, views and designs, throw them loose about us."[3]

Cutler's statement is the earliest expression of a theme echoed by writers in the Old Northwest during the early and mid-nineteenth century. His observation, though significant, was not entirely original or exceptional. His assumptions about the founding of new settlements in the West were widespread and reflect the American experience from the late colonial period onward. Michel Guillaume Jean de Crèvecoeur, (1731–1813), who wrote under the pseudonym of J. Hector St. John Crèvecoeur is an example. Crèvecoeur maintained in the original English edition of his *Letters from an American Farmer* (1782) that "He is an American, who leaving behind him all his ancient prejudices and manners, receives new ones from his new mode of life he has embraced, the new government he obeys, and the new rank he holds." Cutler may well have been paraphrasing Crèvecoeur in applying his own observation on the effects of westward migration. Both Cutler's and Crèvecoeur's comments are essentially rooted in an environmental determinism that dates at least to Montesquieu. It was an article of faith that the melding of different nationalities and cultures in new environments transformed emigrants in the new societies opening westward of the Alleghenies. Crèvecoeur's and Cutler's observations were a set piece.[4]

Cutler was at pains to note that the new settlement at the Muskingum would be established by men of property and virtuous character—men who stood in stark contrast to the "lawless banditti" (squatters of an allegedly dubious character) that would surely overrun public lands unless the national government and its agents (i.e., the Ohio Company) made a concerted effort to attract emigrants to the western country who were of the right sort. The proximity of western Virginia to the lands northwest of the Ohio River made the establishment of squatter settlements an immediate concern. Squatters threatened the sorely needed land-sale revenues of the national government, the orderly settlement of public lands, and the pecuniary interests of the directors, agents, and shareholders of the Ohio Company. One of the primary duties of the 1st American Regiment stationed at Fort Harmar in 1785 was removing unlawful squatters in the Seven Ranges and burning their cabins and fields. Cutler privately betrayed more than a little prejudice towards southerners to his fellow New Englander Nathan Dane, who was then a member of Congress. Writing to Dane in March 1787 Cutler observed that "settlers from the northern states, in which this company is made up, are undoubtedly preferable to those from the southern states. They [northerners] will be men of more robust constitutions, inured to labor, and free from the habits of idleness." While there is no explicit mention of slavery in that passage, critics of slavery, of which Cutler was one, often complained of the idleness of slave owners compared to those who were no strangers to the invigorating and virtuous qualities they attributed to their own labor and the hired labor of others. Tension between New Englanders and upland southerners became palpable as they later vied for leadership in the political culture of the Old Northwest.[5]

Cutler's pamphlet captures the temperament of a rising country. The future prosperity and national influence of the Northwest Territory and its future states were subjects of "sublime contemplation." He speculated that the establishment of new settlements and new states northwest of the Ohio would ultimately make it the center of population in the nation and probably the future site of the national capitol. He also called to witness the testimony of Crèvecoeur in *Letters from an American Farmer,* originally published in 1782. Interest in Crèvecoeur's observations on American society led to a second English edition in 1783, a two-volume French edition in 1784, and a three-volume French edition in 1787. Crèvecoeur traveled down the Ohio from Pittsburgh to Louisville in April 1786. Cutler appended an extract from the third volume of Crèvecoeur's epistles that conveyed some idea of the sentiments evoked when he first beheld the abundant resources of the Ohio Country and its latent potential for development: "Never before had I felt so disposed to meditation and revery [*sic*, i.e., reverie]; involuntarily my imagination darted into the future, the remoteness of which gave me no trouble, because it appeared to be near." He did not doubt that travelers would soon behold beautiful houses, well-cultivated fields, and orchards along the banks of the Ohio.[6]

Crèvecoeur envisioned the lands watered by the Ohio as a future theatre of industry, culture, and commerce. Settlement of the Ohio Country was "one of the greatest enterprises ever presented to man" and made all "the more glorious because it will be legally acquired with the consent of the ancient proprietors and without the shedding of a drop of blood." Here was the cant of conquest and wishful thinking. In reality, the processes of dispossessing the native inhabitants of the land would be contested and far from bloodless. The prospect of peaceful possession of the land was premature, naïve, and forlorn. Yet such was the official line of both the Ohio Company and the national government, at least at the beginning of settlement. Yet few doubted Crèvecoeur's confident prediction that the fertile and well-watered recesses of the Ohio Country were "destined to become the foundation of the power, wealth, and future glory of the United States."[7]

An equally significant expression of regional identity and mission occurred when the Ohio Company settlers at Marietta, together with the garrison at Fort Harmar, greeted the arrival of the Fourth of July in 1788 with elevated sentiments and solemn festivities. James Mitchell Varnum (1748-1789)—one of the judges in the Northwest Territory appointed by Congress—gave an oration on the occasion. A native of Dracut, Massachusetts, Varnum was no stranger to many of those assembled at Marietta to hear him. He graduated with honors from Brown University in 1769, served as Brigadier General in the Continental Army and as Major General in the Rhode Island State Militia, was a delegate to the Continental Congress from 1780 to '81, and again served in Congress in 1787. He was a member of the Society of Cincinnati, a Freemason, and a director of the Ohio Company. Varnum reminded his audience of the common advantages deriving to them with the achievement of American independence and the opportunity to realize "our own particular felicity in being placed upon this happy spot!" His oration was a self-congratulatory yet meaningful discourse carefully tailored to the aspirations and self-perceptions of his audience. The fertility of the soil, salubrious climate, and many navigable rivers and streams in their new home presented the rising prospects of future commerce and trade that welcomed "the admiring stranger."[8]

The new nation was still forming but bespoke a bright future. Varnum drew attention to "Prejudices too deeply imbibed," the effects of "pre-existing opinion," and "local habits" that rendered government under the Articles of Confederation defective and led to the drafting of the new plan of federal government pending adoption. How fortunate were they who had defended their country in its greatest time of need to "here find a safe, and honorable asylum; and may recline upon the pleasure of their own reflections." But there could be no complacency for new challenges now stood before them. So long as Niagara and Detroit remained in British hands there would likely be "disturbances from the natives: but it is our duty as well as interest to conduct towards them humanity and kindness. We must, at the same time, be upon our guard, and by no means suffer the progress of our settlement to be checked by too great a degree of confidence." Promoting humanity and kindness towards the natives while also promoting national expansion were antithetical goals. The northwestern tribes would not be so accommodating as to allow the peaceful possession of their lands through the legalistic extinguishment of their title to lands boldly claimed by the United States. "Difficulties we must expect to encounter in our infant state: but most of the distresses common to new countries, we shall never experience, if we make use of the means in our power to promote our own happiness."

There was also a decided note of class consciousness in Varnum's oration and recognition of the potential for social discord: "Every class of citizens will be equally protected by the laws; and the labor of the industrious will find the reward of peace, plenty, and virtuous contentment." He acknowledged that many of the associates were "distinguished for wealth, education, and virtue; and others, for the most part, are reputable, industrious, well informed planters, farmers, tradesmen and mechanics." Several of the more prominent associates were community leaders before the Revolutionary War, high-ranking officers during the war, founders and directors of the Ohio Company, and members of the Society of Cincinnati—a hereditary group founded in 1783 to preserve the ideals and fellowship of officers in the Continental Army who served in the Revolutionary War. They were accustomed to social deference and were politically well connected. Whose interests would be advanced at the Muskingum and at whose expense were unanswered questions, but it was clearly a concern to those who had cast their lot together at the Muskingum. A concern for prosperity, personal contentment, and future security is a persistent theme in Varnum's oration. He was himself a director of the Ohio Company, a member of the Society of Cincinnati, and a territorial judge. He was very much a party concerned. And he reminded those who had joined him at the Muskingum that theirs was a covenanted identity cemented by mutual experiences during the American Revolution and furthered as members of the Society of Cincinnati and their speculative venture in the Ohio Company. According to Varnum, they were "a band of brothers, connected by the most sacred ties."

Varnum made the association of the principles of the American Revolution with the settlement of the Northwest Territory explicit. He would be the first of many to follow. There was reason to believe, said Varnum, that republican virtue and principles could regenerate humankind: "Mankind, my friends, have deviated from the rectitude of their original formation. They have been sullied and dishonored by the control of ungovernable passion." But there was reason for rejoicing since it appeared that "mankind are [sic] now upon the ascending scale!" Reason, philosophy, and the restraints of law "will cease to degrade us with humiliating distinctions; and the assaults of passion will be subdued by the gentle sway of virtuous affection." Religion and good government would do the rest until they accomplished "in this western world, the consummation of all things.... this new Jerusalem shall form an august temple, unfolding its celestial gates to every corner of the globe!—when millions shall fly to it, 'as doves to their windows,' elevating their hopes upon the broad spreading wings of millennial happiness!"

Adherents of republican ideas and institutions likened the ends of good government with social well-being. The idea resonated widely within the ideology of the founding era. Both Varnum and St. Clair drew attention to the relationship between good government and "happiness" or "felicity," which translated as civil and religious liberty under rational law and orderly government that protected property rights and promoted the public good as defined by those who wielded political power and wrote national law. The ventures of the Ohio Company of Associates were an early and significant instance of that concept of republicanism— one of its presumed virtues. It was a self-evident truth to the veterans of the Ohio Company of Associates and one they pursued in the new territory opening northwest of the Ohio River. Andrew R.L. Cayton aptly described the western venture of the Ohio Company as a search for "a quiet independence" in recompense for services rendered the nation. Like Cincinnatus of old, the associates would beat their swords into plowshares and seek happiness on the banks of the Muskingum as agents of the new American republic.[9]

The inauguration of the first stage of civil government in the Northwest Territory occurred at Marietta on July 15, 1788. It was an important step in the mutual fulfillment of private and public interests. The future prosperity of the Ohio Company venture depended upon the sponsorship and protection of the national government, which in turn had a vested interest in promoting the settlement of the Northwest Territory in an orderly manner by people with vested interests and a strong attachment to the distant national government. Thus, when Arthur St. Clair arrived at Fort Harmar on July 9, 1788, and officially began his duties as the territorial governor, it was a welcome event. Winthrop Sargent, Secretary of the Northwest Territory, read the Northwest Ordinance, the congressional commissions of Governor St. Clair, those of judges Samuel Holden Parsons and James M. Varnum, and his own as secretary. The purposeful merging of the interests of the Ohio Company and those of the national government is clearly seen in those appointments. Parsons, Varnum, and Sargent were all either directors or agents of the Ohio Company. Sargent, who had worked with Cutler in negotiating the particulars of the Ohio Company Purchase with the Treasury Department and Congress in October 1787, was a known and trusted person.

St. Clair's address to the people of the Muskingum settlement further expressed the Ohio Company's mission at the Muskingum. The Northwest Ordinance gave proof, said St. Clair, of the parental concern and attention of Congress to the welfare of those who were removing themselves to the distant settlements of the western country, and the protection of their essential rights, liberties, and interests as citizens of the United States. "A good Government well administered is the first of Blessings to a People—everything desirable in Life is thereby secured to them, & from the Operation of wholesome & equal Laws, the Passions of Men are restrain'd within due Bounds; their Actions receive a proper Direction; the Virtues are cultivated, & the beautiful Fabric of civilized Life is reared & brought to Perfection." Echoing Cutler, it was fortunate for all concerned that individuals of a proper character and social standing were forming the settlement at the Muskingum, for their influence and example would "probably give a tone" to the settlements that would follow. He flattered his listeners by describing them as individuals who recognized the importance of religion and morality to society, had demonstrated a passion for liberty and order, and were "no Strangers to the Decencies & to the Elegancies of Life." As the former president of the Confederation Congress he was intimately familiar with the details of the Ohio Company Purchase and as veterans of the Revolutionary War he knew many of the associates personally.[10]

The type of government under which the residents at the Muskingum were living was temporary only. It was "suited to your infant Situation, & to continue no longer than that State of Infancy shall last." Difficult days lay ahead as the Ohio Company settlers and the national government laid the foundations of a new society:

> The subduing [of] a new Country, notwithstanding its natural Advantages, is alone an arduous Task:—a Task however that Patience & Perseverance will Surmount, & these Virtues so necessary in every Situation, but peculiarly so in your own must resolve to exercise—neither is the reducing a Country from a State of Nature to a State of Civilization so irksome as it may appear from a slight or superficial View—Even very sensible Pleasures attend it;— the gradual Progress of Improvement fills the Mind with delectable Ideas—Vast Forests converted into arable Fields, & Cities rising in Places which were lately the Habitation of wild Beasts give a Pleasure something like that attendant on Creation, if we can form an Idea of it—the Imagination is ravished, & a Taste communicated of even the 'Joy of God to see a happy World.'

St. Clair also struck a cautionary note regarding relations with the Native Americans with whom the residents at the Muskingum shared the land. The inherent difficulties and tensions involved in promoting the establishment of new American settlements and protecting the acknowledged property rights of the region's resident native peoples was not lost on St. Clair or the Ohio Company settlers. The achievement of the former under the authority of the Northwest Ordinance could be accomplished only at the expense of the latter. The dispossessors never doubted the superiority of their own way of life over those they were in the act of dispossessing, nor did they question the certainty of how the "state of nature" they attributed to Indians would soon give way to "a state of civilization." It was genuinely hoped that the settlement of the territory would proceed peacefully, with "justice" toward the recognized land rights of the natives and with due regard for the legitimacy of many of their grievances as greatly injured peoples. But the advance of American settlements and the creation of new republican states were clearly the greater priority and order of the day. The willingness to use force to obtain land-cession treaties, moreover, was the unspoken part of the equation. The imposing attitude of the United States toward the land rights of the northwestern tribes belied the expressions of benevolence.

St. Clair elaborated the precarious and problematic position of the government in self-justifying, ethnocentric, and assimilationist terms:

> Endeavour to cultivate a good Understanding with the Natives, without much Familiarity. Treat them on all Occasions with Kindness & the strictest Regard to Justice—Run not into their Custom & Habits, which is but too frequent with those who settle near them, but endeavor to induce them to adopt yours—Prevent, by every Means, that dreadful Reproach, perhaps too justly brought by them against all the People, they have been yet acquainted with, that, professing the most holy & benevolent Religion, they are uninfluenced by its Dictates & regardless of its Precepts—Such a Conduct will produce on their Parts the utmost Confidence—they will soon become sensible of the superior Advantages of a State of Civilization—They will gradually lose their present Manners, & a way [will] be opened for introducing amongst them the Gospel of Peace; & you be the happy Instruments in the Hand of Providence of bringing forward that Time, which will surely arrive, when all the Nations of the Earth shall become the Kingdom of JESUS CHRIST.

St. Clair learned firsthand, and all too tragically, how unrealistic and impractical the contradictory objectives of honoring Native American land rights, rhetorically at least, and clearing the way for the creation of new American states would be. He led an American army to a disastrous defeat in November 1791, which embarrassed the national government, forever damaged St. Clair's reputation and prestige, earned him a court martial, and emboldened the tribes to continue their resistance against the encroachments of American settlements northwest of the Ohio.

The historically conscious denizens of Marietta commemorated the first anniversary of the settlement at the Muskingum on April 7, 1789, with an oration by Solomon Drowne (1753–1834). Drowne—who graduated from Brown University in 1773—was a physician, surgeon, and revolutionary war veteran. Much was expected of him on the occasion since the directors of the Ohio Company resolved in February of that year that "the 7th Day of April be forever considered as a day of Public Festival in the Territory of the Ohio Company, As their Settlements in this Country commenced upon that Day."[11] Drowne did not disappoint them. He reflected upon what had been accomplished at the Muskingum settlement over the past year and what remained to be done. His would be the first of a long line of celebratory speeches delivered in commemoration of the founding of Marietta. "HAIL glorious birth day of this western region!—On such a day and in the same beauteous season, ancient poets feign'd the earth was then created" (an allusion to Virgil's *Georgics*, Book II, 336). The tide of western migration, the founding of new settlements, and the creation of new American states would be likened to the birth of a new world many times over.[12]

Drowne sanctified the day by praising and applauding "that firm band" that left warm hearths and loved ones in the dead of winter to seek their fortunes in a distant region. Here was the apotheosis of the legendary hardihood and Promethean accomplishments of the pioneers—a recurring theme in the early literature of the American frontier and an enduring one in American popular culture. It was an essential component in creating an origin myth. American historian Forrest McDonald once tellingly observed, "THE FIRST FUNCTION of the founders of nations, after the founding itself, is to devise a set of true falsehoods about origins—a mythology—that will make it desirable for nationals to continue to live under common authority, and, indeed, make it impossible for them to entertain contrary thoughts." What was true of the founding of the American republic itself was no less true of the origin myths relating to the organization and settlement of the Northwest Territory.[13]

Drowne's oration, so far as it relates to the relinquishment of Native American land rights, is a notable case in point. "The origin of most countries," said Drowne, "is lost in the clouds of fiction and romance; and as far up as you can trace their history, you will find they were generally founded in rapacity, usurpation, and blood.... Singular, then, and before unheard of, are the circumstances of your first establishment, in this extensive territory; without opposition, and without bloodshed. How striking the contrast between such a manner of conducting an important enterprise.... The kind and friendly treatment of the Indians by the first settlers, has conducted greatly to the favorable issue of the late treaty [The Treaty of Fort Harmar signed on January 9, 1789]. Such humane conduct, so easy to practice, cannot fail to have great influence, even on savage minds." It was a convenient and comforting fiction; yet a further instance of the cant of conquest. Drowne and his listeners no doubt hoped for the peaceful possession of the lands claimed by the United States and the Ohio Company in preference to war. But it was an impulsive assessment of the situation made from the perspective of April 1789. Only one year later Colonel Josiah Harmar unsuccessfully led the first of three military campaigns against the recalcitrant northwestern tribes. How ironic, then, was Drowne's statement that "Thus fair is the first page of our history, and may no foul blot hereafter stain the important volume which time is unfolding in this Western World."

But it was the practice of husbandry, Drowne predicted, for which the "Western World" would forever be most admired. Agriculture in Drowne's estimation was "that best occupation of mankind" and the source of all true wealth. The lands in which the Ohio Company had planted their settlements were likewise blessed with a mild climate that unerringly marked it as a place where agriculture would flourish. Those natural resources would be "a real treasure to every family that is wise enough to be contented with living nobly independent." Along the Ohio and its tributaries nature's beneficence gave rise to agreeable contemplations. It was amid such delightful rural scenes "that health and rejuvenescency [sic] of soul" were to be found. Agriculture was a virtuous and ennobling pursuit. "There is indeed something great in this employment; ... and has something in it like creation. *Homer, Virgil,* and *Horace,* those greatest geniuses of all antiquity—with how much rapture have they spoken on this universally admired art!" It was a sentiment also endorsed by Thomas Jefferson. Drowne fully shared the opinion of Jefferson that "Those who labor in the earth are the chosen people of God." Cultivators received from their Creator the divine gift of genuine virtue and were the most independent and least corruptible citizens. The farmer's plow was "the philosopher's stone" of a virtuous, prosperous, and independent people. And not the least of the advantages derived from agriculture, said Drowne, was its contrast with "the flattering and too often deceitful prospects afforded by trade and commerce."[14]

Regional identity in the American Midwest begins in the region's distant origins as the Old Northwest. Even though the embryonic Old Northwest was at the time a largely unrealized region of the nation, how it was then perceived by its promoters and beneficiaries identifies themes that moved forward in the rhetoric of region. Several of the conflicts and aspirations of that critical period in the nation's history stand in bold relief, and those early conceptions were shaped by a ready-made assemblage of ideas regarding the West already deeply embedded in American thought. Settling a new country was akin to the act of creation—the quintessential emigrants theme of new land and new beginnings.

Notes

1. [Manasseh Cutler,] *An Explanation of the Map Which Delineates That Part of the Federal Lands Comprehended Between [the] Pennsylvania West Line, the Rivers Ohio and Scioto, and Lake Erie, Confirmed to the United States and Sundry Tribes of Indians, in the Treaties of 1784 and 1786, and Now Ready for Settlement* (Salem: Dabney and Cushing, 1787). The pamphlet is hereafter cited as Cutler, *An Explanation.*
2. Gordon's journal of his trip down the Ohio in 1766 appears in Clarence Walworth Alvord and Clarence Edwin Carter, eds., *The New Regime: 1765–1767, British Series* vol. 2, *Collections of the Illinois State Historical Society* vol. 11 (Springfield: Illinois State Historical Society, 1916), 290–311.
3. William Parker Cutler and Julia Perkins Cutler, eds., *Life, Journals, and Correspondence of Rev. Manasseh Cutler, LL.D.* vol. 2 (Cincinnati: Robert Clarke & Co., 1888), 446 and Cutler, *An Explanation,* 14 and 20.
4. Hector St. John Crèvecoeur, *Letters from an American Farmer: Describing Certain Provincial Situations, Manners, and Customs, Not Generally Known* (London: Printed for Thomas Davies and Lockyer Davis, 1782), 51–52.

5. Cutler to Nathan Dane, letter draft, n.p., 16 March 1787 in Cutler and Cutler, eds., *Life, Journals, and Correspondence of Rev. Manasseh Cutler* vol. 1, 194. See Nicole Etcheson, *The Emerging Midwest: Upland Southerners and the Political Culture of the Old Northwest, 1787–1861* (Bloomington: Indiana University Press, 1996) and Richard Lytle Power, *Planting Corn Belt Culture: The Impress of the Upland Southerner and Yankee in the Old Northwest*, Indiana Historical Society Publications, vol. 17 (Indianapolis: Indiana Historical Society, 1953).
6. Cutler, *An Explanation*, 22 and Crèvecoeur as cited in Cutler, *An Explanation*, 23–24.
7. Cutler's extracts from Crèvecoeur's *Letters of an American Farmer* are from J. Hector St. John de Crèvecoeur, *Lettres d'un cultivateur américain addressées à Wm. Seton, Esq.r depuis l'année 1770, jusqu'en 1786 Tome 3* (Paris: Chez Cuchet Libraire, 1787), 394–95. The three-volume French edition of Crèvecoeur's *Lettres* published at Paris in 1787 contains material not present in either the single-volume English editions published at London in 1782 and 1783 or the two-volume French edition published in Paris in 1784. Crèvecoeur's description of the Ohio Country appears in the third volume of the 1787 French edition only. Cutler hurriedly placed his translated excerpts from Crèvecoeur at the end of his pamphlet even as Dabney and Cushing were printing it at Salem.
8. James M. Varnum, *An Oration, Delivered at Marietta, July 4, 1788, by the Hon. James M. Varnum, Esq., one of the Judges of the Western Territory; the Speech of His Excellency Arthur St. Clair, Esquire, upon the Proclamation of His Commission Appointing Him Governor of Said Territory; and the Proceedings of the Inhabitants of the City of Marietta* (Newport, Rhode Island: Peter Edes, 1788). The quotes appearing in this and the following three paragraphs are taken from Varnum's *Oration*, 4, 5, 6, and 7.
9. Andrew R.L. Cayton, "A Quiet Independence: The Western Vision of the Ohio Company," *Ohio History* 90 (Winter 1981): 5–32.
10. St. Clair's address of 15 July 1788 to the people of the Muskingum settlement in Winthrop Sargent, "Journal of the Executive Proceedings in the Territory Northwest of the River Ohio" in Clarence Edwin Carter, ed., *Territorial Papers of the United States* vol. 3 (Washington, DC: Government Printing Office, 1934), 263–66.
11. Archer Butler Hulbert, ed., *Records of the Original Proceedings of the Ohio Company* vol. 1 (Marietta, Ohio: Marietta Historical Commission, 1917), 86.
12. Solomon Drown[e], *An Oration, Delivered at Marietta, April 7, 1789, in Commemoration of the Commencement of the Settlement Formed by the Ohio Company* (Worcester, Massachusetts: Printed by Isaiah Thomas, 1789), 6.
13. Forrest McDonald, *E Pluribus Unum: The Formation of the American Republic, 1776–1790* (Boston: Houghton Mifflin, 1965), ix.

14. Drowne, *An Oration*, 14. Drowne's ode to agriculture and virgin soil continued to signify the literature of the westward movement. See Henry Nash Smith, *Virgin Land: The American West as Symbol and Myth* (Cambridge: Harvard University Press, 1950), Book Three, 121–262.

Jason S. Lantzer | Forging God's Country

The Northwest Territorial Ordinance, the Second Great Awakening, and the Midwestern Vision for America

The Northwest Territorial Ordinance's significance in shaping the Midwest is undeniable. Best known for Article VI, which declared, "There shall be neither slavery nor involuntary servitude," the document spurred the orderly settlement of America's western territory. While the language used in the Ordinance and the eventual state constitutions of Ohio, Indiana, Illinois, Michigan, Wisconsin, and Minnesota might seem to be "cut and pasted" from other sources, there were other forces at work, most importantly, the Second Great Awakening. The Ordinance fostered religious liberty and freedom of worship in the territory as well. Only by considering how antislavery and religious liberty helped create the Midwest can we truly appreciate the region's contribution to the nation's new freedom during the Civil War.[1]

Genesis of the Ordinance

The War of Independence was scarcely over before Americans turned their eyes towards the western lands they had secured by battles and treaty. The Articles of Confederation gave Congress control of a vast territory, which stretched from the Great Lakes to the Gulf of Mexico. Whether settlement would be sporadic or orderly remained to be seen.[2] Many in the East thought of the West as an area of "contagious disorder," where settlers were bound to become "a mongrel breed, half civilized, half savage," unless proper guidance was offered and order imposed.[3]

Providing that guidance was up to Congress. The Confederation Congress's first attempt at grappling with these issues came when Thomas Jefferson authored the Ordinance of 1784. Though not enacted in full, the ordinance provided a blueprint for the future. Most importantly, Jefferson encapsulated one important criteria: "that they [the new states] shall forever remain a part of this confederacy of the United States of America."[4] Jefferson's ordinance was more aspirational than functional and subsequent Congresses had to shape western policy.[5]

In doing so, Congress had to address the issue of religious liberty. Americans, both in and out of political circles, were discussing the topic with increased regularity. The Confederation Congress, much like its predecessor, the Continental Congress, had a long history of supporting religion. With virtually no opposition, Congress "appointed chaplains for itself and the armed forces, sponsored the publication of a Bible, imposed Christian morality on the armed forces, and granted public lands to promote Christianity among the Indians. National days of thanksgiving and of 'humiliation, fasting, and prayer' were proclaimed by Congress at least twice a year throughout the war." Nearly the only restriction Congress placed on itself was that it did not favor any one Protestant denomination.[6]

Furthermore, the states openly discussed religion in their constitutions. Massachusetts's constitution (1780), for example, opens with an acknowledgment of "grateful hearts, [of] the goodness of the Great Legislator of the Universe, in affording us, in the course of His providence, an opportunity, deliberately and peaceably, without fraud, violence, or surprise, of entering into an original, explicit, and solemn compact with each other." State constitutions like Virginia's and Pennsylvania's (both from 1776) struck a different chord about "the duty to which we owe to our creator," emphasizing "that all men have a natural and unalienable right to worship Almighty God according to the dictates of their own consciences."[7]

The state constitutions were manifestations of a deeper discussion within the founding generation about the role of organized religion in the new American republic.[8] New England states like Massachusetts, Connecticut, and New Hampshire all had "general assessment" plans in place, which allowed the states to raise tax revenues to support religious institutions, as they believed the government benefited from a strong religious presence.[9] Further south, in Virginia, where the Episcopal Church held sway, the situation was different. As the former Church of England lost adherents, new denominations rose up whose members did not want to support the older denomination with their taxes. It was Jefferson who drafted Virginia's 1786 Act for Establishing Religious Freedom. Rather than a wall of separation, it gave equal footing to all denominations by not compelling support or attendance.[10] However, Virginians were hardly of a single mind on the topic, for while Jefferson and James Madison both supported dis-establishment, Patrick Henry and George Washington both favored some kind of general assessment.[11]

Congress tried to reconcile these views with the Ordinance of 1785. One provision to promote settlement was for the New England model of religious liberty, allowing for state support of churches.[12] Congressman Nathan Dane of Massachusetts drafted the general outline for the Ordinance, working alongside Manasseh Cutler (a Congregational minister, future congressman, and advocate for the Ohio Company of Associates), who wanted a land patent for settlement and land sales, and a provision for land to be set aside for religious purposes.[13] Virginians took the lead in challenging the proposed religious land mandate. Doing so, a later historian noted, was "an important step toward freedom of religion in America."[14]

The Confederation Congress had one more chance at creating an ordinance. Meeting at the same time as the Constitutional Convention in Philadelphia, a divided Congress passed a new land ordinance on July 13, 1787.[15] While there was not much discussion about the provision banning slavery, the debate on the proper role of religion in the territory was another matter entirely. The finalized version gave no clear victory to either side, neither granting a stark separation between Church and State nor fully endorsing State sanction of the work of the Church.[16]

What is clear is how different the ordinance was when compared to the Constitution. The Constitution's only mention of religion is to ban the use of religious tests for holding federal office. Unlike the Declaration of Independence and the Articles of Confederation themselves, the Constitution does not mention God. Its Bill of Rights addressed this to a degree via the First Amendment, but the Northwest Ordinance had much more to say on the subject, with three key religious provisions. The first was found in Section 13, which states that "the fundamental principles of civil and religious liberty" are "the basis whereon these republics [the eventual new states], their laws and constitutions are erected." Article I notes, "No person, demeaning himself in a peaceable and orderly manner, shall ever be molested on account of his mode of worship or religious sentiments, in the said territory." Lastly, Article III states, "religion, morality, and knowledge, being necessary to good government and the happiness of mankind, schools and the means of education shall forever be encouraged."[17]

The Constitution's silence on slavery is also remarkable. Before the Revolution, there was little debate about the morality of the institution. However, the war, with its talk of liberty, rights, and equality changed that. Most of the Founders assumed slavery was going to eventually vanish and that gradual emancipation was the way to achieve it. Within this rubric, the Northwest Ordinance came into being.[18] While the Ordinances' Article VI explicitly banned slavery, the Constitution avoided the very word, as a compromise between northern and southern delegates, even as it produced a mechanism for how slaves were to be counted for taxation and representation purposes. Though Article VI was added at the last moment and contained no real enforcement provision or cultural precedent, its ban on slavery was clear. The Ohio River was now a boundary line that defined freedom and slavery.[19]

The ban was a harbinger of things to come. The Ordinance gave antislavery a foothold in the new nation, and its discussion of religion gave Article VI fertile soil to grow. It was "the future Union of the states as it should be," according to Harold M. Hyman. The Ordinance helped convince would-be settlers that settlement was possible, painting the process in almost idyllic, utopian terms and providing for orderly surveying and land sales, a familiar governmental system with easy-to-follow steps to statehood, and the support of the federal government in both administration and in dealing with Native Americans. However, its vision was the utopianism found in its provisions for "religious pluralism" and freedom from slavery.[20]

Advent of the States

Exactly what the Northwest Ordinance's religious liberty and antislavery sections meant would be sorted out only in the process of time, as its provisions on land and statehood came to fruition. From the outset, the Ordinance shaped what citizens thought their fundamental rights were.[21] In the words of the Ordinance, it was "extending the fundamental principles of civil and religious liberty, which form the basis whereon these republics, their laws and constitutions, are erected; to fix and establish those principles as the basis of all laws, constitutions and governments, which forever hereafter shall be formed in said territory."[22]

Settlement of the Midwest happened quickly. Largely due to the work of Generals Arthur St. Clair, Anthony Wayne, and William Henry Harrison, the chief obstacle to settlement, Native Americans, was largely eliminated by the end of the War of 1812.[23] The area's rapid settlement seemed to prove that a territory need not have slavery to attract people. While most settlers were small farmers, not everyone who came to the Northwest was interested in agriculture, making for a dynamic and diverse economy in comparison to the cash crop economy in the South. Here was the creation of what James Bergquist called the "corn-hog economy," a potential paradise for both farmers and businessmen alike.[24]

The new Hoosier state is a great example. Indiana saw a wide variety of settlers from the Upland South, Mid-Atlantic, and New England regions arrive within its boundaries. The intermingling these pioneers did, as Bergquist notes, created a new, midwestern culture, held together by the Northwest Ordinance.[25] It was attractive to utopian groups, such as the Rappites and Owenites of New Harmony, as well as people who felt as though they no longer "fit" in more established parts of the country. This latter group included Upland Southern members of the Society of Friends who had rejected slavery, as well as poor white Southerners, such as Thomas Lincoln and his family, who were antislavery either by religious conviction or for economic reasons. The Friends were given new life in the new states of the Midwest. Having adopted an antislavery position, the Friends found themselves out of step in places like Virginia and North Carolina. Therefore, they left, taking with them their now freed former slaves, to settle in places like Indiana. In the case of the Lincoln family of Kentucky, Thomas Lincoln moved his family to Indiana, where there was easy title to good land, free from competition with slave-owning neighbors, and where they could worship in an antislavery Baptist congregation with more freedom. Antislavery proved a strong attraction to a growing number of Americans who wanted to move west.[26]

Not surprisingly, the new state constitutions adhered to the guidelines set out in the Ordinance. Ohio was the first state to be carved from the Northwest, and its first constitution (1803) not only contained a Bill of Rights (Article VIII), whose Section 2 banned slavery and limited the duration to indenture for African American servants, but also (in Section 3) said "that all men have a natural and indefeasible right to worship Almighty God according to the dictates of conscience; that no human authority can, in any case whatever, control or interfere with the rights of conscience; that no man shall be compelled to attend, erect or support any place of worship, or to maintain any ministry, against his consent, and that no preference shall ever be given, by law, to any religious society or mode of worship, and no religious test shall be required as a qualification to any office or trust or profit. But religion, morality and knowledge being essentially necessary to good government and the happiness of mankind, schools and the means of instructions shall forever be encouraged by legislative provision not inconsistent with the rights of conscience."[27]

Other new states followed Ohio's example of following the Ordinance. Indiana achieved statehood in 1816. Its first constitution used similar language to their neighbor to the east. Calling the "right to worship Almighty God" an "indefeasible right," Hoosiers also wrote an "extremely forceful" antislavery provision into their constitution.[28] In 1818, Illinois became a state, in part due to the work of antislavery citizens who wanted to get through the process before debate could begin on Missouri, a territory that would enter statehood outside the orbit of the Ordinance. Illinois continued the trend of banning slavery and exalting the concept of religious freedom.[29]

Already the new states were going beyond the Ordinance (and Constitutional) provisions on religion, while also staying true to its stance on antislavery. Ohio's constitution, for example, was written within the context of Jefferson's letter to the Danbury Baptists of Connecticut. Dated January 1, 1802, Jefferson's letter talked of the First Amendment, authored by his friend Madison, as "building a wall of separation" between Church and State.[30] However, as Philip Hamburger has pointed out, the Baptists certainly did not seek a wall when it came to having their "Christian obligations" transformed into legislation. What we see in Ohio was an emerging midwestern consensus on the topic for the early republic. Jefferson, as David Scott reminds us, signed off on Ohio becoming a state with this very constitution after he had written about a wall of separation.[31]

Adhering to antislavery came with opposition. Despite being outnumbered, pro-slavery settlers continually demanded votes to allow slavery in the Northwest Territory. Indeed, slavery existed there, despite the provision. Harrison in particular worked to make sure that the institution was allowed to exist, openly flaunting and actively seeking ways to subvert Article VI while he was Indiana's territorial governor.[32] In 1805, Indiana's territorial legislature allowed African American servants to be brought into the state under contract—as a means to get around the antislavery provision. However, such legislation was unpopular with the territory's settlers, who were able to get the law repealed in 1810. The servant law, they argued, was clearly against the Ordinance, which they saw as their constitution.[33] One's stance on slavery became a political issue, and antislavery proved overwhelmingly popular in Indiana. Such sentiment benefited the rise of the state's first governor, Jonathan Jennings, and the ultimate defeat of the Harrison faction.[34]

It was not until 1835 that the Northwest Territory again produced states. They (Michigan in 1835, Wisconsin in 1848, and Minnesota in 1857) continued to emulate each other in their attempts to live up to the Ordinance when it came to religious freedom and antislavery. At times, the language might be grand, other times quite bland, but the spirit never deviated.[35] Politics might dictate compromise on the national level, such as with the Missouri Compromise of 1821 and the Compromise of 1850, but not in these states, where the principles of religious freedom and antislavery were so ingrained. Indeed, even when Illinois (1848), Ohio (1851), and Indiana (1851) wrote new constitutions, their devotion to Ordinance remained steadfast.[36] Doing so was a firm statement about how they saw the future of the United States and further differentiated the emerging Midwest from the South. However, their desire to do so had almost as much to do with the effects of the Second Great Awakening as it did with what was first written in 1787.

A Second Great Awakening

At the same time the Northwest Ordinance was being realized, a religious revival swept over American Protestantism. Known today as the Second Great Awakening, the nationwide revival not only called people back to God but also (at least north of the Ohio River) launched reforms to better American society. Westward expansion created within many evangelical Protestants in the East a fear that pioneers might lose their faith as they moved into the wilderness of the Northwest. These fears, coupled with the notion (expressed in the Northwest Ordinance's Article III) that churches were a mark of civilization, led to missionary efforts, camp revivals, church construction, and denominational proliferation. And in the lands of the Northwest Ordinance, where Article VI barred slavery, the Second Great Awakening also helped fuel in its inhabitants a religiously tinged antislavery (if not always abolitionism), as American Protestants sought to create God's kingdom on the earth.[37]

While older, established (and increasingly dis-established from state coffers) denominations like the Congregational and Episcopal Churches were slow to warm towards westward expansion, and perhaps overly confident that transplanted members would simply wait for their denominational churches to be built,[38] other denominations filled the faith gap.[39] Indeed, evangelical Protestants, like the Baptists and Methodists, were in the best position to take advantage of western migration because they were not interested in forming new congregations based off old membership lists but rather winning new members to their denominational banners. They had no ties to the pre-Revolutionary establishments, and western migration was perfect for them to win converts. Not only did they go where the people were, they also were ready to deal with societal problems brought about by both expansion and eventual industrialization. As a result, evangelical Protestantism became a force to be reckoned with and perhaps the defining expression of religious faith in the country.[40]

The rapid growth of Baptists, Methodists, Presbyterians, and Disciples of Christ (a new denomination that sought to unify American Protestants around New Testament Christianity) after the American Revolution, amongst both whites and blacks, shocked older denominations. As the nation's population grew, and these new churches beside it, Christianity suddenly became, in the words of Nathan O. Hatch, "a mass enterprise."[41] "Of all the denominations, the Methodists were the best equipped for success on the frontier: effective organization, self-sacrificing workers, and popular doctrines assured the wide and rapid spread of their church," thanks to their use of local classes and circuit riding ministers. A close second were the Baptists, with a largely decentralized denominational and pastoral structure. However, all denominations benefited from the rich soil of the Ordinance when it came to religious freedom.[42]

Under the Ordinance, religion was to help foster education. In places like Ohio and Indiana, the presidents of the state's colleges tended to be Presbyterian, which led to some denominational jealousy—and the rise of private, truly denomination-based institutions of higher education.[43] Indiana is a prime example: Hanover (Presbyterian), Wabash (Presbyterian), Franklin (Baptist), Indiana Asbury (now known as DePauw, Methodist), Earlham (Friends), Notre Dame (Roman Catholic), and Northwestern Christian University (Disciples of Christ) were all founded during the first half of the nineteenth century. NWCU was also a direct challenge to the denomination's first institution of higher learning, Bethany College, located in Virginia. The new school's name, Northwestern Christian University, was heavy with symbolism. Organized in 1850 by Ovid Butler and other midwestern Disciples, "Northwest" was not only a geographic but also a political statement, making a case for remembering the Northwest Ordinance at the same time the Compromise of 1850 was being debated.[44]

Indeed, the education-religious matrix brought the Beecher family to the Midwest. Lyman, a New England Calvinist, came west to help run the new Lane Theological Seminary in Cincinnati. The goal was to train a new generation of ministers for midwestern pulpits. Included in the new pastoral ranks were his sons, Edward, Henry, and Charles. Edward became a college president and abolitionist in Illinois, while Henry and Charles both helped found new churches in Indiana, where they preached about reforms the nation needed to enact to usher in God's kingdom on earth, including antislavery.[45]

The Awakening's combination of revival and reform produced a wide variety of activity. While antislavery became the most pronounced, America's churches also advocated for the rights of women, reforms of prisons and asylums, free public schools, and the condemnation of alcohol.[46] Being involved in reforms brought evangelical Protestants directly into politics. While evangelical Protestants were in both the Whig and Democratic parties, their influence was most clearly seen within the Whigs.[47] Though concerning to some, the reforms that the Second Great Awakening launched were preached from pulpits and given a moral hue congregants carried with them into the world beyond their church doors.[48]

With so many denominations taking part in midwestern society, the notion of religious diversity was ingrained in the region. However, it was increasingly Protestantism that was opposed to slavery, at home in a region that not only was free of slavery but also guarded that purity zealously. In the English context, Protestantism meant freedom, not slavery, a notion the Midwest embraced. Northern evangelical Protestants increasingly argued that slavery was both a societal and personal sin. They also believed that removing it would make the nation a better place.[49]

Apostles for the Union

The utopianism of the Ordinance, according to Denis P. Duffey, helped create an idealized notion of citizenship amongst its settlers, not only making them think things could happen to make society better, but that it would happen. That sentiment, fueled by the Second Great Awakening, directly contributed to the Civil War. The antislavery component of the Ordinance insulated those who lived in the Northwest from the realities of slavery. On some level, what they knew was idealized and imagined. But it was also real to them.[50]

Moreover, in the realm of politics, the antislavery provision made the Northwest more open to societal changes in general. The Southwest Territory, made of land that became the states of Tennessee, Alabama, and Mississippi, had a similar ordinance governing their rise from territorial status, save for the provision on slavery. The lack of an antislavery provision diverted many slave owners from even attempting to move to the Midwest. While the same evangelical Protestant denominations arose there during the Second Great Awakening, without the provision, slavery became so joined to the culture of the region that southern evangelicals doubted both the need for any reforms and any theological argument that came from northern pulpits.[51] Southerners who had once talked about ending slavery, no longer did so. So when the great crisis swept the nation, despite strong pro-Union sentiment in some areas, all three states joined the Confederacy. While cash crops, like cotton, and slavery came to define the South, the lack of slavery had the same effect in the Northwest.⁵² The Article VI inoculation thus explains the denominational divisions that happened between the 1830s and early 1840s to the Baptists, Methodists, and Presbyterians.⁵³

Midwesterners were increasingly willing to challenge slavery. The region was at the center of the Underground Railroad. Fugitive slaves received help in Ohio, Indiana, and Illinois at least by 1820, and perhaps as early as 1815.⁵⁴ One of the best-known proponents of the escape network was Levi Coffin. Born into a North Carolina Friends family in 1798, Coffin moved to Indiana in 1826 largely because of pressure his antislavery beliefs were generating. Between 1826 and 1846, Coffin and his wife helped free more than 2000 fugitive slaves while living in Indiana. He continued to use his home as a station on the Underground Railroad after relocating to Ohio in 1847.⁵⁵ Coffin's activities were guided by his faith, which was allowed to flourish in the Midwest thanks to the Ordinance.

Antislavery amongst northern whites did not, out of hand, mean pro-abolition, nor support for racial equality.⁵⁶ Indiana, in Article XIII of its Constitution of 1851, for example, overwhelming banned further black migration into the state. However, any antislavery agitation was increasingly problematic for Southerners, who viewed it as an attack on their region.⁵⁷ By the 1850s, the Ordinance's regional distinctiveness was having an effect even on the friends of the South who lived in the Midwest. Northern Democrats, while willing to permit slavery in the South, refused to embrace it for their region and were divided over if the institution should spread further west. The demise of antislavery voices in the South made notions of abolition seem dangerously radical. The less the regions knew of the other, the less likely they were to seek real compromise.⁵⁸

Congress became a battleground because of the Ordinance.⁵⁹ No president seemed to doubt its authority, with every president from Washington to Buchanan assenting that Congress could allow into the Union states that prohibited slavery, but the Northwest Ordinance did have its opponents. By the end of his life, South Carolina's John C. Calhoun, who was the father of nullification and secessionist thought, saw the Ordinance as a "sin" of the North, as it gave the faster growing antislavery states a false sense of moral authority when it came to the South and its peculiar institution.⁶⁰ For Calhoun, this was brought to the forefront by Pennsylvania's David Wilmot, who cited the Ordinance during the debate over his proviso to ban slavery in any territory acquired during the War with Mexico.[61]

Perhaps the Ordinance's greatest foe was Chief Justice Roger B. Taney. In 1847, under Taney's guidance, the U.S. Supreme Court handed down its *Jones v. Van Zandt* ruling, which said that fugitive slaves in Ohio were not free merely because they had made it out of Kentucky into a state that was created by the Northwest Ordinance. The Taney Court ruled that just because laws like the Ordinance might ban slavery, they could do nothing to slavery where it already existed. Four years later, and in the wake of the Compromise of 1850 (which included a much stronger Fugitive Slave Act), Taney's high court struck at the Ordinance again, in *Strader v. Graham*. Once again, the Supreme Court held that just because a slave entered a free state, such contact with lands made free by the Ordinance did nothing to the condition of the slave as property. Taney disavowed that the Ordinance was even something the high court could consider as having any legal consequence because it mattered only for territorial formation. These volleys were all a buildup to diminish the Ordinance and Congress's authority to extend the rights and liberties under it into the territories for Taney's masterpiece, the *Dred Scott v. Sandford* decision. Not only did Taney's 1857 opinion repeal the Missouri Compromise, it also threatened to extend slavery into the Free states.[62]

It was Taney's assault on the Ordinance that outraged Abraham Lincoln and other Midwesterners.[63] Indeed, Midwesterners and their Northeastern antislavery allies were already forging a counter argument steeped in the Ordinance and a concept of higher law. Abolitionist lawyer James G. Birney (from the *Strader* decision) argued that the Ordinance spoke to higher truths than laws made by Congress.[64] The higher law argument was also advanced by William Seward of New York, who served as one of the attorneys in the *Van Zandt* case.[65] Seward, who eventually became Lincoln's Secretary of State, paid a political price for his support of the concept. However, Lincoln continued to advocate it, using the concept of higher law, along with other biblical allusions for the remainder of his life, perhaps most spectacularly at his Cooper Union address in 1860, which made him a contender for the Republican presidential nomination that fall.[66] The Republicans were a new political party that emerged in the Midwest in 1854, based (in part) on the principle that slavery should not be allowed to spread into the western territories.[67]

And into this charged political and legal debate over slavery came the Beechers. Perhaps no other family better displayed the power of the Second Great Awakening's focus on slavery and the forging of a North out of the Midwest and New England. While Henry was but one of many Protestant ministers giving sermons about the evils of slavery, his older sister Harriet became the author of *Uncle Tom's Cabin*. The book blended the Christian message the family embodied with the actual experience of having lived on the border of slave states and observing the institution firsthand. Its message captivated northern readers, helped galvanize public opinion against the Fugitive Slave Act of 1850, and, according to Abraham Lincoln, brought on the Civil War.[68]

Once war began in 1861, Midwesterners were prepared to give their last full measure of devotion for the Union. Of the approximately 2.1 million men who bore arms for the United States during the war, 47 percent hailed from Ohio, Indiana, Illinois, Michigan, Wisconsin, or Minnesota. Those six states were just a quarter of the entire loyal Union states. In Indiana, the mix of religious freedom and antislavery helped compel some Hoosier Quakers to enlist in the fight against the Confederacy, not to preserve the union as it had been, but to make it anew, without the stain of slavery.[69] The war was the ultimate rejection of southern influence in the Midwest.[70]

None of this was surprising for Midwesterners, however. Ohioan Jordan Pugh said of the Ordinance, "its impress is upon our character."[71] Those growing up after statehood believed its provision on antislavery was a "sacred text." It made them who they were. However, the Ordinance also made them view the nation in their terms—a lens that did not have slavery and increasingly saw no place for it in a United States that was being defined by Northwesterners. Here, there was no "incubus of slavery" to be found. And so it should be, from sea to shining sea—and from the Great Lakes to the Gulf of Mexico.[72]

A Renewed America

The importance of the Northwest Ordinance not just to the creation of the midwestern states but to how Americans came to define their country is undeniable. Mixing religious liberty and antislavery produced a region that was fertile ground for sentiments ranging from "free soil and free men" to abolition, all under the flag of the United States. Indeed, the freedom of free soil and antislavery was steeped in a religious understanding of freedom of worship, in a place where religious voices freely advocated for their version of creating God's kingdom on the earth. The earth in question was free of slavery, and the people advocating for rights believed increasingly not only in the region's uniqueness but that such a place was the way all America should be.[73]

Rather than American Exceptionalism, what we see is Midwestern Exceptionalism grounded in the Ordinance—a belief that Midwesterners carried with them wherever they went.[74] Rather than an outlier, Midwestern Exceptionalism became the norm. While the region shared much with the Northeast and the South, it was more than just a hybrid of the original states. The Ordinance gave it an understanding of what the United States could be. Free, in very real ways from the colonial past, the Midwest developed its own understanding of liberty, one that did not allow for human bondage. The marriage in the Ordinance of religious liberty and antislavery had profound consequences. For even though we find the same denominations in the North and South, antislavery sentiment grew in northern pews and wilted in southern ones. And in those northern pews grew leaders like Abraham Lincoln. When civil war came, Midwesterners were ready not just to preserve the union but also to give it a new birth of freedom, free of slavery. Here, in the Midwest, religious freedom met freedom from slavery, and the result was a nation destined for liberty.[75]

Notes

1. Frederick D. Williams, ed., *The Northwest Ordinance: Essays on Its Formulation, Provisions, and Legacy* (East Lansing: Michigan State University Press, 1989), ix.
2. Peter S. Onuf, *Statehood and Union: A History of the Northwest Ordinance* (Indianapolis: Indiana University Press, 1992), 1.
3. Denis P. Duffey, "The Northwest Ordinance as a Constitutional Document," *Columbia Law Review*, 95 (May 1995), 939, 953–54.
4. "The Ordinance of 1784," https://founders.archives.gov/documents/Jefferson/01-06-02-0420-0006, 3 December 2018.
5. Onuf, *Statehood and Union*, 52.
6. Library of Congress, "Religion and the Founding of the American Republic: Religion and the Congress of the Confederation," https://www.loc.gov/exhibits/religion/rel04.html, 5 December 2018.

7. "Fundamental Documents: Massachusetts Constitution 1780," http://press-pubs.uchicago.edu/founders/print_documents/v1ch1s6.html, 12 January 2018; "Constitution of Pennsylvania, 1776," http://avalon.law.yale.edu/18th_century/pa08.asp, 10 January 2018.
8. Michael I. Meyerson, *Endowed by Our Creator: The Birth of Religious Freedom in America* (New Haven: Yale University Press, 2012), 8; Lloyd A. Hunter, ed., *Pathways to the Old Northwest: An Observance of the Bicentennial of the Northwest Ordinance* (Indianapolis: Indiana Historical Society Press, 1989), 2.
9. Library of Congress, "Religion and the Founding of the American Republic: Religion and the State Governments," https://www.loc.gov/exhibits/religion/rel05.html 5 December 2018.
10. Philip Hamburger, *Separation of Church and State* (Cambridge: Harvard University Press, 2002), 5; "Thomas Jefferson and the Virginia Statue for Religious Freedom," https://www.virginiahistory.org/collections-and-resources/virginia-history-explorer/thomas-jefferson, 4 December 2018; "A Bill for Establishing Religious Freedom 18 June 1779, https://founders.archives.gov/documents/Jefferson/01-02-02-0132-0004-0082, 3 December 2018.
11. Library of Congress, "Religion and the Founding of the American Republic."
12. Williams, ed., *Northwest Ordinance*, vii; Ronald A. Smith, "Freedom of Religion and the Land Ordinance of 1785," *Journal of Church and State* 24 (Autumn 1982): 589–92, 597.
13. Duffey, "Northwest Ordinance," 937; Meyerson, *Endowed by Our Creator*, 123–24; David Scott, "The Ohio Constitution of 1803, Jefferson's Danbury Letter, and Religion in Education," *Ohio History* 121 (2014): 77; "Manasseh Cutler," New England Historical Society, http://www.newenglandhistoricalsociety.com/manasseh-cutler-ipswich-minister-set-great-westward-migration/, 3 December 2018. "Ohio Company of Associates," http://www.ohiohistorycentral.org/w/Ohio_Company_of_Associates, 5 December 2018; Hunter, ed., *Pathways*, 3–5.
14. Smith, "Freedom of Religion and the Land Ordinance of 1785," 590; Meyerson, *Endowed by Our Creator*, 122.
15. Duffey, "Northwest Ordinance," 929; Meyerson, *Endowed by Our Creator*, 124–25.
16. Meyerson, *Endowed by Our Creator*, 121, 124.
17. "Northwest Ordinance: July 13, 1787," http://avalon.law.yale.edu/18th_century/nworder.asp, 13 February 2018.
18. David M. Potter, *The Impending Crisis: 1848–1861* (New York: Harper Torch Books, 1976), 38–39.
19. Phillip R. Shriver, "Freedom's Proving Ground: The Heritage of the Northwest Ordinance," *The Wisconsin Magazine of History* 72 (Winter, 1988–1989): 131; Williams, ed., *Northwest Ordinance*, 63, 67–68, 73, 76;

"Northwest Ordinance: July 13, 1787." The Ordinance did allow for the recapture of fugitive slaves in the territory.
20. Duffey, "Northwest Ordinance," 938, 963–64.
21. Matthew J. Hegreness, "An Organic Law Theory of the Fourteenth Amendment: The Northwest Ordinance as the Source of Rights, Privileges, and Immunities," *The Yale Law Journal* 120 (May 2011): 1827.
22. "Northwest Ordinance: July 13, 1787."
23. John D. Barnhart and Dorothy L. Riker, *Indiana to 1816: The Colonial Period* (Indianapolis: Indiana Historical Society, 1994), 311; "American Settlements," http://iagenweb.org/jefferson/1879History/AmerSettlements.html, 3 December 2018.
24. James M. Bergquist, "Tracking the Origins of a Midwestern Culture: The Case of Central Indiana," *Indiana Magazine of History* 77 (March 1981): 28; Gordon S. Wood, *Empire of Liberty: A History of the Early Republic, 1789–1815* (New York: Oxford University Press, 2009), 363–65.
25. Bergquist, "Tracking the Origins of a Midwestern Culture," 1–32; Jon K. Lauck, Gleaves Whitney, and Joseph Hogan, eds., *Finding a New Midwestern History* (Lincoln: University of Nebraska Press, 2018), 14.
26. William E. Bartelt, *There I Grew Up: Remembering Abraham Lincoln's Indiana Youth* (Indianapolis: Indiana Historical Society Press, 2008); Williams, ed., *Northwest Ordinance*, 83.
27. "Ohio Constitution of 1803," http://www.ohiohistorycentral.org/w/Ohio_Constitution_of_1803_(Transcript), 12 January 2018; Scott, "The Ohio Constitution of 1803," 78.
28. "Indiana's Constitution of 1816," https://www.in.gov/history/2460.htm, 13 February 2018; "Indiana's Constitutional Past by Justice Brent E. Dickson, Justice, Indiana Supreme Court," https://www.in.gov/history/2609.htm, 13 February 2018.
29. R. Carlyle Buley, *The Old Northwest: Pioneer Period, 1815–1840 Volume 1* (Bloomington: Indiana University Press, 1978), 80; Donald F. Carmony, *Indiana, 1816–1850: The Pioneer Era* (Indianapolis: Indiana Historical Bureau and Indiana Historical Society, 1998), 470; *Constitution of the State of Illinois* (Washington City, IL: E. De Karafft, 1818), 14–16.
30. "Jefferson's Letter to Danbury Baptists," https://www.loc.gov/loc/lcib/9806/danpre.html, 7 August 2018.
31. Scott, "The Ohio Constitution of 1803," 74–75, 81–82, 87.
32. Williams, ed., *Northwest Ordinance*, 61; Beverley W. Bond Jr., *The Civilization of the Old Northwest: A Study of Political, Social, and Economic Development, 1788–1812* (New York: The MacMillan Company, 1934), 154–55; Stanley Harrold, *Border War: Fighting Over Slavery Before the Civil War* (Chapel Hill: The University of North Carolina Press, 2010), 19; Barnhart and Riker, *Indiana to 1816*, 347–48; Wood, *Empire of Liberty*, 362. Harrison remained ambivalent on slavery. In 1838, he said he believed in the "sovereign" independence of states to decide the issue, while also

supporting the free speech efforts of Free states to alter the status quo. See, "William Henry Harrison Discusses the Politics of Slavery," http://www.digitalhistory.uh.edu/disp_textbook.cfm?smtID=3&psid=347, 5 December 2018.
33. Onuf, *Statehood and Union*, 117–19; Bond, *Civilization*, 156–58, 165, 176–77.
34. Randy K. Mills, *Jonathan Jennings: Indiana's First Governor* (Indianapolis: Indiana Historical Society Press, 2005); Onuf, *Statehood and Union*, 120–23.
35. "Constitution of Michigan of 1835," http://www.legislature.mi.gov/documents/historical/miconstitution1835.htm, 10 January 2018; "Constitution of Wisconsin of 1848," http://content.wisconsinhistory.org/cdm/ref/collection/tp/id/71796, 10 January 2018; "Constitution of Minnesota of 1857," http://www.mnhs.org/library/constitution/pdf/democraticversion.pdf, 10 January 2018.
36. "New Constitution of Illinois (1848), http://www.idaillinois.org/cdm/ref/collection/isl2/id/211, 13 February 2018; "Ohio Constitution of 1851," https://www.legislature.ohio.gov/laws/ohio-constitution/section?const=1.07, 12 January 2018; "Indiana's Constitution of 1851," https://www.in.gov/history/2473.htm, 13 February 2018; "Indiana's Constitutional Past," https://www.in.gov/history/2609.htm, 13 February 2018.
37. Williams, ed., *Northwest Ordinance*, ix, 40, 53; Duffey, "Northwest Ordinance," 931; Hegreness, "An Organic Law Theory," 1850; R. Carlyle Buley, *The Old Northwest: Pioneer Period, 1815–1840 Volume 2* (Bloomington: Indiana University Press, 1978), 417, 421–24, 487; Bergquist, "Tracking the Origins of a Midwestern Culture," 22; Dickson D. Bruce Jr., *And They All Sang Hallelujah: Plain-Folk Camp-Meeting Religion, 1800–1845* (Knoxville: University of Tennessee Press, 1974); Jason S. Lantzer, *Rebel Bulldog: The Story of One Family, Two States, and the Civil War* (Indianapolis: Indiana Historical Society Press, 2017), 19; Jason S. Lantzer, *"Prohibition Is Here to Stay": The Reverend Edward S. Shumaker and the Dry Crusade in America* (Notre Dame, Indiana: University of Notre Dame Press, 2009), 13; Jason S. Lantzer, *Mainline Christianity: The Past and Future of America's Majority Faith* (New York: New York University Press, 2012), 29.
38. Jon Butler, *Awash in a Sea of Faith: Christianizing the American People* (Cambridge, Massachusetts: Harvard University Press, 1990), 258–59; Buley, *The Old Northwest: Pioneer Period, 1815–1840 Volume 2*, 428–29; Williams, ed., *The Northwest Ordinance*, 41, 50–52. Congregationalists were divided as to where missionary activity should take place, as Maine, Vermont, and New York needed church plants.
39. Williams, ed., *The Northwest Ordinance*, 50.

40. Lantzer, *Mainline Christianity*, 29; Lauck, Whitney, and Hogan, eds., *Finding a New*, 202.
41. Nathan O. Hatch, *The Democratization of American Christianity* (New Haven: Yale University Press, 1989), 3–4; Buley, *The Old Northwest: Pioneer Period, 1815–1840 Volume 2*, 424–27; Lantzer, *Rebel Bulldog*, 26; Lantzer, *Mainline Christianity*, 31; Bond, *Civilization*, 465. Jon Butler asserts that the Midwest is the nation's "most religiously complex region" still today. See, Lauck, Whitney, and Hogan, eds., *Finding a New*, 196.
42. Buley, *The Old Northwest: Pioneer Period, 1815–1840 Volume 2*, 449–51, 461–64, 469–86. While Roman Catholics, the Society of Friends, Shakers, Moravians, Millerites, Lutherans, Mennonites, United Brethren, Universalists, Unitarians, and Jews all found homes in the Midwest, there were limits to what took root. Most notably, the case of the Church of Jesus Christ of Latter-Day Saints (the Mormons). Joseph Smith was murdered in Illinois, in large part because of the doctrines he taught.
43. Williams, ed., *Northwest Ordinance*, 97, 102.
44. Lantzer, *Rebel Bulldog*, 28–29. After the Civil War, NWCU took the name of its founder, becoming Butler University.
45. Milton Rugoff, *The Beechers: An American Family in the Nineteenth Century* (New York: Harper and Row, 1981); Lyman Beecher Stowe, *Saints, Sinners, and Beechers* (Indianapolis: The Bobbs-Merrill Company, 1934); Debby Applegate, *The Most Famous Man in America: The Biography of Henry Ward Beecher* (New York: Doubleday, 2006); Lantzer, *Rebel Bulldog*, 19, 32.
46. Lantzer, *Mainline Christianity*, 31.
47. Daniel Walker Howe, *The Political Culture of the American Whigs* (Chicago: University of Chicago Press, 1984).
48. Philip Hamburger, *Separation of Church and State* (Cambridge, Massachusetts: Harvard University Press, 2002), 200, 243–45.
49. Butler, *Awash in a Sea of Faith*, 132; Charles Kettleborough, ed., *Constitution Making in Indiana: Volume II, 1851–1916* (Indianapolis: Indiana Historical Bureau, 1975), 62–67; Lantzer, *Rebel Bulldog*, 30.
50. Duffey, "The Northwest Ordinance," 965–66.
51. Harrold, *Border War*, 4–5, 65, 86–87; Henry Clyde Hubbart, *The Older Middle West, 1840–1880* (New York: D. Appleton-Century Company, 1936), 44–45.
52. "Southwest Territory 1790–1796," http://www.tngenweb.org/tnletters/territories/sw-terr.html, 13 February 2018; Hegreness, "An Organic Law Theory," 1846–47; David M. Potter, *The Impending Crisis: 1848–1861* (New York: Harper Torch Books, 1976), 53–54; Daniel Walker Howe, *What Hath God Wrought: The Transformation of America, 1815–1848* (New York: Oxford University Press, 2007), 136; Christine Leigh Heyrman, *Southern Cross: The Beginnings of the Bible Belt* (Chapel Hill: The University of North Carolina Press, 1997), 158; Hamburger, *Separation of Church and State*, 265–66; Lantzer, *Rebel Bulldog*, 31; Hunter, ed., *Pathways*, 14.

53. Lantzer, *Mainline Christianity*, 33.
54. Harrold, *Border War*, 27.
55. "Levi Coffin," https://www.nps.gov/people/levi-coffin.htm, 3 December 2018.
56. Lantzer, *Rebel Bulldog*, 32–33.
57. Ibid., 31.
58. Ibid., *Rebel Bulldog*, 32–33.
59. Joanne B. Freeman, *The Field of Blood: Violence in Congress and the Road to Civil War* (New York: Farrar, Straus and Giroux, 2018).
60. Steven E. Woodworth, *Manifest Destinies: America's Westward Expansion and the Road to the Civil War* (New York: Alfred A. Knopf, 2010), 346; Onuf, *Statehood and Union*, 127.
61. Potter, *The Impending Crisis*, 21.
62. *Jones v. Van Zandt*, 46 U.S. 215 (1847); *Strader v. Graham*, 51 U.S. 82 (1851); *Dred Scott v. Sandford*, 60 U.S. 393 (1857); Hegreness, "An Organic Law Theory," 1836, 1862–65, 1869–72.
63. Hegreness, "An Organic Law Theory," 1872; Hunter, ed., *Pathways*, 15.
64. Onuf, *Statehood and Union*, 139.
65. Jane H. Pease, "The Road to the Higher Law," *New York History* 40 (April 1959); 117–36.
66. Harold Holzer, *Lincoln at Cooper Union: The Speech That Made Abraham Lincoln President* (New York: Simon and Schuster, 2004). Lincoln's address was originally scheduled for Henry Ward Beecher's Plymouth Church in Brooklyn.
67. *Chicago Tribune*, 19 October 1993.
68. David S. Reynolds, *Mightier Than the Sword: Uncle Tom's Cabin and the Battle for America* (New York: W.W. Norton and Company, 2011); Lantzer, *Rebel Bulldog*, 36–37.
69. Jacquelyn S. Nelson, *Indiana Quakers Confront the Civil War* (Indianapolis: Indiana Historical Society, 1991); Shriver, "Freedom's Proving Ground," 131.
70. Lauck, Whitney, and Hogan, eds., *Finding a New*, 39
71. Duffey, "Northwest Ordinance," 929; Shriver, "Freedom's Proving Ground," 127. As Paul Finkelman notes, the Ordinance became an "icon" in the region. See, Hunter, ed., *Pathways*, 2.
72. Williams, ed., *The Northwest Ordinance*, 62; Onuf, *Statehood and Union*, 145, 151–52.
73. Eric Foner, *Free Soil, Free Labor, Free Men: The Ideology of the Republican Party Before the Civil War* (New York: Oxford University Press, 1995).
74. Duffey, "Northwest Ordinance," 930, 933; Scott, "The Ohio Constitution of 1803," 88; Lauck, Whitney, and Hogan, eds., *Finding a New*, 7.
75. Wood, *Empire of Liberty*, 70, 122; Hegreness, "An Organic Law Theory," 1820, 1824, 1831; Lauck, Whitney, and Hogan, eds., *Finding a New*, 18; Hubbart, *The Older Middle West*, 173.

Marcia Noe | The Innocent Midwest and the New Midwestern Pastoral

"In 1896 the purity of the inner United States was proclaimed by both political parties jointly and severally," wrote Thomas Beer in *The Mauve Decade* (83). Beer noted that nineteenth-century American drama often coded the rural as innocent and noble: "These shows included a pure farmer, a pure country girl, a villain from the city, and an urban adventuress ... The specific of these plays was simple: the country mice might have foibles or even stumble into sin but their hearts were in the right place."[1]

Such plays participate in the construction of the Midwest as the region that, in the words of cultural geographer James R. Shortridge, "came to symbolize Arcadian idealism ... This identification is the unwavering fact of Middle-western existence—a root identity equivalent to New England's puritanism."[2] Over time and throughout multiple media—newspaper and magazine articles, television shows, films, and advertisements—this pastoral ideal has been central to the notion of the Midwest as the locus of all that is simple, pure, good-hearted, and, above all, innocent.

In 1827, Ohio journalist Timothy Flint published a description of the Midwest that emphasized such beneficent qualities:

> Thousands of independent and happy yeomen, who have emigrated from New England to Ohio and Indiana ... with the ample abundance that fills their granaries, with their young orchards ... beside their beautiful rivers, and beech woods ... would hardly be willing to exchange the sylvan range of their fee simple empires, their droves of cattle, horses, and domestic animals, and the ability to employ the leisure of half of their time as they choose, for the interior of square stone or brick walls, to breathe floccules of cotton, and to contemplate the whirl of innumerable wheels for

> fourteen hours of six days of every week in the year.... But we may still be permitted to believe the condition of the yeoman's children, to be more conducive to health, *innocence* and happiness.... Farmers and their children are strong, and *innocent* and moral almost of necessity.² (emphasis mine)

In this encomium of the Ohio Valley, Flint makes some rhetorical moves that are also found in several early American novels set in the Midwest. He emphasizes the Edenic quality of its rural beauty and abundance; he draws a contrast between the agrarian Garden of the West and another, less beneficent locale; and he asserts its potential for creating a democratic social order where citizens are free, equal, happy, and independent and, above all, innocent. This notion of midwestern innocence, grounded in the foundational ideology of our nation, persists today as an identifying characteristic of the region.

Midwestern innocence is rooted in the democratic ideology that has informed our larger culture.⁴ Andrew R.L. Cayton and Susan E. Gray emphasize that the birth of the region occurred nearly simultaneously with that of American citizenship; midwestern values and institutions were deeply informed by the legislation that not only brought it into being but also laid the groundwork for the new nation: the Land Ordinance of 1785 and the Northwest Ordinance of 1787. Theses foundational documents of our democracy endorsed and promoted widespread land ownership, public education, protection for civil and religious liberties, and free—as opposed to slave—labor.⁵ As David D. Anderson remarks, "The impact of [the Northwest Ordinance] on popular thinking in the nineteenth century, as the Old Northwest became the Midwest, can hardly be over-estimated."⁶

Early American statesmen and authors promulgated this democratic ideal, based on the Enlightenment theory of natural rights and the promise of agrarianism. The latter ultimately derives from the pastoral poetry of Hesiod, Theocritus, and Virgil that posits the city as decadent and the country as a refuge where jaded urbanities can find rest and refreshment through communion with Nature. This pastoral tradition carried over into the Renaissance, as John Armstrong Crow points out: "Nature becomes the symbol of perfect harmony, goodness, and peace. The shepherd, or "natural man" embodies these same qualities of perfection, and his loves, too, are perfect. Poets, novelists, and courtiers become shepherds in this pastoral literature in order to make the pattern complete."[7] David Stouck more directly addresses this kind of literature, positing innocence at the heart of the pastoral tradition:

> In its simplest form a pastoral of *innocence* marks a retreat in time and place to an enclosed, green world, a retreat expressing man's dream of a simplified, harmonious existence from which the complexities of society and natural process (age, disease, and death) are eliminated ... The pastoral landscape is ultimately a place of *innocent* erotic fulfillment wherein the imagination is reunited to the world in a maternal embrace."[8] (emphases mine)

Echoing the French Physiocrats' theory of Nature as a source of goodness that produces virtue in those who work the land, the writings of J. Hector St. John de Crèvecoeur, George Washington, Benjamin Franklin, and Thomas Jefferson laid the groundwork for a strong agrarian orientation in America that ultimately gave rise to legislation such as the Homestead Act of 1862, which awarded 160 acres to those who would farm and improve them for at least five years, and the Morrill Act, also passed in 1862, which established a system of land-grant universities that focused on agricultural education.[9]

The first of these writers asserts that becoming a freehold farmer was an essential step in becoming an American, calling such farmers "the most respectable set of people in this part of the world ... for their industry, their happy independence, the great share of freedom they possess" and observing that "[t]his formerly rude soil has been converted by my father into a pleasant farm, and, in return, it has established all our rights; on it is founded our rank, our freedom, our power as citizens, our importance." Crèvecoeur's notion that the middle border, situated between the lawless western wilderness and the problem-filled cities of the eastern seaboard, was the ideal location for settlement was an early manifestation of the innocent Midwest.[10]

The founders of our nation conveyed a similar agrarian message. Writing of the Northwest Territory, George Washington asserts that "[t]he Citizens of America, placed in the most enviable condition, as the sole Lords and Proprietors of a vast Tract of Continent ... [are] to be considered as the Actors in a most conspicuous Theatre, which seems to be peculiarly designed by Providence for the display of human greatness and felicity."[11] In his autobiography, Benjamin Franklin suggests that it might be God's will that Native Americans be removed from their ancestral lands "in order to make room for the Cultivators of the Earth."[12] Similar sentiments appear in Thomas Jefferson's *Notes on the State of Virginia*, as he states that "[t]hose who labor in the earth are the chosen people of God ... whose breast he has made his peculiar deposit for substantial and genuine virtue."[13] "The myth of small-town goodness, neighborliness, mutuality and good will was a direct descendant of Thomas Jefferson's agrarian myth of rural virtue and superiority," concludes John E. Miller.[14]

Equally significant in the construction of the innocent Midwest were the Calvinist doctrines and traditions that informed American culture from the earliest days of its existence. As Max Weber argues, Calvinism fueled the belief that "[t]he earning of money within the modern economic order is, so long as it is done legally, the result and the expression of virtue and proficiency in a calling." According to Weber, one of the most significant consequences of the Protestant Reformation was the belief that "the fulfillment of worldly duties is in all circumstances the only way to live acceptably to God."[15] From this point, it was only a small step to the mindset that wealth earned through labor was a sign of virtue and salvation, a worldview that nicely complemented and reinforced prevailing agrarian notions and gave rise to a work ethic that has become fundamental to the American character.

In "New England, Ohio's Western Reserve, and the New Jerusalem in the West," Anderson acknowledges this Calvinist influence on midwestern identity formation, writing of the migration of New Englanders to Ohio that "the settlers brought a determination to succeed as clear proof of God's favor and a greater determination to reform and civilize and purify the West in obedience to God's will and the dictates of their consciences as heir to John Calvin." Anderson emphasizes that this early grounding in Calvinism in the Ohio Western Reserve resulted in midwestern social movements, such as temperance and abolition, that aimed at the moral improvement of individuals and the consequential betterment of society. "The settlers," concludes Anderson, "were determined to fuse God's will, nature's promise, and moral certainty as they pursued their varied causes with remarkably similar single-mindedness."[16] By the nineteenth century, this religious emphasis was reflected in the central role that Christianity played in sentimental domestic novels such as Susan Warner's *The Wide, Wide World*, in which the orphaned heroine achieves self-sufficiency and domestic happiness through hard work and Christian virtue. Ann Douglas, in *The Feminization of American Culture*, emphasizes the significance of religion in nineteenth-century American life, crediting the influence of Protestant clergymen, in concert with the efforts of middle-class Christian ladies, with instilling Christian dogma and values at the core of nineteenth-century American cultural production. "Between 1820 and 1875," Douglas concludes, "religion became the message of America's conventional and cultural life."[17]

Linking the Christianity that Douglas demonstrates as having informed Victorian culture to the agrarianism enshrined in American life through legislation and literature, Weber writes that "[t]he high esteem for agriculture as a peculiarly important branch of activity, also especially consistent with piety, which the Puritans shared, applied ... not to the landlord, but to the yeoman and farmer."[18] Unsurprisingly, antebellum novels with these ideological underpinnings often portray the Midwest as a rural Eden where contact with abundant Nature through agricultural labor forms the basis for a new start and the good life among happy, virtuous people. As Cayton and Gray remark, "[C]ontemporaries thought of the territory north of the Ohio River as a promised land."[19] Caroline A. Soule's *The Pet of the Settlement* (1860) exemplifies this belief. Henry Nash Smith writes that Soule's novel makes the case that "frontier farmers are noble and that the process of advancing the agricultural frontier yields vast consequences for the good of mankind" but argues that "[f]or all her four years on the prairie, Mrs. Soule can not find the literary means to embody the affirmation of the agrarian ideal that her theory calls for."[20] Despite Smith's poor opinion of the novel's aesthetic value, *The Pet of the Settlement* does succeed in clearly articulating the paradisiacal qualities of frontier Iowa: "The golden air was fragrant with balmy winds; the sky was splendid, a thousand flitting tints of blue and amber chasing over its zenith, while pale, purplish mists hung about its horizon; the woodland grew each day more gorgeous in its coloring; the river sang more softly, while the prairies were more magnificent than ever ... It seemed to Margaret like Eden."[21]

Passages very much like this idyllic description of an Iowa prairie can be found in a number of early American novels that represent the Midwest as a beautiful, fertile Garden of Eden where contact with Nature facilitates harmonious living and moral regeneration in contrast to the decadence and superficiality of life in cities on the eastern seaboard, the South, or Europe. In Soule's novel, a blonde, blue-eyed baby girl, abandoned on the Iowa prairie and adopted by the people of the "borderland, the only spot we have yet found where the brotherhood of men is recognized as an actual as well as an ideal thing" functions as a metonym for the innocent Midwest.[22]

Like Soule, a number of early American novelists wrote in this pastoral mode. But while the old pastoral looks wistfully backward with longing for a more innocent life of rural community in harmony with Nature, this new midwestern pastoral novel looks forward and westward. Grounded in the ideologies of Christianity and democracy that drive their structures of feeling and values, such novels feature characters who leave the corrupt Old World, the urbanized eastern seaboard, or the decadent South for the Edenic Midwest; through contact with this bucolic region, they are ennobled and reborn, financially, socially, and morally. These novels, governed by East-West, South-West, Europe-America, or city-country dichotomies, are organized through their tying binary oppositions such as vanity-virtue, indolence-industry, and profligacy-frugality to these respective locales. A rhetorical strategy employed in some of these novels is to privilege the latter term of each binary by identifying it with Christianity, a powerful rhetorical appeal for many readers of that time.

More consistently, these early novels oppose the aristocratic, elitist culture of other locales with the Jeffersonian democracy of the West, identifying the latter as the source of true happiness, order, and virtue and emphasizing that democratic values lie at the heart of the good life by featuring characters who promote or become involved with representative democracy. In part because these works link the region to the above-discussed ideologies, they have been effective in perpetuating the notion of the innocent Midwest that lives on today in the American cultural imaginary.

Perhaps the earliest manifestation of the New Midwestern Pastoral is Gilbert Imlay's novel, *The Emigrants* (1793), which recounts the story of a British family, deeply in debt from profligate living, who immigrate to Illinois territory to rebuild their lives. Ruined morally and financially, the T. family discovers in the region a natural beauty and abundance that are morally restorative: "Everything seemed to be enchanted as we passed the extensive plains of the Illinois country.... The fertile and boundless savannas were covered with flocks of buffalo, elk, and deer ... we seemed to have regained Paradise."²³ The pastoral tradition seems especially apparent in passages such as this one: "It is impossible for any country to appear to advantage after you have seen the Illinois ... and could you see the naivete of the inhabitants ... you would believe you was [sic] living in those Arcadian days, when the tuneful shepherd used to compose sonnets to his mistress and when the charms of love were propitiated in sequestered groves, and smiling meads."²⁴

This Arcadian novel of the innocent Midwest, which W.M. Verhoeven describes as "extraordinarily influential" and as achieving "immense popularity" in England, is thrown into high relief through contrast with the decadent shores of Europe that were so recently abandoned by the financially ruined T. family.²⁵ When Caroline, the novel's heroine, is advised by her uncle not to return to England, he cautions her to "contrast in your mind, the genial charms of the social pleasures of this hospitable country, with the unnatural customs of the European world—and then recollect, that you would pass from a state of *innocence* and joy, into perturbed elements of folly and dissipation"²⁶ (emphasis mine).

The innocent Midwest not only rehabilitates the Ts but provides the foundation for Arl—ton's vision of democracy in action. In contrast to the hierarchical social world of England so recently abandoned, Arl—ton's notion of social perfection involves his purchasing 256 square miles of land on the Ohio River on which to found a model society. He plans to give Revolutionary War veterans "a fee-simple in the soil he occupies," each one eligible to sit in a house of representatives of twenty members meeting each Sunday "to take into consideration the measures necessary to promote the encouragements of agriculture and all useful arts, as well as to discuss upon the science of government and jurisprudence" (295), a plan that echoes provisions of the Northwest Ordinance.[27]

A similar structure of values is inscribed in *Mabel Vaughan* (1857), written by popular novelist Maria Susanna Cummins, author of *The Lamplighter*.[28] *Mabel Vaughan*'s action takes place in the years immediately following the Panic of 1833 and alternates from country to city, a place that Baym says the novel constructs as "a realization of an acquisitive economic system where money shapes human relations" and that is placed in contrast with an "ideal community in the West."[29] As the book progresses, these two terms, as well as the values associated with each, work in opposition to each other and function rhetorically, directing the reader's sympathy to the latter term in the binary: Urban society is opposed to rural home and community, social prominence to familial affection, fashion to feeling, vanity to virtue, business to farming, and idleness and speculation to hard work. This pattern is established in the first chapter in a paradigmatic scene in which a twelve-year-old Mabel is torn between playing with her chums and studying her lessons. Mabel's schoolgirl vacillations foreshadow the conflict she will experience when, as a beautiful young woman, she will be forced to choose between duty and pleasure. And the moral lesson that she learns when her teacher points out that the apple orchard is not conducive to study is also prophetic: Choose the appropriate environment and you will be more likely to make subsequent wise choices.

When she leaves school to reside in her father's mansion in New York City, eighteen-year-old Mabel finds herself in a sophisticated urban world of upper-middle-class socialites obsessed with clothes, admirers, and parties. Although Mabel enjoys her new status as a brilliant belle, she is brought up short and faced with her neglect of duty by the Christian example set by the poor but loving Hope family, particularly that of the youngest daughter, Rose, who, despite her ill health, functions as a source of spiritual strength for her brother Jack, who is continually tempted by bad companions and alcohol. Reflecting upon her nearly estranged relationship with her own brother, Harry, who is succumbing to those same temptations, Mabel, after much soul searching, forgoes an excursion with her fashionable friends to accompany her brother to the country, where he is to reform his character and study law. Mabel successfully negotiates this crisis of conscience by basing her choice upon the Christian ethos that her teacher had sought to inculcate in her: "Beware of self-love and cultivate to the utmost degree a universal charity."[30]

Having been thus fortified by Christian virtue, Mabel is armed with the moral and emotional resources to cope with the adversity that befalls her family. First, Mr. Vaughan is ruined financially; then Louise falls ill and dies after learning of her own husband's bankruptcy and death. Consequently, Mabel takes her two orphaned nephews to join her father and brother on a farm in eastern Illinois near Lake Michigan, extolling the regenerative powers of the Garden of the West: "But these boundless woods, and lakes, and prairies, are well able to defend themselves;—they excite one's activity and energy, too, by their richness and munificence. I am sure I never look upon them without feeling strengthened for everything that is good, and great, and generous."[31]

Thus, the midwestern environment plays a crucial role in the rejuvenation of Mabel's family, as the decadence of the East, represented in large part by her sister Louise's frivolous, shallow, and selfish life, is contrasted with the moral potency of the West. Harry, who has gone to Illinois to help his father through his crisis, recognizes the beneficent effects of frontier living when he writes his sister, "This is indeed a glorious country. I feel a larger life stirring within me, when I breathe the free air of these noble woods and prairies. It inspires me with new energy, and gives me strength to believe that with God's help I may yet live to some worthy purpose."[32] In the Garden of the West, Harry is able to give up drinking and gambling and become a successful farmer and family man, choosing a minister's daughter to wed instead of the silly socialite he flirted with in New York City.

Mabel, too, achieves a happy and productive life on the prairie; she is rewarded by the love of Bayard Percival, a hard-working and articulate young farmer-lawyer who asks her to be his wife. Christianity and democracy are coupled in Percival's strong commitment to keep the frontier free of slavery. His election to the United States Congress on an antislavery platform signals the triumph of western democratic values over an eastern elitist ethos. Another such coupling of democratic values to Christian beliefs is seen in the working-class Hope family, who practice the Christian virtues of faith, hope, and charity and end up prospering on the frontier while the wealthy idlers and social climbers either die or are left behind in New York.

A novel closely paralleling *Mabel Vaughan* in ideological undergirding and structure is the prolific Mrs. E.D.E.N. Southworth's eighteenth novel, *India: The Pearl of Pearl River* (1853).[33] As Annette Kolodny observes, "[t]he domestic novel of relocation ... provided the major vehicle through which a decade of American Eves imaginatively took their place in Eden ... The two most able practitioners of the form ... (E.D.E.N) Southworth and Maria Susanna Cummins—clearly intended to portray the removal from east to west as the rejection of a blighted garden and the attainment of one 'not only undiminished, but almost untouched.'"[34] While the action in *Mabel Vaughan* alternates between city and country, Southworth's novel is set in the South, the East, and the Midwest during the decade that immediately preceded the Civil War and, like many works of that period, deals with the issue of slavery. A Bildungsroman that traces the maturation and moral evolution of Mark Sutherland, a Yale graduate and a Mississippian who will inherit three lucrative plantations, *India* not only exposes the evils of slavery but also offers a solution: Liberate your slaves and find a new future on the free soil of the Midwest.

When Mark accepts his classmate Lauderdale's invitation to travel to New York and attend an abolitionist meeting before returning to Mississippi, this experience turns out to be a defining moment for a young man whose aristocratic and patriarchal values were previously reflected in his frequent use of the phrase, "Enter life, and take possession."[35] Influenced by what he has learned about slavery in the North, Mark writes home, denouncing the institution that was to provide his patrimony. His fiancé, India Sutherland, attributes his change of attitude to the more democratic social conventions of the North: "Here, for weeks past, he has been mingling freely with these sorts of persons—mixing in their assemblies, where people of all colors and castes meet on equal terms, in a stifling crowd."[36] Enamored of a life of luxury, pleasure, and indolence underwritten by a slave economy, she breaks their engagement, rejecting Mark's democratic plan to free his slaves, sell his land, and relocate to the Illinois frontier to practice law.

Despite much hard work, Mark is at first unable to succeed as a lawyer on the Illinois frontier, so he takes a position as a tutor to the sons of Colonel Ashley, a wealthy Virginia plantation owner. Here he meets and falls in love with Rosalie Vivian, visiting there with her stepmother. Shortly thereafter, Mark and Rosalie marry and depart together for Rock River country in Illinois. Although Kolodny accurately points out that Southworth's descriptions of Mississippi's Pearl River Valley are more numerous, detailed, and appealing than her depictions of the novel's Illinois setting, Rosalie's response to her new environment is similar to that of Mabel Vaughan's in its emphasis on its restorative powers:

> I know something inspires me with unlimited hope just now.... there is about this country an air of youth, vigor, hope, promise, unlimited, indescribable.... here, the age, the weariness, and the sorrow of the old world has been left behind. That this is a breaking out in a new place, or rather that this country and people, and we ourselves, are a new creation, fresh from the hand of God, and with a new promise!"[37]

The trajectory of the narrative juxtaposes Mark's struggles with adversity and subsequent rise in the West, aided by the loving support of Rosalie, with the deterioration of St. Gerald Ashley in the South, corrupted by the indifference of his selfish wife India. Here Southworth opposes aristocratic and democratic ways of life most effectively by contrasting the environments in which each way of life flourishes. Her description of India in her boudoir suggests a sultan's seraglio. By contrast, Southworth's description of Mark and Rosalie's Illinois homestead emphasizes its Edenic and democratic qualities:

> The grounds were unpretending, too—behind the house a kitchen garden and young orchard; in front and at the sides a spacious yard, where single great forest trees were left standing, with rural seats fixed under their shade. In that rich and fertile soil the favorite rose flourished luxuriantly.... Mark Sutherland approached this sweet home. Every care and sorrow dropped from his spirit as he opened the little wicker-gate that separated his garden of Eden from the wilderness."[38]

Here Southworth endorses an ethic of achievement and hard work, linked to the West and opposed to an aristocratic mindset that values being, owning, and having, which she associates with the South. Lincoln Lauderdale, a Northerner who will have to work for a living, articulates this structure of values when he suggests that despite Mark's wealth and social status, he has what it takes to make it on his own: "My dear Mark, I think that I, that you, even you possess those very qualities out of which really distinguished men are formed, and that if destiny had not 'thrust' a sort of moneyed and landed greatness upon you, that even you would 'achieve' some judicial, political, diplomatic, or intellectual greatness of some sort."[39] Rosalie Vivian, who will one day become Mark's wife, echoes Lauderdale's sentiments: "We have no royal road to distinction in our country. We have no ready-made great men. None are 'born great'; none have 'greatness thrust upon them.' If any would be great, he must 'achieve greatness.' Nearly all of our heroes and statesmen have struggled up from the humblest places in society."[40]

In this book, as in *Mabel Vaughan*, the democratic ideology that informs the novel dictates a plot in which a self-made man achieves the good life, domestic happiness and political success in the Midwest. Just as Cummins makes her hero, Bayard Percival, relinquish his inherited wealth before he can succeed on the Illinois frontier through hard work on his own farm, so Southworth first has Mark Sutherland repudiate his inheritance and start from scratch as a frontier lawyer before he is allowed to enjoy success and happiness. This novel also parallels *Mabel Vaughan* in its foregrounding of representative democracy, as Mark, like Bayard Percival, so successfully articulates his antislavery views on the frontier that he wins a seat in Congress.

Southworth employs a second rhetorical strategy similar to that used by Cummins in *Mabel Vaughan* by linking the ethos of Christianity to the democratic values that the novel endorses. Mark's conversion to the antislavery movement was begun when he was cared for while imprisoned after a fight by "some excellent men, and women also— persons whose disinterestedness, benevolence, gentleness, and perfect sincerity gave me such a deep and beautiful impression of the Christian character as I had never received from book or pulpit."[41] Although Mark has been repudiated by his mother, uncles, and fiancé, his resolve to carry through with his plan to free his slaves is strengthened when Rosalie sends him her Bible, with this passage from the twenty-seventh Psalm marked: "When my mother and father forsake me, the Lord will take me up."[42]

Later, linking the promise of the West to the promise of Christian salvation, Rosalie adds, "Let us be faithful to our part of the covenant. Oh, let us be faithful; let no sin, selfishness, injustice of ours cause us to lose the glorious promise."[43] The Christian ethos of the novel is also revealed in its ending: Rosalie's untimely death offers Mark the opportunity to renew his relationship with the now-widowed India, who, chastened by a bad marriage and repentant of her sinful ways, frees her slaves, pays off her father's creditors, and begins to earn an honest living as a teacher. The two then marry and start a family in Illinois.

Although Kolodny asserts that the novels she discusses "seem to have left no lasting imprint on our shared cultural imagination," a review of mainstream midwestern cultural productions from *Adventures of Huckleberry Finn* through *The Music Man* to *The Prairie Home Companion* and beyond indicates otherwise.[44] Kolodny appears not to have perceived that the strong grounding of these novels in Christian, democratic, and agrarian ideologies was powerful enough, if not to ensure their longevity and canonicity, then to enable their participation in the construction of the innocent Midwest in our national consciousness. Contrary to Kolodny's assertion, the notion of the innocent Midwest has been an enduring one, surviving assault by the prairie realists of the late nineteenth century and the village rebels of the early twentieth, as well as by modernist and postmodernist debunkers and deconstructors. The novels discussed in this essay helped to shape the notion of the innocent Midwest and, in so doing, reinforced the ideologies in which American culture is grounded.

As several scholars have observed, the Middle West has come to function synechdochally in our culture as the most American part of America.[45] The reasons that the notion of midwestern innocence lies at the very core of the region's identity can be traced not only to the strong hold that its foundational ideologies have on the American psyche but also to the way in which the idea of the innocent Midwest meets deep-seated national needs. Americans need the Midwest to be innocent, to be the moral center of an often transgressive nation dominated by coastal elites who continually practice unconscionable politics; in other words, we need the innocent Midwest so that we can like ourselves as Americans. Moreover, we need the innocence of the Midwest to function as the foundation of our national myth, to be the matrix of a democratic society where free, equal, and independent citizens can achieve the Jeffersonian dream—the good life as successful farmers, businessmen, workers, and professionals—to enable us to believe, as Cayton declares, that "[t]he fortunate residents of the Old Northwest had the power to perfect this world" and that this power still obtains today.[46] The novels discussed here participate in the social construction of the innocent Midwest by enacting narratives in which the Edenic promise of the region comes true.

Notes

1. Thomas Beer, *The Mauve Decade* [1926] (New York: Vintage Books, 1961), 79.
2. James R. Shortridge, *The Middle West: Its Meaning in American Culture* (Lawrence: University Press of Kansas, 1989), 7.
3. Timothy Flint, review of *America*, by Alexander Hill Everett, *Western Monthly Review* 1 (July 1827): 169–76, 170.
4. Definitions of ideology abound. The two most pertinent to the way the term is used here are Sally Haslanger's definition of ideology as "the beliefs, concepts, and practices that constitute one's social identity" (qtd. in Jason Stanley, "The War on Thugs," *The Chronicle Review* 26 June 2015, B10–12, B10) and Martin Seliger's definition of ideology as "sets of ideas by which men [sic] posit, explain and justify ends and means of organized social action, and specifically political action, irrespective of whether such action aims to preserve, uproot, amend, or rebuild a given social order" (qtd. in Terry Eagleton, *Ideology: An Introduction*. London: Verso, 1991, 6).
5. Andrew R.L. Cayton and Susan E. Gray, "The Story of the Midwest: An Introduction," in Cayton and Gray, eds., *The American Midwest: Essays on Regional History* (Bloomington: Indiana University Press, 2001), 1–26.
6. David D. Anderson, "Notes Toward a Definition of the Mind of the Midwest," *MidAmerica* 3 (1976): 7–16, 12.
7. John Armstrong Crow, *Spain: The Root and the Flower* (New York: Harper and Row, 1963), 187.
8. David Stouck, *Willa Cather's Imagination* (Lincoln: University of Nebraska Press, 1975), 36.
9. Henry Nash Smith. *The Virgin Land: The American West as Symbol and Myth* (New York: Vintage Books, 1957), 145; 190–200.
10. J. Hector St. John de Crèvecoeur, *Letters from an American Farmer and Sketches of Eighteenth-Century America* [1782] (New York: The New American Library of World Literature, 1963), 79, 48, 65–67.

11. Qtd. in Gleaves Whitney, "The Upper Midwest as the Second Promised Land," in Jon K. Lauck, Gleaves Whitney, and Joseph Hogan, eds., *Finding a New Midwestern History* (Lincoln: University of Nebraska Press, 2018), 281–302, 281.
12. Benjamin Franklin, *The Autobiography of Benjamin Franklin*, Louis P. Masur, ed. and intro., The Bedford Series in American History and Culture (New York: Bedford Books, 1993), 120.
13. Thomas Jefferson, *Notes on the History of Virginia* [1785], William Peden, ed. and intro. (Chapel Hill: University of North Carolina Press, 1982), 164–65.
14. John E. Miller, "Midwestern Small Towns," in Lauck, Whitney, and Hogan, eds., 129–42, 130.
15. Max Weber, *The Protestant Ethic and the Spirit of Capitalism*, trans. Talcott Parsons, foreword R.H. Tawney (New York: Charles Scribner's Sons, 1958), 53–54, 81.
16. David D. Anderson, "New England, Ohio's Western Reserve, and the New Jerusalem in the West," *MidAmerica* 18 (1991): 31–43, 38, 39.
17. Ann Douglas, *The Feminization of American Culture* [1977] (New York: Anchor Books, 1988), ix, 6.
18. Weber, *The Protestant Ethic*, 173.
19. Cayton and Gray, "The Story of the Midwest," 10.
20. Smith, *Virgin Land*, 249, 250.
21. Caroline A. Soule, *The Pet of the Settlement: A Story of Prairie-Land* (Boston: A Tompkins, 1860), 79.
22. Soule, *Pet of the Settlement*, 56.
23. Gilbert Imlay, *The Emigrants* [1793] Facsimile Edition (Gainesville, FL: Scholars Facsimiles and Reprints, 1964), 258–59.
24. Ibid., 259.
25. W.M. Verhoeven, "'New Philosophers' in the Backwoods: Romantic Primitivism in the 1790s Novel," *The Wordsworth Circle* 32, no. 3 (Summer 2001): 130–33, 130, 132. Attesting to the novel's influence, Verhoeven reports that a number of novels were written in imitation of *The Emigrants*, citing Frances Jacson's *Disobedience* (1797), George Walker's *The Vagabond* (1799), and the anonymously authored *Henry Willoughby* (1798) and *Berkeley Hall* (1796).
26. Imlay, *Emigrants*, 279.
27. Ibid., 295.
28. Nina Baym, *Women's Fiction: A Guide to Novels by and about Women in America, 1820–70* (Urbana: University of Illinois Press, 1993), 164. Baym reports that Cummins's earlier novel, *The Lamplighter* (1854) sold 40,000 copies during the first two months after publication and 70,000 copies overall that year.
29. Ibid., 172.

30. Maria Susanna Cummins, *Mabel Vaughan* (Boston: John P. Jewett and Company, 1857), 10.
31. Ibid., 390.
32. Ibid., 318.
33. Baym reports that according to Frank Luther Mott, Southworth was "the greatest publishing success in nineteenth-century America.... it seems fair to say that Southworth's fiction was widely known and widely read in America for some forty years of the nineteenth century, between the publication of *Retribution* [1849] and her death in 1899," 114. First appearing as a serial in the *National Era* as *Mark Sutherland* in 1853, *India* was published two years later.
34. Annette Kolodny, *The Land Before Her: Fantasy and Experience of the American Frontiers, 1630–1860* (Chapel Hill: The University of North Carolina Press, 1984), 202; qtd. in *India*, 269.
35. E.D.E.N. Southworth, *India; or The Pearl of Pearl River* [1855] (Philadelphia: T.B. Peterson and Brothers, 1859), 26.
36. Ibid., 63.
37. Ibid., 269.
38. Ibid., 345.
39. Ibid., 31.
40. Ibid., 192.
41. Ibid., 101.
42. Ibid., 151.
43. Ibid., 269.
44. Kolodny, *Land Before Her*, 225.
45. See Andrew R.L. Cayton and Peter S. Onuf, *The Midwest and the Nation: Rethinking the History of an American Region* (Bloomington: Indiana University Press, 1990), 85; R. Douglas Hurt, "Midwestern Distinctiveness," in Cayton and Gray, eds., 162–63; and Shortridge, 33.
46. Cayton and Gray, "The Story of the Midwest," 10.

Wayne Duerkes | Travel Literature and Midwestern Identity

The Case of Illinois

In the summer of 1848, Rebecca Burlend was besieged with visitors during her return trip to England to visit family. In 1831, her husband, John, had decided that "it would tend to the good of the family" to immigrate to the United States.[1] He had chosen to settle in Pike County, Illinois, based off of letters sent home from an acquaintance.[2] Like most of her visitors, before the move, Rebecca had never traveled very far from her home. Now, upon her return, as an experienced American frontier settler, friends confronted Rebecca with requests to regale them with stories of her adventures. By the time of her visit, the English laboring class had developed a keen interest in emigration across the Atlantic and voraciously devoured all news on the subject. Rebecca, not highly educated, enlisted the talents of her son to "profess ... a true picture" of her experiences that were to be based on fact, not fiction.[3] By setting her experience to paper, Rebecca could answer the flood of questions that dealt with as many aspects of emigration as she felt obligated to pass on to the hopeful travelers in a concise, efficient, and straightforward manner. Her little guide sold over 2000 copies locally, requiring a second edition to meet the demand.[4]

With their decision to emigrate, the Burlends had unconsciously decided to redefine themselves as migratory settlers to Illinois, and as such they were not alone. During the first several decades of Illinois's statehood, thousands of new settlers migrated to the frontier state, which created a broad community established on a similar experience of emigration. This new identity became the basis of a new genre of travel literature. Shared experiences form group identity and historians have discussed several types of experience that contribute to identity. In his work on Jacksonville, Illinois, Don Harrison Doyle discusses how a "voluntary community" came together to establish social order from formal institutions as a shared experience.[5] Family relationships also formed communities of shared experiences. John Mack Faragher's insightful study of "kinship communities" elucidates the role that endogamous relationships played in building group identity.[6] Other scholars discuss the role place plays in group identity. Douglas K. Meyer explores migration to Illinois by groups of different cultural origins that created their own communities.[7] Additionally, Kristin L. Hoganson demonstrates how one community's local history, as a component of place within the state and globally, shaped identity in central Illinois.[8] Each endeavor lends itself to the further discussion of regionalism, but before these communities and regions exist as culturally defined institutions, initial settlement played an early role in identity creation.

During the antebellum period, authors like Burlend published a myriad of narratives to describe travel experiences that specifically focused on Illinois. They wrote narratives to describe the journey, the new home, and more importantly, what would be required of future immigrants to make it permanently in the American West.[9] Travelers produced roughly 400 separate works concerning the Illinois country in the three decades after statehood in multiple languages.[10] The collective body of literature became its own genre of narrative histories and solidified itself as an indelible mark on the period's travel culture and the people. This genre, which portrayed the West as a fertile land full of abundant vitality through descriptive imagery, contributed to the population growth in the Illinois country during the epoch. Additionally, the narratives' descriptions of daily life demonstrate the pervasive shared experience of the settlers. Shared experience is the foundation of group and regional identity.

The success of these works was based on the imagery presented to its audience. Colorful imagery built from carefully formulated descriptive language offered potential settlers a portrait of the landscape and of daily life on the Illinois prairies. The imagery's consistency throughout most of the works is obvious in both its splendor, possibilities, and challenges. Despite the authors' various original backgrounds, the common threads in the writing spoke to the general concerns that potential immigrants had concerning a place they had never seen. Very little direct evidence links a particular immigrant to a travel narrative, but the volume of works and quantities printed indicate both their popularity and influence. This collective body of work, with its repetitive imagery, appealed to travelers seeking a new start, an underlying component towards forming a group dynamic.

As the subject of the narratives, the author must undergo "a process of change from one condition to another while remaining identifiable," and their story describes the process.[11] This transformative process brings these seemingly diverse, yet inherently similar people closer together through a shared, integrative experience. The travel narratives repeatedly identify four main phases of the experiences: the journey to their destination, the establishment of the home, life in the new surroundings, and finally reflection. The chronologically based phases became an unofficial template to the travel narratives that demonstrate the consistency of not just the imagery but of the experience itself. During the pioneer years, the actual experience of settling on the Illinois frontier became a connective fiber from which these individuals found continuity in their lives and decisions with which others back East could not identify.

During this period, events that transpired all over Europe, from famines to revolts, forced increasing numbers of the lower class to migrate for better opportunities. Also, the Industrial Revolution modernized much of the artisan's work, which stimulated emigration. Most authors recognized that better opportunity lay elsewhere, and their tone called for patience and perseverance. Burlend recalled the increased financial strain that caused "the gradual diminution of our little property and the entire absence of ... being able to supply the wants of a large family."[12] Not all migrants suffered from financial concerns, but whether they struggled or were comfortable, a brighter opportunity was a consistent theme.

In contrast, others vigorously embraced the future possibilities. In 1827, Frances Trollope excitedly states of her imminent departure, "tomorrow to fresh fields and pastures new," despite traveling alone with her children.[13] In 1838, Abner Dumont Jones wrote that he "besought ... the 'land of promise,'" upon leaving New England.[14] Years after settling in the West, Christina Holmes Tillson wrote that most settlers wished "to grow up with the land."[15] Their pastoral imagery elicited a sense of bounty and promise. For farm workers—who had grown accustomed to cramped conditions, nutrient-poor soil, dismal crop yields, and the financial stress associated by these land-poor conditions—images of abundance from a rich land were powerfully motivating. Trollope's use of "to-morrow" made such images feel imminent.

The first phase of the narratives centered on the journey. The authors' tone in their writing during the travel phase displayed the most stress. Expectantly, this phase could be wrought with emotional response, and for most this was their first real experience in leaving home. The shift from a world of known variables to the veritable unknown was a momentarily difficult mental transition to acknowledge. For the nascent authors, the articulation of such deep emotional events, such as loss, separation, fear, and uncertainty, are most evident in this phase. Once on the journey, the imagery briefly shifted to heartache and reflection of their homeland. "I ... enviously looked upon the vessels that were approaching the shores I was leaving," decried Rebecca Burlend.[16] Most emigrants knew they would probably never see their homeland again. This sense of loss would become a strong unifier amongst frontier settlers.

Once on the eastern seaboard, European travelers met up with their American counterparts to swell the ranks of sojourners flowing west. The land-travel descriptions ran from the mundane to the fantastic, all of which were new to the travelers. Once the migrants closed in on their intended destination, the imagery universally changed to beauty and possibility. "I can scarcely hope to give you any impression of our feelings when we began to descend the last ridge," Timothy Flint declared, "and the boundless valley ... began to open upon our view."[17] The bucolic imagery, first imaged in their hopes back home, had materialized once finally within the West. John Woods used appealing language to describe the landscape: Waterways and creeks were "navigable" and "swift," the trees were "of immense size," the hills and soil were of "fine appearance" and "rich," and the wild game was "plentiful."[18] Traveling in between the settlements, roughly five or six miles apart, gave the region a sense of grand openness, abundance, and freedom. The landscape changed from the used-up and overcrowded farms and smoke-filled, industrious cities to which they were accustomed to lush, life-filled groves of timber and massive prairies that ran for miles. The travelers also began to transform as people and writers. Flint summarized that "nothing can be more beautiful than these little bottoms, upon which these emigrants ... deposite [sic] their household gods."[19] Eliza W. Farnham declared that "the variety and excellence of [the prairie's] production are unrivaled in our own country, if not on the globe."[20] The despair of family separation and trans-Atlantic travel was replaced by the realization that the land could fulfill their expectations, which validated their decision to emigrate.

The settlers came to a very important realization at the end of the first phase: They were not alone in their journey to the West. "Our boat was calculated to accommodate thirty persons; we had sixty-five," quipped Abner Dumont Jones.[21] In 1819, William Faux noted in his journal that "two hundred and fifty emigrants arrived" in just one week at Baltimore.[22] Every other author continually described numerous encounters with other settlers and travelers along the journey. Flint wrote that, "It is no uncommon spectacle to see a large family ... all embarked, and floating down on the same bottom," on his trip down the Ohio River. The travelers began to see themselves as frontier settlers that were members of a larger, indescribable community of like-minded individuals despite their remoteness. The growing sense of camaraderie amongst the settlers could fill the void created by leaving family behind in the old country, as many settlers sought out, found, and readily identified with others with similar regional origins.

With the long journey completed, phase two, the process of settling in and creating a new life, began. Many settlers' new surroundings elicited responses that were elegant in their descriptiveness. One of Eliza W. Farnham's great desires was to behold the vista that was the Illinois prairie. As she rode in a wagon to her sister's house, she was delighted to see the "[large] smooth openings among the groves," but her elation was amplified upon hearing the driver declare that those were only "little meadows."[23] As she later encountered the fullness of the open prairie, she exclaimed it was "a vast ocean, teeming with life; redolent of sweet odors!"[24] Eliza R. Steele reacted similarly when she first saw the splendid prairie: "How shall I convey to you the idea of a prairie ... what a new and wonderous world of beauty!"[25] William Oliver provided a more pragmatic assessment of the rolling prairies as full of "rich impalpable loam" and described the superiority of the landscape as it "facilitates drainage ... and induces a more abundant growth."[26] During the pioneer era in the Illinois country, when land was plentiful and open, the immigrants selected acreage that fit their idea of pastoral beauty and economic benefits, usually based on ample resources for farming:

timber, water, arable land, and transportation access. The settlers had overcome great adversity to achieve their little piece of heaven and, being accustomed to strenuous labor, the sweat and toil of carving out a new home was superseded by the possibilities. Most narratives tell of a relatively smooth transition to life on the prairies after a brief learning period peppered with various minor challenges. These transition stories were commonly shared amongst neighbors at social events of the day.

The description of the people on the frontier was as informative as the description of the landscape in producing an image of the West. Some settlers were links in chain migration, who initially settled with family, but most encounters were with completely new people. However, the transition, for most, occurred quickly. "In short, we met with as good treatment as we should in a tour through England," declared John Woods.[27] The majority of the settlers were cordial and receptive to new immigrants. "Much of [the people] on the prairies and purely agricultural districts consists of decent people of simple manners," Oliver recounted.[28] He continued to describe a popular communal event that instilled camaraderie: "[N]ot long after arriving ... we were invited ... to a corn husking or husking frolic."[29] A frolic brought many families from the surrounding area to help a specific family with a major chore. Cabin raising and corn husking were two of the more common frolics. The host family supplied sufficient amounts of whiskey to attract the free labor and a festive, picnic-like atmosphere ensued. The task at hand was completed in short order to the satisfaction of the host family, which also spoke well of the neighborly support. The host family would return the favor to many of their neighbors as time and circumstances dictated. Thus, the sense of a broader community was palpable in the narratives. J.M. Peck partook in several community husking frolics and declared that "these gatherings end in sobriety and good feeling [unless the whiskey flowed too freely, then] they proved scenes of unbridled merriment."[30]

For some of the authors, Illinois was far from a Utopian dream. The rich, alluvial soil and loam, which was so desirable for crops and gardens, also supported the perpetual growth of a menagerie of weeds and overgrowth. The endless miles of prairie grasses were intrinsically linked with the dense vegetation and this made clearing the land troublesome. It was also home to an array of the loathsome life forms despised by settlers. Authors recalled mosquitoes categorically as numerous and troublesome.[31] Also grasshoppers were so abundant and voracious at times that "a hat left in a field was devoured in a night."[32] Another creature, abhorred by settlers, that all authors universally mentioned was snakes. It seemed as if only phenomenal prairie fires could rid the settlers of any of these pests, but the fires were also, of course, extremely dangerous to human inhabitants of the prairie. Eliza W. Farnham would stand on a roof and watch "a sea of fire which appeared to be unbroken for miles," but thought them "magnificent spectacles" as they lit up the night sky all around.[33] Another awe-inspiring natural phenomenon that narratives described with stunning language was the prairie storm. Farnham stated that "a little cloud ... rises on the horizon, and in fifteen minutes the earth is deluged, and the pealing heavens seem on fire."[34] Faux explained how "an awful tempest darkened and illuminated the mountainous forest this evening."[35] Writers described these simple and common events to help create imagery easily recognized by the growing local population.

In addition to local imagery, there was one more universal component to the possibilities and challenges of Illinois, and that involved financial concerns. First, Illinois had land, lots of inexpensive, productive land that every author described in detail. Second, immigrants risked all they had and knew in an attempt to ameliorate their condition; therefore, they equated land and opportunity to an increased financial benefit. Relocation costs and a home (and for farmers, arable land) figured high on the list of financial concerns. The question of whether they could afford the expense of the new home once they arrived was one that concerned many. Discussions, within the narratives, on land prices were common and unchanging.[36] The authors also mentioned the possibility of purchasing land on credit if needed, but with land prices running from $100 to $320 for a small farm, the land was relatively affordably priced.[37] To accentuate the affordability, the authors discussed the other expenses that were normally associated with land ownership by informing readers that there was no additional tithe or poor's rate and that taxes were small and in Illinois deferred for up to five years from the year of purchase.[38] Taxes and tithes, on their own, were strenuous enough to force some English farmers to lose their farms and livelihoods; therefore advertising that these cumbersome expenses were no longer an annual burden was quite attractive to a financially strapped reading audience. The frequency of financial topics also indicates the consistency of discussion amongst early Illinois settlers.

Another financial component that authors employed descriptive language with which to attract immigrants concerned the one aspect of financial capital that practically all immigrants carried with them: labor. Burlend reminded her audience that her family's success on the prairie was due to the fact that "our industry and perseverance have been unremitting."[39] Birkbeck informed his readers that "the working farmer, by the amount of capital required in England, as a renter, may own and cultivate a much better farm in this country."[40] Labor in the West was in great demand and all the authors witnessed this first hand. Labor was so important that it was even announced that "it is better to do a great deal in a middling way than to do a little well."[41] Abner Dumont Jones instructed his readers to utilize their labor as capital in the West.[42] Industrious young men could rent land to cultivate by agreeing to surrender up to a third of the yield delivered to the landowner. In this manner, by strength of character and with the sweat off his brow, an able-bodied individual could make his way in the West with no cash down. John B. Newhall shared this sentiment by declaring that "the industrious and prudent man can not only succeed, but may lay the foundation of a handsome property."[43] The imagery of financial possibilities, based off labor conditions the working-class were accustomed to, gave them hope beyond the mere value of their cash holdings.

To this end, this group of authors agreed their new society should encourage economic growth based on a free labor market. To them, slavery was an unacceptable institution.[44] With a majority of the authors originating from the British Isles and the upper East Coast, these sentiments are not surprising. The federal government designated the land of the Northwest Ordinance a free territory, which induced some to settle there exclusively. In Birkbeck's initial tour, the peculiar institution influenced his search for productive settlement land: "again, —Slavery, 'that broadest, foulest blot,' which still prevails ... will circumscribe my choice within still narrower limits."[45] Some immigrants initially located in the South but soon found slavery incentive enough to relocate north of the Ohio River. William Oliver met many migrants in his time in Illinois: "[T]here are Dutch, Germans, Swiss, Yankees, Irish, Scotch, a few English, and a number from the more southern states; the latter, as I understood, having immigrated to this part of the country, owing to the dislike they had to slavery."[46] John Woods spoke for many when he wrote that living in a slave state would be "a disgrace [to] myself and family."[47]

The investment of their time, labor, and money in emigrating was all in hopes of a better future for the whole family, especially for their children. In their original homes, the prospects of obtaining enough land to maintain a productive and financially stable farm was usually cost prohibitive.[48] Birkbeck declared that the West offered the opportunity "with a certainty of establishing his children as well or better than himself."[49] Woods openly announced that "a man with a family may get a good living, in a plain way, and leave his children in a situation to do the same."[50] Such proclamations allowed the reading audience to dream of a future for their children that normally had been unthinkable.

The heterogeneous frontier community initially developed along egalitarian lines based on shared experiences and pragmatic social cohesion. The pluralistic community design allowed freedom for families to capitalize on who they were as individuals but also inexplicably linked the members of the broader community, or as Birkbeck described "the good of all is promoted in perfect accordance with individual interest."[51] The authors all felt as if they were a part of something while in the West. As a member of this community, the authors, in the transformation of the narrative, embraced the role of purveyor of truth and reality and felt incumbent to inculcate the next wave of their fellow like-minded community members. The majority of the authors had been transformed personally by their experiences and their surroundings. They knew the old stories and now they could assess those narratives for accuracy and relay the truth, as they saw it. The success of the authors in the West gave them a sense of obligatory and proprietary right to disseminate that truth. In their mind, individuals of stout heart and sound character that could appreciate the value of the western landscape and industrious labor needed the correct facts and substantive data to emigrate with an informed mind and a clear conscious. The final phase of their writing transformed as well to meet this role as communal educator. The passing of this education became critical to establishing Illinois's regional identity across generations.

The authors also discussed local issues about which they were personally knowledgeable, topics ranging from domestic issues to cultivation and crop yield, to local customs for animal husbandry. The manner in which they wrote of these daily events was colloquial, instructive, and usually dry in nature. Farnham described the multiple utilities and time management of a Franklin stove; William Oliver discussed the planting and harvesting of corn and textually demonstrated the correct method of plowing a field; etc.[52] The key to these discussions was that the author had achieved a sense of expertise in the performance of the tasks as required by the surroundings. Readers could contextualize this information with comparisons to methodologies utilized back home. The value of these simple presentations of daily and occupational life, though rhetorically bland, was immeasurable in helping readers mentally prepare for their new surroundings.[53]

The authors' reflective assessments, made after they were established, were the final aspect of their writing. With their land bought, homes built, and first winter passed, the start of a new year brought about a rebirth of pastoral life and imagery. "As spring approached we felt some symptoms of those hopes which had animated us in England with reference to our success as emigrants," Burlend rejoiced, and her rapture at their continued success on the prairie made her feel "more at home."[54] John Woods proclaimed that "I never liked my living in England better than I do here."[55] The authors implied that a sense of home and community, despite the distance, separation, and feelings of loss, could be reconciled within the West. The authors also portrayed not only a new home, but also a better home. Birkbeck's assessment of his settlement in Illinois convinced him to deduce that "I have no doubt of its being greatly to the advantage of an industrious working family to exchange a rented farm in England for a freehold, west of the Ohio."[56] Freedom was a line of continuity that threads the narratives together firmly. The freedom to choose for oneself and the freedom to be the beneficiary of one's own labor, or at least the possibility of these in a short span of time, were strong aspirations. Many second or third sons of farmers in the land-starved East and Europe saw the monotony of wage labor in a factory as a noose to strangle the remaining bit of freedom out of their lives; and relocation to a land where many extolled the enduring sense of freedom was intoxicating. To this end, Farnham, on reflecting on members of her community in regards to the freedom of the West, announced that they "loved the country and … mode of life."[57] The sense of freedom felt by many relieved pressures that burdened the mind. After a period, Woods wrote of his community that "I was much struck ... to find in what harmony [the] people ... lived together, and I have since had no reason to alter my opinion."⁵⁸ Simon A. Ferrall witnessed this phenomenon while touring throughout the United States, proclaiming, "The inhabitants of these prairies, generally speaking, are much more agreeable than those of most other parts of the western country."⁵⁹

In the authors' reflections, many attempted to answer a self-imposed question they undoubtedly thought was on the minds of a majority of their readers: Should I (the reader) emigrate to the West? Christiana Holmes Tillson described that "going to Illinois was more an event than a trip."⁶⁰ Any person could take a trip, but an event was experienced and life-altering, and the authors wanted their readers to be cognizant of what the event entailed and to make the decision for themselves based on the information presented in the text. "Were I asked what is my opinion respecting emigration, I would refer the enquirer to the foregoing narrative; here are facts, let him consider and judge for himself ... our success has been ultimately greater than at one time we anticipated," Burlend summarized.⁶¹ The authors did not desire to make a strong and direct case for emigration; rather they presented the facts so that the reader could judge for themselves and live with the consequences of their own decisions.

Towards the end of the antebellum period, the travel literature's focus on Illinois began to wane. The national rail system had linked the Midwest and the East Coast and was spreading throughout the Illinois frontier to the lands beyond the Mississippi, forever changing the dynamics of settlement patterns. New immigrants settled along economic corridors that allowed the transportation of goods and services in the most cost-effective manner available. The ocean of vast prairies waiting to be settled diminished at an alarming rate, gobbled up in rectangular sequence set by the surveyor decades before. The travel literature that helped attract hordes of settlers to Illinois had evolved and took its story further west where new images of America and opportunity drew a new generation of settlers to the hopes of greener pastures. "The memory of immigrants is a complex story that still awaits its exposition," and this expository examination must demonstrate how writers' experiences shaped the foundation for understanding the character of the western immigrant and the identity that became synonymous with the Midwest.⁶² Through their colorful, instructive, and heartfelt imagery, these narratives gave a voice to the similar experiences of a generation that descendants took pride in identifying themselves with. In 1901, at an Old Settlers' Association meeting, Harvey B. Hurd summed it all up: "[G]reat things have come to pass during the time of which we are speaking and great progress has been made in almost everything that concerns our well-being, in all of which Illinois has borne a foremost part."⁶³

Notes

1. Rebecca Burlend, *A True Picture of Emigration* (1848; repr., Lincoln: University of Nebraska Press, 1987), 12.
2. Ibid., 8.
3. Ibid., 5.
4. Ibid., xxvii.
5. Don Harrison Doyle, *The Social Order of a Frontier Community: Jacksonville, Illinois, 1825–70* (Urbana: University of Illinois Press, 1978).
6. John Mack Faragher, *Sugar Creek: Life on the Illinois Prairie* (New Haven: Yale University Press, 1986).
7. Douglas K. Meyer, *Making the Heartland Quilt: A Geographical History of Settlement and Migration in Early-Nineteenth-Century Illinois* (Carbondale: Southern Illinois University Press, 2016).
8. Kristin L. Hoganson, *The Heartland: An American History* (New York: Penguin Press, 2019).
9. The American West, during this time, was considered to be the states and territories bordering the Mississippi River.
10. Solon Justus Buck, *Travel and Description 1765–1865* (Springfield: Illinois State Historical Library, 1914), 63–206.
11. Hayden White, *The Fiction of Narrative: Essays on History, Literature, and Theory, 1957–2007* (Baltimore: Johns Hopkins University Press, 2010), 113.
12. Burlend, *True Picture*, 7–8.
13. Frances Trollope, *Domestic Manners of the Americans* (1832; repr., New York: Dodd, Mead and Co., 1927), 4.
14. Abner Dumont Jones, *Illinois and the West* (Boston: Weeks, Jordan and Co., 1838), 13.
15. Christiana Holmes Tillson, *A Woman's Story of Pioneer Illinois* (1870; repr., Carbondale: Southern Illinois University Press, 1995), 7.
16. Burlend, *True Picture*, 17.
17. Timothy Flint, *Recollections of the last ten years, passed in occasional residences and journeyings in the valley of the Mississippi, from Pittsburg and the Missouri*

to the Gulf of Mexico, and from Florida to the Spanish Frontier; in a series of letters to the Rev. James Flint, of Salem, Massachusetts (Boston: Cummings, Hilliard, and Company, 1826), 11.
18. John Woods, *Two Years' Residence on the English Prairie of Illinois* (Chicago: Lakeside Press, 1968), 67, 82, 71, 90.
19. Flint, *Recollections*, 40.
20. Eliza W. Farnham, *Life in Prairie Land* (1846, repr, Urbana: University of Illinois Press, 1988), xxxiii.
21. Abner Dumont Jones, *Illinois and the West* (1838, repr, N.p.: BiblioLife, 2009), 16.
22. William Faux, *Memorable days in America: being a journal of a tour to the United States, principally undertaken to ascertain, by positive evidence, the condition and probable prospects of British emigrants; including accounts of Mr. Birkbeck's settlement in the Illinois* (London: W. Simpkin & R. Marshall, 1823), 110.
23. Farnham, *Life in Prairie Land*, 26.
24. Ibid., 45.
25. Eliza R. Steele, *Summer Journey in the West* (New York: John S. Taylor, 1841), 125.
26. William Oliver, *Eight Months in Illinois* (1843; repr., Ann Arbor: University Microfilms, Inc., 1966), 23.
27. Woods, *Two Years' Residence*, 105.
28. Oliver, *Eight Months in Illinois*, 29.
29. Ibid., 32.
30. J.M. Peck, *A Guide for Emigrants, Containing Sketches of Illinois, Missouri, and the Adjacent Parts* (Boston: Lincoln and Edmands, 1831), 155.
31. Woods, *Two Years' Residence*, 85; Simon A. Ferrall, *A Ramble of Six Thousand Miles Through the United States of America* (1832, repr, D.N. Goodchild, 2009), 94.
32. Faux, *Memorable Days in America*, 137.
33. Farnham, *Life in Prairie Land*, 108–09.
34. Ibid., 41.
35. Faux, *Memorable Days in America*, 64.
36. Depending on publication date, most authors merely regurgitated policy verbatim from land offices as there was little actual change in federal policy during the era.
37. Morris Birkbeck, *Notes on a Journey in America, from the Coast of Virginia to the Territory of Illinois* (1818; repr., New York: Augustus M. Kelley, 1971), 59–60; Jones, 136; Woods, 106–07.
38. Morris Birkbeck, *Letters from Illinois* (Philadelphia: M. Carey & Son, 1818), 5; Jones, 136.
39. Burlend, *True Picture*, 153.
40. Birkbeck, *Notes*, 57–58.
41. Oliver, *Eight Months in Illinois*, 100.

42. Jones, *Illinois and the West*, 194.
43. John B. Newhall, *The British Emigrants' "Handbook."* (London: T. Stutter, 1844), 62.
44. The southern portion of Illinois was heavily populated by migrants from the South during the antebellum period and most of these settlers brought their ideologies with them. Some also found ways to bring all their property into Illinois. The region, though legally a non-slave region, was decidedly a mixture of anti- and proslavery sentiment.
45. Morris Birkbeck, *Notes on a Journey in America, from the Coast of Virginia to the Territory of Illinois* (London: Severn and Co., 1818), 7.
46. Oliver, *Eight Months in Illinois*, 29.
47. Woods, *Two Years' Residence*, 24.
48. For further examination on this issue, review Christopher Clark's *The Roots of Rural Capitalism: Western Massachusetts, 1780–1860* (Ithaca: Cornell University Press, 1990).
49. Birkbeck, *Letters*, 18.
50. Woods, *Two Years' Residence*, 201.
51. Birkbeck, *Notes*, 115.
52. Farnham, *Life in Prairie Land*, 116; Oliver, *Eight Months in Illinois*, 86–87.
53. All the narratives are rife with these descriptions. The majority of the discourse, of course, leaned towards an agrarian readership as this was one of the leading draws to the region. There were also several mentions throughout the narratives to the prosperity of merchants and shopkeepers as well as the need for mechanics of all sorts: blacksmiths, carpenters, bricklayers, and such.
54. Burlend, *True Picture*, 75, 122.
55. Woods, *Two Years' Residence*, 200.
56. Birkbeck, *Notes*, 55.
57. Farnham, *Life in Prairie Land*, 83.
58. Woods, *Two Years' Residence*, 177.
59. Ferrall, *Ramble of Six Thousand Miles*, 117.
60. Tillson, *A Woman's Story*, 11.
61. Burlend, *True Picture*, 152–53.
62. John Lukacs, *Confessions of an Original Sinner* (South Bend: St. Augustine's Press, 2000), 113.
63. "Address of Hon. Harvey B. Hurd delivered before the Old Settlers' Association of DeKalb County," Manuscripts Division, Abraham Lincoln Presidential Library & Museum, Springfield, Illinois.

Michael J. Sherfy

Place-Making in the Midwest

Pioneer Memoirs in Early Illinois History

In 1833, Black Hawk—the Sauk war-leader whose short-lived resistance to American expansion marked the end of the "Indian Wars" in the Old Northwest—dictated his autobiography and saw it published for an audience unlikely to fully understand him. Through its words, he offered a glimpse into his world and described a cultural and geographical region already more memory than reality.[1] While fascinating and tragic, the outlines of Black Hawk's story are unsurprising to modern audiences. His is a narrative of self-vindication and of displacement brought about by adversaries he deemed less admirable than himself.

Ironically, the very people who had pushed Black Hawk and his people from their homeland found themselves in an analogous situation just a few decades later. They had come westward to what they considered a new country, made it their own, and reckoned their experiences to be distinctive and important. Some, however, lived long enough to see that country transformed again—socially, physically, demographically, and culturally—into something new. The region they had known was vanishing and their stories along with it. Like Black Hawk, some of them resisted that process by turning to the printed word.

Although professional historians arrived late to the scene, the people who had displaced Black Hawk and his Native contemporaries in the 1830s possessed a keen sense of history and recognized their own importance in making it. By surveying memoirs written between 1850 and 1880, one can observe how the region's pioneer-authors—voices of a generation who had *made* the Midwest but who were not necessarily *of* it—created a set of tropes that afforded them a sense of primacy and which placed them on a higher social, moral, and historical level than newer arrivals. Authors described a "wilderness" abundant in game but undisturbed by railroad or plow. They presented a time and a society whose values exceeded those of their present day. Nostalgically, they recounted anecdotes of men and women—both Native and white—who appear more vital and perhaps more admirable than the farmers and businessmen who came later. By the time their works were published, few traces remained on the landscape of the region these authors described. But, in their pages, that vanished history lived on.

Among the earliest of the region's residents to set his life on paper was Illinois Governor John Reynolds.[2] Never a humble man, Reynolds saw his life as being inextricably intertwined with the history of Illinois, so he explicitly intended *My Own Times* (1855) to serve as both an autobiography and a firsthand account of the transformation of Illinois from an Indian-filled wilderness to one of the most important states in the Union—a transformation for which Reynolds reckoned himself in no small way responsible.[3] While Reynolds discussed a wide range of topics, the campaign against Black Hawk—the Governor's defining moment as a military leader and the key event of his political career—forms the core of his story.

Reynolds noted that he had met Black Hawk prior to the 1832 conflict but was not impressed by him. "He seemed to possess a mind of more than ordinary strength, but slow and plodding in its operations," Reynolds recalled. "He appeared to me to possess not such genius or talents that would enable him to take the lead in a great emergency and conduct a great enterprise to a successful conclusion." "He might have had the talents to conduct a small marauding party with success," Reynolds allowed, "but he possessed not such intellect as could combine together great discordant elements into harmonious operation."[4]

For Reynolds, the "Old Ranger" whose public persona derived from his skills as a soldier and a politician, to denigrate Black Hawk's skills as a warrior and as a leader among his people was to attack the core of his identity as a man. By focusing on Black Hawk's ineffectualness, Reynolds emasculated him. As further insult, Reynolds compared Black Hawk unfavorably to other Native American leaders, including his chief rival, the accommodating Keokuk."[5]

Reynolds portrayed Black Hawk as the sole fomenter of disturbances on the frontier, a liar, a treaty-breaker, and a deceiver with "the fire of war and hatred of the whites impressed strongly in his heart."[6]

But denigrating Black Hawk's character was not John Reynolds's primary motivation for writing his story. If, as David Brumble claimed, Black Hawk's Life was a "self-vindication narrative," the same label applies equally well to Reynolds's autobiography.[7] The "Old Ranger" spent much of his section on the conflict against Black Hawk explaining the reasoning behind his own actions and justifying his decisions. Consistently, Reynolds claimed that he had responded to provocation only with great reluctance. "Not a single good and intelligent man in the State desired a collision with an insignificant and infatuated band of Indians," he alleged, "but at the same time, the peaceable citizens, residing on their own lands, must be protected from the assaults of a contemptible and ignorant foe."[8]

Even after receiving several petitions from settlers living near Rock Island, Reynolds claimed to have felt conflicted over the proper course of action. "If I did not act, and the inhabitants were murdered, after being informed of their situation, I would be condemned 'from Dan to Bersheba,'" he wrote, "and if I levied war, by raising troops, when there was no necessity for it, I would also be responsible."[9]

After Reynolds decided to call out the state militia (which, he pointedly reminded his readers, he did only after it became clear that the settlers would receive no satisfaction from the Indian agents or federal troops in the region), he heaped praise upon the volunteers who responded to his call to arms. "It is astounding, the war-spirit the western people possess," he began. "As soon as I decided to march against the Indians at Rock Island, the whole country ... responded with the war clamor."[10] Their "war-spirit" drove them to do their duty even at great personal sacrifice. "It was the most busy [sic] time in the year with the farmers," Reynolds noted, "yet hundreds of them unhitched their horses from the plow, left their cornfields, and appeared in the army."[11]

Even when Reynolds acknowledged the limitations of the Illinois volunteers—especially their unruliness and lack of discipline—he did so in the form of praise. "This small army was composed of the flower of the country, and possessed strong sense and unbounded energy," he said of the militiamen—who apparently did not feel so strongly the desire for peace that Reynolds claimed for himself. "They also entertained rather an excess of *Indian ill-will*, so that it required much gentle persuasion to restrain them from killing, indiscriminately, all the Indians they met."[12]

In his introduction, Reynolds explicitly stated his purpose in writing:

> The leading object of the writer is to record facts and the progress of events, which may do service to the present and future generations. The rise and progress of a great country is, and always will be interesting to an intelligent and enlightened public. The valley of the Mississippi is fast becoming an important and interesting country, and in it the State of Illinois is assuming a very high character. The important facts and public measures that had a tendency to develop the resources of this great State, and to advance its growth and prosperity, will always be interesting and, the writer hopes, serviceable to the people.[13]

Reynolds, therefore, deemed two themes important enough to record for posterity. First, he believed Illinois to be destined for greatness. In only a generation, much of the state had been transformed from an apparent wilderness peopled only by "wandering savages" into some of the richest farmland in the world. Moreover, with its rapidly growing population, its northern lead mines, its southern coal mines, and the beginnings of major industry in the northeast, Illinois stood poised to become one of the most important states in the Union. By the time Reynolds published, Illinois ranked fourth among the states in population, and its economy boomed. Second, Reynolds made clear that these improvements came about only because men like himself and the region's first American settlers had made them happen. *They*—not the come-lately newcomers from Europe, New England, and New York—had tamed the wilderness and tapped into the wealth of its natural resources. Theirs was the *real* frontier experience, as exemplified by the Black Hawk War. Further, these men—in Reynolds's account, men are the only prominent actors—had paid for the land with their toil and with their blood. American casualties in the conflict against Black Hawk had been few, but the blood of the fallen had nonetheless sanctified the process of clearing the land of its Native residents. Reynolds and the other frontiersmen of his era had, by their efforts and sacrifice, simultaneously made the country and made it their own.

In certain ways, *My Own Times* closely parallels Black Hawk's *Life*. Both were written by men who had once been prominent among their people but had been pushed into obscurity by younger and more polished rivals. Both authors lived during periods of rapid transition and massive change that made them appear to have outlasted their own eras. Further, both Black Hawk and Reynolds lamented a loss of virtue—the rugged masculinity of the frontier that existed (or was at least assumed to exist) on both the white and Native sides of the cultural divide—and the failure of the younger generations to fully embrace the values of their predecessors. Finally, both men described the loss—either by physical or political removal—of a land to which they had forged deep personal connections. John Reynolds, like his old enemy had done more than two decades earlier, told a story that attempted to pass along the importance of his region and of his cultural values to a public that did not necessarily care to hear him. He emphasized that he had been *here*, that he had been here *first*, that this was who he was, and—at least insofar as the life he lived reflected the values of his culture and his generation—Reynolds believed that his story offered important lessons that readers would do well to embrace.

Ideas like these permeate nearly all the published memoirs of frontier life during this period. Despite individual variations in tone and emphasis, frontier memoirists recorded and published their life stories largely to establish their presence on the region's historical and physical landscapes and to publicly assert their families' deep connections to the places in which they had lived. Juliette M. Kinzie's *Wau-Bun* (1856) is good example of this—and an effective counter-weight to John Reynolds's male-dominated and politically oriented narrative.[14]

Juliette (Magill) Kinzie was born into a respectable middle-class Connecticut family in 1806. At a young age, her progressive parents sent her to Troy Female Seminary in New York—an institution devoted to the principle that women deserved an educational experience equal to that available to men. While there, she studied music, natural history, and art and developed a taste for literature. She came to enjoy "a wide and intimate acquaintance with the 'best families' of the city."[15] Save for one factor, young Juliette Magill seemed destined to become a prominent member of some of the Northeast's better social circles: She acquired a passion for the West.

Her uncle had gone to the frontier to practice medicine and took a position at Chicago's Indian Agency in 1819. His letters home told of adventures in "Indian Country" and his romantic tales thrilled his favorite niece, as (apparently) did his descriptions of his associate and brother-in-law, John Kinzie.[16] In 1830, Kinzie traveled east and, after a brief courtship, married Juliette Magill. Almost immediately, the newlyweds embarked for Fort Winnebago in Wisconsin, to which Kinzie had been appointed U.S. Indian Sub-Agent for over 4000 Ho-Chunk (Winnebago) people.

That Juliette M. Kinzie was excited about her new life on the frontier can easily be seen in *Wau-Bun* (an Ojibwe term that translates roughly as "dawn" or "the break of day"), but she stated her feelings most succinctly in a posthumously released novel in which a fictional version of herself was asked whether she expected to become bored by life in the West. "Certainly not," the character answered. "On the contrary I expect to be continually more and more delighted. I have enjoyed myself a thousandfold more than I had anticipated, although I am but at the very outset of my adventures. I am prepared to be in a continuous state of rapture when I get to the wild woods and prairies beyond the bounds of civilization."[17]

For Kinzie, the frontier was not the sole province of men as portrayed in so many history books and adventure stories. Nor did she suppose western women to be peripheral characters with little to contribute to the region's history. Like their husbands, fathers, and brothers, women in Kinzie's account experienced the frontier as active and vital participants—sometimes playing more important roles than their men. They also offered insights and perspectives that male-oriented histories missed altogether.

Unlike John Reynolds and other historians of the period who frequently reprinted documents verbatim, Kinzie made little use of standard historical sources. Government archives, court records, newspapers, and public letters do not appear in *Wau-Bun*. Instead, she believed that the actual lived experience of ordinary human beings provided the most effective source material for writers of history. Kinzie's narrative, therefore, drew from firsthand observations and consultations with the individuals around her—especially the women of her husband's family who had shared the hardships, romance, and excitement that she had traveled west to experience. Women thus constituted the primary actors and storytellers in Kinzie's account.

From her vantage at Fort Winnebago, Kinzie was ideally situated during the Black Hawk War—far from scenes of hostilities but near enough to receive news quickly ... and that news was delivered not by distant newspapers of questionable reliability but by the Native people with whom her husband worked. Kinzie got along well with her husband's charges and approached them with an attitude that sounds remarkably sympathetic and modern. "I was obliged for my part," she explained, "to confess that being almost a stranger to the Indian character and habits, I was going among them with no settled plans of any kind—general good-will, and a hope of making them my friends."[18] This open-minded approach served her well, and, during the summer of 1832, her Ho-Chunk friends lived in particularly close proximity to the Indian Sub-Agency.

Anxious to assure American officials that they did not support Black Hawk's cause, several bands of Winnebagoes crowded around the fort. While whites elsewhere in the territory saw this as threatening, Kinzie and most of the white residents on the scene believed that the presence of so many friendly Native people would protect them from harm should hostiles approach. Even so, their nerves were excited by wildly circulating rumors and, on a few occasions, Kinzie's resolve left her and she imagined her friendly neighbors as the fearsome "savages" that frontier residents most feared.

The most striking such incident occurred when the Ho-Chunks invited Fort Winnebago's few white residents to join them in a "war dance" just outside the walls of the fort. Kinzie described the scene:

> The performance commenced, and as they proceeded, following each other round and round in the progress of the dance, my sister[-in-law], Mrs. Helm, remarked to me, "Look at that small dark Indian, with green boughs on his person—that is a *Sauk!*"... [H]is countenance was truly ferocious. He held his gun in his hand, and every time the course of the dance brought him directly in front of where we sat, he would turn his gaze full upon us, and club his weapon before him with what we interpreted into an act of defiance. We sat as still as death, for we knew it would

not be wise to exhibit any appearance of fear, but my sister remarked in a low tone, "I have always thought that I was to lose my life by the hands of the Indians—this is the third Indian war I have gone through, and now, I suppose, it will be the last."[19]

Already nervous, frightened by the Sauk dancer and obviously not comforted by her sister-in-law's observations, Kinzie recalled that she began to tremble—yet continued to watch the frenzied dancers from her porch. Then it began to rain and, "with whoopings and shoutings," the Indians rushed as a body for the doorway of the Kinzie home. Screaming, the women fled into a bedroom and secured the door. Despite the coaxing of their husbands, they refused to come out. "Of all forms of death, that by the hands of savages, is the most difficult to face calmly," Kinzie explained, "and I fully believed that our hour was come."[20]

Kinzie was later told that the dancer she believed to be a Sauk warrior had been only a young Ho-Chunk man dressed up purposefully to frighten the white women. "Such a trick would not be unnatural in a white youth," Kinzie allowed, "and perhaps since human nature is everywhere the same, it might not be out of the way in an Indian."[21] By admitting this, Kinzie not only recognized a fundamental parity between Natives and whites but also suggested that the unwarranted fears of American settlers—even those like the Kinzies with every reason to know better—had done much to escalate the conflict and the suffering of the area's Native people.

This incident, however, was an aberration. For most of her narrative, Native people inspire admiration rather than fear—especially the women, to whom Kinzie devoted far more attention than did male writers of her day. For instance, she brings into the historical record such individuals as "Madame Four-Legs," the Mesquakie wife of a Winnebago chief who often interpreted for and advised her husband, and of Elizabeth Decoray (called "the Cut-Nose" because of an injury inflicted upon her by an ex-husband), with whom Juliette M. Kinzie developed an especially close relationship. Kinzie even allowed a few Native women to tell their own stories by including their folk tales and personal accounts.

Among the most poignant of the stories that Kinzie presented were those of the Sauk refugees who had been brought to Fort Winnebago after being captured by American troops. After the battle at Wisconsin Heights, a group of women and children had broken away from the main body of Black Hawk's band, lashed together several canoes, and set off downriver to join relatives west of the Mississippi. Soldiers fired on them shortly after their departure, and the canoes overturned. Starving and exhausted from weeks of travel, the women saved only a few children from drowning in the tumult. Kinzie's mother-in-law described the survivors as being "wretched and reduced beyond anything she had ever seen." One Sauk woman provided details of her ordeal—how they had subsisted on acorns, elm-bark, and grass, how they had left the bodies of those who had starved to be found by their pursuers, how her husband had fallen in battle, how her children had drowned, and how her only wish was to join them.[22] To this, Kinzie added, "Poor Indians! It is no wonder that they do not love the whites."[23]

Whether because of her attitude towards the Indians, her failure to rely on traditional historical sources, or for other reasons, *Wau-Bun* found little favor among the Midwest's early professional historians. Milo Quaife was particularly dismissive of the work. "To the present writer it seems clear that Mrs. Kinzie had but the vaguest comprehension of the historian's calling," he charged, "and that in approaching *Wau-Bun* the reader should regard her as a literary artist whose primary ambition was to produce an entertaining narrative."[24] Quaife represented the general attitude of his academic generation when he offered a historian's perspective on *Wau-Bun*:

> In large part the volume is autobiographical, and to this extent it belongs to the category which in the shop-talk of historians is denominated source material.... The scenes depicted by her have commonly a certain factual basis, but into the recital of this much imaginative fiction is interwoven. Accuracy of statement is clearly not her *forte*, while to the objective detachment of the historian she is a complete stranger.[25]

Quaife makes at least one good point in his assertions. Juliette Kinzie did not adopt the "objective detachment of the historian." She had her own viewpoint and beliefs about the role of women in society and about the poor treatment of Native Americans and she did not hesitate to display them in her narrative. But Kinzie also had another major goal in mind: She presented a history that emphasized her family and firmly and publicly rooted it in the history of the places where they had lived.

The Kinzie family once owned much of what became downtown Chicago. Though family members sold most of their holdings too soon to become fabulously wealthy, John and Juliette Kinzie became rich beyond the typical expectations of frontier fur traders and minor government officials. Juliette remained a prominent citizen of Chicago until her death in 1870, and her home became a center of the city's social and cultural life. But there was a significant gulf between the pulsing commercial city of the 1850s and the fur trade outpost of three decades earlier. In a city of newcomers and immigrants, the Kinzies ranked among the few who spanned it—going back to a time beyond which the local memory did not run. In producing *Wau-Bun,* Juliette M. Kinzie celebrated her family's deep connections to the region—even if it meant being occasionally selective with the truth.[26]

To Quaife's chagrin, she was quite successful. "So thoroughly has her narrative of the Kinzie family ... permeated the local mind, that not all the efforts of all the historians, probably, will ever succeed in replacing it with a more correct and judicial concept," he complained. "Through her literary exploit, John Kinzie has become the Captain John Smith of Chicago history."[27]

By the time she wrote *Wau-Bun,* Chicago had already grown regionally paramount—and showed no signs of slowing in terms of increased prosperity and population growth. Her work firmly attached her family to a city whose history had yet to be written but whose importance was already recognized and ensured. Others, from less booming regions, used their memoirs not only to assert their connection to a particular place, but also to remind their readers of that place's past significance. By the 1870s, the frontier of the Old Northwest was well on its way to becoming the American Midwest and the world known by the "Old Settlers"—and by the Native people who had long preceded them—had been wholly re-made. Those who had witnessed and guided that transformation wanted that vanished world to be remembered.

John W. Spencer, a Vermont-native who became one of the earliest white settlers in the Rock Island area, keenly felt that responsibility.[28] In

1872, he published a few dozen copies of his memoir, *Reminiscences of Pioneer Life in the Mississippi Valley,* for distribution to younger members of his family.[29]

Spencer explained his motivations for writing in his preface:

> The record of the Old Settlers can never be written. Nearly all of them are gone, and lie with the faded leaves which have fallen over their graves. The history of the settlement of this part of the Mississippi Valley can never be recovered, as it was transcribed only in the memories of those who came here before the Indians had been driven from their hunting grounds, to find new homes beyond the great river.... The real character of the early settlers, and of the Indians, who have faded away before a stronger race, is well nigh lost, : those who knew both classes being only represented here and there by a survivor, who has lived long beyond that hardy generation who here commenced the conquest of the wilderness.... To save a few pages of this early history— pages rendered even more valuable by the destruction of the rest—is the object of this publication.[30]

Spencer's account illustrates how even events of wide importance are experienced and organized not in terms of grand national—or even regional—narratives but in terms much more local.[31] Broad events prove too complex and their effects too diffuse to be experienced fully by individuals. Instead, people break them down into segments related to their personal experiences. These are then passed down as family stories with little connection to a larger narrative. Most history-making, in the nineteenth century as well as today, was very much a family affair.

Spencer made no attempt to narrate the Black Hawk War. *That* story resided elsewhere and was in no danger of being lost. Nor was it particularly relevant to his project. The stories that he wanted to preserve were those that, by the 1870s, belonged only to a few elderly survivors from the period before the conflict and that recalled a moment when American settlers and the people to whom Spencer affectionately refers as "our Indians" lived together in the Rock Island area. From the very start, the relationship between them was tense. Spencer began:

We were here but a few days when two Indians came—
the first we had seen. One of them commenced talking
in a loud voice in the Indian language, of which we could
not understand a word. By pointing to the wigwam, saying
'Saukie wigiop,' then pointing to the ground, saying 'Saukie
aukie,' and repeating this many times, we understood
he claimed the land and the wigwam belonged to the
Indians.[32]

The irate Native homeowner was Black Hawk, an individual with whom Spencer and his neighbors were at the time unfamiliar. At his winter hunting camp in Iowa, Black Hawk had received word that Americans had come to Saukenuk and were living in its temporarily unoccupied homes.[33] He returned and found the rumors all too accurate. Not only was an American family living in his house, their fire had damaged it—for which, according to Spencer, Black Hawk vigorously scolded them.[34]

In his account of this first encounter, Spencer not only provided another perspective on an event included in Black Hawk's autobiography, he also acknowledged that Black Hawk and his associates had legitimate grievances.[35]

Like Kinzie's memoir, Spencer's account described Natives and newcomers living together in a tense but workable peace. The boundaries between the cultures were visible but permeable and peaceful interactions were commonplace during those early days. Spencer told, for instance, of a time when he and a delegation of settlers cultivated Keokuk's friendship by offering to plow his field. The Sauk chief accepted their proposition and, throughout the day, brought the laborers cool water sweetened with maple sugar, which "was considered by the Indians a very nice drink."[36]

Even when problems arose, Spencer described them as largely surmountable—so long as whites and Natives were willing to accommodate one another. For example, he recalled that in the spring of 1829 Keokuk had visited each of the settlers to request they pen their cattle at night to keep them out of the Sauks' cornfields. The Sauk leader pledged also that young men would guard the crops and the cattle in the daytime to avoid further problems. "All the settlers agreed to the preposition except Mr. Rinnah Wells," Spencer noted, "who thought it too much trouble."³⁷

Wells paid for his stubbornness. "When the corn got in good order for roasting ears, Mr. Wells's cattle came out one night to near Mr. Corker's old place, and ate up the corn of several Indian families," Spencer recalled. "Mr. Wells had corn on the opposite side of the road…. The next night, when the cattle returned for another meal, the Indians turned them into his own field. After that, Mr. Wells took care of his cattle."³⁸

Even Black Hawk, demonized in the press and denounced by historians, is portrayed as having usually gotten along well with Spencer and his fellows. Living less than a quarter mile from Black Hawk's lodge, Spencer became well-acquainted with him and described him as "a very quiet, peaceable neighbor."³⁹ Spencer said little about the war, but included many stories about Black Hawk—several of which served as lessons for his readers.⁴⁰

Although he had served as a Lieutenant in the local Ranger company, Spencer remained on friendly terms with Black Hawk after hostilities had concluded. When the Sauk war-leader returned to Rock Island in 1833 after his tour of the East coast, he showed Spencer some of the presents he had received and told him of the many impressive sights he had witnessed, including a balloon ascent in New York.⁴¹ Spencer also recorded Black Hawk's excitement at being reunited with his family. Black Hawk had fought an unsuccessful war with the United States and had been driven from the country he and the American settlers had briefly shared, yet Spencer still found much about the man to admire."⁴²

For Spencer, though, the individuals most worthy of admiration were his fellow pioneers. These individuals had come to a place that, while perhaps not quite wilderness, was definitely "Indian Country," and in a remarkably short time they had transformed it into a vibrant part of the United States. They had left their mark on the land and made it their own—and in the process they had forged a common identity that more recent arrivals did not fully comprehend. He concluded:

> I now feel it not only a duty, but a great pleasure, to make some mention of the old settlers of Rock Island County. I came to the State at such an early day, and traveled over it so extensively … that I had a great opportunity of judging

frontier life, and of frontier men. Of all my knowledge of the settlement of the State, our old settlers were the most intelligent and best informed of any who came under my notice.... Our relation to the Indians, after the first summer, was very peculiar. We having had a good title to our lands from the Government, felt we were entitled to be protected in our rights, while the Indians claimed the lands to be theirs with just as much assurance. Under such conflicting circumstances ... we lived almost three seasons together without any serious outbreak among us, which seems to be flattering to both whites and Indians. I feel that the Old Settlers of Rock Island County are very nearly related to me. Our privations and hardships brought us very near to each other, and I cannot but sympathize in the sorrows of each Old Settler, and rejoice in their well-being.[43]

Collectively, these memoirs illustrate the development of a regional identity based on a shared frontier experience centered largely on the era during which Black Hawk and his people were driven across the Mississippi. The settlers who came to Black Hawk's country had arrived in a country fraught with difficulties—some natural and others man-made—and they had overcome them. Their experiences instilled in them a particular identity and set of values. But this identity—like their claims to the land and its history—was jeopardized by the rapid influx of settlers who flooded the region after the mid-1830s. From more long-established states in the East and from Europe, these newcomers changed the region's culture and seemed little interested in those who had preceded them. In an odd way, the early settlers—victors in the campaign against Black Hawk—had wrested the region away from its Native people only to find themselves culturally (if not physically) displaced a generation later. Like him, they reacted by putting their lives on paper and preserving in words a world that was rapidly vanishing from the landscape and from living memory.

America happened to Black Hawk and his people; the Midwest happened to the early settlers and their generation. By mid-century, their stories were fast disappearing, but publication preserved a few before those capable of telling them had quite passed from the scene. Their authors could only hope that future generations would care enough to listen.

Black Hawk might have appreciated the irony.

Notes

1. J.B. Patterson, ed. *Life of Ma-ka-tai-me-she-kia-kiak, or Black Hawk: embracing the tradition of his nation—Indian wars in which he has been engaged—cause of joining the British in their late war with America, and its history—description of the Rock-River village—manners and customs—encroachments by the whites, contrary to treaty—removal from his village in 1831: with an account of the cause and general history of the late war, his surrender and confinement at Jefferson Barracks, and travels through the United States. Cincinnati, OH: 1833.* For a thorough discussion of the production, content, and publication of Black Hawk's autobiography, see Chapters 4–6 of Michael J. Sherfy "Narrating Black Hawk: Indian Wars, Memory, and Midwestern Identity." PhD diss, University of Illinois, Urbana-Champaign, 2005.
2. Born in Pennsylvania in 1788, John Reynolds had been raised in St. Clair County, Illinois, and educated in Tennessee. He returned to Illinois permanently during the War of 1812 and, while serving in that conflict, managed also to be admitted to the Illinois bar and establish a law practice in Cahokia—an indication of how little time Reynolds spent in active military campaigning. Before becoming Illinois's fourth governor in 1830, Reynolds served in the state legislature and sat on its Supreme Court. He would later resign his governorship to serve in Congress.
3. John Reynolds, *My Own Times: Embracing Also the History of My Life* (Chicago: Chicago Historical Society. Fergus Printing Company, 1879; Rpt. 1968).
4. Reynolds, *My Own Times,* 203.
5. Ibid.
6. Ibid., 206.
7. See David Brumble, *American Indian Autobiography* (Berkeley: University of California Press, 1988) and Chapter 4 of Sherfy, "Narrating Black Hawk."
8. Reynolds, *My Own Times,* 207.
9. Ibid., 208.
10. Ibid., 209.
11. Ibid., 209–10.
12. Ibid., 214.
13. Ibid., n.p. Perhaps not incidentally, Reynolds's book was initially not so "interesting" or "serviceable to the people" as he might have hoped. At least, his publishers and potential readers didn't believe so. Reynolds ended up paying for the first printing himself and sold only a few copies. Reynolds

brought most of his first-edition memoirs to a Chicago warehouse where they burned, unread, in an accidental fire.
14. Mrs. John H. Kinzie, *Wau-Bun: The "Early Day" in the Northwest* (Chicago: D.B. Cooke, 1856).
15. Reuben Gold Thwaites, ed., "Introduction" to *Wau-Bun: The Early Day in the North-West* (Chicago: Caxton Club, 1901), n.p.
16. John Kinzie was born at Sandwich, Upper Canada, into a well-known fur trading family. He worked as an agent of the American Fur Company at Mackinac Island and later at Prairie du Chien. In 1825, he served as an interpreter and secretary to Lewis Cass at treaty negotiations with several of the region's Native tribes. Following the conclusion of the Winnebago War of 1827, Kinzie was appointed federal sub-agent to the Winnebago (Ho-Chunk) at Fort Winnebago.
17. Milo M. Quaife, "Historical Introduction" to *Wau-Bun* (Chicago: Lakeside Press, 1932), xlix. To this quote, Quaife added, "If the statement does not represent with entire precision her [Juliette Kinzie's] own state of mind on coming to Wisconsin in 1830, it at least discloses what as an old woman, dwelling upon the memories of her past, she imagines herself to have felt" (xlix).
18. Kinzie, *Wau-Bun*. (1992 ed.), 64. For more on Juliette Kinzie's relationship to Native people, see Margaret Beattie Bogue, "As She Knew Them: Juliette Kinzie and the Ho-Chunk, 1830–1832," *Wisconsin Magazine of History* 85, no. 2 (2001–2002): 44–57.
19. Kinzie, *Wau-Bun* (1901 edition, Milo M. Quaife, ed.). 481–82.
20. Ibid., 482.
21. Ibid., 483.
22. Kinzie (1992 ed.), 242.
23. Ibid.
24. Quaife, "Historical Introduction," lii–liii. Nina Baym also pointed out Kinzie's tendency to produce very literary narrative. She, however, attributed this not to Kinzie's failure as a historian but to her educational background—her "literariness"—which made her frame her experiences in a literary way. According to Baym, Juliette Kinzie did not falsify her perceptions to make them literary. Rather, as a gifted and fully literate individual, Kinzie genuinely had lived her entire life as a story. Nina Baym, "Introduction" in Juliette M. Kinzie, *Wau-Bun: The "Early Day" in the North-West* (Chicago: University of Illinois Press, 1992), xiv.
25. Ibid. Quaife's criticism sounds somewhat specious when one considers that virtually every history of the region uses Kinzie's account of the Fort Dearborn Massacre (which was based on her mother-in-law's eyewitness memories and had been anonymously published as a pamphlet in 1844) as their primary source materials.
26. By no stretch of the imagination did Juliette Kinzie portray her family "warts and all." Much that she found troubling about her relatives (including the

Michael J. Sherfy 83

existence of a branch of the family descended from her father-in-law's first "wife," a Virginian taken captive by Indians) did not find its way into the pages of *Wau-Bun.*
27. Quaife, "Historical Introduction," liii–liv.
28. Spencer arrived in Illinois in September 1820 and reached St. Louis on October 25 of that year. The following spring brought Spencer to the Illinois River country to help his uncle stake his land claim. In 1827, Spencer traveled to Galena to work in the lead mines and passed Rock Island on his way there. Admiring the possibilities of the land in the vicinity of Fort Armstrong, he returned there to settle permanently in 1829. Spencer would later become a Rock Island County Commissioner and served as the county's first judge (and performed the first marriage ceremony in that place). In 1847 he was a delegate to the Illinois Constitutional Convention. He died in 1878.
29. J.W. Spencer, *Reminiscences of Pioneer Life in the Mississippi Valley* (Davenport: Griggs, Watson, and Day, printers, 1872; Rpt. Chicago: Lakeside Press, 1942).
30. Ibid., n.p.
31. This relates to some of the conclusions found in Roy Rosenzweig and David Thelen's *The Presence of the Past: Popular Uses of History in American Life* (New York: Columbia University Press, 1998).
32. Spencer, *Reminiscences of Pioneer Life,* 24–25. In this story, Spencer took great pains to explain exactly where the events of this story took place in relation to landmarks better known to his audience, usually the still-standing homes of other white settlers. Spencer also, perhaps for the pleasure of their descendants in the audience when he presented portions of his memoir to the Rock Island County Old Settler Society, named every other American that he remembered as having moved into temporarily vacated Sauk lodges in March 1829. Clearly, his was an intensely local history of a particular place. This, however, made it *more* important in Spencer's estimation rather than less so.
33. Saukenuk was the principle village of the Sauk people (though it was also home to Mesquakies, Ho-Chunks, Kickapoos, and others by the 1830s) and was the most populous Native village in the region during the early 1800s. Located on the Illinois side of the Mississippi, it stood on the site of today's Rock Island, Illinois.
34. Spencer, *Reminiscences of Pioneer Life,* 24–25.
35. For Black Hawk's version of this incident, see Donald Jackson, *Black Hawk: An Autobiography* (Chicago: University of Illinois Press, 1990), 99–100. For further discussion of Black Hawk's account of this incident, see Chapter 4 of Sherfy, "Narrating Black Hawk."
36. Spencer, *Reminiscences of Pioneer Life,* 26. Unfortunately, Spencer says little about Native women. "Keokuk's fields," after all, belonged to the women of his family and, in plowing the soil, Spencer and his associates were saving

them from having to work, not Keokuk himself. One must wonder whether it was Keokuk or his wives who sent out the maple drinks—and what the Sauks and Mesquakies thought about white men performing the work of Indian women.

37. Ibid. Spencer cites Rinnah Wells, a settler who came to the frontier to set up a trading operation, as fomenting a great deal of difficulties between the Native residents of Saukenuk and the Americans. Most of the other white settlers in Spencer's account are presented as having been on reasonably good terms, while Wells is consistently portrayed as being unwilling to live in close proximity to the Indians. Wells was among the leaders of those who, after receiving no satisfaction from Indian Agent Thomas Forsyth, William Clark, or the military commanders at Fort Armstrong and St. Louis, circulated a petition calling on Governor John Reynolds to muster the State Militia. One can only speculate whether Spencer revised history through nostalgic lenses or whether individuals like Rinnah Wells were indeed greatly outnumbered on the immediate scene by white settlers willing to compromise—even co-exist with the Natives for an indefinite period—in order to prevent hostilities.
38. Ibid., 26–27.
39. Ibid., 27.
40. A good example of this is an account of Black Hawk's infamous encounter with a whiskey peddler. Ibid., 27–28.
41. Ibid., 77.
42. Ibid., 28.
43. Ibid., 84–85.

Barton E. Price | The Protestant Imagination and the Making of the Midwest as America's Heartland

T.H. Cunningham was a farmer in Russellville, Illinois, whose 1876 journal recorded the weather and a few lines about his morning and evening activities. He spent the beginning and end of the year in the same fashion: hauling manure and fodder and chopping wood. He planted in the spring, and he harvested late in the summer. He wrote about a woman named Carrie, possibly his wife, and his annual accounting mentioned a "helper boy" and a man named Dick who helped chop wood. Cunningham's world was one bound to his local setting. He did venture to nearby towns to visit friends and family, but he rarely stayed the night. In the summer, he visited a local doctor for treatment of an ailment that kept him in bed and limited his work. He spent the centennial Independence Day mending a harness and piling manure. He had "intended to go to Robinson to celebration," but the rain changed his plans. Religious gatherings were a social outlet for Cunningham. He went to a Methodist meeting at Dollahaus Chapel, where he listened to a Mr. Boyer preach and infrequently attended Sunday school. In sum, Cunningham listed fifteen times that he went to church that year.[1]

Many of the residents in the middle Mississippi Valley (i.e., Illinois and Missouri) were like Cunningham. Their daily lives were bound by their immediate, domestic experiences. For example, George R. Goodman, a Methodist minister in southern Illinois, remembered his childhood on a farm in Lawrence County, Illinois, as being so common that it needed little detail or explanation. Instead, he recounted that his upbringing consisted of tasks "as are common and familiar to all farmers [sic] boys."[2] Growing up in the same county, Goodman and Cunningham shared many of the same experiences. These experiences were common for rural Midwesterners in the nineteenth century, and they reflected a growing awareness that midwestern life lie at the core of American life. Before either Cunningham or Goodman had come to think of the

Midwest as the center of their lives, Protestants had projected on the Midwest an imagination that the region was heartland in North America.

This chapter contends that the American Protestant imagination made the Midwest into America's heartland. In the nascent years of the American republic, Protestant missionaries imagined that the Mississippi Valley was a future center of Christendom. They planned and organized an expansive missionary and literary empire to extend from the Atlantic seaboard to the continental interior. At stake was the future religious identity of the new nation. Particularly threatening to Protestants was the established and growing Catholic presence in the Midwest during the early decades of the nineteenth century. Therefore, Protestant missionary work was an effort to redeem the American heartland from heathenism and Catholicism. The Protestant evangelical imagination of the Midwest inspired another religious community to come to think of the region as the center of their own cosmology. The Mormon founder Joseph Smith's prophecies that the Mississippi Valley was to house the new Jerusalem reflected the themes of Smith's evangelical forebears. Evangelical Protestants found themselves vying for control of the Midwest with Catholics and Mormons during the Jacksonian era. By mid-century, they also experienced their own internal sectional tensions. Throughout this contest between northern and southern factions within the church, there was an emerging consciousness among residents within the Midwest that their region was at the center of America's postwar future.

Evangelicals who were swept into the Manifest Destiny fever were ambitious to redeem the frontier. As the federal government acquired more land and removed the indigenous population, it introduced new states to the west. The frontier progressed westward, leaving territorial lands left to be inhabited by white settlers and acculturated to Euro-American mores. The field of missions lay open to evangelicals. As they prepared to extend what they considered their righteous empire, evangelicals participated in a discourse to evaluate the promises and perils of the frontier.[3]

At stake in this enterprise was the future religious and moral caliber of the nation, and this caliber was contingent on demographic and electoral changes.[4] The westward migration of Americans increased the frontier population. Indiana and Ohio experienced growth of more than 400 percent between 1800 and 1810, while Illinois grew by more than 300 percent and Missouri saw a 225 percent increase by 1820. As residents moved westward, the demographic shifts led to the West having greater political influence. Ohio added five seats to the House of Representatives after the 1810 Census, and Indiana three after the 1820 Census and another four after the 1830 Census. Illinois, which had only one seat after the 1820 Census, added two more seats in the 1830s. Due to changes in the ratio of representation, eastern states lost thirty-one members of Congress between 1830 and 1840, even though they gained new districts due to population increases. The difference meant a swing of forty-two seats in favor of the Midwest.[5]

The growth of the western population and the accompanying growth of political influence informed the evangelical imagination about the Midwest. As Lyman Beecher wrote in his *A Plea for the West* (1835):

> It is equally plain that the religious and political destiny of our nation is to be decided in the West. There is the territory, and there soon will be the population, the wealth, and the political power.... the West is destined to be the great central power of the nation, and under heaven, must affect powerfully the cause of free institutions and the liberty of the world.[6]

Beecher's words found resonance in the sentiments of evangelicals who shared his view of American destiny. A writer in the *Christian Observer* commented that "in this great [Mississippi] valley will be the centre of power—of political influence in our country. The millions that will here exist, will control the destinies of our Republic."[7] Rev. Elms Lyman Magoon, addressing the American Baptist Home Mission Society, also claimed that the American frontier was soon to be the sacred capital of Christendom. Magoon recognized that population shifts westward meant that the West was gradually becoming the new center of political power. Magoon was concerned about the implications of this shift in politics: "Where the population is thus rapidly increasing, taking with it a transfer of supreme power from one section of the Union to another, and when the stupendous result which this state of things is working is so near at hand, every consideration of patriotism and religion which relates to it is of utmost importance."[8] With the population swell and growing political strength, there were indications that the empire was indeed headed west. Evangelical Protestants believed that what stood in the way of the progress of morality and religion were a lack of religious information and the presence of Roman Catholicism.

Advocates of evangelical Protestant missionaries decried the lack of religious institutions and literature among the settlers of the Midwest. These missionaries often used the term "destitute" to refer to this condition on the frontier. The first observation was the paucity of trained and able clergy to meet the spiritual needs of the pioneers. John F. Schermerhorn, a Plan of Union missionary on tour through Illinois and Missouri in 1814, wrote to his patrons, "In this whole Territory is not a solitary Presbyterian minister."[9] John Mason Peck observed that the family he had visited in 1818 "had not seen a Baptist preacher since they had lived in the territory some eight or ten years."[10] In his *Condensed Geography and History of the Western States* (1828), Timothy Flint observed that "there are very few settled pastors, in the sense in which that phrase is understood in New England and the Atlantic States."[11] Rufus T. Babcock addressed the Massachusetts Baptist Missionary Society in 1829, stressing that home missions were necessary. According to his report, there was less than one preacher for every 10,000 pioneers.[12]

Missionaries and Bible societies also described people without the scriptures as destitute. Samuel J. Mills "found the inhabitants in a very destitute state; very ignorant of the doctrines of the Gospel; and in many instances without Bibles, or any other religious books."[13] In a report Mills sent to the Massachusetts Missionary Society the following year, he observed the pioneers pleading for Bibles and tracts. Writing from Shawneetown, Illinois Territory, Mills lamented, "We could not ascertain, that there had ever been any Bibles or Testaments sent into this Territory ... Some, who are anxious to obtain the Bible, and able to purchase it, have been for years destitute."[14] In response to the absence of Bibles in the Midwest, missionaries began to provide copies at no charge. John Mason Peck, "having long known that multitudes of families in this country are destitute of the Scriptures," set about distributing Bibles and tracts through the Missouri Bible Society, an auxiliary of the American Bible Society.[15] The Pennsylvania Bible Society aimed at supplying "the destitute families in the State with a copy of the Bible without note or comment."[16] True to their Protestant values about the unmediated Bible placed in the hands of the people, missionary and Bible societies that distributed Bibles provided those texts "without note or comment" in order to supply the riches of the Gospel to impoverished souls.

Boosters for Sunday Schools believed education was a necessary effort to complement evangelical preaching in the Mississippi Valley. The American Sunday School Union (ASSU) estimated in 1842 that 97,000 children in Missouri were "destitute of Sunday School instruction, and only 3,000 enjoying it. Multitudes of children are growing up ignorant of the Sabbath and its blessed purposes, and exposed to all evils of neglected and perverted minds."[17] For this reason, the ASSU established a fundraising campaign to supply children in the Mississippi Valley with more religious literature and Sunday School teachers. The ASSU also appropriated $3000 "to the supply of destitute Sunday-schools in the Mississippi Valley, with libraries wholly or partially gratuitous."[18] This was not the first time that the ASSU had embarked on an aggressive campaign to promote the growth of Sunday Schools and the distribution of Sunday School literature. In 1830, the ASSU launched its Mississippi Valley Campaign. The aim of the Valley Campaign was to establish "a Sunday School in every destitute place where it is practicable, throughout the Valley of the Mississippi."[19]

Evangelical Protestants feared that the Catholic presence in the Mississippi Valley threatened the republic. To many Protestants, the swelling Catholic population appeared as though Roman Catholicism would become the dominant religion in the United States. Protestants maintained a suspicion that Catholics were deferential to the Pope's leadership, who Protestants presented as a despotic tyrant seeking to overthrow democratic republicanism. Such suspicions were unsubstantiated. But the data on Catholic immigration showed growth during the first half of the nineteenth century. According to historian Gerald Shaughnessy's estimates, the number of Catholics grew from 35,000 in 1790 to more than 700,000 in the 1840s. By 1850, the Catholic population had swelled to 1.6 million.[20] In the Midwest, Catholicism grew at a rate that alarmed Protestants. Historian Robert Frederick Trisco estimated that Catholics in the West numbered roughly 7500 in 1826. Within twenty-five years, Catholics made up 400,000 in the region between the Ohio and Mississippi Valleys.[21]

The inflammatory anti-Catholic rhetoric of Samuel F.B. Morse and Lyman Beecher stressed the importance of Protestant missionary activity in the Midwest. Specifically, they were concerned that the growing Catholic population was the result of immigrants, who Protestants believed brought a foreign faith and foreign civic values. Morse pointed to Catholic missionary societies, particularly the Leopold Association and the Association for the Propagation of the Faith, as participating in a conspiracy to set up a papal colony in the American interior. His articles soon became the book *Foreign Conspiracy* and won wide readership and popular acclaim. Evangelicals affirmed Samuel Morse's writings, and they sponsored a propaganda campaign to promote awareness of the Catholic conspiracy and to encourage continued efforts in home missions to the Midwest. Morse's *Foreign Conspiracy* found its most publicized endorsement by Lyman Beecher. After accepting the presidency of Lane Theological Seminary in 1832, Beecher moved to Cincinnati from Boston, positioning himself at the front line of the conflict with Catholics. In 1834, he returned to Boston and preached a sermon series railing against Catholics and raised funds for Protestant missionary activity. Along with other preachers in the city, Beecher provoked the anger of the Protestant Bostonians, an anger that erupted in the burning of the Ursuline convent in Charlestown. Beecher's fundraising sermon *Plea for the West* became a book that convinced readers of the necessities of Protestant efforts in the West.[22]

Morse and Beecher were not alone in their suspicions of Catholics in the Midwest. Anti-Catholic nativism ran throughout evangelical periodical literature in the antebellum decades. An article in the *Christian Secretary* warned that Catholics were infiltrating the Mississippi Valley and promoting their religion through their parochial schools.[23] The *Christian Watchman* printed an article titled "The Valley of the Mississippi," which stated that European immigrants were "filling up" the valley rapidly. These "foreigners" brought with them "their particularities and prejudices; and that some of them have loose notions about liberty, which are too near akin to licentiousness."[24] Evangelicals feared that not only would immigration plant Catholicism in the center of the continent, but that immigrants would corrupt the morality of the republic by offering a religion and governance alternative to the Anglo-Protestant ideal.

Evangelicals were equally anxious regarding the influx of Mormon emigrants into the Midwest. The Mormon prophet Joseph Smith had inherited and appropriated the Protestant evangelical imagination in his own conception about the American Midwest. Soon after officially establishing the Church of Jesus Christ of Latter-Day Saints, Smith began to prophesy that the new Jerusalem—the seat of the Mormon kingdom on earth—would be located in Missouri. In July 1831 and again in September 1832, Smith proclaimed that the city of Zion would be established in western Missouri and would be the site of the gathering of all saints.[25]

The Mormons had tried to establish their kingdom in Kirtland, Ohio, in the middle of the 1830s but found the non-Mormon neighbors unwelcoming. After a series of financial controversies, Smith determined that it was time for the Saints to remove to Missouri and realize their destiny. But they soon found that their new non-Mormon neighbors—called gentiles—were just as apprehensive. The Upland Southerners who moved into Missouri transplanted their own mores, replete with their suspicions about religious outsiders and Protestant backsliders. They were also wary of the extension of Yankee culture with its free soil values and moral superiority. This was a volatile mix that did not bode well for Mormons in northwestern Missouri, many of whom had relocated from New England, upland New York, and Ohio. Historian Kenneth Winn acknowledged that the shared Yankee heritage in New York and Ohio may have tempered anti-Mormonism, whereas the southern population in Missouri and Illinois likely contributed to a new level of vitriol.[26] Consider, for example, Samuel Lucas's description of the emigrant Saints as "a tribe of human locusts" who plagued Missouri "from their pestilent hive in Ohio and New York."[27] Moreover, there appeared to be a persistent alarm among transplanted Southerners that the Yankee Mormons would seek to upend the slave economy. Residents in Clay County used this as one of the charges against the Saints, prompting a series of articles in the *LDS Messenger and Advocate* in April 1836 and a subsequent letter from Joseph Smith and the church Presidency to clarify the Church's position on abolition.[28]

Despite claims by some Missouri residents that Mormons would have been tolerated had they been "respectable citizens in society" whose religion was "deluded," there was evidence that gentiles objected to Mormons nonetheless. Evangelicals viewed Mormonism as an aberration of Christianity.[29] Missouri was an especially prominent site for encountering and objecting to Mormonism's more enthusiastic religious experiences such as glossolalia.[30] Given observations made by Peter Cartwright in Illinois in the late 1830s and early 1840s, it is reasonable that evangelical Protestants like Methodists and Baptists who employed similar mechanisms of enthusiasm found Mormon worship to be too similar that they had to resort to chastising Mormonism as delusional and fanatical in order to maintain some distance.[31] This was all the more critical given that the Saints often recruited from Campbellite and Methodist ranks.[32]

If Mormonism represented to evangelicals a corruption of Christianity, it might have also represented a corrupted republicanism, especially at the heart of the new American nation. In their complaints about Mormons, gentiles often used the same rhetorical devices about their anxieties concerning the religious and political fate of the Mississippi Valley that had animated evangelical missionaries and anti-Catholic rhetoric of the same era. One cause for concern was the rapid influx of Saints into Missouri, which had increased nearly ten-fold between 1833 and 1837.[33] Mormons aggressively purchased land, often at prices higher than the market rate. Smith himself purchased 78.56 acres in Lexington, Missouri, in June 1836.[34] Such growth could have shifted the electoral power in the relatively young state and consolidated local authority among LDS members. One anti-Mormon tirade decried, "the civil government will be in their [Mormons'] hands ... or persons wishing to court their favor."[35]

Gentile Missourians also may have likened the LDS structure, and its chief authority, to Catholicism, which Protestants had claimed was antithetical to republicanism. The Mormons' primary allegiance was to the Kingdom of Christ according to Joseph Smith's prophecies, causing alarm from other Missourians.[36] This devotion to that Kingdom and to its prophecies could easily be interpreted as devotion to the prophet. In August 1834, Joseph Smith acknowledged as much, recounting to the Saints in Missouri that some in his own congregation in Kirtland had begun to claim that he was a "Tyrant—Pope—King—Usurper," but that these accusations were "as black as the author of lies himself."[37] Despite Smith's efforts to reinvigorate the Protestant ethos of the priesthood of all believers,[38] he was nevertheless painted as a Pope.

Smith and his Saints posed just as much of a threat to the Protestant imagined ideal of the Midwest and its role in a North American Christendom. However, what is striking is that both Saints and gentiles shared a common assumption about how the valley fulfilled their millennial aspirations and prophetic imaginations. In northwestern Missouri, those competing claims to the capital of God's continental empire converged. Yet they diverged in violent clashes—such as the Mormon War in Missouri and the mob violence in Nauvoo, Illinois—with neither vision being realized. In the end, Mormons thrice attempted to establish a godly kingdom in the Midwest only to be thwarted by their gentile neighbors.

Evangelicals distinguished themselves from their Catholic and Mormon neighbors by emphasizing that the revival tradition, along with its print media, facilitated this new regional imagination. Itinerant circuits, revivals, and camp meetings collected people into new social organizations, and the emotional ethos of evangelicalism further served as a cohesive element.[39] And in time, denominational publications recreated and reinforced these experiences. In 1868, a reader of the *Central Baptist* from Burnt Prairie, Illinois, recognized how reading the paper was akin to a meeting of Baptists who were knit together by their ingathering. He wrote:

> We are by means of our paper, drawn so near to each other every week, that it is [the] next thing to a warm personal greeting. The same words of good cheer greet us, the same principles animate us, and we become daily more and more endeared to each other, until the names of brethren who may never see each other in the flesh, become household words. Indeed, it is the next thing to a great gathering of the Baptists of a whole State ...[40]

While Protestants stressed that immigrant Catholic and Mormon populations were unwelcome in the Midwest, they also stressed their own cohesion, which formed a new American identity. As Americans from various points of origin converged in the Midwest to establish new homes, they created a rhetoric that midwestern people shed old sectional identities. In the 1820s, an Illinois judge named James Hall published a series of letters that testified to the character and qualities of western inhabitants. His "Letters from the West" originally appeared in his newspaper in Shawneetown, but later they captured the imagination of readers in Philadelphia. In "National Character," Hall described how the western settlers had forged the national character by fusing northern and southern qualities into a new class of people. It was in the convergence of the Midwest that Americans from the North and the South met and established the quintessential national character. "The western states derive their inhabitants," Hall stated, "from New England and Virginia." While Hall admitted "at the first glance, there would be no more resemblance between the Boston merchant, the Virginia planter, and the hunter of the west," he suggested that all three persons share "the same American spirit." Hall described that the pioneer "soon becomes a different man; his *national character* will burst the chains of local habit."[41]

In 1858, the article "Traits of the Western People" described westerners as the amalgam of all positive traits from both north and south and presented westerners as the true Americans who were neither Yankee nor Cavalier. "There is a certain universality in the type of the Western man," claimed the author of the article, "and a certain freedom and eclecticism in his social life, which enable them to reflect a partial likeness of the better traits and qualities, peculiar to either section of the country, however much these sections may differ in their standard of morals and manners."[42] The article claimed that westerners represented the true essence of democracy by demonstrating the harmony between north and south.

This projection was misleading, given the instances of sectional animosity and violence in the Midwest. Additionally, both Baptists and Methodists dissolved over slavery in 1844. These schisms created ruptures as local congregations debated their alliances to the northern and southern factions of their respective denominations. The Civil War widened the evangelicals' sectional division in the Midwest.[43]

The martial law in Missouri during the war and the immediate period of Reconstruction forced ministers to sign oaths of loyalty to the Union. Baptists in Missouri divided further over this issue. Southern Baptists who experienced what they considered the injustices of martial law and the imposition of the test oath believed northern Baptists were apathetic to the southern Baptists' plight. In February 1866, the *Missouri*

Baptist Journal printed the test oath that ministers in that state had to sign. The editor reprinted the oath so that readers could be aware of the situation. The editor introduced the oath by writing, "As many of our Eastern brethren seem to be ignorant of the nature of the famous oath which ministers in this State are required to take, we insert it for their benefit."[44]

Despite these tensions, Missouri Baptists chose to reunite and to merge institutions. Baptist periodicals in Missouri also merged. One such effort was to merge the two Baptist newspapers in the state. In 1866, the General Association founded the *Missouri Baptist Journal*. The prospectus for the paper said that it would exclude any discussion of politics. Those persons involved in the formation of the *Missouri Baptist Journal* wished to keep the paper from belonging to any "clique, company or section."[45] Despite its claims to objectivity, the *Journal* had readers who objected to the perceived factionalism. One reader returned his copy of the February 12, 1866, issue with marginalia telling the editor, "I do not wish to read the publications of any man that cannot or will not take the oath of loyalty to his Government!" The editor, feeling more righteous than his disgruntled reader, called the reader "an Apostle of State Religion and old Puritan Bigotry."[46] In order to provide to pro-loyalty readers a paper with fidelity, the Baptist State Convention had commenced the *Baptist Record*. While the two Baptist groups and their respective periodicals remained independent of one another, they soon joined together in order to rally Baptists to one central organization.[47]

This new paper, the *Central Baptist*, formed in 1868 out of a merger between the *Journal* and the *Record*. Many observers hailed the merger of the Baptist papers and the reunification of Baptists in Missouri as foreshadowing the reunification of America. The editor of the *Central Baptist* considered the new merger "a step that marks the return of good feeling and fraternal co-operation between Baptist[s] of the North and the South." He continued, "It is a coming together of the Baptists of Missouri in fraternal concord. It is a necessary preliminary step to the establishment of a paper that shall truly serve and represent the Baptist interests of this great valley."[48]

The editors of the *Central Baptist* continually reinforced the claim that the paper was not factional. Its mission was "not to carry bitterness of controversy to the Christian fireside; not to kindle the fires of sectional or sectarian hate in Baptist households ... to breathe forth a spirit of reconciliation; [and] to plead for the unity of God's people in spirit and action."⁴⁹ The Baptist reunification also signified a return to Missouri's role and purpose within Christian history. In 1868, a correspondent from Washington, DC, recognized that the Mississippi Valley was the seat of a new evangelical empire. "I rejoice in the union formed in your paper enterprise and the union progressing among Baptists in your great central State," he wrote. Reiterating the praises that Beecher, Magoon, and others heaped on the Mississippi Valley, the correspondent continued that Missouri was "soon destined to be an empire itself."⁵⁰

The Protestant evangelical hope that the Midwest would be at the heart of North American Christendom was never realized. In part, this was due to the inability among Protestants to maintain their own cohesion amidst the sectional crisis of the nineteenth century. In part, because evangelicals chose to exclude Christians of other traditions. The Midwest maintains a heavy proportion of Protestants. According to a Pew Research study in 2014, the Midwest had the second-highest data of self-described Protestant Christians at 45 percent, behind the South at 48 percent. Within the Midwest itself, there is an evangelical subregion with states that report more than 25 percent of residents identify as Evangelical Protestants. These include the states Iowa (28%), Missouri (36%), Michigan (25%), Indiana (31%), and Ohio (29%).⁵¹ The region has become a symbol of the quintessence of American culture and values. Thus, although the Midwest was never the seat of American Christianity, it did become an imagined heartland.

Notes

This chapter combines portions from my Ph.D. dissertation, noted below. I appreciate Jon Lauck for putting together this volume and including my contribution. I am also grateful to Randall Stephens and Elesha Coffman for their comments and constructive criticism.

1. T.H. Cunningham Diary 1876, M27, St. Louis Mercantile Library (StLMerc), University of Missouri–St. Louis, St. Louis, Missouri.
2. "Biographical and Historical Notes Contributed by Rev. George R. Goodman to the Historical Society of Southern Illinois Conference," Methodist Archives, Box 25, Holman Library, McKendree University, Lebanon, Illinois.
3. R.W. Van Alstyne, *The Rising American Empire* (New York: Oxford University Press, 1960), 78–123; Richard Kluger, *Seizing Destiny: How*

American Grew from Sea to Shining Sea (New York: Alfred A. Knopf, 2007), 181–231, 270–399; Walter Nugent, *Habits of Empire: A History of American Expansion* (New York: Knopf, 2008), 3–72; and Daniel Walker Howe, *What God Hath Wrought: The Transformation of America, 1815–1848* (New York: Oxford University Press, 2007), 701–43. A recent essay has explored the three complementary and competing visions of the Old Northwest during the early federal period. See Gleaves Whitney, "The Upper Midwest as the Second Promised Land," in Jon K. Lauck, Gleaves Whitney, and Joseph Hogan, eds., *Finding a New Midwestern History* (Lincoln: University of Nebraska Press, 2018), 281–302.
4. Laurie Maffly-Kipp, *Religion and Society in Frontier California* (New Haven, CT: Yale University Press, 1994), 35–36; Colin B. Goodykoontz, *Home Missions on the American Frontier with Particular Reference to the American Home Missionary Society* (1939; reprint, New York: Octagon Books, 1971), 38–39.
5. Based on data from Stanley B. Parsons, William W. Beach, and Dan Hermann, *United States Congressional Districts, 1788–1841* (Westport, CT: Greenwood Press, 1978); and Kenneth C. Martis and Ruth Anderson Rowles, *The Historical Atlas of the United States Congressional Districts, 1789–1983* (New York: Free Press, 1982). This affinity for the Midwest and its potential importance to the nation's destiny continued throughout the nineteenth century and into the twentieth. For examples, see Jon K. Lauck, *From Warm Center to Ragged Edge: The Erosion of Midwestern Literary and Historical Regionalism, 1920–1965* (Iowa City: University of Iowa Press, 2017), 1–2.
6. Lyman Beecher, *A Plea for the West*, 2nd ed. (Cincinnati: Truman and Smith, 1835; reprint, Bedford, MA: Applewood Books, 2009), 11–12.
7. *Christian Observer*, 16 April 1847.
8. "Remarks of Rev. E.L. Magoon, before the Home Mission Society," *Christian Secretary*, 2 June 1848.
9. John F. Schermerhorn and Samuel J. Mills, *A Correct View of That Part of the United States Which Lies West of the Allegany Mountains, with Regard to Religion and Morals* (Hartford: Peter B. Gleason and Co. Printers, 1814), 31–32, reprinted in Edwin S. Gaustad, ed., *To Win the West: Missionary Viewpoints, 1814–1815* (New York: Arno Press, 1972).
10. Rufus T. Babcock, ed., *Forty Years of Pioneer Life: Memoir of John Mason Peck D.D., Edited from his Journals and Correspondence* (1864; reprint with introduction by Paul M. Harrison, Carbondale: Southern Illinois University Press, 1965), 101.
11. Timothy Flint, *A Condensed Geography and History of the Western States, or the Mississippi Valley* (Cincinnati: E.H. Flint, 1828), I:217.
12. "Baptist Missionary Society of Massachusetts," *Christian Watchman*, 29 May 1829.
13. Schermerhorn and Mills, *Correct View*, 48.

14. Samuel J. Mills and Daniel Smith, *Report of a Missionary Tour through That Part of the United States Which Lies West of the Allegany Mountains; Performed under the Direction of the Massachusetts Missionary Society* (Andover: Flagg and Gould, 1815), 13, reprinted in Gaustad, ed., *To Win the West*.
15. Babcock, ed., *Forty Years*, 186. See also David Paul Nord, *Faith in Reading: Religious Publishing and the Birth of Mass Media in America* (New York: Oxford University Press, 2004); and John Fea, *The Bible Cause: A History of the American Bible Society* (New York: Oxford University Press, 2016), 30–50.
16. "Claims of the Bible Cause," *Christian Observer*, 18 November 1842.
17. "What Can Be Done to Supply Sunday School Libraries in the West," *Christian Observer*, 18 November 1842.
18. "Sunday School Libraries at the West," *New York Evangelist*, 9 November 1843. See also "Selected Summary," *Christian Secretary*, 10 November 1843; and "Three Thousand Dollars; For Sunday-School Libraries in the Valley of the Mississippi," *Christian Reflector*, 15 November 1843.
19. American Sunday School Union, *Sixth Annual Report* (1830), 3, quoted in Robert W. Lynn and Elliott Wright, *The Big Little School: Sunday Child of American Protestantism* (New York: Harper & Row, 1971), 18. See also Lynn and Wright, 15–38; Anne Boylan, *Sunday School: The Transformation of an American Institution* (New Haven, CT: Yale University Press, 1988), 69–70; and Ryan Ruggles Smith Jr., "'In Every Destitute Place': The Mission Program of the American Sunday School Union, 1817–1834" (Ph.D. Dissertation: University of Southern California, 1973), 124–51.
20. Gerald Shaughnessy, *Has the Immigrant Kept the Faith?: A Study of Immigration and Catholic Growth in the United States, 1790–1920* (New York: Macmillan, 1925; reprint, New York: Arno Press, 1969).
21. Robert Frederick Trisco, *The Holy See and the Nascent Church in the Middle Western United States, 1826–1850* (Rome, Italy: Gregorian University Press, 1962), 22.
22. Ray Allen Billington, *The Protestant Crusade, 1800–1860: A Study of the Origins of American Nativism* (New York: Macmillan, 1938; reprint, New York: Rinehart & Co., 1952), 72–73. See also Maura Jane Farrelly, *Anti-Catholicism in America, 1620–1860* (New York: Cambridge University Press, 2018), 134–57. On American nativism and Catholicism, see John L. Higham, *Strangers in the Land: Patterns in American Nativism, 1860–1925*, rev. ed. (New Brunswick, NJ: Rutgers University Press, 2011). It comes as no surprise to this author that the anti-Catholic and anti-immigrant sentiments should persist within the Midwest throughout the nineteenth and twentieth centuries, giving rise to the American Protective Association (APA) in Iowa in the 1880s. For additional overviews of nativism and anti-Catholicism in the Midwest, including the APA, see also Jon Lauck, "'You Can't Mix Wheat and Potatoes in the Same Bin': Anti-Catholicism in Early Dakota," *South Dakota History* 38, no. 4 (Spring 2008): 1–46; and Jon

Butler, "The Midwest's Sacred Landscapes," in Lauck et al., eds., *Finding*, 196–210.
23. "What Catholics Expect from Their Schools," *Christian Secretary*, 5 July 1834.
24. "Valley of the Mississippi," *Christian Watchman*, 6 April 1832.
25. *Doctrine and Covenants* 57:1–2; *Doctrine and Covenants* 84:2–3.
26. Kenneth Winn, *Exiles in the Land of Liberty: Mormons in America, 1830–1846* (Chapel Hill: University of North Carolina Press, 1989), 83–84.
27. Samuel Lucas, "Jackson County," in *Gazetteer of the State of Missouri*, compiled by Alphonso Wetmore (St. Louis, 1837), 96. Quoted in Winn, *Exiles*, 89.
28. "Letter to John Thornton and Others, 25 July 1836" in *Joseph Smith Papers Documents, Volume 5: October 1835 – January 1838* (Salt Lake City: Church Historian's Press, 2017), 258–68.
29. Joseph Smith, *History of the Church*, I:375. Quoted in Winn, *Exiles*, 89.
30. J. Spencer Fluhman, *"A Peculiar People": Anti-Mormonism and the Making of Religion in Nineteenth-Century America* (Chapel Hill: University of North Carolina Press, 2012), 56.
31. *Autobiography of Peter Cartwright, Backwoods Preacher* (1856) with an Introduction, Bibliography, and Index by Charles L. Wallis (Nashville: Abingdon Press, 1956), 225–28, 250–51, 260–61.
32. Winn, 64. See also Christopher C. Jones "'We Latter-Day Saints are Methodists': The Influence of Methodism on Early Mormon Religiosity" (M.A. Thesis: Brigham Young University, 2009), 13–39.
33. Winn, *Exiles*, 129.
34. "Application for Land Patent, 22 June 1836," in *Joseph Smith Papers Documents, Volume 5*, 253–58.
35. Benjamin F. Johnson, *My Life's Review* (1947), 28. Quoted in Winn, *Exiles*, 93.
36. Winn, *Exiles*, 93.
37. Smith, *History of the Church* 2:144.
38. "Revelation on Priesthood," *History of the Church* 2:210. Accessed from *BYU Studies* at https://byustudies.byu.edu/content/volume-2-chapter-14.
39. Barton Price, "Evangelical Periodicals and the Making of America's Heartland, 1789–1900" (Ph.D. dissertation, Florida State University, 2011), 165–211.
40. "The Value of a Religious Paper," *Central Baptist*, 17 September 1868.
41. James Hall, *Letters from the West; containing Sketches of Scenery, Manners, and Customs; and Anecdotes Connected with the First Settlement of the Western Sections of the United States* (London: Henry Colburn, 1828), 234–47. See also, Robert P. Swierenga, "The Settlement of the Old Northwest: Ethnic Pluralism in a Featureless Plain," *Journal of the Early Republic* 9, no. 1 (Spring, 1989): 73–105; Douglas K. Meyer, *Making the Heartland Quilt: A Geographical History of Settlement and Migration in Early-Nineteenth-Century*

Illinois (Carbondale: Southern Illinois University Press, 2000); Gregory S. Rose, "Hoosier Origins: The Nativity of Indiana's United States-Born Population in 1850," *Indiana Magazine of History* 81, no. 3 (September 1985), 201–32; Russel L. Gerlach, *Settlement Patterns in Missouri: A Study of Population Origins with a Wall Map* (Columbia: University of Missouri Press, 1986), 15–29; William O. Lynch, "The Influence of Population Movement on Missouri Before 1861," *Missouri Historical Review* 16, no. 2 (1922): 506–16; John C. Hudson, "North American Origins of Middlewestern Frontier Populations," *Annals of the Association of American Geographers* 78, no. 3 (September 1988): 395–413; and Stewart H. Holbrook, *The Yankee Exodus: An Account of Migration from New England* (New York: Macmillan, 1950).

42. "Traits of the Western People," *Central Christian Advocate*, 22 September 1858.
43. Robert Andrew Baker, *Relations Between Northern and Southern Baptists* (1948; reprint, New York: Arno Press, 1980); Donald G. Mathews, *Slavery and Methodism: A Chapter in American Morality, 1780–1845* (1965; reprint, Westport, CT: Greenwood Press, 1978); C.C. Goen, *Broken Churches, Broken Nation: Denominational Schisms and the Coming of the American Civil War* (Macon, GA: Mercer University Press, 1985). The sectional crisis of the 1840s and 1850s followed by the Civil War fomented tremendous crises of faith within American Protestantism. See especially Mark Noll, *The Civil War as a Theological Crisis* (Chapel Hill: University of North Carolina Press, 2006), 31–94. Additionally, the Civil War brought a crisis of faith in America's divine mission and moral uprightness, espoused in its civil religion. Harry Stout explored these themes in *Upon the Altar of the Nation: A Moral History of the American Civil War* (New York: Viking Press, 2006).
44. "The Test Oath," *Missouri Baptist Journal*, 12 February 1866; see also Thomas S. Barclay, "The Test Oath for the Clergy in Missouri," *Missouri Historical Review* 18, no. 3 (April 1924), 345–81.
45. "Prospectus," *Missouri Baptist Journal*, 8 January 1866.
46. "One out of Fifteen Hundred!" *Missouri Baptist Journal* 19 February 1866.
47. Robert Sidney Douglass, *History of Missouri Baptists* (Kansas City, MO: Western Baptist Publishing Company, 1934), 238–42; and Harvey Eldon Truex, *Baptists in Missouri: being a brief account of the early struggles, the organization, etc. of the denomination in the state* (Columbia, MO: E.W. Stephens, 1904), 60.
48. "The New Paper," *Central Baptist*, 6 August 1868.
49. "Our Paper," *Central Baptist*, 6 January 1870.
50. "Letter from the National Capital," *Central Baptist*, 10 September 1868.
51. Pew Research Center, "Religious Landscape Study" (2014) <http://www.pewforum.org/religious-landscape-study/> Accessed 2 May 2018.

Kenyon Gradert | Walt Whitman's Heartland Romance

"The fear of conflicting and irreconcilable interiors, and the lack of a common skeleton, knitting all close, continually haunts me."
—Whitman, *Democratic Vistas*

"Of you, my Land—your rivers, prairies, States—you, mottled Flag I love,
Your aggregate retain'd entire—Of north, south, east and west, your items all;
Of me myself—the jocund heart yet beating in my breast."
—Whitman, "A Carol Closing Sixty-Nine," *Leaves of Grass*

Walt Whitman never wrote about the American "heartland," a term that wouldn't become common until after the Second World War. But he did praise "the dominion-heart of America," what he imagined as the nation's geographical and agro-industrial heart in the Mississippi River Valley and especially its cultural life-source, a region that might bind together the country's tensions and contradictions.[1] In fact, more than any single writer, Whitman laid the groundwork for the Heartland as an idea, a feeling, and a myth that remains potent today.[2] Shortly after the 2016 presidential election, *The New York Times* polled readers on what they considered the best map of "The Heartland": 11 percent chose a map of where farmland held the highest share of total land (a.k.a., the "Breadbasket") and 12 percent a map where Donald Trump won the highest share of votes. Significantly, second place (18 percent) went to a map of everything but the United States's eastern and western coasts, and first place (22 percent) to a map of the midwestern states (the Dakotas, Nebraska, Kansas, Minnesota, Iowa, Missouri, Wisconsin, Michigan, Illinois, Indiana, and Ohio).[3] This variety of answers hints at the

Heartland's porous borders but also at the associations it evokes and the political-cultural role it serves. Our sense of the Heartland today—some hazy but distinctly noncoastal, fecund, and conservative region hovering around the Midwest—descends from Whitman's "dominion-heart."[4]

While the rest of the nation grew infatuated with the romance of the westward frontier or a vanishing "Old South," Whitman especially nursed a fondness for what he simply called "the prairies," the "Inland," or the "interior" alongside the Mississippi River that watered them. He would not see any of this in person until a trip in 1879 that took him through Indiana, Illinois, and Missouri, with a final stretch through the Kansas prairie on the Kansas Pacific Railroad from Kansas City to Denver, a journey that led him to declare in an interview with the *St. Louis Globe-Democrat*, "I am called a Western man. Although born in New York, I am in sympathy and preference Western—better fitted for the Mississippi Valley." But long before this trip, Whitman had sung the Heartland's praises repeatedly—from the very first edition of *Leaves of Grass* in 1855.[5] "I, from the banks of the running Missouri, praise nothing, in art, or aught else, / Till it has breathed well the atmosphere of this river—also the western prairie-scent, / And exudes it again," he wrote in "Others May Praise What They Like" (2–4).[6] In "Night on the Prairies," he similarly breathes in a starry sky, "absorb[ing] immortality and peace" while breathing out benediction upon the nation and its landscape: "How plenteous! How spiritual!" (5, 7).[7] When he would finally see these landscapes in person, Whitman concluded that "the Prairies and Plains, while less stunning at first sight, last longer, fill the esthetic sense fuller, precede all the rest, and make North America's characteristic landscape." Their "boundless prodigality" surpassed the more typical symbols of American nature—Yellowstone, Niagara Falls, even Yosemite—while "the valley of the Mississippi river and its tributaries ... is by far the most important stream on the globe, and would seem to have been marked out by design."[8]

Steven P. Schneider argues that Whitman loved the prairies and inland states because "the far circle-line of the horizon" created by their flatness was "an analog for his own expansive consciousness and for his idealized conception of Americans living free of constraint."[9] In addition to the prairie's expansiveness, Whitman loved its grass as his favored symbol for democracy. The very title of his hymn to America,

Leaves of Grass, was his persistent image for a democratic nation, a collection of individual spears knit together by common roots. Finally, beyond its expansiveness and grassland was the prairie's fertility, ready for any yeoman with resolve to plow a patch into a self-sufficient farm. Mountains were the play-place of aristocrats, prairies the stuff of a Jeffersonian republic.

But Whitman's attraction to this "dominion heart" did not wholly grow from its associations with boundless freedom and unconstrained democracy. In fact, Whitman more often evoked this interior as a symbol for the cultural unity that he hoped would counteract the destructive potential of unconstrained democracy. His celebration of the American interior began in response to the profound national unrest around slavery in the 1850s and grew stronger only after the deadly Civil War that nearly destroyed his beloved republic. Into the uncertainties of Reconstruction and beyond, Whitman returned repeatedly to the American interior as a cultural anchor during volatile decades of national uncertainty. "The fear of conflicting and irreconcilable interiors, and the lack of a common skeleton, knitting all close," he wrote, "continually haunts me."[10] His imaginative dominion heart would use the nation's geographic interior to assert a cultural and political unity via poetic fiat.

Whitman hinted at this conservative role for the heartland already in the Preface to the first edition of *Leaves of Grass* (1855). There he described his poetic vocation as that of the truly American poet who "incarnates its geography and natural life and rivers and lakes." He followed with the first of many rhapsodic catalogues of the American landscape, flying like a westward pioneer from "the sea off Massachusetts and Maine and over Manhattan bay and over Champlain and Erie ... and over the Texan and Mexican and Floridian and Cuban seas and over the seas off California and Oregon." But rather than glossing over this American interior as "flyover country," the true American poet especially "spans between them also from east to west and reflects what is between them." Thus he opened his magnum opus with special praise for America's interior and its river arteries, the "Mississippi with annual freshets and changing chutes, Missouri and Columbia and Ohio." Paralleling himself with these rivers and the prairies they feed, Whitman poses as a poet fertile and expansive enough to sustain and incorporate the diversity of American life: whether it be "the perpetual coming of immigrants," "the perfect equality of the female with the male," "the fluid movement of the population—the factories and mercantile life," or even "slavery and the tremulous spreading of hands to protect it, and the stern opposition to it which shall never cease till it ceases"—all shockwaves are absorbed by the vast "unsurveyed interior" of poet and nation. Within such a heart, "the haughty defiance of '76" is balanced by the "peace and formation of the constitution" and "the union always surrounded by blatherers and always calm and impregnable."[11]

This theme became at once more political, personal, and provocative with the homoerotic *Calamus* poems, added to the 1860 edition of *Leaves of Grass* as the nation careened ever closer towards a crisis over slavery. The *Calamus* cluster especially celebrated the kind of brotherly camaraderie and affection that Whitman would himself later feel as a nurse during the Civil War, a *cri de couer* for brotherly love among Americans at a moment in which such relationships felt increasingly impossible. Here too the "prairie" and the "interior" served as Whitman's frequent backdrop (if not a character in its own right), its geographic centrality and lush fertility the perfect setting for brotherly love and national unity. "Come, I will make the continent indissoluble," he wrote, "I will plant companionship thick as trees along all the rivers of America, and along the shores of the great lakes, and all over the prairie; / I will make inseparable cities, with their arms about each other's necks; / By the love of comrades, / By the manly love of comrades" ("For You O Democracy," 1, 6–9). Elsewhere in *Calamus*, this prairie camaraderie became more explicitly sexual:

> THE prairie-grass dividing—its special odor breathing,
> I demand of it the spiritual corresponding,
> Demand the most copious and close companionship of men,
> Demand the blades to rise of words, acts, beings,
> Those of the open atmosphere, coarse, sunlit, fresh, nutritious,
> ...
> Those that look carelessly in the faces of Presidents and Governors, as to say, *Who are you?*
> Those of earth-born passion, simple, never constrain'd, never obedient,
> Those of inland America. ("The Prairie-Grass Dividing," 1–5, 8–10)

Such poems provoked an antebellum audience, but for Whitman, any true celebration of "inland America" as the nation's throbbing heart and fertile seedbed could not ignore the sexual overtones of such metaphors. During and after the Civil War, Whitman placed his moral allegiance with the Union and the end of slavery as the only course for a true democracy, and several poems added to the 1867 *Leaves of Grass* reflect his admiration for the thousands of young westerners who aided what Lincoln called in his Gettysburg Address the "new birth of freedom" with higher per capita enlistment rates than any other regions of the North. In "O Tan-Faced Prairie-Boy," Whitman hailed one such volunteer as "more than all the gifts of the world" (5), while the image became more heroic in "Virginia—the West," (added to the 1881 *Leaves of Grass*): against fallen southern gentry brandishing "The insane knife toward the Mother of All,"

> The noble son on sinewy feet advancing,
> I saw, out of the land of prairies, land of Ohio's waters and of Indiana,
> To the rescue the stalwart giant hurry his plenteous offspring,
> Drest in blue, bearing their trusty rifles on their shoulders. (5–9)

A more tender variation of this theme arises in "Come Up from the Fields Father" (1867), telling the story of an Ohio farm family that belatedly learn of their son's death in war, marring the pastoral promise of the West with death and war: "Down in the fields all prospers well / But now from the fields come father … / … Ah now the single figure to me, / Amid all teeming and wealthy Ohio with all its cities and farms, / Sickly white in the face and dull in the head, very faint, / By the jamb of a door leans" (11–25). The son's death is made more poignant by the fertility of the western home he's left behind. In an 1863 letter to Ralph Waldo Emerson, Whitman wrote of his desire "to write a little book out of this phase of America, her masculine young manhood … genuine of the soil, of darlings and true heirs to me the first unquestioned and convincing western crop, prophetic of the future."[12] Many of his later poems did precisely this.

But in addition to praising Union westerners for squelching a rebellious slaveocracy, Whitman also hoped that the nation's sectional wounds would heal after the war, and he again turned to "inland America" as a place where North and South could again become tender-hearted "comrades" and "companions" of the sort he had imagined in *Calamus*, as in his well-known "Pioneers, O Pioneers!":

> From Nebraska, from Arkansas,
> Central inland race are we, from Missouri, with the continental blood intervein'd,
> All the hands of comrades clasping, all the Southern, all the Northern,
> Pioneers! O pioneers! (33–36)

In *Democratic Vistas* (1871), Whitman especially clarified why he placed so much hope for America's future in this dominion heart: Its economic and industrial strength would provide a solid material foundation for a united American culture. His first major prose work was occasioned as a response to Thomas Carlyle's 1867 article "Shooting Niagara," which argued that Reconstruction and the foolishness of black suffrage in particular would be the undoing of the American republic and definitive proof of democracy's tendency towards self-destruction. In response, Whitman energetically defended the prospects of democracy in America, and his faith grew in large part from the growing strength of the western states to provide a firm foundation for its future success. In particular, he cited the 1870 apportionment number revealing that the young western states (Ohio, Michigan, Indiana, Illinois, Wisconsin, Minnesota, Iowa, Missouri, Nebraska, Kansas) had gained twenty-four representatives in Congress for a grand total of ninety-eight, already larger than the entire South and one short of gaining more representatives than the rest of the States combined.[13] These young middlewestern states would be the future of not only the nation's political power but also its economic and industrial strength, for like its population, its prosperity "has risen so high that it has overflow'd all barriers, and has fill'd up the back-waters, and establish'd something like an approach to uniform success" among its eastern and southern brethren. Quite simply, America was still booming thanks to these inland states. In the wake of the War and Reconstruction, Whitman hoped that the emerging power of midwestern politics, agriculture, and industry would bind all states and territories around this literal interior of the continent just as Whitman's poetic self attempted to incarnate the entire country in *Leaves of Grass*. More so, he hoped that the unifying power of this dominion heart's material strength would also unite the country culturally, even spiritually. After "the planning and putting on record the political foundation rights of immense masses of people," the nation secured a second stage of "material prosperity" while "the Third stage, rising out of the previous ones," would be to achieve "a native expression-spirit."[14]

Whitman's choice to begin *Democratic Vistas* on this second stage of material prosperity responded directly to real historical currents. The Midwest was quickly on its way to becoming not only the agricultural but industrial heartland of the States. David Meyer bluntly declares that "the Midwest was an industrial colossus by 1870 compared to the South." Western states "industrialized significantly during the 1860s, far outpacing the eastern sections. Its share of the nation's manufacturing increased dramatically between 1860 and 1920, with almost half of this increase occurring in the 1860s," largely due to decreased transportation costs after a burst of track-laying and canal-digging linked the raw materials of the western states with New England and Mid-Atlantic industries.[15] Thus is the historical backdrop of Whitman's "The Prairie States" (1881), in which readers witness a return to reverence for the past and geological language of "iron interlace" and "time's accumulation":

> A NEWER garden of creation, no primal solitude,
> Dense, joyous, modern, populous millions, cities and farms,
> With iron interlaced, composite, tied, many in one,
> By all the world contributed—freedom's and law's and thrift's society,
> The crown and teeming paradise, so far, of time's accumulations,
> To justify the past. (1–6)

As his early footnote implies, Whitman hoped that the recent population growth and economic boom of the western states had "risen so high that it has overflow'd all barriers, and has fill'd up the back-waters, and establish'd something like an approach to uniform success." That is, the Midwest's wealth was the nation's wealth.[16]

Whitman's faith in western fecundity was also fueled by his long correspondence with his favorite brother, Jeff, who worked as a prominent engineer in St. Louis. Instrumental in designing water and sewer systems, Jeff was to Walt the perfect mix of science and application, eastern intellect with western pragmatism. "Displaying that desire for new ideas and broad vistas that Walt admired in the national character," Berthold and Price note that "Jeff showed particular interest in the West" and "as an engineer in the West who had asked Walt for publications concerning the transcontinental railroad, embodied the poem's ideals."[17] Whitman stopped in St. Louis on his famous western trip with the Old Settlers of Kansas Committee. David Reynolds brings to life the trip's influence:

> Whitman waxed ecstatic when they reached the midwestern prairies ... He saw in the prairie states a rugged naturalness and, at the same time, an almost utopian promise for a new industrial future. The trip answered Whitman's love of primal nature and restored his hope for modern technology. The American economy was on the rebound. Even as he traveled through the vast open lands that he thought were the basis for all future American poetry and art, he resumed his almost transcendental stance towards machines and business.[18]

As in "Passage to India," in many ways a poetic complement to the prose of *Democratic Vistas,* canals and railroad tracks were literally binding together the States in increasing material wealth and technological splendor. Though Promontory Point captures the American imagination, the tracks' mythic significance more rightly came from the knot in Council Bluffs, Iowa, "Tying the Eastern to the Western sea, / The road between Europe and Asia" (III.23–24).

The literal capital of the States, Whitman even hinted, would soon be West of the Alleghenies. "In a few years the dominion-heart of America will be far inland, toward the West," he wrote, for "the main social, political, spine-character of the States will probably run along the Ohio, Missouri and Mississippi rivers ... [regions which] will compact and settle the traits of America, with all the old retain'd, but more expanded, grafted on newer, hardier, purely native stock. A giant growth, composite from the rest, getting their contribution, absorbing it, to make it more illustrious."[19] Ever a strong unionist, this "composite" would be Whitman's utmost political and cultural goal in his later years. Whitman's millennial hopes would fluctuate between different saviors—New York City's bustling cosmopolitanism often offered itself as a candidate for this spiritual fusion—but nothing ever quite captured the poet's imagination like the West. "At different times," Reynolds says, "he found further 'solutions' in the railroad, in the Mississippi River basin, in the geography and people of the American West, to name a few phenomena he discussed in this way."[20]

Many critics emphasize Whitman's love of industry in his later poetry and prose, but this quality persisted alongside rhapsodic images of agricultural fecundity that also abetted his heartland millennialism. Within a metaphysical framework of popular Hegelianism and Darwinism, Whitman practiced a kind of geo-cultural surveying in his later work, marking the growth of the western states and the fecundity of their soils, sensing in their vast prairies the space and fertility necessary for democracy to grow a strong American soul. Language of fertility and growth dominates *Democratic Vistas* and usually overlaps with an inland setting to sketch the contours of his dominion heart: Literature, Whitman writes, must "stamp the interior ... of this American continent" and "tills its crops in many fields"; democracy, too, is safe, for it "resides, crude and latent, well down in the hearts of the fair average of the American-born people, mainly in the agricultural regions"; Whitman speaks repeatedly of this "democratic principle" that results when "individuality" "breaks up the limitless fallows of humankind, and plants the seed, and gives fair play, that its claims now precede the rest." Weaving all of these threads together, Whitman declares that the American experiment in democracy will succeed because, like a farmer, it plows the unused lands of humanity and creates plenty of space for varied types of "crops."[21]

But lest such rousing defenses of democracy sound like the stuff of a radical, Whitman also invoked western agriculture and geology—stolid, slow-moving, cyclical forces—to counter Carlyle's charge that democracy breeds an excess of dangerous dissent. "The eager and often inconsiderate appeals of reformers and revolutionists are indispensable," Whitman claims, "to counterbalance the inertness and fossilism making so large a part of human institutions. The latter will always take care of themselves—the danger being that they rapidly tend to ossify us." Elsewhere he concluded that "Nature's stomach is fully strong enough not only to digest the morbific matter" of excess political zeal, "even to change such contributions into nutriment for highest use and life—so American democracy's," literally grounded in a fecund heartland with room to absorb discontent. Here especially, Whitman's dominion heart binds together the nation by counteracting the forces of dissent and schismatism that would threaten it.[22]

Just as the Midwest functioned as a literal geographic center to America's vast interior, Whitman viewed the political and cultural future of America as one of increasing centralization. After the war, Whitman had a growing faith in centralized politics and a strong federal government, and especially looked up to the western politicians who represented these shifts. Lincoln, of course, is the oft-touted example and Whitman's personal hero. The man who was a tyrant to southern democrats would approach divinity status in Whitman's later poetry and became the star of Whitman's most often recited poem "O Captain! My Captain!" Eulogizing Lincoln's assassination in "When Lilacs Last in the Dooryard Bloom'd" (1865), Whitman would anticipate the vision of "Passage to India" of the railroad as a centralizing national force. Winding through the States, Lincoln's funeral train finds pastoral rest in a maternal, fecund prairie-land:

> Over the breast of the spring, the land, amid cities,
> Amid lanes and through old woods, where lately the violets peep'd
>   from the ground, spotting the gray debris,
> Amid the grass in the fields each side of the lanes, passing the
>   endless grass,
> Passing the yellow-spear'd wheat, every grain from its shroud in
>   the dark-brown fields uprisen,
> Passing the apple-tree blows of white and pink in the orchards,
> Carrying a corpse to where it shall rest in the grave (26–31)

Not only would Lincoln be Whitman's "powerful western fallen star" (7) and his "western orb sailing the heaven" (52)—a steady guide in troubled times—but a representative of the geographic "dominion-heart" that

Whitman hoped would hold America together. "Sea-winds blown from east and west, ... / ... till there on the prairies meeting" (66–68) is the only perfume acceptable to Lincoln's grave, the scent of America's geographic union. Building America, Whitman begins with the body of the North and South, working towards the soul of the western states: "Lo, body and soul—this land, / My own Manhattan with spires ... / ... The varied and ample land, the South and the North in the light, Ohio's shores and flashing Missouri, / And ever the far-spreading prairies cover'd with grass and corn" (83–86). Quite simply, the land of Lincoln had much to do with the president's stature as "the greatest, best, most characteristic, artistic, moral personality" in American life, as Whitman deemed him.

For similar reasons, Whitman remained surprisingly loyal to the questionable presidential administrations of Johnson, Grant, and Garfield, as well, for all were invested in centralized national unity at high costs, and all had come from the "inland" states of the West. When Whitman wrote of President Grant's return from a tour of Europe in "What Best I See in Thee" (1881), he painted the old general far more the Jacksonian democrat of the common folk than Grant ever was during his administration. The best he sees in Grant's tour is how

> in foreign lands, in all thy walks with kings,
> Those prairie sovereigns of the West, Kansas, Missouri, Illinois,
> Ohio's, Indiana's millions, comrades, farmers, soldiers, all to the front,
> Invisibly with thee walking with kings with even pace the round world's promenade,
> Were all so justified. (7–11)

The fact that Grant's administration bolstered a strong central government boosted his appeal to Whitman's imagination as a member of nation's dominion-heart, kin to these same western fields and farmers that knit together the nation.

As Whitman declares in "The Eighteenth Presidency" and elsewhere, his democratic vistas especially prize "farmers and mechanics" as symbolic representatives of the kind of culture he hopes to see poets realize in America: "I should demand a programme of culture, drawn out, not for a single class alone, or for the parlors or lecture-rooms, but with an eye to practical life, the west, the working-men, the facts of farms and jack-planes and engineers, and of the broad range of the women also of the middle and working strata."[23] In like manner, Whitman speaks in "Thoughts" (*Songs of Parting*, 1866) of "how few see the arrived models, the athletes, the Western states, or see freedom or spirituality" (6). In the wake of the purgative war, these athletes are ripe with promise as Whitman sings "of seeds dropping into the ground, of births, / of the steady concentration of America, inland, upward ... / ... of this Union welded in blood ... / ... Of all sloping own there where the fresh free giver the mother, the Mississippi flows, / of mighty inland cities yet unsurveyed ... / ... Of immense spiritual results future years far West" (16–40). The kind of people who Whitman prizes above all are productive and hearty, practical and pure, usually "Westerners" autocthonously sprung from the nation's dominion heart.

As in "Passage to India" and *Democratic Vistas*, the material prosperity of the American interior would not suffice in itself until it formed a foundation for a higher "third stage" of spiritual prosperity. Here too he placed millennial hopes in the Heartland as the region where all hopes of a new world would culminate. Quite literally, the history of western exploration and advancement would culminate in the geographic heart of America. "The manly and womanly personalism of our western world, can only be, and is, indeed, to be, (I hope,) its all penetrating Religiousness," he wrote. "Now arise these States. We see that while many were supposing things established and completed, really the grandest things always remain; and discover that the work of the New World is not ended, but only fairly begun."[24]

Notes

1. I am indebted to Ed Folsom's work on Whitman's midwestern connections: see especially "Walt Whitman at Iowa," *Books at Iowa* 39 (November 1983): 17–37; "Walt Whitman and the Prairies," *Mickle Street Review* 17/18; and "Walt Whitman's Prairie Paradise," in Robert F. Sayre, ed., *Recovering the Prairie* (University of Wisconsin Press, 1999), 47–60. Briefer notes of the significance of the interior for Whitman can be found in Jon K. Lauck, *From Warm Center to Ragged Edge* (Iowa City: University of Iowa Press, 2017), 1–3 and Robert F. Sayre, *Recovering the Prairie* (Madison: University of Wisconsin Press, 1999), 50–57.

2. "Rethinking the Heartland," *Frontier to Heartland*, The Newberry Library, 2009, https://publications.newberry.org/frontiertoheartland/exhibits/show/perspectives/rethinkingheartland
3. Emily Badger and Kevin Quealy, "Where Is America's Heartland? Pick Your Map," *The New York Times*, 3 January 2017, https://www.nytimes.com/interactive/2017/01/03/upshot/where-is-americas-heartland-pick-your-map.html
4. On the emergence of the Heartland as a conservative "signifier" opposed to "coastal liberal elites," see Frank Tobias Higbie, "Heartland: The Politics of a Regional Signifier," *Middle West Review* I, no. 1 (Fall 2014): 81–80; and especially Kristin L. Hoganson, *The Heartland: An American History* (New York: Penguin, 2019).
5. "Walt Whitman, the Poet," *St. Louis Globe-Democrat*, 13 September 1879, https://whitmanarchive.org/criticism/interviews/transcriptions/med.00528.html
6. Whitman, "Others May Praise What They Like," *Leaves of Grass* (New York: W.E. Chapin & Co., Printers, 1867), 68.
7. "Night on the Prairies," ibid., 287, *The Walt Whitman Archive*. https://whitmanarchive.org/published/other/CompletePoetry.html. From here on, all poems are quoted from the first original edition in which they appeared, as digitized by the Whitman Archive. Line numbers follow.
8. Whitman, *Specimen Days* (1882), from *Complete Prose Works* (Philadelphia: David McKay, 1892), 150. *The Walt Whitman Archive*. https://whitmanarchive.org/published/other/CompleteProse#leaf105r1.html
9. Ibid., 94; Steven P. Schneider, "The Great Plains and Prairies," J.R. LeMaster and Donald D. Kummings, eds., *Walt Whitman: An Encyclopedia* (New York: Garland Publishing, 1998).
10. Whitman, *Democratic Vistas* (1871), *Complete Prose Works* (Philadelphia: David McKay, 1892), 209. *The Walt Whitman Archive*. https://whitmanarchive.org/published/other/CompleteProse#leaf105r1.html
11. Walt Whitman, *Leaves of Grass*, Brooklyn, NY, 1855, iv. *The Walt Whitman Archive*. https://whitmanarchive.org/published/LG/1855/whole.html
12. "Walt Whitman to Ralph Waldo Emerson, 17 January 1863," Clifton Waller Barrett Collection, University of Virginia. The transcription presented here is derived from *Walt Whitman, The Correspondence*, ed. Edwin Haviland Miller (New York: New York University Press, 1961–1977), 1: 68–70. Digitized by the Walt Whitman Archive, https://whitmanarchive.org/biography/correspondence/tei/uva.00344.html
13. For a recent historical review of this moment of explosive midwestern growth, see Jon K. Lauck, ed., *The Midwestern Moment* (Hastings, NE: Hastings College Press, 2017).
14. Whitman, *Democratic Vistas*, 205, 244.

15. David Meyer, "Midwestern Industrialization and the American Manufacturing Belt in the Nineteenth Century," *The Journal of Economic History* 49, no. 4: 937.
16. Whitman, *Democratic Vistas*, note, 205.
17. Dennis Berthold and Kenneth M. Price, eds., *Dear Brother Walt: The Letters of Thomas Jefferson Whitman* (Kent, OH: Kent State University Press, 1984).
18. David Reynolds, *Walt Whitman's America: A Cultural Biography* (New York: Vintage, 1996), 532.
19. Whitman, *Democratic Vistas*, 222.
20. Reynolds, *Walt Whitman's America*, 468.
21. Whitman, *Democratic Vistas*, 207, 208, 226, 228.
22. Ibid., 221, 220.
23. Ibid., 231.
24. Ibid,, 257.

Nicole Etcheson | The Making of Midwesterners

The Fletcher Family in Indiana

Calvin Fletcher left Vermont as a poor youth and became one of the early settlers of Indianapolis, where he prospered as a lawyer and businessman. His "relentless pursuit of respectability and success" distinguishes Fletcher, in the view of his biographer, as a classic nineteenth-century middle-class American. Indeed, Calvin Fletcher's life illustrates many facets of mid-nineteenth-century life: the migration to the western frontier, the market revolution, the Second Great Awakening, and the growing sectional crisis. But the story of the Fletcher family in Indiana also reveals the shaping of the Midwest out of the migration streams that populated the region.[1] Although Fletcher lived in Indiana for two-thirds of his life, he retained family connections in New England and was particularly close to a slave-owning brother in Virginia. Such relationships are chronicled in Fletcher's diaries, which reveal that "Indiana's population fashioned a blend of the distinctive regional cultures of the Atlantic seaboard: New England, middle state, and southern."[2] The story of how the Fletchers became Midwesterners is a story of how the Midwest became a unique region.

In the summer of 1817, nineteen-year-old Calvin Fletcher borrowed $7.50 from an uncle to finance a move from his native Vermont to Ohio. En route to the West, he worked as a farm laborer and in a brickyard. "Destitute of mo[n]ey," he settled near Urbana, Ohio, where he taught school and read law. In 1821, Fletcher married one of his pupils, Sarah Hill. That year, the Fletchers settled in Indianapolis, where Calvin became one of the first lawyers in the town. After a brief political career as state senator from 1826 until 1833, he was elected a director of the state bank by the Indiana General Assembly in early 1834.[3] By then he had established "a very fine business in the law," but "the most profitable part" of his work was in collecting debts. By the end of his life, he was the "highest income taxpayer" in Indianapolis.[4]

Calvin Fletcher's leave-taking of New England involved a wrenching separation from his family. Upon departing for the West, he was clearly uneasy about "launch[ing] into the world without a Parent to protect or friends to assist [him] in time of need."⁵ Teaching school in Urbana, Fletcher reflected, "I have no desire to return to Vt, though I frequently draw involuntary sighs when I think of home!"⁶ Almost two decades later, Fletcher still spoke of a desire to see his "native hills."⁷ Fletcher arrived in the Midwest at a time when Upland Southern settlers dominated. Although parts of the upper Midwest would be incorporated into the "universal Yankee nation," Fletcher always lived in a region dominated by Upland Southerners who viewed New England characteristics in a negative light: New Englanders' capitalist orientation seemed greedy and their emphasis on religion and school sanctimonious and elitist.⁸

From his first arrival in Ohio, Fletcher noted differences between the West and New England. In Ohio, dancing was not so popular as whist, singing, and riding. Girls married younger, and wedding celebrations lasted for days. Farm communities gathered for communal harvests and drank a great deal of whiskey on such occasions, which led "Kentuckyans and Virginians" to do "pi[t]ched Battle." Although dueling was illegal, it frequently occurred.⁹ After two years in Indianapolis, Fletcher wrote that Westerners were not like people from New York and New England:

> They are bold & independent in their sentiments as to public men or measures the most ignorant man here knows who governs him & who administers justice—In NE the government are becoming aristocratical & the common people put all credence in great men—The language here among the common people has many provincial expressions and would be diverting to a New Englander.¹⁰

Indiana had been heavily settled from the Upland South, which influenced its culture, language, food, religion, and politics. Just as Fletcher formed opinions about his Upland Southern neighbors, they had their own sectional prejudices about New Englanders. When Fletcher rose "from poverty ... to plenty," the family attributed his success to "his industrious habits."¹¹ But the Upland Southern settlers saw Calvin Fletcher's business acumen as rooted in his regional origins:

"[H]e is a Yankee he can get rich any where," locals thought. In turn, New Englanders believed that it was easy for men of mediocre talents to prosper in the West. Calvin acknowledged that "even the most pious & moral" New Englanders "desired to see their children to[o] '*sharp*' ... in all their dealings as to be a little *dishonest*."[12]

Having married into Upland Southern culture, Fletcher was not just a transplanted New England observer. His father-in-law had migrated from Kentucky, and both of Sarah Hill's grandfathers had been Virginians, although one was originally from Boston. Sarah identified herself as a western woman. It was perhaps because of Sarah's influence that the Fletchers, unlike some transplanted New Englanders, did not celebrate the Pilgrim Thanksgiving. Even so, the Fletchers maintained strong ties to other regions. All but two of the Fletchers' eleven children went to school in the East and visited family in New England and Virginia.[13] Fletcher even endowed his marriage's fecundity with regional meaning: He had always desired "a goodly number" of children, "differing widely from the fashionable of New England, who are dissatisfied if they have not some, & are mad if they have many—"[14]

As westerners, the Fletchers were aware not just of regional differences but animosities. Sarah ventured that Calvin's sister would like Ohio, "notwithstanding most N.E. people dislike it."[15] Yankees were held to be guilty of "cultural imperialism," viewing their ways as superior and intent on imposing them on the region. The Fletchers themselves were capable of a certain New England disdain for the West. Calvin Fletcher sent his children to schools in the East, where he believed scholarship was more highly "esteemed" than in Indiana.[16] His second son, Elijah, concluded that "Indiana (and so in fact is the whole west) at the present day is sadly deficient in literrary attainments."[17] Hoosier educational shortcomings reflected the lack of a "disposition to improve."[18] While a professor at Indiana Asbury (later DePauw) University in western Indiana, Calvin's son Miles visited the "dilapidated" town of Putnamville, which he described as occupied by "geese, drunken Kentuck Hoosiers, and bloated Irishmen."[19] Even the college town of Greencastle was a "low, dirty, ignorant Kentucky town," without "energy or public spirit."[20] Yet Miles, a Brown University graduate, nonetheless maintained that Indiana Asbury was "not at all inferior" to New England colleges, having students as good as any in New England.[21] The Fletchers were constantly comparing Indiana and the West to other sections. When another son, Calvin Jr., attended an agricultural fair in Kentucky, he judged Indiana superior in horses and machines but "far-far behind" in "fat cattle." Kentucky's men were "independent and gentlemanly," and the "Ladies fat sociable and *ignorant*."[22]

The clearest impact of western values on Calvin Fletcher was in religion. Raised as a Congregationalist, Fletcher did not at first attend church in the Midwest because "the ministers are uncooth low bread Methodist whom I despise."[23] But within a decade, he would nevertheless join the Methodists. At the time of Fletcher's conversion, the South and Lower Midwest were the locus of Methodist strength. Fletcher's brother-in-law was a Methodist minister, and the Hill family seems to have been influential in Fletcher's conversion. John H. Wigger cites Fletcher as an exemplar of Methodist values.[24] Fletcher's conversion brought him into spiritual fellowship with Midwesterners of southern descent.

All the Fletcher children were born in the Midwest, where all but the oldest lived the majority of their lives. They retained a consciousness of their New England background, but absorbed the attitudes of southern-stock Hoosiers. While their father would always be a transplanted New Englander, the Fletcher children were Westerners. Among their New England relatives, they called themselves the "hoosier cousins."[25] One of the younger sons, Stephen, who worked in a hardware store in Greencastle, referred to another man as "the little yanke that has the stump mashine."[26] Stephen did not evidently identify as a Yankee himself. In turn, the New Englanders also saw the Fletchers as different. A Vermont relative called Elijah "a <u>live Hoosier</u> right from the west."[27]

The Fletcher children were proud to be Hoosiers. In Elijah's view, western boys had more "<u>spunk</u>" and western girls were "handsomer."[28] Spending a winter with his grandmother in Vermont, Elijah complained, "I am getting so tired of seeing nothing but snow and hearing nothing but sleigh bells." He vividly described for his younger brothers in Indiana a "yankee winter" in which the sun appeared only once every two weeks and the snow piled up as high as their corn crib roof at home.[29] In contrast, his New England cousin wrote that it must be "delightful" to "have plenty of snow for sleigh riding."[30]

Although proud of Indiana, this second generation of Fletchers held New England as the standard to which they aspired. When Calvin's oldest son, Cooley, left for schooling at Phillips Exeter, a family friend wrote with the hope that he would "do credit to himself, his friends & the 'Hoosier land'—"³¹ Studying at a college-preparatory academy in Ludlow, Vermont, Elijah wrote home, "I have burned out oil but I have been paid for it. I have yielded to no yankee. I finished Cicero last week."³² He celebrated his brother Calvin's ability to make India crackers, writing, "Several yankee boys have tried to make them, but with all their boasted ingenuity they have failed."³³ While Elijah was away at school, his younger brother Calvin wrote how their two sisters had grown into young ladies, quoting a visitor to Indianapolis who remarked that "he never saw more health intelligence and beauty in the same number of young ladies in N.E."³⁴

Admitted to Brown University, Elijah categorized his classmates by region: "The Southerners that come here are generally good speakers, and great ladies men.... But the Yankees like fools run after them, and will make themselves niggers to gain their good will." Elijah, one of only three Westerners, found the "intelligent" New Englanders actually very "ignorant" about the West: "I have had those who were the smartest ask me how many slaves my father had. I generally stuff them, saying about a hundred and fifty[.] If they are too much engrossed with Yankeedom to learn what states of the Mississippi valley are free and those that are not I say let them sleep on in their ignorance."³⁵

Although Indiana was indeed a free state, Elijah's casual use of the derogatory term "nigger" indicated that racial attitudes in the Midwest were not that different from those in the South, especially in heavily southern-settled states such as Indiana. Calvin Fletcher did not engage in the casual prejudice of the era. He spoke of African Americans as "colored" or "negro." When Miles objected to his father giving advice, Calvin responded that he would accept counsel from "a beggar or old negro woman" if the intentions were good.³⁶ One of Calvin Fletcher's brothers, Elijah, settled in Virginia and became a slaveowner and successful planter. Elijah's family adopted the values of the planter class. Lucien Fletcher, Calvin's Virginia-born nephew, rejected Calvin's stricture that Lucien should black his own shoes. Lucien insisted "he is no negro to do such work."³⁷ Despite Calvin's assertion that he was not too good to take an elderly black woman's advice, the force of the contrast lay in the differences in their status: he a well-off white male and she a poor black female. When Calvin Jr. plowed the lot of a black man, "The rest of the childrin laughed at him for ploughing for a negro." The younger Calvin told them "that he had a right to experiment on a negro while he was trying to learn a thing."[38] Rather than avow a kind act or a service to a black man, Calvin Jr. sought to indicate that he did keep racial lines—and his father did not rebuke this assertion.

When Stephen and Billy Fletcher served in the Union Army, they described African Americans in the vulgar terms employed by other Indiana soldiers but not found in their father's vocabulary. Stephen described black refugees with the Union Army in Nashville as "a big case full of Monkeys," called them "*cussed niggers,*" and insisted that western men would never consent to fight alongside black soldiers.[39] Like many Union soldiers, Stephen acquired a black servant, Norris Allen, who had been fathered by his owner and sold by his half-brother. Even knowledge of the poor treatment Allen had received from his kin did not stop Stephen from referring to Allen as property, "my darky," or from casually saying that Allen would come home with him without any indication of Allen's wishes. Billy luxuriated at a tavern in Virginia, where he and other members of his regiment drank mint juleps and were "carefully attended by 'Samson' the biggest blackest and politest of niggers." Calvin regretted the soldiers' attitudes about African Americans, but seemed not to notice that his sons shared those attitudes.[40]

Despite Calvin's fondness for his slave-owning Virginia relatives, there was no question as to the Indiana Fletchers' allegiances when the Civil War broke out. When Confederates fired on Fort Sumter, two of Calvin's younger children, Stephen and Lucy, were visiting their uncle's family. Calvin praised Stephen's "coolness" in getting himself and his sister home. Stephen enlisted in fall 1861, maintaining that it was a "just war, that all that is dear & near depends on the result of the struggle."[41] When Stephen left for the war, Billy was already a prisoner in Richmond, having been captured while scouting for the army. Although Miles had gone east in an effort to secure Billy's exchange, Calvin worried that his Virginia relatives would try to help Billy: "I wanted no aid from them as they are rebels."[42]

Nor did the Fletchers tolerate the disloyal in Indiana. Stationed in Kentucky, Stephen was outraged when anti-war Democrats captured the Indiana legislature in the 1862 election. Many of the Peace Democrats were of southern birth or ancestry.⁴³ "Where ever I have been I never have heard more *disloyal* sentiments spoken, than have been in the Ind. Legislature," he wrote. "I am *disgusted*, with it. They ought to be *hung*, shot down like *dogs*." Indiana's "brave boys now in the field" had brought the state "to the highest pitch of *honor*," but Indiana's name was "now to be *disgraced*, & be brought on an equal with *South Carolina*." Stephen's remedy was to "Send 20,000 of us back to Ind. & we'll make the whole *cowardly set* tremble in their boots. The whole *Set* will be *exterminated*. They will not receive the mercy that would be shown to a *Southern Reble*.... *Northern* Rebles I am afraid will be more trouble than Southern ones."⁴⁴ The Fletchers may have been influenced by Upland Southerners in religious and racial attitudes, but they maintained a firm adherence to the Union—even when it meant cutting ties to southern relatives. Although Indiana did have a strong Peace Democrat faction, the state was second among Union states in the percentage of men of military age who served in the Union army.⁴⁵

Fletcher also drew his interest in philanthropy from his New England heritage, becoming one of the most noteworthy of Indiana philanthropists. Robert A. Gross has written that Southerners and southern-influenced Midwesterners viewed missionary societies and many charitable associations as agents of New England cultural imperialism.⁴⁶ In the South, where civil society revolved around the needs of a slave society, the "sprawling array of highly autonomous charitable, educational, and social reform movements" that characterized the North failed to emerge.⁴⁷ But Fletcher was extremely active in associational culture, participating in and helping to found a library, a thespian society, agricultural societies, Sunday schools, a temperance society, and a colonization society in Indianapolis. Plowing matches for Indiana's first state fair were held on Fletcher's Indianapolis farm. Fletcher took a strong interest in education. Like Fletcher, Caleb Mills, who was Indiana's most prominent school reformer, also hailed from New England. When Fletcher served in the legislature, he considered the school bill the most important legislation.⁴⁸ Throughout the 1850s, he served as a school trustee in Indianapolis. The trustees were responsible for hiring teachers, implementing a graded school system, inspecting schools, and examining students. Fletcher described the position as "one of the most important offices in the gift of the people."⁴⁹ He attended lectures by William H. McGuffey, author of the noted schoolbooks.⁵⁰

Fletcher's philanthropy included support for the black community. He represented a number of African Americans in court, including "a poor but honest *colored* man" who had been cheated by a grandson of the first Chief Justice of the United States, a runaway slave woman and her three children who were contesting recapture by their owner, and a black man who was working to buy his freedom from his owner.⁵¹ Fletcher played a role in the most celebrated fugitive slave case in Indiana, raising money to help John Freeman, an Indianapolis restaurateur who was claimed under the 1850 Fugitive Slave Act. During the Civil War, Fletcher was elected president of the Freedman's Aid Society and donated land on his farm as the camp for Indiana's black regiment. But Fletcher was never a radical. On July 4, 1845, an Indianapolis mob attacked and killed John Tucker, a former Kentucky slave. Fletcher and Henry Ward Beecher, who then served as pastor to an Indianapolis church, approached the editor of an antislavery newspaper, Henry Depuy, in order to dissuade him from publishing an account of the atrocity lest it provoke more bloodshed. Depuy published it anyway.⁵² Fletcher's long support of colonization only faded with the Civil War, when he adopted aiding freedmen as "a solemn duty reserved perhaps to me as the last public act of my life."⁵³

Although moderate by the standards of many reformers, Fletcher's reformism stood in contrast to that of many Hoosiers. He was a zealous advocate of public education in a state that provided little support for schools, a temperance man in a culture where alcohol fueled farm labor, and a defender of African Americans in a state that held abolitionists in "utter abhorrence." Fletcher was also active in causes such as freedman's aid, which did not get broad support in the North except in abolitionist circles.⁵⁴

Freedman's Aid did indeed prove to be Fletcher's last "solemn duty." He died in May 1866, two months after taking a fall from his horse. His legacy endured in the institutions he helped build in Indiana, including the historical society and his bank. Many of his children remained deeply rooted in Indiana, contributing both as businessmen and philanthropists. His two oldest sons, Cooley and Elijah, became ministers. Several of his sons pursued careers in business. Calvin

Fletcher Jr., whose Owen County mansion was named Ludlow Hall after the Fletchers' Vermont home, was a railroad executive. Stoughton was president of an Indiana gas company and then an engine works. Stephen owned a brick manufactory. Ingram and Albert became partners in Fletcher's bank; when it failed in the Panic of 1873, they struggled to recover by working in a variety of fields, including insurance, real estate, and sales. Other sons devoted themselves to public service. Cooley was a diplomat. Miles was serving as state superintendent of public education when he died in a railroad accident during the Civil War. Stoughton, initially a businessman, became the first president of the Indiana Reformatory for Women and Girls. And Billy, who was a successful physician, became superintendent of Indiana Central Hospital for the Insane.[55]

The Fletcher children continued to be active philanthropists: Stoughton was active with the state board of charities, Billy was a temperance advocate who wrote books on treating alcoholism, and Stephen—noted for his philanthropy—founded a mission for the Indianapolis poor. The two Fletcher daughters, although they did not have business careers, also continued the Fletcher legacy of charitable works. The oldest daughter, Maria, taught school and Sunday School, participated in temperance activity, and served on the state fair committee for butter and preserves. She died of complications after childbirth at the age of twenty-six. The other daughter, Lucy, was seventeen years old when Maria died, and often cared for her nieces and nephews, becoming such a fixture in her widowed brother-in-law's household that they married (despite Calvin's reservations) two years after Maria's death. In addition to caring for her siblings' children, Lucy taught Sunday School.[56]

The story of the Fletcher family in Indiana from the 1820s through the Civil War is a story of shifting regional identities. The Fletchers retained a sense of themselves as New Englanders and therefore as different in certain ways from their neighbors; but while they increasingly accommodated themselves to the southern-influenced society in which they lived, they rejected the proslavery culture of the South. The Fletchers' transformation into Midwesterners is a microcosm of the region's formation of midwestern identity out of the diverse migrant groups that populated the Midwest.

Notes

1. Daniel Blake Smith, *Our Family Dreams: The Fletchers' Adventures in Nineteenth-Century America* (New York: St. Martin's Press, 2016), 2. See J.M. Opal, *Beyond the Farm: National Ambitions in Rural New England* (Philadelphia: University of Pennsylvania Press, 2008); Charles Sellers, *The Market Revolution: Jacksonian America, 1815–1846* (New York: Oxford University Press, 1991); John H. Wigger, *Taking Heaven by Storm: Methodism and the Rise of Popular Christianity in America* (New York: Oxford University Press, 1998); and Nicole Etcheson, *The Emerging Midwest: Upland Southerners and the Political Culture of the Old Northwest, 1787–1861* (Bloomington: Indiana University Press, 1996).
2. George Geib, "The Diary of Calvin Fletcher and the Historians," *Traces of Indiana and Midwestern History* 10 (Winter 1998): 23–25.
3. Gayle Thornbrough, ed., *The Diary of Calvin Fletcher, vol. 1: 1817–1838* (Indianapolis: Indiana Historical Society, 1972), xi–xiii, xvi, xxxiii, 4, 8, 14; "Early Indianapolis: The Fletcher Papers—Third Instalment," *Indiana Magazine of History* 2 (no. 1): 187–90.
4. Thornbrough, ed., *Diary of Calvin Fletcher, vol. I*, xiii, 202.
5. Calvin [Fletcher] to Dear Parents, 10 April 1817, folder 1, box 1, Calvin Fletcher Papers (Indiana Historical Society, Indianapolis).
6. Calvin Fletcher to Dear Father, 24 January 1818, folder 1, box 3, Fletcher Papers, IHS.
7. Calvin Fletcher to Mother, 1 June 1834, folder 7, box 1, Fletcher Papers, IHS.
8. Susan E. Gray, *The Yankee West: Community Life on the Midwestern Frontier* (Chapel Hill: University of North Carolina Press, 1996), 1–4; Richard Lyle Power, *Planting Corn Belt Culture: The Impress of the Upland Southerner and the Yankee in the Old North* (Indianapolis: Indian Historical Society, 1953), 1–3; R. Carlyle Buley, *The Old Northwest: Pioneer Period, 1815–1840* (2 vols., Indianapolis: Indiana Historical Society, 1950), I, 47–48. See also Robert W. McCormick, *New Englanders on the Ohio Frontier: Migration and Settlement in Worthington, Ohio* (Kent, OH: Kent State University Press, 1998).
9. C. Fletcher to Cousins, 2 May 1818, folder 1, box 1, Fletcher Papers, IHS; Calvin to [Jesse], 25 July 1818, ibid.
10. Calvin Fletcher to Brother Michael, 23 February 1823, folder 1, box 1, Fletcher Papers, IHS.
11. Etcheson, *Emerging Midwest*, 1–14; Sarah H. Fletcher to Father & Mother, May 1829, folder 4, box 1, Fletcher Papers, IHS.
12. W.O. Hill to [Calvin Fletcher], 3 April 1842, folder 7, box 2, Fletcher Papers, IHS; S. Yandes to [Calvin Fletcher], 1 June 1839, folder 4, box 2, ibid.; Calvin Fletcher to Mother, 22 December 1833, folder 6, box 1, ibid.
13. Sarah H. Fletcher to Louisa Fletcher, 22 June 1821, folder 1, box 1, Fletcher Papers, IHS; Calvin Fletcher to Mother, 26 December 1835, folder 8,

box 1, ibid. They may have eventually adopted the custom of celebrating Thanksgiving, because Fletcher's son Miles spoke of bringing his son to his parents' for Thanksgiving in 1857. Miles J. Fletcher to Father, 24 November 1857, box 8, folder 9, ibid. See also Ransom Hawley to Father, 8 December 1851 box 3, Ransom Hawley Papers, Manuscripts of the Indiana Division (Indiana State Library, Indianapolis); Thornbrough, ed., *Diary of Calvin Fletcher, vol. I,* xvi.

14. Calvin Fletcher to Mother, 28 June 1835, folder 8, box 1, Fletcher Papers, IHS.
15. Sarah H. Fletcher to Louisa Fletcher, 22 June 1821, folder 1, box 1, Fletcher Papers, IHS.
16. Power, *Planting Corn Belt Culture*, 5–25; C. Fletcher to Elijah, 21 January 1843, folder 1, box 3, Fletcher Papers, IHS; Gayle Thornbrough, Dorothy L. Riker, and Paula Corpuz, eds., The Diary of Calvin Fletcher (9 vols., Indianapolis: Indiana Historical Society, 1978), vol. VI, xvi.
17. E.T. Fletcher to Father, 7 May 1843, folder 1, box 3, Fletcher Papers, IHS.
18. William N. Holiday to Calvin Fletcher, 14 January 1843, folder 1, box 3, Fletcher Papers, IHS.
19. Miles to Father, 24 April 1858, folder 10, box 8, Fletcher Papers, IHS.
20. Miles to Father, 6 June 1853, folder 2, box 7, Fletcher Papers, IHS.
21. Miles J. Fletcher to Father, 31 August 1853, folder 3, box 7, Fletcher Papers, IHS; Miles to Father, 26 September 1852, folder 7, box 6, ibid.
22. Calvin [Jr.] to Father, 14 September 1853, folder 4, box 7, Fletcher Papers, IHS. For Upland Southern prejudice against New Englanders, see Kenneth M. Stampp, *Indiana Politics during the Civil War* (orig. 1949, Bloomington: Indiana University Press, 1978), 12, 54; Etcheson, *Emerging Midwest*.
23. Wigger, *Taking Heaven by Storm*, 103; Thornbrough, ed., *Diary of Calvin Fletcher, vol. I,* 13.
24. Christine Leigh Heyrman, *Southern Cross: The Beginnings of the Bible Belt* (Chapel Hill: University of North Carolina Press, 1997), 254; Thornbrough, ed., *Diary of Calvin Fletcher, vol. I,* 150–51; Wigger, *Taking Heaven by Storm,* 103.
25. Charlotte F. Bulton to Cousin Elijah, 20 March 1843, folder 1, box 3, Fletcher Papers, IHS.
26. S.K. Fletcher to Father, 27 May 1860, folder 3, box 9, Fletcher Papers, IHS.
27. Ryland Fletcher to [Calvin Fletcher], 6 April 1843, folder 1, box 3, Fletcher Papers, IHS.
28. Elijah to Calvin [Jr.], 26 March 1843, folder 1, box 3, Fletcher Papers, IHS.
29. E.T. Fletcher to Father, 12 March 1843, folder 1, box 3, Fletcher Papers, IHS.
30. DuBois Fletcher to Cousin, 24 March 1843, folder 1, box 3, Fletcher Papers, IHS.
31. Andrew Ingram to Elijah, 22 September 1839, folder 4, box 2, Fletcher Papers, IHS.

32. E.T. Fletcher to Father, 23 May 1843, folder 1, box 3, Fletcher Papers, IHS.
33. E.T.F. to Father, February 1843, folder 1, box 3, Fletcher Papers, IHS.
34. Calvin Fletcher [Jr.] to Elijah, 11 March 1843, folder 1, box 3, Fletcher Papers, IHS.
35. E.T. Fletcher to Dick, February 1844, folder 3, box 3, Fletcher Papers, IHS.
36. Thornbrough, ed., *Diary of Calvin Fletcher, vol. I,* 455–56; Gayle Thornbrough, Dorothy L. Riker, and Paula Corpuz, eds., *The Diary of Calvin Fletcher* (9 vols., Indianapolis: Indiana Historical Society, 1980), vol. VII, 171. For the lower Midwest's strong connection to the South, see Nicole Etcheson, "First Cousins: The Civil War's Impact on Midwestern Identity," in Jon K. Lauck, Gleaves Whitney, and Joseph Hogan, eds., *Finding a New Midwestern History* (Lincoln: University of Nebraska Press, 2018), 39–52; Etcheson, *Emerging Midwest.*
37. E. Fletcher to Brother, 19 March 1830, folder 4, box 1, Fletcher Papers, IHS.
38. Calvin Fletcher to Wife, 31 July 1838, folder 3, box 3, Fletcher Papers, IHS.
39. Thornbrough, Riker, and Corpuz, eds., *Diary of Calvin Fletcher, vol. VII,* 308–09; Gayle Thornbrough, Dorothy L. Riker, and Paula Corpuz, eds., *The Diary of Calvin Fletcher* (9 vols., Indianapolis: Indiana Historical Society, 1981), Vol. VIII, 55–57.
40. Thornbrough, Riker, and Corpuz, eds., *Diary of Calvin Fletcher, vol. VIII,* 61, 289; Loriman S. Brigham, ed., "The Civil War Journal of William B. Fletcher," *Indiana Magazine of History* 57 (March 1961): 43–76, esp. 68.
41. Thornbrough, Riker, and Corpuz, eds., *Diary of Calvin Fletcher, vol. VII,* 103–04, 208.
42. Thornbrough, Riker, and Corpuz, eds., *Diary of Calvin Fletcher, vol. VII,* xii, 293.
43. Nicole Etcheson, *A Generation at War: The Civil War Era in a Northern Community* (Lawrence: University Press of Kansas, 2011), 102–03.
44. Thornbrough, Riker, and Corpuz, eds., *Diary of Calvin Fletcher, vol. VIII,* 17, 19.
45. Jennifer L. Weber, *Copperheads: The Rise and Fall of Lincoln's Opponents in the North* (New York: Oxford University Press, 2006); Emma Lou Thornbrough, *Indiana in the Civil War Era, 1850–1880* (Indianapolis: Indiana Historical Society, 1995), 124.
46. Robert A. Gross, "Giving in America: From Charity to Philanthropy," in Lawrence J. Friedman and Mark D. McGarvie, eds., *Charity, Philanthropy, and Civility in American History* (Cambridge: Cambridge University Press, 2003), 29–48, esp. 45.
47. Kathleen D. McCarthy, *American Creed: Philanthropy and the Rise of Civil Society, 1700–1865* (Chicago: University of Chicago Press, 2003), 141–42.
48. Thornbrough, ed., *Diary of Calvin Fletcher, vol. I,* 22, 34, 153, 157, 259, 290, 296, 361; Grover L. Hartman, *A School for God's People: A History of the Sunday School Movement in Indiana* (Indianapolis: Central Publishing

Co., 1980), 220; "First State Fair in Indiana," *Indiana Magazine of History* 3 (September 1907): 144–45; William J. Reese, "Indiana's Public School Traditions: Dominant Themes and Research Opportunities," *Indiana Magazine of History* 89 (December 1993): 289–334, esp. 302.
49. Gayle Thornbrough, Dorothy L. Riker, and Paula Corpuz, eds., *The Diary of Calvin Fletcher* (9 vols., Indianapolis: Indiana Historical Society, 1977), vol. V, p. xvi; Miles to Father, 31 October 1853, folder 4, box 7, Fletcher Papers, IHS; E N C Travis to Mr. Fletcher, 22 June [1853], folder 2, box 7, Fletcher Papers, IHS.
50. Thornbrough, ed., *Diary of Calvin Fletcher, vol. I,* 447.
51. Ibid., 167–68, 322–23, 442, 455–56.
52. Ibid., 167–68, 322–23, 442, 455–56; Calvin Fletcher Sr. to Dear Wife, 27 June 1853, folder 2, box 7, Fletcher Papers, IHS; Calvin Fletcher Sr to My Dear Wife, 22 June 1853, folder 2, box 7, ibid.; Thornbrough, ed., *Diary of Calvin Fletcher, vol. I,* 322–23; Thornbrough and Corpuz, eds., *Diary of Calvin Fletcher, VIII,* 200–01; George P. Clark and Shirley E. Clark, "Heroes Carved in Ebony: Indiana's Black Civil War Regiment, the 28th USCT," *Traces of Indiana and Midwestern History* 7 (Summer 1995): 4–16; Debby Applegate, *The Most Famous Man in America: The Biography of Henry Ward Beecher* (New York: Doubleday, 2006), 188–89.
53. *Diary of Calvin Fletcher, VIII,* 200–01.
54. "The Early Schools of Indiana from the Papers of D.D. Banta," *Indiana Magazine of History* 2 (March 1906): 41–48, esp. 48; E.L. Fletcher to Father, 14 March 1853, folder 2, box 7, Fletcher Papers, IHS; Emma Lou Thornbrough, *Indiana in the Civil War Era,* 466–68, 472–74; Thornbrough, Riker, and Corpuz, eds., *Diary of Calvin Fletcher, vol. VI,* 172–73; Thornbrough, Riker, and Corpuz, eds., *Diary of Calvin Fletcher, Vol. VII,* 54; Thornbrough, ed., *Diary of Calvin Fletcher, vol. I,* 11. Fletcher's temperance principles seem to have been rooted in part in reaction against his father's dram drinking. William N. Holiday to Calvin Fletcher, 14 January 1843, folder 1, box 3, Fletcher Papers, HIS. See also, Robert H. Bremner, *The Public Good: Philanthropy and Welfare in the Civil War Era* (New York: Knopf, 1980), 102.
55. Gayle Thornbrough and Paula Corpuz, eds., *The Diary of Calvin Fletcher* (9 vols., Indianapolis: Indiana Historical Society, 1983), IX, 256, 265–71, 273–76.
56. Thornbrough and Corpuz, eds., *Diary of Calvin Fletcher, IX,* 265–71, 273–76; Gayle Thornbrough, Dorothy L. Riker, and Paula Corpuz, eds., *The Diary of Calvin Fletcher* (9 vols., Indianapolis: Indiana Historical Society, 1975), IV, 346, 350, 355, 397, 404; Thornbrough, Riker, and Corpuz, eds., *Diary of Calvin Fletcher, V,* 467, 606; Thornbrough, Riker, and Corpuz, eds., *Diary of Calvin Fletcher, VI,* 430, 437, 442, 532–44, 560, 645–46; Thornbrough, Riker, and Corpuz, eds., *Diary of Calvin Fletcher, VII,* 55, 174, 202, 311, 313, 375–76.

A. James Fuller | A Copperhead Construction

The Northwestern Confederacy and the Making of the Midwest during the War of the Rebellion

On January 8, 1862, the Indiana Democratic Party held its state convention in Indianapolis on Jackson Day, the anniversary of Andrew Jackson's victory at the Battle of New Orleans. Selected as president of the convention, Thomas A. Hendricks delivered a fiery speech condemning Republican leadership in the War of the Rebellion. He played the race card, accusing Republicans of wanting emancipation, arguing that the end of slavery was at the heart of Abraham Lincoln's agenda, despite the president's contentions that freeing the slaves would be a necessary war measure. Such arguments appealed to Hoosier voters who believed in white supremacy but also worried about emancipation being a violation of constitutional limits and an unwarranted overreach of government power. Calling on his party to defend the republic against the growing tyranny of the federal government, Hendricks claimed that the Republicans were in the pocket of powerful businessmen in the Northeast. He then defined the states of the old Northwest Territory against the Northeast and hinted that the region might have to create their own confederacy: "[W]e are now being so crushed that if we and our children are not to become the hewers of wood and drawers of water for the capitalists of New England and Pennsylvania, we must look to the interest of our section." Hendricks made an economic argument, saying that states like Ohio, Indiana, and Illinois were tied by the Ohio and Mississippi Rivers to trade with the South. If the Republicans continued to violate the Constitution and their policies threatened to destroy the Union forever, "then the mighty Northwest must take care of herself and her own interests. She must not allow the arts and finesse of New

England to despoil her of her richest commerce and trade by a sectional and selfish policy—Eastern lust of power, commerce and gain."[1]

Hendricks was not the first Democrat to conjure up images of a Northwestern Confederacy defined in opposition to the northeast as well as the southern states. Nor would he be the last. His speech underscored the divisions the Civil War created across the region that would later become known as the Midwest. Although the factions within the party were not always clear and individuals often moved between them, the rebellion created three general types of northern Democrats. The War Democrats supported the Union and the war effort, usually cooperating with the Republicans to put down the rebellion. Some of them would go so far as to eventually switch parties, while others tried to separate themselves from the Republicans by disagreeing on issues related to the conduct of the war. Then, there were the Peace Democrats, those who wanted to resolve the conflict as quickly as possible. Some of them hoped to restore the Union with some sort of compromise, but others were willing to let the South go and break up the country. A third faction were the Copperheads, whose opposition to the war took them to extreme positions. Named after the poisonous snake, some of the Copperheads went so far as to organize secret societies and plot schemes to sabotage the war effort, assassinate political figures, and even overthrow state governments. Such plans often included the creation of a separate Northwest Confederacy that defined the region that later came to be called the Midwest. In the midst of the Civil War, the roots of midwestern identity sprang from a Copperhead construction.[2]

A former U.S. Congressman, Hendricks would be elected to the U.S. Senate in 1863 and later served as Indiana's governor before being elected as Vice President of the United States as Grover Cleveland's running mate in 1884. During the war, he became one of the elected leaders associated with the Copperheads, although he was not known to be a member of any of their secret societies. He and other Democrats tied to the Copperheads reached back to the Northwest Territory in defining their regional affiliation, linking Ohio, Indiana, and Illinois to the river trade that utilized New Orleans as a commercial entrepot. Aimed at winning votes and achieving political power, their rhetoric reflected opinions held by many in southern Indiana, southern Ohio, and southern Illinois. Those areas were populated largely by "Butternuts" (a term derived from the use of the white walnut or butternut to dye their homespun clothing), whose ancestors had immigrated from the southern states—especially Virginia and North Carolina by way of Kentucky. The Democratic appeal included racism, but also rejected slavery while recognizing the South's right to continue the institution. Their regional identity was geographic, racial, and economic and was formed in opposition not only to the slave South, but also against the Northeast.[3]

Vallandigham Conceives the Northwest Confederacy

One of the first to publicly formulate this construction of a northwestern identity was the most infamous of the Copperheads, Clement L. Vallandigham. A congressman who represented a district in southwestern Ohio, he was a staunch defender of state's rights and limited government who also resisted the abolition of slavery. The Buckeye Democrat opposed the war on principle and believed that Abraham Lincoln was a tyrant. Accused of being a traitor and southern sympathizer, he saw himself as a defender of liberty. He lobbed attacks on Lincoln and the Republicans in his bombastic speeches against the war and his activities would eventually lead to his arrest and exile.[4]

In a speech on December 10, 1860, he called for compromise between the opposing sides and expressed the economic interests of the Northwest: "I speak now as a western man ... We of the Northwest have a deeper interest in the preservation of this Government in its present form, than other section of the Union." Vallandigham pointed out the situation caused by being located in the heartland, "Hemmed in, isolated, cut off from the sea-board upon every side; a thousand miles and more from the mouth of the Mississippi, the free navigation of which ... we demand, and will have at every cost." Yes, the region had the Great Lakes, but he worried that their connection to the Atlantic went through "a foreign country." Faced with the realities of geography, the citizens of the region could not but ask, "What is to be our destiny?" He asked, "Where is to be our outlet? What are we to do when you shall have broken up and destroyed this government?" The Buckeye turned bellicose when he cried out that the area now known as the Midwest did "not mean to be a dependency or province either of the East or of the South; nor yet an inferior ... if we cannot secure a maritime boundary upon other terms, we will cleave our way to the sea-coast with the sword." He swore that "A nation of warriors we may be; a tribe of shepherds never."[5]

Oliver P. Morton's Nationalist Conception

The Ohio Democrat was not the only one to see the economic and geographic interests of the Northwest being vitally connected to the South. Newly elected Republican Oliver P. Morton, soon to serve as the war governor of Indiana, had outlined similar issues in a speech on November 22, 1860. Morton noted that if the right of secession were accepted and the southern states withdrew, then so too could other states leave the Union. As a result, the Northwest might find itself "shut up in the interior of a continent, surrounded by independent, perhaps hostile nations, through whose territories we could obtain egress to the seaboard only upon such terms as might be agreed to by treaty." But Morton disagreed completely with Vallandigham's call for compromise. Instead, the Republican called for crushing the very idea of secession. He said that, "If South Carolina gets out of the Union, I trust it will be at the point of the bayonet, after our best efforts have failed to compel her to submission to the laws." In his eyes, the nation was sacred and perpetual—it could not be divided: "Seven years is but a day in the life of a nation, and I would rather come out of a struggle at the end of that time, defeated in arms and conceding independence to successful revolution, than to purchase present peace by the concession of a principle that must inevitably explode this nation into small and dishonored fragments." His fighting words bespoke the differences between compromise and conflict even when leaders held similar views of some of the problems at hand. Vallandigham wanted a compromise to save the Union but believed secession was a right. Morton refused to accept that withdrawal from the nation was a right and would suppress it as rebellion.[6]

Vallandigham's Four Sections and the Origins of the Midwest

When secession occurred, Vallandigham again tried to prevent war, this time by offering seemingly outlandish ideas to head-off the looming prospect of bloodshed. On February 7, 1861, he delivered a speech in Congress that called for amending the constitution in such a way to recognize the existence of four separate sections of the country: the North, the West, the South, and the Pacific. Vallandigham's West consisted of Ohio, Indiana, Illinois, Michigan, Wisconsin, Minnesota, and Kansas, plus all of the territory north of the 36°-30' line out to the crest of the Rocky Mountains. This area is the region that many scholars today consider the Midwest.[7] On February 20, he followed up on his idea and again proposed "to establish four instead of two grand sections of the Union, all of them well known or easily designated by marked, natural, or geographical lines and boundaries." With only two sections, the division hinged on the politics and morality of slavery as an issue. But with four sections, he thought the "forty years of strife" could be put behind the country: "I propose, therefore, to multiply the sections, and thus efface the slave-labor and free-labor division, and at the same time, and in this manner, to diminish the relative power of each section." His sections would be given power in the U.S. Senate by allowing "a vote in the Senate by sections, upon demand of one third of the Senators of any section" and requiring a "concurrence of a majority of the Senators of each section in the passage of any measure in which, by the Constitution, it is necessary that the House, and therefore, also, the President, should concur." Thus, Vallandigham's plan would add another check in the system of checks and balances, this one designed to recognize the already existing regions of the country. The Ohio Democrat went on to say that his plan "would not prohibit totally the right of secession," but that "no State shall secede without the consent of the Legislatures of all of the States of the section to which the State proposing to secede may belong." However outlandish the plan seems now and whatever merits it lacked for making peace—he was dividing up the free states into three parts, giving the South even more power—Vallandigham's scheme pointed toward an identity for the section that would come to be called the Midwest.[8]

Thomas A. Hendricks Defines the Northwest Economically and Racially
Thomas A. Hendricks' Jackson Day speech in Indianapolis in 1862 echoed what Vallandigham had already expressed. Like his Ohio ally, Hendricks made his case in the name of opposing the war and the policies of the Republicans. In typical Jacksonian style, he claimed to defend

liberty and the nation as a whole even as he attacked his opponents for their cause of freedom and Union. He rallied his party, "Do we not now hear the wailing cry of our country? ... does not the sobbing voice of civil liberty, coming from out of the ruins of a violated Constitution, and the broken pillars of our institutions, call us to the rescue?" The Hoosier orator passionately urged his fellow Democrats to pass the word along throughout the party ranks: "Every man to his post, every man for his country." The Copperhead construction of a regional identity was couched in the language of freedom and Union, promoted in the name of defending the nation even as it meant breaking up the country.[9]

Hendricks was clear: The Republicans were to blame for the crisis at hand. If the Democrats failed to rally to save the country, they would leave the government in "the hands of the leaders of the Republican party, the most proscriptive and intolerant ever known to the country—the very men who for years have labored to build up a sectional party." The Democrat charged the Republicans of having used sectionalism merely "for the sake of political power," and they were thus the ones who were responsible for the war. They had "taught the people of the North that they have separate and opposing interests to the people of the South." He claimed that the Republicans had used "sectional pride and prejudice" to stir up hatred and envy between the North and South "until now the power of the sections is embodied in terrible armies." Hendricks said that the Republicans had rejected all attempts at compromise because they wanted a war to achieve their own ends. He charged them with corruption and fraud, claimed that they had plundered the treasury and denied the soldiers what they needed in order to enrich themselves. For him, Lincoln and his party were nothing but evil thieves bent on the destruction of the United States.[10]

For the Northwest, this meant economic disaster, as the region suffered from "a disturbed commerce and interrupted trade" and all of the problems associated with "a deranged currency, and the low prices of all our valuable productions." To those who wondered about the economic situation, Hendricks responded, "[A]re we now as secure, as we were before the Republican party came into power? ... Your depreciated estates and the bonds of Indiana refused in the market, at eighty cents on the dollar, furnish the answer." In addition to financial ruin, he reminded his audience that the Lincoln administration had suspended habeas corpus and arrested those who dared to criticize the government. Hendricks urged the audience to hear "the groans of men confined without a charge, and denied the privilege of a trial."

Race also mattered. Hendricks had used racist appeals in his campaign for governor in 1860 and now he did it again, noting that the question of slavery had been raised by the war. He asked his audience, "[F]or what purpose is the war waged?" If Lincoln was honest in saying that it was being fought to put down the rebellion and preserve the Union, then slavery had nothing to do with the war. Hendricks dismissed arguments that emancipation might be undertaken as a war measure, to help defeat the rebellion. He sneered at the idea that former slaves would add needed manpower because the North already outnumbered the South. And, besides, how could the freed slaves help in battle without training? Hendricks also denied the ability of black men to fight because he thought they were "lacking those high intellectual and moral qualities, that make the efficient soldier." For him, emancipation was the plan of another "class, too cowardly to fight, and too malevolent to be gratified by the results of civilized warfare." These were the abolitionists who demanded "a carnival of blood, and feast of horrors, amid scenes of servile insurrection." Hendricks despised the opponents of slavery who wanted the slave to rise up against their masters. He argued that the Founding Fathers had "detested the foe that would incite the forest savage to ... midnight massacre" and he decried the notion that Union men would want to be guilty of "calling up the foul spirit of insurrection, and making indiscriminate and uncontrolled war upon men, women, and children, amid scenes too horrible to be described." The Hoosier Democrat raised the specter of black men raping and murdering whites to whip up resistance to emancipation.[11]

Making race and slavery an issue, then, Hendricks went on to attack in detail the arguments some Republicans made for using slaves to help with non-combatant military work like building fortifications and, especially, the legal grounds for allowing the government to free the slaves. For the Indiana Democrat, such notions insulted white soldiers and violated the Constitution. Furthermore, Hendricks argued that Southerners were vital to the economic well-being of the Northwest. Without the South being part of the Union, the river trade would be lost—denying many in the region the ability to move their products easily and cheaply. And Southerners were important consumers who "depend upon and buy from us the production of our lands and labor." He argued that the South needed the Northwest and the Northwest needed the South "and that political party that would destroy that market is our greatest foe." Thus, Hendricks contended, if the Republicans emancipated the slaves, it would destroy the country and would mean "the ruin, forever, of our rich trade and the value of our products." Claiming to defend all that Hoosiers held dear, Hendricks cried that the "first and highest interest of the Northwest is in the restoration and preservation of the Union upon the basis of the Constitution." And if the Republicans made such a restoration impossible, then it was incumbent on the Northwest to protect its own interests.[12]

Daniel W. Voorhees and the Politics of Taxation

Such interests almost always revolved around economics for the Copperheads. Daniel W. Voorhees was another Indiana Democratic congressman unofficially affiliated with the Copperheads. A true Jacksonian on economic policy, he supported free trade and free markets and railed against the eastern banking and business interests who he thought controlled the Republican Party. Like Hendricks, he held racist views that tainted his libertarian positions on limited government and individual freedom. He continually argued that slavery was protected by the Constitution and that the government had no right to emancipate the slaves. When Fort Sumter fell, the Terre Haute congressman declared that "he would not vote one cent or one man to put down the rebellion." Throughout the war, Voorhees complained about taxes, especially the War Tax and the protectionist tariffs favored by Republicans. His opponents countered the Copperhead congressman's attacks on higher taxes by insisting that he never paid taxes himself and arguing that his hatred of taxation stemmed from his treasonous anti-war views and pro-southern sympathies. On February 20, 1862, he spoke on "The Pledges of the Government," arguing that the federal authorities had no right to interfere with the institutions of the states—such as slavery. He stated unequivocally, "I shall oppose unalterably, in all constitutional method, and to the utmost of my ability, the prosecution of this war for the purpose of subjugating the Southern States, reducing them to the condition of

Territories, subverting their institutions, or liberating their slaves." That summer, the Indiana Democratic Party held its convention and pledged to uphold the Union and suppress the rebellion. The convention also denounced secret societies working against the government. But they also protested "against the mischievous measure of negro emancipation," called upon the public authorities to enforce the law prohibiting "the entrance of free negroes and mulattoes into the State," and expressed alarm at the "reckless extravagance which pervades every department of the Federal Government." Officially, the state party distanced itself from the Copperheads and the idea of a Northwestern Confederacy. But they still agreed with the extremists when it came to many of the important questions of the day.[13]

Tax policy remained a potent issue and the Democratic factions came together in their opposition to higher taxes. Voorhees pushed to repeal the Morrill Tariff Act of 1861. The protectionist tariff was supported by most Republicans, but most Democrats thought it odious, especially those in the South and West. While contentions that tariff policy caused the war were over-blown, the tax on imports did clash with Jacksonian notions of free trade and had been extremely unpopular in the slave states. Voorhees hated the tariff and introduced a resolution in the House of Representatives calling for its repeal on April 7, 1862. In doing so, the Copperhead congressman couched his arguments in the language of a Northwestern identity. The *Indiana Sentinel*, the Hoosier state's leading Democratic newspaper, praised Voorhees for leading the movement against the tariff and informed readers that the congressman's resolution embodied the ideas of "all northwestern Democrats" and contained sound, rational thinking that promised to help "work out the destiny of the great agricultural States." Voorhees expressed the views of "that self-dependent people who are in the future to control the policy of the government." The congressman argued that the tariff was "a system of injustice and oppression toward the agricultural portion of the country and toward the laboring consumers generally, and especially so toward the people of the Northwest." Like Morton, Vallandigham, and Hendricks before him, Voorhees bound the region together with economic ties.[14]

The *Sentinel* lamented that, no sooner had the Indiana representative introduced his resolution than Republican Thaddeus

Stevens of Pennsylvania moved to table the measure. Stevens, a leading Radical Republican, supported the tariff, which he thought helped workers in his district. The voice of Indiana Democrats called him "the false-teethed, wig-crowned, and club-footed abolition chairman of the Committee of Ways and Means." The paper denounced those who voted to table the resolution, but the Republican majority easily swept aside Democratic attempts to thwart their agenda.[15]

William A. Richardson, Illinois Copperhead

Illinois Copperheads were also at work constructing the idea of a Northwest Confederacy. Among them was William A. Richardson, a member of the House of Representatives who was elected to the U.S. Senate in 1863. While still in the House, he took the offensive against the Republicans and the possibility of emancipation. In a congressional speech on May 19, 1862, he blasted away at the idea of "Abolition Schemes of Negro Equality" and argued in racist terms that the taxpayers of the United States did not want to pay for the radical social experiments of the Republican majority. Later that year, Richardson continued his assaults on President Lincoln, arguing that the president's annual message ignored the brave soldiers fighting to save the Union while devoting too much space to blacks. He denounced emancipation and criticized Lincoln for turning the war for Union into a crusade against slavery: "To feed, clothe, buy, and colonize the negro we are to tax and mortgage the white man and his children. The white race is to be burdened to the earth for the benefit of the black race." The Copperhead Democrat accused the president of ruining the country and destroying its institutions in the name of abolition. All that the Republicans cared about was the black man, he argued, and "rivers of blood and countless millions of treasure are not enough for his benefit and advantage." He denounced Lincoln's abuse of executive power in issuing the emancipation proclamation and declared that he would not support any legal measures, including constitutional amendments, to legitimize the confiscation of property in the name of abolition. He rejected the president's call for compromise: "For whom does he propose a compromise? What for? In order that [he] may have more power to advance the negro." Playing the race card and pleading fiscal conservatism, Richardson and other Illinois Democrats fanned the flames of dissent. John A. Logan, a Union general and long-time Prairie State Democrat, denounced the Copperheads in the summer of 1863, but confirmed the existence of plans for a Northwestern Confederacy even though he denied he had ever been part of such schemes. Meanwhile, Illinois newspapers like the *Chicago Daily Tribune* regularly reported on Richardson and other Copperheads and their plans for a Northwestern Confederacy.[16]

Conspiracies, Treason Trials, and the Roots of Midwestern Identity

When he moved to the Senate, Richardson continued his criticism of the Republicans, but like Voorhees and Vallandigham, he could do little to stop them, and such powerlessness fed into the Copperhead movement. As the war went, so did the opposition. Higher taxes, the draft, emancipation, and battlefield setbacks all strengthened the Copperheads. But the resolve of the majority of the citizens of the Northwest to win the war also strengthened. It was true that many in the region opposed the Republican conduct of the war, especially on issues that they saw as violating their rights, but that did not mean that they wanted to help the South win its independence. Nor did it mean that they wanted their own confederacy composed of the states of the old Northwest Territory. Seeing the failure of their party through the political process, some Copperheads went underground. They tried to assassinate Governor Morton, derailed troop and supply trains, and held protests against taxes and the draft. By the summer of 1864, the clandestine organizations working against the government had concocted plans for a full-scale uprising. In Indiana, they planned on taking over the state government and cooperating with other Copperheads to create a Northwestern Confederacy, fulfilling the geographic and economic destiny that they believed lay at the heart of the region if the Union could not be preserved within the constitutional bounds of the republic. Convinced that the Republicans had gone too far and were a threat to country, they stepped up their efforts, stockpiling weapons and setting dates for their insurrection.

    The U.S. Army, cooperating with state officials like Governor Morton, had sent spies and detectives to investigate the secret societies.

By that time, Clement Vallandigham had already been arrested and exiled. The other high-ranking elected Democrats distanced themselves from the Copperheads and neither Hendricks nor Voorhees were caught up in the investigation, although there was some evidence that they had corresponded with some of the conspirators. Late that summer, the army moved in and began arresting the leading Copperheads, who were brought before a military tribunal in the Indianapolis Treason Trials. The sensational newspaper accounts of the "fire in the rear" recounted the plans of the Copperheads and helped rally support for the Republicans in the elections that fall. The reports revealed that the Copperheads had not only conspired against the government, but also met with Confederate agents in hopes of cooperating with the South. The trials also revealed their plans for a Northwestern Confederacy based on ideas about liberty, race, economics, limited government, and geography. Although their treasonous dreams were not fulfilled, that Copperhead construction served as a foundation for a later midwestern identity.[17]

Notes

1. For Hendricks's speech, see *Indiana Daily State Sentinel*, 9 January 1862. The speech is also found in Thomas A. Hendricks, "The Issues of the War. Speech Delivered to the Democratic State Convention, Metropolitan Hall, Indianapolis, Jan. 8, 1862," in John W. Holcombe and Hubert M. Skinner, eds., *Life and Public Services of Thomas A. Hendricks with Selected Speeches and Writing*, (Indianapolis: Carlton and Hollenbeck, 1886), 451–65. For a long-neglected study, see William C. Cochran, "The Dream of a Northwestern Confederacy," *State Historical Society of Wisconsin, Separate No. 175, From the Proceedings of the Society for 1916* (1917): 213–53.
2. For more on the Democrats during the rebellion, see Joel H. Silbey, *A Respectable Minority: The Democratic Party in the Civil War Era, 1860–1868* (New York: Norton, 1977). For a long-standing interpretation of the Copperheads, see Frank L. Klement, *The Copperheads in the Middle West* (Chicago: University of Chicago Press, 1960). For challenges to Klement, see Jennifer L. Weber, *Copperheads: The Rise and Fall of Lincoln's Opponents in the North* (New York: Oxford University Press, 2006) and Stephen E. Towne, *Surveillance and Spies in the Civil War: Exposing Confederate Conspiracies in America's Heartland* (Athens: Ohio University Press, 2015).
3. There is no full biography of Hendricks, but a brief treatment is found in Ralph D. Gray, "Thomas A. Hendricks," in Linda C. Gugin and James E. St. Clair, *The Governors of Indiana* (Indianapolis: Indiana Historical Society Press and Indiana Historical Bureau, 2006), 160–65.

4. We need a new biography of Clement L. Vallandigham, but until then, see Frank L. Klement, *The Limits of Dissent: Clement L. Vallandigham and the Civil War* (Lexington: University Press of Kentucky, 1970).
5. *Congressional Globe, 36th Cong. 2nd Sess.*, 10 December 1860, 38.
6. For a reprint of Oliver P. Morton's 22 November 1860, speech delivered in Indianapolis, see *Richmond Palladium*, 13 December 1860.
7. To be sure, the debate over what states make up the Midwest continues. Admitting my own stance, I reject Vallandigham's geography in favor of restricting the region to the states carved from the Northwest Territory, adding only the rest of Minnesota.
8. *Congressional Globe, 36th Cong., 2nd Sess.*, 7 February 1861, 794–95; Clement L. Vallandigham, "The Great American Revolution of 1861. Speech of Hon. C. L. Vallandigham of Ohio, in the House of Representatives, 20 February 1861," in *Congressional Globe, 36th Cong., 2nd Sess., Appendix*, 235–43.
9. *Indiana Daily Sentinel*, 9 January 1862.
10. Ibid.
11. Ibid.
12. Ibid.
13. *Richmond Palladium*, 19 April 1862; *Evansville Daily Journal*, 7 April 1862; Daniel W. Voorhees, "The Pledges of the Government, Speech of Hon. Daniel W. Voorhees in the House of Representatives, Feb. 20, 1862," in Indiana Democratic Convention, *Speeches of Hon. D.W. Voorhees & Hon. T.A. Hendricks on the Civil War and Present Condition of the Country* (Indianapolis: State Sentinel Steam Press, 1862). For Voorhees complaining about taxes and the Republican response, see *Evansville Daily Journal*, 24 June 1862. Until a new biography of Voorhees appears, see the outdated Leonard S. Kenworthy, *The Tall Sycamore of the Wabash: Daniel Wolsey Voorhees* (Boston: Bruce Humphries, Inc., 1936).
14. *Indiana Daily Sentinel*, 15 April 1862.
15. Ibid.
16. William A. Richardson, *Speech of Hon. W.A. Richardson, of Illinois. Delivered in the House of Representatives, May 19, 1862* (Washington, DC: L. Towers & Co., 1862); William A. Richardson, *Speech of Hon. W.A. Richardson, of Illinois: on the President's message, delivered in the House of Representatives, December 8, 1862* (Washington, DC: L. Towers & Co., 1862). Richardson was consistent throughout the war, see *Joliet (IL) Signal*, 14 May 1861 and William A. Richardson, *Address of the Democratic Members of Congress to the Democracy of the United States* (Washington, DC: n.p., 1864). For more on Richardson, see Holt, Robert D. "The Political Career of William A. Richardson," *Journal of the Illinois State Historical Society* 26 (October 1933): 222–69. For Logan's denials, see *Chicago Daily Tribune*, 13 August 1863. For examples of Illinois newspaper reports on the Northwestern Confederacy, see *Chicago Daily Tribune*, 30 October 1862; 14 January 20,

29, 1863; 15 April 1863; 13 November 1863; 12 March 1864; 23 July 26, 1864; 20, 21 October 1864.
17. For the details of the 1864 arrests and Indianapolis Treason Trials, see the trial transcripts in Ben Pittman, ed., *The Trials for Treason at Indianapolis* (Cincinnati: Moore, Wilstach, and Baldwin, 1865); Towne, *Surveillance and Spies,* 221–306.

Edward O. Frantz | When the Midwest Controlled the Presidency, 1860–1930

The Midwest reached political maturity during the period stretching from the Civil War to World War I. Although the term *Midwest* or its close cousin *Middle West* was not in circulation during the early part of the period, its residents increasingly were drawn to thinking about it as a distinctive region. This was most true in electoral politics and the presidency in particular. Although many observers have made casual observations about the number of Midwesterners who occupied the presidency, few have ventured to describe how that came to be and what that says about midwestern identity during the late-nineteenth and early-twentieth centuries. This chapter corrects this oversight by examining the importance of Midwesterners to the presidency between 1860 and 1930.

During the period between 1860 and 1930, 69% (or 9 of 13) of the men elected president were born or raised in the Midwest. This sample starts with Abraham Lincoln, who was born in Kentucky but moved to Indiana in 1816 when he was seven years old. It ends with Herbert Hoover—the first president born west of the Mississippi River—who spent the first eleven years of his life in West Branch, Iowa, before moving west to live with an uncle in Oregon. It includes a president who was *not* a Midwesterner but whose last name, Cleveland, makes it seem as if he were. Ohio lays claim to seven of the nine elected Midwesterners, with Iowa, Illinois, and Indiana laying a claim or partial claim to the other two (see Table 1). This analysis does not include major third parties or smaller parties, both of which frequently ran presidential candidates during the period between 1880 and 1920. Although those parties might often nominate a Midwesterner for president (most notably Socialist Party candidate and Indiana native Eugene V. Debs, who ran for president five times), they never successfully elected a president. All of the successful midwestern candidates ran as Republicans, although simply receiving the nomination was not enough to ensure victory.

Table 1. Presidents Hailing from the Midwest*

Year	Republican Candidate (home state in parentheses)	Democratic Candidate
1860	**Lincoln** (IN, IL)	Douglas (IL)
1864	**Lincoln** (IN, IL)	McClellan (PA)
1868	**Grant** (OH, IL)	Seymour (NY)
1872	**Grant** (OH, IL)	Greeley (NY)
1876	**Hayes** (OH)	Tilden (NY)
1880	**Garfield** (OH)	Hancock (PA)
1884	Blaine (ME)	**Cleveland** (NJ, NY)
1888	**Harrison** (OH, IN)	Cleveland (NJ, NY)
1892	Harrison (OH, IN)	**Cleveland** (NJ, NY)
1896	**McKinley** (OH)	Bryan (IL, NE)
1900	**McKinley** (OH)	Bryan (IL, NE)
1904	**Roosevelt** (NY)	Parker (NY)
1908	**Taft** (OH)	Bryan (IL, NE)
1912	Taft (OH)	**Wilson** (VA, NJ)
1916	Hughes (NY)	**Wilson** (VA, NJ)
1920	**Harding** (OH)	Cox (OH)
1924	**Coolidge** (VT, MA)	Davis (WV)
1928	**Hoover** (IA, CA)	Smith (NY)

*Note: Victorious candidates noted in bold. Table simplified in cases of multiple candidates such as 1860, and labels for parties, such as 1872, when Greeley, running as a Liberal Republican, also received the Democratic nomination. Cases where more than one midwestern state claims the president are noted, too. All election data taken from *The American Presidency Project*, http://presidency.proxied.lsit.ucsb.edu/elections.php

As essays in this volume indicate, the nineteenth century witnessed the maturation of the region that we now think of as the Midwest. Stretching from Ohio in the east to the Dakotas in the west, the region contained in it places that were still in their infancy, as well as other locales with sophisticated political economies. When Abraham Lincoln ran for president in 1860 the western tier of midwestern states, including the Dakotas, Nebraska, and Kansas, were still in territorial stages. By the election of 1892, all the former territories had achieved statehood, which also meant votes in the electoral college.

A trio of historians, hailing from divergent eras and interests, have commented most perceptively on the Midwest's dominance of the presidency during this time period. First among them, not surprisingly, is Frederick Jackson Turner. Although Turner is best known for his "Significance of the Frontier in American History," a number of his essays examine the economics and culture of the region we now think of as the Midwest. In "Dominant Forces in Western Life" Turner observes, "This region seemed to represent and understand the various parts of the Union." After the Civil War, the country entered a period that Turner claims rendered the region particularly meaningful. "Sharing the interest of the East and West, as once before those of North and South," the historian remarked, the region was "forced to give her voice on issues of equal significance for the destiny of the republic."[1] In another essay, he taps into the romantic imagery of the Old Northwest, claiming that the region was "more American, but less cosmopolitan than the seaboard." He predicted that "in the long run," the part of the country that he called the "Center of the Republic," "may be trusted to strike a wise balance between the contending ideals."[2]

A second historian, David S. Brown is a midwestern native like Turner. Brown's *Beyond the Frontier: The Midwestern Voice in American Writing* analyzes historians who made their profession in the Midwest, as opposed to midwestern politicians. Linking the growth of history departments to the prominence of the region as a whole, Brown observes that the region contained in it "critical swing states, vital to both parties' success and conscious of their growing significance in a nation politically balkanized by a solid Democratic South and a static Republican Northeast."[3] Brown's assertion of the Midwest's political vitality is key. It would drive both parties to look to the Midwest during the 1860 to 1930 period.

Richard White is the third historian observing the Midwest's political importance. Following the Civil War, White asserts, "The rest of the century would in many ways belong to the Midwest.... Men and women born in the Midwest, if not always living there, would soon dominate American culture and politics." Within the political realm, according to White, "the presidency would be the special province of Midwesterners." Part of the reason midwestern politicians were so successful, White maintains, was their ability to let basic concepts symbolize their politics, even those that might not otherwise have been perceived as political. "The creation and growth of the home," White argues, "became the great trope of Lincoln's Midwest." In this reading, the ability for Lincoln and other midwestern politicians to use the trajectory of their lives, stretching from log cabin to the White House, offered a narrative of "triumphant individualism" in which "American republicanism" and the home were inextricably linked.[4]

Although these historians help make the case about the political importance of the Midwest, in truth, each is interested in some component other than presidential elections. Probing from observation into explanation requires a deeper dive into the evidence. The factors explaining the midwestern presidencies are manifold, but it is useful to think of them as falling into two main camps. The first are structural or functional explanations. These types of explanations look at the mechanics of electoral votes, for instance, in helping to identify key factors that explain why major parties so often looked to midwestern presidential candidates. The second set of explanations are cultural or psychological. Although harder to pin to precise categories, these cultural explanations touch on many beliefs that Americans ascribe to midwestern natives and many beliefs that Midwesterners hold about themselves.

The most important structural explanation is that the Midwest simply had a high number of electoral votes. Farther east in the region some areas both had become heavily industrialized and boomed with urban growth. In fact, four of America's largest ten cities in 1890 were in the Midwest. As the Midwest grew in population, its share of the electoral college increased, too. As work compiled by Burdett Loomis indicates, during the first decade of the 1900s, no region held a higher percentage of electoral votes than the Midwest. At its peak strength, the Midwest commanded fully one-third of the nation's electoral votes in 1908, for a total of 160.[5] Moreover, the mean center of the American population was located within the borders of the Midwest during the entirety of the time period, ranging from Pike County, Ohio, in 1860, to Greene County, Indiana, in 1930.[6] Thus, in terms of population, development, and votes, there are a number of practical explanations for the Midwest's presidential prominence.

If the number of electoral votes in the region was one important factor, a second, and related factor, was that states in the Midwest tended to be battleground states the major parties recognized they would have to carry if they wanted to win the presidency. Many of these states were closely divided, with a tradition of support for both of the major parties. Down-ballot candidacies including governors and congressional races were critical in helping to ensure electoral success. In contrast to the so-called Solid South, which from 1880 through 1924 devoted nearly all of its electoral votes to Democratic candidates, midwestern states did not return monolithic electoral returns on the presidential level. This meant that with the right candidate, the two major parties could expect to be competitive in the Midwest, or at least in enough midwestern states to help propel their candidate to victory.[7]

Two states had enough electoral votes and enough Republicans and Democrats in them to garner substantial attention: Ohio and Indiana. Although Republicans carried the electoral votes for the former consistently throughout the period between 1860 and 1930, the elections were quite close, and the Democratic Party did well in state and congressional races. With twenty-three electoral votes between 1884 and 1908 and twenty-four electoral votes from 1912 until 1930, Ohio trailed only Illinois in its number of midwestern electoral votes. Indiana, on the other hand, saw its electoral vote go to Democratic candidates in 1876, 1884, 1892, and 1912. With fifteen electoral votes for most of the period under analysis, Indiana offered a ripe political plum for prospective presidents.

Party conventions were a third major factor that explain the plethora of midwestern candidates between 1860 and 1930. Although presidential primaries would increase in frequency throughout the time period, candidates were still chosen at party conventions. This meant that party leaders had an opportunity to shape the ticket in a manner they believed would lead to victory. Electability was one of the factors party leaders considered when nominating their candidates. The presence of a favorite son on the presidential ticket was bound to drive up voter enthusiasm and help with turnout. In states where the margin of victory could be razor thin, this could represent the difference between victory and defeat. Moreover, a majority of the political conventions were held in the Midwest during this time period, as Chicago alone hosted ten

Republican and four Democratic National Conventions. Republicans held their national conventions in midwestern locales 83.3% of the time, further demonstrating just how important the region was to the party's political viability.

The fourth—and final—structural reason explaining the frequency of midwestern candidacies follows from the dominance of party conventions: Midwestern candidates made ideal compromise candidates when more polarizing figures also sought a party's nomination. Rutherford B. Hayes, James Garfield, and Warren G. Harding all fit into this mold. Harding's case is the most memorable, if mostly because his status as the "available man" had been so presciently predicted by his campaign manager (and future Attorney General) Henry Daugherty. In an interview with the *New York Times* on February 21, 1920, Daugherty predicted that none of the frontrunners for the nomination would be able to secure the nomination. He thought that in the early morning hours of the convention, "fifteen or twenty men, somewhat weary," would be "sitting around a table," wondering, "Who will we nominate?" At that time, he predicted "the friends of Senator Harding can suggest him and can afford to abide by the result." Just a few months later, of course, party leaders emerged from the proverbial smoke-filled room in Chicago's Blackstone Hotel on the night of June 11, 1920, with an agreement that Harding would heal the party chasms and lead their party to victory.[8]

Harding's presidency would later become synonymous with greed and corruption, thereby serving as a segue from the structural explanations to the cultural explanations of the preponderance of midwestern presidents between 1860 and 1930. No Ohioan has secured a presidential nomination since Harding. In fact, following the exposure of corruption during the Harding years, the "Ohio Gang" represented qualities that Americans reviled. Chosen because of their ability to get along with the genial Harding, or as political favors in exchange for their support, these officeholders, many of whom were not actually from Ohio, would prove to be the last of a group of Midwesterners who believed that somehow the presidency was theirs by birthright. Although Daugherty could boast that Ohio was "*the* pivotal State of the Nation," "the battle ground of the Republic," and the "training ground of political athletes," he had helped to sour Americans on Ohio-born presidents, thereby hastening the end of an era that reached back to the Civil War.[9]

Long before the Harding presidency signaled a change in midwestern politics, the region had served as a political battleground; the states comprising the Midwest would famously nominate two of the four leading candidates during the fateful 1860 nomination. Abraham Lincoln had lived longer in the Midwest than Democratic nominee Stephen Douglas, who had moved to Illinois from his native Vermont in 1833, but until the 1860 election, Lincoln had stood in the political shadow of the "Little Giant." As one of two Democrats to receive the nomination, along with a Constitutional Union candidate running in the border states, Douglas was doomed to win only twelve electoral votes in the contest: three split votes from the New Jersey delegation and all nine of Missouri's electoral votes. Even in Missouri, Douglas would barely eke out a victory, defeating Constitutional Union candidate John Bell by fewer than 500 votes. Lincoln won a majority of votes in all the other Midwest states, for a total of sixty-six of the region's seventy-five electoral votes. Although issues of North and South had fixated a nation, the region of the Midwest held the political balance of power. This trend accelerated during the war.[10]

Many of the most prominent Union war heroes to emerge during the war were Midwesterners, including not only Lincoln, but Generals Ulysses S. Grant, William Tecumseh Sherman, and Philip Sheridan. The latter three, first associated with the western theatre of war, were known as "fighting generals." They all three had also "grown up in provincial Ohio towns," as historian David S. Brown observes.[11]

While midwestern generals were battling to save the Union, the course of the war was seeming to vindicate the Republicans' free labor ideology. In other hands, what has sometimes been called "the myth of the self-made man," the social mobility possible among those with talent in the Midwest proved to be a useful political tool for midwestern Republicans in particular. They celebrated the economic and social mobility in which a person might possibly be born into humble origins and yet achieve the highest political office in the land. Critically, during the decade preceding the Civil War, politicians residing in midwestern states had learned to compare the upward trajectories possible within their region to what they saw in the slave states.[12] Slavery, they maintained, retarded growth and prevented such mobility. Abraham Lincoln put this formulation most powerfully when he boasted that within what we would now recognize as the Midwest, "The man who labored for another last year, this year labors for himself, and next year he will hire others to labor for him."[13] Lincoln's own life symbolized this dream, which contained within it incredible appeal. Not only could voters marvel that a candidate like Lincoln could rise from such humble origins, in casting a vote for Lincoln, they could also hope that their own lives would follow the same upward socioeconomic trajectory.

If the positive ideology stressing free labor was not powerful enough, midwestern Republicans soon learned to master patriotic appeals as they stumped for votes. Throughout the war Republicans articulated an argument that loyalty to the Union was paramount. To vote otherwise was to follow the lead of reviled Ohio Democrat Clement Vallandigham, who was the leading Copperhead in the United States, prosecuted for treason in 1863, and sent through enemy lines to the Confederacy. Beginning in the election of 1864, Republicans succeeded in painting all Democrats with the Copperhead brush. Thus, a vote for a Democrat was a vote against the region and a vote against the Union. Indiana War Governor Oliver P. Morton, who later became Senator, was one of the earliest practitioners of what became known as "waving the bloody shirt." In a June 20, 1866, speech in Indianapolis, Morton thundered with invective: "Every man who labored for the rebellion in the field, who murdered Union prisoners by cruelty and starvation, who conspired to bring about civil war in the loyal States ... calls himself a Democrat." This disloyalty should never be forgotten, according to Morton, because the Democratic party was nothing more than a "common sewer and loathsome receptacle into which is emptied every element of treason North and South."[14]

The bloody shirt strategy did not always work, but it was effective enough to secure Rutherford B. Hayes most of the Midwest's electoral votes in the infamous 1876 election. (Hayes carried every midwestern state except Indiana and Missouri, or 74.5% of the region's electoral votes.) Republicans learned that patriotism led to success: They wrapped themselves in the glory of the Civil War by nominating a veteran for president in every election between 1868 and 1900, with the lone exception of 1884. Coincidentally, the nominee that year, James G. Blaine, was also the only non-midwestern Republican nominee during the same period. It would be a mistake to make a causal claim linking

Blaine's narrow 1884 defeat to his lack of military service or residency in the Midwest. Blaine lost Missouri and Indiana to Democrat Grover Cleveland, but his showing in the popular vote was not substantively worse than that of Hayes in 1876 (50.1% for Blaine as compared to 51% for Hayes). But it is also revealing that no candidate from outside the region emerged as the party's nominee until 1904, when Theodore Roosevelt sought to continue the presidency he had inherited from William McKinley. As parties searched for new issues to connect with the electorate, including civil service reform, currency, and the tariff, the patriotism of the Civil War provided a key organizing principle. Linking courage on the battlefield to political courage, Republican presidential candidates from the Midwest boasted about their duty to home and country. Northern patriots, they pledged to serve their country as they had served their region during the war.

If appealing to the legacy of the Civil War was one method that midwestern presidential candidates could employ to connect to voters, another was a technique employed by four midwestern candidates beginning with James Garfield in 1880: the front-porch campaign. If historian Richard White is correct in his assertion that midwestern politicians revered the home in their public discourse, then getting a chance to showcase a presidential candidate in his own hometown was particularly powerful. Seeing where a candidate lived gave voters some insight into who the candidate might be and allowed them to forge a connection with him in a novel way. James Garfield's foray into the technique was nearly accidental; as described by historian Jeffrey Bourdon, it developed as an afterthought and did not really begin in earnest until October 1880.[15] Still, Garfield delivered roughly seventy speeches during the 1880 campaign, which were well received as citizens descended on Mentor, Ohio, to see the Republican candidate at his Queen Anne–style home in the bucolic Buckeye village. This was a way to seek votes without breaking the existing norm that presidents should not actively campaign for themselves. Garfield was able to swing Indiana back into the Republican column with a narrow margin of victory of just under 7000 votes.[16]

In 1888 Benjamin Harrison put more deliberate thought (and resources) into his front-porch efforts. The Republican National Committee contained shrewd operatives who understood the importance of a well-financed operation. By bringing audiences to Indianapolis, Republicans could orchestrate speeches, audiences, and experiences that seemed spontaneous and natural. According to historian Charles W. Calhoun, Harrison gave as many as ninety speeches to approximately 300,000 people in Indianapolis during the 1888 campaign, ranging in topic and interest group.[17] When he narrowly won the presidency by carrying the electoral college but losing the popular vote, many thought that front-porch gatherings had helped to propel Harrison to victory.

William McKinley perfected the front porch technique in 1896 and 1900. Although these are well known in political circles as demonstrations of the organizational genius of McKinley's campaign manager, Mark Hanna, they generally have not been analyzed in the context of their midwestern connections. As noted by historian Margaret Leech, all of McKinley's hometown of Canton, Ohio, seemed to be involved in the campaign. "For eight weeks, every day but Sunday was circus day in Canton," Leech claimed. On Saturdays in particular McKinley might receive multiple delegations, including one day when Leech reports over 20,000 people arrived via train to see the Republican nominee. McKinley's invalid wife, Ida, was a source of constant sympathy from onlookers.[18] Although the visits were scripted, the remarks tailored, and the episodes choreographed in a way that would have surprised many citizens, those who made it to Canton consumed an image of McKinley that was at once dedicated statesman, husband, and dutiful son. In sum, he was the embodiment of the ideal Midwesterner. Historian Charles Calhoun estimates that McKinley addressed 750,000 people at his Canton home in 1896, in over three hundred speeches. Importantly, all were publicized and widely available throughout the country, thereby selling the image of home even to those who could not journey to Canton.[19]

McKinley needed to project an image of calm, in part, because his opponent, Nebraskan William Jennings Bryan, was taking his appeal to the people with hundreds of speeches. The election of 1896 has achieved symbolic status as a "realigning election" among American political scientists and has long fascinated historians, many of whom have noted that Bryan's advocacy of "Free Silver" and the Republican platform endorsing the Gold Standard were based on different visions for the nation's future. They were also based on different locales that each candidate called home. Kevin Phillips, who gained fame as a political strategist for describing the emerging Sunbelt during the Richard Nixon presidency, perceptively argues that McKinley's Midwest was more urban and urbane, more industrial, and diverse than Bryan's. He notes that the candidates were "both in their ways remarkable men," and that too often scholars have presented them as caricatures of their constituents. He maintains, however, that McKinley's midwestern background made him uniquely able to mute portions of Bryan's appeal.[20] In other words, an eastern candidate who could not identify with the middle of the country may well have suffered defeat at the hands of the young Democrat from Nebraska.

The 1920 election offered a coda to front porch campaigning as well as to some of the small-town symbolism that many midwestern candidates had touted. Following the progressive era and World War I, the country was dramatically different when Warren Harding was campaigning than it had been when his fellow Buckeye William McKinley sought the presidency. Yet as the Republican Party brought voters to Harding's hometown of Marion, Ohio, many of the familiar attributes of home were on display. In the hands of advertising expert and Chicago Cubs owner Albert Lasker, Warren Harding's hometown could serve as an ideal campaign spot. The Harding campaign sought to evoke calm in an era of uncertainty. It worked: Harding captured 60% of the popular vote throughout the country, 64% of the popular vote in the Midwest, and all 167 of the region's electoral votes, thereby ushering an era of Republican dominance in the region that would persist through the end of the 1920s. No Democrat would win a midwestern electoral vote during that decade, and only Robert La Follette's ability to garner his home state of Wisconsin's thirteen electoral votes during his quixotic 1924 campaign as a third-party candidate prevented Republicans from a decade-wide clean sweep of the Midwest's electoral votes.[21]

1920 also famously was the first official recognition that America had become a more urban than rural nation, as reported in the Fourteenth United States Census. If much of the appeal of midwestern candidates seemed to be that they came from a place that was "typically American," over ensuing decades, as the centers of population moved increasingly to urban areas and increasingly toward the sunbelt, the small midwestern towns that once had produced presidential candidates no longer seemed the ideal staging ground. Herbert Hoover could run as a small-town Iowan in 1928 even though he was a consummate technocrat, creature of Washington, and an international mining expert who amassed a personal fortune that made him a multimillionaire. But the Great Depression of the 1930s killed off most of the allure that rustic small towns had among the American electorate, as a series of global conflicts and complex internal politics demanded new sets of attributes and new sets of symbols. The 1930s politically belonged to Franklin Roosevelt and the New Deal and the 1940s to World War II, as national and international forces appeared triumphant over regional distinctions.

William Dean Howells, the noted midwestern writer, once remarked that the "best sort of American" was a "Westerner ... with Eastern finish."[22] Howells wrote the official campaign biography for Rutherford B. Hayes in 1876. When Howells made this observation, in a letter to Whitelaw Reid about the ideal American in 1880, he voiced a myth that many of his countrymen helped to construct in the period following the Civil War. As midwestern identity solidified during the nineteenth century, many of its residents became particularly preoccupied with their region's distinctiveness. At a time of national transition between agrarian and industrial, rural and urban, it is only fitting that the region that contained a balance of those elements became the center of American political life.

Notes

1. Frederick Jackson Turner, "Dominant Forces in Western Life," in *The Frontier in American History* (New York: Holt, 1920), 229–31.
2. Frederick Jackson Turner, "The Problem of the West," in *The Frontier in American History* (New York: Holt, 1920), 219–21.
3. David S. Brown, *Beyond the Frontier: The Midwestern Voice in American Historical Writing* (Chicago: University of Chicago Press, 2009), 5.
4. Richard White, *The Republic for Which It Stands: The United States During Reconstruction and the Gilded Age, 1865–1896* (New York: Oxford University Press, 2017), 16–19.
5. See Burdett A. Loomis, "Center Ring or Sideshow? The Role of the Midwest in National Politics," in Richard Sisson, Christian Zacher, and Andrew Cayton, eds., *The American Midwest: An Interpretive Encyclopedia* (Bloomington: Indiana University Press, 2007), 1622.
6. For more on mean center of population in the country, see https://www.census.gov/geo/reference/centersofpop/animatedmean2010.html

7. Warren G. Harding carried Tennessee in the 1920 election. In 1928, due in large part to Democratic candidate Al Smith's Roman Catholic affiliation, Republican nominee Herbert Hoover carried Tennessee, Virginia, North Carolina, Texas, and Florida.
8. "Sees Harding as Compromise Choice," *New York Times*, 21 February 1920, 3. Historians have long focused on Daugherty's prediction. See, for example, William E. Leuchtenburg, *The Perils of Prosperity, 1914–1932*, 2nd ed. (Chicago: University of Chicago Press), 85.
9. Harry Daugherty attempted to embrace the term "Ohio Gang," claiming in his memoirs that he wore the "badge as a mark of honor." Harry M. Daugherty with Thomas Dixon Jr., *The Inside Story of the Harding Tragedy* (New York: Churchill, 1932), 5.
10. Missouri's voting history between 1860 and 1916 adheres far more closely with the states of the upper South than with its other midwestern neighbors. Prior to 1920, Republicans rarely carried the state. In terms of its political behavior, it might be better to consider Missouri separate from the Midwest for most of this period. It has been included here for purposes of consistency throughout the volume.
11. Brown, *Beyond the Frontier*, 5.
12. The classic discussion of the free labor ideology is Eric Foner, *Free Soil, Free Labor, Free Men: The Ideology of the Republican Party Before the Civil War* (New York: Oxford University Press, 1970).
13. Abraham Lincoln, "Speech at Kalamazoo, Michigan," in Abraham Lincoln, *Speeches and Writings* (New York: Library of America, 1989), 1:380.
14. William Dudley Foulke, *Life of Oliver P. Morton: Including His Important Speeches* (Indianapolis: Bowen-Merrill, 1899), 1:474–75.
15. Jeffrey Normand Bourdon, "Germans, Jubilee Singers, and Axe Men: James A. Garfield and the Original Front-Porch Campaign for the Presidency," *Ohio History* 121 (4 March 2014): 112–29, https://doi.org/10.1353/ohh.2014.0006.
16. The definitive volume on presidential travel is Richard J. Ellis, *Presidential Travel: The Journey from George Washington to George W. Bush* (Lawrence: University Press of Kansas, 2008).
17. Charles W. Calhoun, *Benjamin Harrison* (New York: Times Books, 2005), 52.
18. Margaret Leech, *In the Days of McKinley* (New York: Harper & Brothers, 1959), 88–93.
19. Charles W. Calhoun, *From Bloody Shirt to Full Dinner Pail: The Transformation of Politics and Governance in the Gilded Age* (New York: Hill and Wang, 2010), 91.
20. Kevin Phillips, *William McKinley* (New York: Times Books, 2003), 84. Phillips synthesizes and summarizes the work of the so-called ethnocultural approach of historians such as Richard Jensen and Paul Kleppner.

21. More on the Harding campaign can be found in Francis Russell, *The Shadow of Blooming Grove: Warren G. Harding in His Times* (New York: McGraw-Hill, 1968), and John Dean, *Warren G. Harding* (New York: Times Books, 2004), 68–78. Dean notes that Harding delivered 112 additional speeches beyond his front porch, thereby refuting an interpretation that Republican handlers deliberately kept the malaprop-prone candidate off the hustings.
22. William Dean Howells to Whitelaw Reid, 22 October 1880, in W.D. Howells, *Selected Letters,* vol. 2: 1873–1881, George Arms and Christoph K. Lohmann, eds., 269. I am indebted to Richard White for the quotation, which appears on pp. 16–17 in *The Republic for Which It Stands*.

Gregory S. Rose

On the Path Toward
National Eminence

Economic Development
in the Old Northwest,
1850–1860

Already in the decade prior to the Civil War, Ohio, Indiana, Illinois, Michigan, and Wisconsin were well along the economic development path toward national eminence, and their distinctive mix of agricultural/industrial and rural/urban was emerging. This region, traditionally referred to as the Old Northwest but identified as the East North Central region by the U.S. Census, represented the third most economically developed area of the United States in 1860 behind the Middle Atlantic (New Jersey, New York, Pennsylvania) and New England regions, ahead of the South Atlantic region (Maryland and Delaware to Florida), and well ahead of the other comparatively new trans-Appalachian area, the East South Central region (Alabama, Kentucky, Mississippi, Tennessee).

Ranking the Old Northwest as the third most economically developed region by the Civil War predates its seemingly sudden rise following 1865, with the 1893 World's Columbian Exhibition marking the "coming out" of Chicago and its region on the world stage.[1] As the second most economically developed region in 1900, the Old Northwest surpassed New England, trailed closely behind the Middle Atlantic, and far exceeded any other region. According to the 1900 Census, "The most striking phenomenon of the manufacturing development of the United States in the half century has been the rapid advance of the Central states from a comparatively insignificant position to second place among the geographic groups.... Nowhere else in the world has there been so rapid a transformation of the occupations of the population."[2] The rise of Illinois from fifteenth among states in 1850 to third in 1900 represented "the most notable and rapid advance in position which has occurred in our industrial history."[3] The Old Northwest's trajectory continued upward: By 1920, propelled by the exponentially expanding automobile industry, it had surpassed the Middle Atlantic region to become the nation's industrial and agricultural heartland.[4]

Rapid advancements in four key components of economic development—agriculture, transportation and communication, population growth and urbanization, and industrialization—carried the Old Northwest from barely settled by non–Native Americans in 1800 to a leading region within the United States by 1860.

Agriculture

The censuses of 1850 and 1860 collected production data from 1849 and 1859 for most crops and livestock. Agricultural production in the five census divisions east of the Mississippi River varied due to territorial extent, amount of non-agricultural territory in each region, and environmental factors such as climate, length of growing season, precipitation amounts, topography, and soil types influencing suitability for specific crops.[5] The proportion of "improved" and "unimproved" land in farms also differed from region to region and state to state.[6] The census defined unimproved acreage as "in occupancy and necessary to the enjoyment of the improved," including owned woodlots and forested or prairie grazing lands supporting farm operations but excluding unclaimed acreage or areas such as the pineries of northern Michigan and Wisconsin.[7] In 1850, 52.6 percent of the Middle Atlantic region was in farms as was 49.9 percent of the East South Central region. Farms accounted for 26.0 percent of the Old Northwest's area, ranging from 62.7 percent in Ohio to 7.1 percent in Michigan and Wisconsin, whose northern areas, with limitations of climate, soil, and heavy timber cover, were notably less settled. By 1860, the farmed proportion of the Old Northwest increased to 37.4 percent, compared to 63.7 percent of the East South Central states (the most of any region), while the total acreage in farms was similar.

Average farm size provides a glimpse into the types of agriculture practiced. Reflecting the presence of large-scale plantation farming in the South Atlantic and East South Central regions, average farm size ranged from 271 to 317 acres in both census years. Yet in the Upland South areas and on poorer soils in both regions, smaller semi-subsistence farms using family labor, a hired hand, or a few slaves generated modest surpluses of animals or corn, sometimes in liquid form.[8] In the North, average farm size varied from 110 to 139 acres in 1850 and 1860, less than the national average.[9] These grain-farming and livestock-raising agricultural units aligned more closely with the stereotypical family farm reliant upon family labor or a hired hand or two as wage laborers.[10] Even in the Old Northwest, where agricultural output rapidly increased, the comparatively smaller northern farm model remained typical and formed one basis for the region's unique development. Here the average farm consisted of 139 acres in 1850 and 121 acres in 1860, with farm sizes in the latter year ranging from 111 acres in Ohio to 146 acres in Illinois.

Corn, wheat, and oats, basic crops grown for livestock feed and human consumption, represented key markers of national agricultural output according to data from the most recent growing seasons, 1849 for the 1850 census and 1859 for 1860 (Table 1). The Old Northwest led the nation in corn grown in 1849, producing over one third of the total, and again in 1859, when it accounted for forty-three percent of bushels. Total bushels raised also dramatically increased, from 177.3 million in 1849 to 280.3 million in 1859. Yields in the next most productive region, the East South Central, rose from 162.1 million bushels in 1849 to 178.6 million in 1859, but its proportional share declined. In 1849, the five leading corn-producing states came from those two regions: Ohio (11.3 percent), Kentucky (11.2), Illinois (11.1), Indiana (10.2), and Tennessee (10.0). By 1859, states in those two regions again topped productivity but rankings and percentages changed. Illinois led (17.7 percent), followed by Ohio (11.3) and Indiana (11.0); Kentucky was fourth (9.8 percent) and Tennessee fifth. The South Atlantic region ranked third in corn production both years. Corn production in the South, used to feed livestock and the local population, free and slave, remained high even as national and international demand for cotton, the South's characteristic commercial crop, continued to rise.[11] By 1850, the Old Northwest's dominance in production of maize, sustained by advantageous climate and soil, rapid development of surpluses and markets, and use in expanding hog and cattle operations, launched the Corn Belt as reality well before the term first appeared in the 1880s.[12]

The Old Northwest also formed the nation's Wheat Belt during this period.[13] The region produced 32.3 percent of bushels in 1849 and 54.0 percent in 1859, more than any other area in both years. The

Table 1. Corn, Wheat, and Oat Production East of the Mississippi River, 1849 and 1859

	Corn Production				Wheat Production				Oat Production			
	1849		1859		1849		1859		1849		1859	
	Rank	% of total	Rank	% of total	Rank	% of total	Rank	% of total	Rank	% of total	Rank	% of total
New England	5	2.0%	5	1.5%	5	2.4%	5	0.7%	5	6.0%	4	6.9%
Middle Atlantic	4	8.9%	4	7.6%	2	31.5%	3	15.9%	1	37.9%	1	42.9%
South Atlantic	3	24.1%	3	20.4%	3	21.3%	2	19.4%	3	17.2%	3	12.8%
East South Central	2	31.1%	2	27.4%	4	12.5%	4	9.9%	4	12.9%	5	4.9%
Old Northwest	1	34.0%	1	43.1%	1	32.3%	1	54.0%	2	26.1%	2	32.4%

Source: *Agriculture of the United States in 1860*; 185, 189.

Middle Atlantic, a close second in 1849, dropped considerably to third place in 1859. Ohio was the only Old Northwest state among the top five producers in 1849, leading the nation with 19.9 percent of the yield, followed by Pennsylvania (15.8), New York (14.7), Virginia (12.1), and Kentucky (5.8). By 1859, the Old Northwest accounted for four of the top five producers: Illinois (11.6 percent), Indiana (11.4), Wisconsin (10.6), and Ohio (10.2). The South Atlantic region surpassed the Middle Atlantic to achieve second place in 1859, producing 19.4 percent of wheat. While tobacco or cotton fit the stereotype for South Atlantic crops, decades previously George Washington and others had promoted wheat for the region's worn-out soils.[14] Climate and disease, heavy cropping of corn, and a focus on cotton placed the East South Central region next to last in wheat, mostly grown in Kentucky and Tennessee.[15] The Middle Atlantic region raised 37.9 percent of oats in 1849 and 42.9 percent in 1859, about half coming from New York. The Old Northwest ranked second in both census years, with Ohio raising 10 percent of oats both years and 10 percent from Illinois in 1859.

In 1849, depending upon the animal, the Old Northwest ranked no less than third in livestock population and value; by 1859, the region ranked first for both (Table 2). The Old Northwest featured the leading proportion of horses, primarily used for farm work, in 1849 and 1859, housed about one-third of sheep in both years (the largest percentage), and produced more pounds of wool than any other region, including nearly 40 percent of the 1859 total.[16] The Old Northwest ranked second in milch cows and other cattle in 1849, behind the Middle Atlantic region; by 1859, it led in both types of livestock. In 1849, the East South Central region contained the largest proportion of swine, 31.0 percent, and the South Atlantic was second, but by 1859 the Old Northwest had advanced from third place to house the largest percentage of swine.

Already by the Civil War, the Old Northwest was the nation's leading livestock producer, raising animals on small plains, prairie grasslands, partially harvested fields, and proto-feedlots from Ohio to Wisconsin.[17] The Old Northwest was in fourth place in value of animals slaughtered in 1849 but by 1859 jumped to first place, accounting for 25.8 percent of value.[18] Some animals walked to eastern markets and some rode the rails; many were slaughtered, salted, and packed into barrels within the region.[19] Although packinghouses appeared around

Table 2. Livestock Production and Value East of the Mississippi River, 1849 and 1859

	Horses				Milch Cows				Other Cattle			
	1849		1859		1849		1859		1849		1859	
	Rank	% of total	Rank	% of total	Rank	% of total	Rank	% of total	Rank	% of total	Rank	% of total
New England	5	4.9%	5	5.3%	5	9.7%	5	8.7%	5	5.5%	5	6.8%
Middle Atlantic	2	19.3%	2	20.9%	1	24.7%	2	28.9%	4	13.7%	4	16.4%
South Atlantic	4	17.9%	4	16.1%	3	19.5%	3	18.5%	1	26.0%	2	26.4%
East South Central	2	19.3%	3	18.3%	4	14.7%	4	14.3%	3	16.8%	3	19.1%
Old Northwest	1	26.3%	1	40.2%	2	20.1%	1	29.1%	2	18.2%	1	31.9%

	Sheep				Swine				Total Value of Livestock			
	1849		1859		1849		1859		1849		1859	
	Rank	% of total	Rank	% of total	Rank	% of total	Rank	% of total	Rank	% of total	Rank	% of total
New England	5	10.5%	5	8.2%	5	1.2%	5	1.0%	5	9.2%	5	6.2%
Middle Atlantic	2	26.4%	2	20.3%	4	7.6%	4	6.5%	1	23.1%	3	17.4%
South Atlantic	3	17.2%	3	11.8%	2	24.8%	3	21.5%	2	19.3%	4	15.1%
East South Central	4	12.6%	4	11.3%	1	31.0%	2	23.8%	4	18.5%	2	19.0%
Old Northwest	1	33.2%	1	32.0%	3	21.5%	1	25.6%	3	19.1%	1	21.7%

Source: *Agriculture of the United States in 1860*, 184–85, 188–89.

the region, their early concentration in Cincinnati and its dominance as a processor of hogs using innovative methods earned it the not-necessarily-complimentary moniker of "Porkopolis."[20] However, Chicago's rise as the railroad and packinghouse hub effectively transferred that title to it and added another one: "Beefopolis."[21]

Transportation and Communication
Internal improvements were top of mind in the nation's consciousness during the nineteenth century. Old Northwest politicians promised to introduce, improve, or support roads, waterways, canals, railroads, and the telegraph to make it possible for farmers to haul or walk their surplus products to market, to facilitate connections between their district or state and the nation's expanding economy, and to nurture tiny hamlets into regional centers.[22] Abraham Lincoln was not alone in including "government support for internal improvements" in his platform for his first run for political office.[23] Ascribing great importance to internal improvements, many states undertook major canal projects undaunted by cost, distance, and the engineering required to overcome difficult topography, resulting in bankruptcy for some.[24] Federal monies also supported the National Road and other arteries in the early 1800s.[25]

Although in the 1780s George Washington and fellow investors sought to connect the East Coast to the Ohio Valley via the Patowmack Canal, the Erie Canal truly provided "proof of concept" in 1825.[26] Pennsylvania and other states sought to replicate New York's success, with most states containing canals by 1853 (Table 3). The Middle Atlantic region accounted for the most canal miles in 1853, and New York had more than any other state. In the Old Northwest, canal advocates succeeded in linking the Ohio River to the Great Lakes, generating sufficient mileage to place the region in second place; Ohio had the third most miles of any state. In 1860, the Middle Atlantic region still featured the most miles of canals, but Pennsylvania's mileage surpassed New York's. Again, the Old Northwest was second and Ohio ranked third among states. The Middle Atlantic region had the most canals per square mile and feet of canals per person in 1853 and 1860, with the Old Northwest second both years. Even as most states modestly expanded mileage and canals remained an integral piece of the transportation

Table 3. River, Miles of Canals in Operation in 1853 and 1860, East of the Mississippi

	\multicolumn{3}{c	}{1853}	\multicolumn{3}{c}{1860}
	Rank	Miles of Canals	% E of Miss. R.	Rank	Miles of Canals	% E of Miss. R.
New England	5	222	4.6%	5	77	1.4%
Middle Atlantic	1	2072	43.2%	1	2411	44.8%
South Atlantic	4	458	9.5%	4	515	9.6%
East South Central	3	537	11.2%	3	821	15.3%
Old Northwest	2	1388	28.9%	2	1553	28.9%
Total Miles		4798			5377	

Source: *Statistical View of the United States, 1850*, 189; *Statistics of the United States, 1860*, 335, 336.

network, aging infrastructure required costly repair and railroads increasingly became the preferred transportation investment.[27]

Railroad mileage statistics did not appear in the 1850 census. However, reports and abstracts in the next few years contained miles in operation and under construction, and the Eighth Census in 1860 included data for that year and 1850, plus an essay outlining the impact of railroads on agricultural commodity shipments.[28] The smallest region, New England, contained the most miles of railroad in 1850 and accounted for nearly 30 percent of the nation's trackage, with the Middle Atlantic having nearly the same length (Table 4). New York featured the most railroad miles, followed by Massachusetts and Pennsylvania. The Old Northwest ranked fourth among regions, and Ohio's 575 miles of railroad placed it fourth among states.

Railroad mileage more than tripled between 1850 and 1860, with expansion occurring in every region. But the real focus was westward extension: The Old Northwest added more miles and contained more miles than any other region in 1860, accounting for over one-third of trackage east of the Mississippi River. Ohio's 3000 miles of railroads exceeded that of any other state. Illinois was second, New York third, Pennsylvania fourth, and Indiana fifth. By 1860, eleven railroads served Chicago: It was "the ultimate objective for the eastern railroads" and

Table 4. Railroad Miles in Operation in 1850 and 1860, East of the Mississippi River, and Increase in Miles, 1850 to 1860

	1850			1860			Growth, 1850–60			
	Rank	Miles in Oper.	% E. of Miss. R.	Rank	Miles in Oper.	% E. of Miss. R.	Rank	Miles Added	% Growth in Region	% Growth E. of Miss R.
New England	1	2508	29.5%	4	3670	12.9%	5	1162	46.3%	5.8%
Middle Atlantic	2	2431	28.6%	3	5804	20.3%	3	3373	138.7%	16.8%
South Atlantic	3	2010	23.6%	2	5971	20.9%	2	3961	197.1%	19.8%
East South Central	5	286	3.4%	5	3383	11.9%	4	3097	1082.9%	15.5%
Old Northwest	4	1276	15.0%	1	9715	34.0%	1	8439	661.4%	42.1%
Total Miles		8511			28,543			20,032		

Source: *Statistics of the United States, 1860*; 325–34.

"had become the undisputed railroad center of the nation."[29] Michigan's railroad miles more than doubled to 799 in 1860, and Wisconsin's grew from 20 to 922. New England had the most feet of railroads compared to area and population in 1850, with the Old Northwest fourth in both measures. Following a decade of intense construction, the Old Northwest achieved the greatest density of tracks per person in 1860, although the Middle Atlantic had the most feet of railroad per square mile, followed by New England. The Old Northwest's rank rose to third, from 22.4 feet of track per square mile to 170.2 in 1860, and its railroad network continued to expand after the Civil War.[30]

Starting with a mere 40 miles of telegraph lines in 1844, approximately 12,000 miles existed in 1850, 23,281 in 1853, and 76,000 in 1866.[31] The census did not list miles of lines per state, but telegraph operators in each appeared among the occupational data for 1850 and 1860 (Table 5).[32] In 1850, 175 telegraph operators, the greatest number, worked in the Old Northwest, twelve more than in the most populous and developed Middle Atlantic region. As adoption of the telegraph and employment of operators increased by 1860, the Middle Atlantic took over leadership with nearly 40 percent of workers, dropping the Old Northwest to second place. However, expansion in the Middle Atlantic and Old Northwest exceeded overall growth rates during the decade.

When most of the Old Northwest's agricultural output flowed down the Ohio and Mississippi Rivers, New Orleans served as the key collection point and prime outlet, but its importance declined

Table 5. Telegraph Operators East of the Mississippi River, 1850 and 1860

	1850		1860	
	Rank	% of Total	Rank	% of Total
New England	4	10.8%	3	10.5%
Middle Atlantic	2	30.4%	1	39.9%
South Atlantic	3	16.2%	4	8.6%
East South Central	5	9.9%	5	6.4%
Old Northwest	1	32.6%	2	34.5%

Source: *Seventh Census of the United States, 1850*, lxxii, lxxvii; *Population of the United States in 1860*, 676–77.

as transportation networks expanded and commercial traffic bent northward and eastward to shorten haulage to eastern and overseas markets and return flows of manufactured goods.[33] The Erie Canal and canals in Ohio, Indiana, and Illinois and railroads rapidly reaching westward from major East Coast cities captured an increasing share of the Old Northwest's agricultural exports. Settlement around the Great Lakes and development of shoreline port and shipping cities like Cleveland, Toledo, Chicago, and Milwaukee supported expanded lake shipping of agricultural goods and raw materials for industrialization. One researcher identified 1835 as the date when transportation infrastructure improvements "integrated the Midwest, linked its regions to the East, and brought about substantial declines in the costs of transporting agricultural products, manufactures, and passengers."[34] Another chose 1847, adding ocean-going steamships to the innovations and pointing to the telegraph as critical for effectively managing the new transportation systems.[35]

Population and Urbanization

Fecund natural increase and rising foreign immigration after 1820 lifted the nation's population from 3.9 million in 1800 to 31.4 million in 1860. Growth was especially spectacular in the Old Northwest. From 792,719 inhabitants in 1820 (three-quarters Ohioans), the Old Northwest grew to 4.5 million in 1850 and 6.9 million in 1860, becoming the third most populous region, gaining more people than any region during that last decade and increasing in diversity.[36] In both census years, the Old Northwest had the second highest proportion of population born in foreign countries: first in Germans, second in natives of England and Canada, and third in Irish-born.[37] It housed a modest number of African Americans, all free but neither unrestricted nor fully accepted. Sprinkled among the predominant Methodists, Presbyterians, and Baptists were Roman Catholics, Quakers and Shakers, German Lutherans, Moravians, and Dutch Reformed.

In 1850 and 1860, New England and the more densely populated Middle Atlantic represented the first and second most urbanized regions based on the census definition of an urban center containing 2500 people or more (Table 6). The Old Northwest ranked fourth in urbanization

Table 6. Urban Population and Population Density East of the Mississippi River, 1850 and 1860

	1850				1860			
	Urban Centers	% Urban Population	Rank by Percent	Pop. per Sq. Mile	Urban Centers	% Urban Population	Rank by Percent	Pop. per Sq. Mile
New England	73	28.8%	1	37.9	94	38.2%	1	43.6
Middle Atlantic	59	25.5%	2	54.0	91	35.4%	2	68.2
South Atlantic	28	9.8%	3	17.4	38	11.7%	4	19.5
East South Central	16	4.2%	5	18.3	22	5.9%	5	21.9
Old Northwest	48	9.0%	4	15.0	104	14.1%	3	23.0

Source: *Sixteenth Census of the United States, 1940*, 69–1161.

in 1850 but last in population density. By 1860, the Old Northwest had become the third most urbanized region, third in population density, and contained over 100 urban centers, more than in any other region. Cincinnati was the nation's sixth largest city in both years, and modestly sized cities such as Cleveland, Detroit, Milwaukee, and especially Chicago, were poised for rapid growth following the Civil War.

Industrialization

The Old Northwest's strong economic foundation—a dominant agricultural sector, well-developed transportation and communication networks, rapidly growing population, increasing urbanization—included an expanding and diversifying industrial base.[38] Timber, another of the Old Northwest's surface resources, provided essential material for building, fuel, and manufacturing at all stages of development. In 1849, Michigan and Ohio each produced between 4 and 8 percent of the nation's lumber; in 1859 Indiana and Wisconsin also met that production level, with Illinois generating between 2 and 4 percent of lumber.[39] Even measured by the midpoint of each range, the Old Northwest in 1860 accounted for nearly 30 percent of the nation's lumber production, a level which only increased in subsequent decades.[40] In 1850 and 1860, the Old Northwest contained the second largest number of saw and planing mills and accounted for the second highest value of product, surpassed only by the Middle Atlantic region; in 1850 it employed the second largest number of mill workers and led the nation in this category in 1860.[41] In an era when commodities of all sorts were moved in wooden barrels, hardwood timber and coopers to construct them were in demand. The Old Northwest employed more coopers than any other region in 1850 and 1860, around 40 percent of the total, and Ohio had more coopers than any state except New York.[42] The wood so abundantly available also provided the material for "cabinet" furniture production, for which the Old Northwest was the second largest producer in 1860.[43] Within a few decades, the region became the center of furniture manufacturing, with Grand Rapids, Michigan, described as "the nation's furniture capital by the end of the nineteenth century."[44]

The enormous agricultural productivity of the Old Northwest provided commodities to support processing industries. Meatpacking and milling of grain within the region increased the value per ton for products bulky to transport.[45] In 1850, the Old Northwest was third according to flour and gristmills present, employment, and product value; by 1860 it had moved into first place in employees and product value (Table 7). The region's proportion of mills also increased but remained third ranked, perhaps indicating fewer but larger establishments. Distilling corn into other products also increased its value. In 1849, the Old Northwest used the most bushels of corn for distilling and produced the most gallons of whiskey and "high wine" (Table 8). By 1859, the region was first according to the value of liquor distilled and gallons of wine produced, much coming from along the Ohio River and the Great Lakes.[46] And, housing as it did the second largest number of milch cows in 1849 and the most in 1859, the Old Northwest occupied second place both years in butter production and the third spot in cheese making in 1849, rising to second place in 1859.[47]

Below-ground resources such as coal and iron ore, revealed in increasing abundance as prospectors explored the Old Northwest in greater detail, were exploited early on to support industrial development. Following the flow of population, manufacturing activities first appeared along the Ohio River, with Cincinnati as the leading center.[48] But as population expanded north and west, manufacturing of all types began to appear in other settlement centers.[49] While production initially focused on local use, as manufacturing matured, demand increased, and transportation systems improved, regional markets in the Old Northwest for many products were secured by mid-century.[50]

One example of this evolution occurred with agricultural equipment. By the Civil War, numerous small and many large manufacturers of agricultural implements and machinery, such as Deere and Company, Oliver Chilled Plow Works, McCormick Harvesting Machine Company, and J.I. Case Threshing Machine Company, were present in the Old Northwest.[51] In 1850, the region was in second place but close behind the Middle Atlantic states in the number of implement manufacturing establishments, workers employed, and product value (Table 9). Rapid growth in the next decade drove the Old Northwest into first place across the board. Whereas in 1850 it accounted for less than 30 percent in each category, by 1860 it generated 37 to 45 percent of each. Perhaps representing a precursor to the region's future dominance in

Table 7. Flour and Grist Mills East of the Mississippi River, 1850 and 1860

	Number of Establishments				Number Employed				Value of Product			
	1850		1860		1850		1860		1850		1860	
	Rank	% of Total	Rank	% of Total	Rank	% of Total	Rank	% of Total	Rank	% of Total	Rank	% of Total
New England	5	6.3%	5	7.8%	5	4.9%	5	6.3%	4	5.0%	5	6.7%
Middle Atlantic	1	38.3%	1	30.7%	1	36.5%	2	31.6%	1	48.5%	2	23.1%
South Atlantic	2	27.2%	2	25.6%	2	26.1%	3	20.4%	2	16.3%	3	19.5%
East South Central	4	9.0%	4	10.3%	4	8.6%	4	9.1%	5	4.0%	4	7.5%
Old Northwest	3	19.2%	3	25.6%	3	23.9%	1	32.7%	3	16.2%	1	43.2%

Source: Abstract of the Statistics of Manufactures, 1850, 51; Manufactures of the United States in 1860, 14–662.

Table 8. Production of Wine (1849 and 1859), Whiskey and High Wine (1849), Liquor Distilled (1859), and Corn Used in Distilling (1849), East of the Mississippi River

	Wine Production, Gallons				Whiskey / High Wine, Gallons		Liquors Distilled, Value		Corn Used in Distilling, Bushels	
	1849		1859		1849		1859		1849	
	Rank	% of Total	Rank	% of Total	Rank	% of Total	Rank	% of Total	Rank	% of Total
New England	4	7.3%	5	7.1%	4	7.1%	4	6.1%	5	0.4%
Middle Atlantic	2	29.2%	4	9.1%	2	35.4%	2	31.5%	2	31.6%
South Atlantic	3	16.0%	3	11.4%	5	5.8%	5	5.4%	4	4.9%
East South Central	5	5.4%	2	16.5%	3	10.8%	3	7.0%	3	7.6%
Old Northwest	1	42.0%	1	55.9%	1	40.9%	1	50.0%	1	55.6%

Source: *Statistical View of the United States, 1850*, 182; *Agriculture of the United States in 1860*, 186, 190.

Table 9. Agricultural Implement Production East of the Mississippi River, 1850 and 1860

	Number of Establishments				Number Employed				Value of Products			
	1850		1860		1850		1860		1850		1860	
	Rank	% of Total	Rank	% of Total	Rank	% of Total	Rank	% of Total	Rank	% of Total	Rank	% of Total
New England	3	16.9%	3	11.8%	3	25.3%	3	11.2%	3	24.6%	3	11.6%
Middle Atlantic	1	31.2%	2	34.7%	1	27.4%	2	32.7%	1	32.5%	2	32.0%
South Atlantic	4	12.2%	4	8.9%	4	14.6%	4	7.7%	4	11.6%	4	6.1%
East South Central	5	11.2%	5	7.3%	5	7.0%	5	5.5%	5	6.3%	5	5.5%
Old Northwest	2	28.4%	1	37.4%	2	25.7%	1	42.9%	2	24.9%	1	44.8%

Source: *Abstracts of the Statistics of Manufacturing, 1860*, 5.

motor vehicle production, the Old Northwest was fourth in production of carriages in 1850 and third in 1860, and second in production of wagons and carts (potentially more applicable to farm needs) in 1860. It employed the second largest number of wheelwrights in 1850 and the most in 1860.[52]

Skilled laborers, most commonly found in the more developed Northeast, supported the Old Northwest's growing industrialization. With over 40 percent of machinists, toolmakers, tinsmiths, and ironworkers in 1850 and 1860, the Middle Atlantic led the nation, and New England typically ranked second.[53] The Old Northwest was in third place but rose from housing 7.3 percent of machinists and toolmakers in 1850 to 14.0 percent in 1860, and from 14.7 percent of tinsmiths and ironworkers in 1850 to 18.7 percent in 1860. The number of tinsmiths and ironworkers increased sufficiently to move the Old Northwest into second place in 1860. Hardware manufacturing typically occurred in the Northeast, but by the Civil War the Old Northwest ranked third in establishments, employees making hardware, and product value.

Statistics of manufacturing in 1850 and 1860, a period of substantial growth nationwide, reveal the increasing significance and emerging strength of Old Northwest industrialization. The region ranked third, behind the Middle Atlantic and New England, in employees and value of production in both years but by 1860 had moved from third to second place in number of manufacturing establishments (Table 10). Although its rankings remained similar, the Old Northwest's proportional share in each category rose by three to four percentage points. New York, Pennsylvania, and Massachusetts typically occupied the top three spots in these measures, but Ohio was third in establishments in 1850 and 1860, third in employees in 1850, and fourth in value of manufactures in both years, ahead of early industrializing states like Connecticut and New Jersey.[54] The South Atlantic and East South Central regions ranked fourth and fifth, respectively, in number of establishments, employees, and value of production both years. Taken together as the South, these two regions in 1860 accounted for just over 20 percent of employees but, far more importantly for the upcoming military conflict, less than 15 percent of industrial capacity, measured by number of employees and value of production. By itself, the third-place Old Northwest exceeded

Table 10. Statistics of Manufacturing East of the Mississippi River, 1850 and 1860

	Number of Establishments				Number Employed				Value of Manufactures			
	1850		1860		1850		1860		1850		1860	
	Rank	% of Total	Rank	% of Total	Rank	% of Total	Rank	% of Total	Rank	% of Total	Rank	% of Total
New England	2	18.7%	3	16.9%	2	32.6%	2	32.3%	2	28.6%	2	27.2%
Middle Atlantic	1	42.6%	1	40.3%	1	42.0%	1	41.9%	1	45.0%	1	43.3%
South Atlantic	4	8.0%	4	13.5%	4	5.6%	4	9.0%	4	5.0%	4	8.8%
East South Central	5	7.2%	5	6.9%	5	4.9%	5	3.8%	5	4.4%	5	4.2%
Old Northwest	3	18.4%	2	22.3%	3	10.2%	3	13.0%	3	12.4%	3	16.4%

Source: *Manufactures of the United States in 1860*, 729, 730.

the South's manufacturing might; adding the Northeast's industrial capacity tipped the scales irreversibly toward the North.

By the cusp of the Civil War, the Old Northwest region looked far different from Thomas Jefferson's vision of yeoman farms blanketing the plains west of the Appalachians. His ideal called for small agricultural units, largely self-contained and self-sufficient in food and simple homemade goods, selling surpluses only to purchase manufactured items not created on the farm.[55] Certainly in 1860, agriculture remained the Old Northwest's predominant economic activity as the Old Northwest led the nation in corn, wheat, and livestock production. But farmers quickly sought markets for their surplus, and accessing markets required internal and external improvements. Developing transportation systems—canals within and outside the region, railroads reaching westward and expanding in the interior, improved lake shipping—enhanced connections to the East Coast and shifted economic networks away from New Orleans. Ties eastward linked the Old Northwest to established northeastern industrial and commercial centers and European markets.

Responding to regional demand, entrepreneurs in the Old Northwest rapidly developed their own industrial production. Cultivating the heavier clay and prairie soils of the Old Northwest required stronger, more effective plows. The call for machines rather than labor to farm more land and harvest more crops encouraged agricultural implement and equipment manufacturing. The demand for more equipment, more materials, and more expertise stimulated further development of manufacturing and supported the expanding industrial base clearly present in the Old Northwest before the Civil War. This base would play a significant role in the North's ultimate victory in the Civil War. And this base was the foundation supporting the Old Northwest's sweeping industrialization during the next hundred years, adding to existing agricultural dominance and making the Midwest what it is today.

Notes

1. David R. Meyer, "Midwestern Industrialization and the American Manufacturing Belt in the Nineteenth Century," *Journal of Economic History* 49, no. 4 (1989): 921–22; Richard White, *The Republic For Which*

It Stands: The United States during Reconstruction and the Gilded Age, 1865–1896 (New York: Oxford, 2017); Erik Larson, The Devil in the White City: Murder, Magic, and Madness at the Fair That Changed America (New York: Vintage, 2004).
2. Twelfth Census of the United States Taken in the Year 1900, Vol. VII, Manufactures, Part I, United States by Industries (New York: Norman Ross Publishers, 1997), clxxvii.
3. Ibid., clxxvi.
4. Gregory S. Rose, "The Midwest as a National and International Economic Powerhouse by 1920," in Sara Kosiba, ed., A Scattering Time: How Modernism Met Midwestern Culture (Hastings, NE: Hastings College Press, 2018), 119–40.
5. For consistency, regional economic development in 1850 and 1860 is compared to total production within the five census regions east of the Mississippi River. Tables in this paper substitute "Old Northwest" for the "East North Central" term used in the U.S. Census.
6. Agriculture of the United States in 1860 (New York: Norman Ross, 1990), 188, 184.
7. Statistical View of the United States … Seventh Census (New York: Norman Ross, 1990), 169.
8. Agriculture of the United States in 1860, 222; Sam Bowers Hilliard, Hog Meat and Hoecake: Food Supply in the Old South, 1840–1860 (Carbondale: Southern Illinois University Press, 1972), 25, 186–99; Douglass C. North, The Economic Growth of the United States 1790–1860 (Englewood Cliffs, NJ: Prentice-Hall, 1966), 130–31.
9. Agriculture of the United States in 1860, 188, 184.
10. Gregory Rose, "Yeoman Farmer," in Richard Sisson, Chris Zacher, and Andrew Cayton, eds., The American Midwest: An Interpretive Encyclopedia (Bloomington: Indiana University Press, 2006), 85–88.
11. Hilliard, Hog Meat, 150–60; Donald L. Kemmerer, "The Pre-Civil War South's Leading Crop, Corn," Agricultural History 23, no. 4 (1949): 236–39; North, Economic Growth, 123–29.
12. Cynthia Clampitt, Midwest Maize: How Corn Shaped the U.S. Heartland (Urbana: University of Illinois Press, 2015), 26–34, 174–77; Clarence H. Danhof, Change in Agriculture: The Northern United States, 1820–1870 (Cambridge MA: Harvard University Press, 1969), 27–48; John C. Hudson, Making the Corn Belt: A Geographical History of Middle-western Agriculture (Bloomington: Indiana University Press, 1994), 1–14, 45–60; Christopher R. Laingen, "The Agrarian Midwest: A Geographical Analysis," in Jon K. Lauck, Gleaves Whitney, and Joseph Hogan, eds., Finding a New Midwestern History (Lincoln: University of Nebraska Press, 2018), 145–50; North, Economic Growth, 136, 143.
13. John G. Clark, The Grain Trade in the Old Northwest (Urbana: University of Illinois Press, 1966), 197–211; Paul W. Gates, The Farmer's Age: Agriculture

1815-1860 (New York: Holt, Rinehart, and Winston, 1960), 156-69; Hildegard Binder Johnson, "King Wheat in Southeastern Minnesota: A Case Study of Pioneer Agriculture," *Annals of the Association of American Geographers* 47, no. 4 (1957): 350-62; Alan L. Olmstead and Paul W. Rhode, "The Red Queen and the Hard Reds: Productivity Growth in American Wheat, 1800-1940," *The Journal of Economic History* 62, no. 4 (2002): 933-41; Louis Bernard Schmidt, "The Westward Movement of the Wheat Growing Industry in the United States," *Iowa Journal of History and Politics* 18, no. 3 (1920): 396-412.

14. Harold B. Gill, "Wheat Culture in Colonial Virginia," *Agricultural History* 52, no. 3 (1978): 380-93.
15. "Ecological Requirements for Wheat Cultivation," last modified 21 June 2018, http://agriinfo.in/default.aspx?page=topic&superid=1&topicid=1173; Gates, *Farmer's Age*, 163-65; Olmstead and Rhode, "The Red Queen," 947-61.
16. *Agriculture of the United States in 1860*, lxxxvi, 184-85, 188-89.
17. Paul Wallace Gates, "Cattle Kings in the Prairies," *Mississippi Valley Historical Review* 35, no. 3 (1948): 379-412; Gates, "Hoosier Cattle Kings," *Indiana Magazine of History* 44, no. 1 (1948): 1-24; Paul C. Henlein, "Early Cattle Ranges of the Ohio Valley," *Agricultural History* 35, no. 3 (1961): 150-54; Hudson, *Corn Belt*, 61-74; Laingen, "The American Midwest," 149-50; North, *Economic Growth*, 152-53.
18. *Statistical View*, 171; *Agriculture of the United States in 1860*, 187.
19. Paul C. Henlein, "Cattle Driving from the Ohio Country, 1800-1850," *Agricultural History* 28, no. 2 (1954): 83-95; Charles T. Leavitt, "Transportation and the Livestock Industry of the Middle West to 1860," *Agricultural History* 8, no. 1 (1934): 20-33.
20. Steve C. Gordon, "From Slaughterhouse to Soap-Boiler: Cincinnati's Meat Packing Industry, Changing Technologies, and the Rise of Mass Production, 1825-1870," *IA. The Journal of the Society for Industrial Archeology* 16, no. 1 (1990): 55-67; Margaret Walsh, "Pork Packing as a Leading Edge of Midwestern Industry, 1835-1875," *Agricultural History* 51, no. 4 (1977): 702-17; Walsh, *The Rise of the Midwestern Meat Packing Industry* (Lexington: University Press of Kentucky, 1982).
21. Jim Edwards and Wynette Edwards, *Chicago Entertainment Between the Wars, 1919-1939* (Chicago: Arcadia, 2003), 47; Gordon, "From Slaughterhouse," 66.
22. Jeremy Atack and Fred Bateman, "Self-Sufficiency and the Marketable Surplus in the Rural North, 1860," *Agricultural History* 58, no. 3 (1984): 296-313; Gates, *Farmer's Age*, 165-69; David E. Schob, *Hired Hands and Plowboys: Farm Labor in the Midwest, 1815-60* (Urbana: University of Illinois Press, 1975), 43-66.
23. Doris Kearns Goodwin, *Leadership in Turbulent Times* (New York: Simon and Schuster, 2018), 11-12.

24. Goodwin, *Leadership in Turbulent Times*, 17–18; North, *Economic Growth*, 206–10; George Rogers Taylor, *The Transportation Revolution, 1815–1860* (New York: Holt, Rinehart, and Winston, 1951), 32–55.
25. Gregory S. Rose, "Extending the Road West," in Karl Raitz, ed., *The National Road* (Baltimore: Johns Hopkins University Press, 1996), 159–92; Taylor, *Transportation Revolution*, 15–31; Joseph S. Wood, "The Idea of a National Road," in Raitz, *The National Road*, 93–122.
26. Robert J. Kapsch, *The Potomac Canal: George Washington and the Waterway West* (Morgantown: West Virginia University Press, 2007); Roger L. Ransom, "Interregional Canals and Economic Specialization in the Antebellum United States," *Explorations in Economic History* 5, no. 1 (1967): 12–35; Roger L. Ransom, "Public Canal Investment and the Opening of the Old Northwest," in David C. Klingaman and Richard K. Vedder, eds., *Essays in Nineteenth Century Economic History: The Old Northwest* (Athens: Ohio University Press, 1975), 246–68; Harvey H. Segal, "Cycles of Canal Construction," in Carter Goodrich, ed., *Canals and American Development* (New York: Columbia University Press, 1961), 171–73, 184–85; Taylor, *Transportation Revolution*, 52–55.
27. Albert Fishlow, *American Railroads and the Transformation of the Ante-Bellum Economy* (Cambridge, MA: Harvard University Press, 1965), 18–22; Harvey H. Segal, "Cycles of Canal Construction," 169–215; Segal, "Canals and Economic Development," in Goodrich, *Canals and American Development*, 216–48; Taylor, *Transportation Revolution*, 54–55.
28. *Agriculture of the United States in 1860*, clxiv–clxix; *Statistics of the United States ... in 1860* (New York: Norman Ross, 1990), 323–64; *Report of the Superintendent of the Census for December 1, 1852* (Washington: Robert Armstrong, Public Printer, 1853), 98–104; John F. Stover, *American Railroads* (Chicago: University of Chicago Press, 1997), 35; Taylor, *Transportation Revolution*, 74–103.
29. Kevin Hillstrom and Laurie Collier Hillstrom, eds., *The Industrial Revolution in America, Volume 2, Railroads* (Santa Barbara, CA: ABC-CLIO, 2005), 13; James E. Vance Jr., *The North American Railroad: Its Origin, Evolution, and Geography* (Baltimore: Johns Hopkins University Press, 1995), 139.
30. *Statistics of the United States*, 335–36; Fishlow, *American Railroads*, 30–31, 163–204, 262–70; Stover, *American Railroads*; Taylor, *Transportation Revolution*, 87; Vance, *The North American Railroad*, front end papers, 13–124, 139–44.
31. Richard R. John, *Network Nation: Inventing American Telecommunications* (Cambridge: Harvard University Press, 2010), 51, 55; Robert Luther Thompson, *Wiring a Continent: The History of the Telegraphic Industry in the United States, 1832–1866* (Princeton: Princeton University Press, 1947), 241–43; *Report of the Superintendent of the Census*, 106–16; *Statistical View*, 189; Richard Sutch and Susan B. Carter, eds. *Historical Statistics of the United States, Earliest Times to the Present, Millennial Edition, Volume 4, Part*

D, *Economic Sectors* (New York: Cambridge University Press, 2006), Table Dg8-21, 4-1001.
32. *The Seventh Census of the United States: 1850* (New York: Norman Ross, 1990), lxvii–lxxix.
33. *Agriculture of the United States in 1860*, cxxxvi–clix; Clark, *Grain Trade*, 32–171, 212–88; Fishlow, *American Railroads*, 205–36, 275–98; Gates, *Farmer's Age*, 174–78; Gordon, "From Slaughterhouse," 56, 66; Hilliard, *Hog Meat*, 201–08; North, *Economic Growth*, 102–21, 140–55, 196, 249–62; Taylor, *Transportation Revolution*, 161–64.
34. Meyer, "Midwestern Industrialization," 927.
35. Alfred D. Chandler Jr., "The Organization of Manufacturing and Transportation," in David T. Gilchrist and W. David Lewis, eds., *Economic Change in the Civil War Era* (Greenville, DE: Eleutherian Mills-Hagley Foundation, 1965), 137–41.
36. "Population of States and Counties of the United States: 1790–1990," last modified 14 July 2016, 69–1,161, https://www.census.gov/population/www/censusdata/PopulationofStatesandCountiesofthe UnitedStates1790-1990.pdf
37. Gregory S. Rose, "American and European Immigrant Groups in the Midwest by the Mid-Nineteenth Century," in Lauck, Whitney, and Hogan, eds., *Finding a New Midwestern History*, 73–95.
38. Jeremy Atack and Fred Bateman, "The Development of Industrial Steam Power in the Midwest with Special Reference to Indiana," *The Old Northwest* 8, no. 4 (1982–1983): 329–51; John A. James, "Structural Change in American Manufacturing, 1850–1890," *Journal of Economic History* 43, no. 2 (1983): 433–59; Isaac Lippincott, *A History of Manufactures in the Ohio Valley to the Year 1860* (New York, Arno Press, 1973); David R. Meyer, "Midwestern Industrialization," 921–37; Meyer, "Emergence of the American Manufacturing Belt: An Interpretation," *Journal of Historical Geography* 9, no. 2 (1983): 145–74; North, *Economic Growth*, 153–55; Margaret Walsh, *The Manufacturing Frontier: Pioneer Industry in Antebellum Wisconsin, 1830–1860* (Madison: State Historical Society of Wisconsin, 1972); Harry L. Wilkey, "Infant Industries in Illinois: As Illustrated in Quincy, 1836–1856," *Journal of the Illinois State Historical Society* 32, no. 4 (1939): 474–97.
39. Michael Williams, "Clearing the United States Forests: Pivotal Years 1810–1860," *Journal of Historical Geography* 8, no. 1 (1982): 12–28, 23.
40. Thomas R. Cox, *The Lumberman's Frontier: Three Centuries of Land Use, Society, and Change in America's Forests* (Corvallis: Oregon State University Press, 2010), 125–89; Theodore J. Karamanski, *Deep Woods Frontier: A History of Logging in Northern Michigan* (Detroit: Wayne State University Press, 1989).
41. *Abstracts of the Statistics of Manufactures According to the Returns of the Seventh Census* (New York: Norman Ross, 1990), 72; *Manufactures of the*

United States in 1860 (New York: Norman Ross, 1990), 113, 144, 275, 486, 658.
42. Seventh Census, 1850, lxix; Population of the United States in 1860 (New York: Norman Ross, 1990), 660–61.
43. Manufactures of the United States in 1860, 14–658, 736.
44. Scott Richard St. Louis, "A 'Self-Made Town': Semi-Annual Furniture Expositions and the Development of Civic Identity in Grand Rapids, 1878–1965," Michigan Historical Review 44, no. 2 (2018): 40.
45. Abstracts of the Statistics of Manufactures, 51; Danhof, Change in Agriculture, 31–33; Gates, Farmer's Age, 158–59; Fishlow, American Railroads, 226–30; Manufactures of the United States in 1860, 14–662; North, Economic Growth, 154.
46. Agriculture of the United States in 1860, clix–clxiii; Lippincott, A History of Manufactures, 88–89.
47. Fred Bateman, "The 'Marketable Surplus' in Northern Dairy Farming: New Evidence by Size of Farm in 1860," Agricultural History 52, no. 3 (1978): 345–63; R. Douglas Hurt, "Dairying in Nineteenth-century Ohio," The Old Northwest 5, no. 4 (1979–1980): 387–99.
48. Lippincott, A History of Manufactures in the Ohio Valley.
49. Walsh, The Manufacturing Frontier; Wilkey, "Infant Industries in Illinois."
50. Meyer, "Midwestern Industrialization," 929–36.
51. Cochrane, Development of American Agriculture, 67–110, 189–208; Danhof, Change in Agriculture, 181–250; Gates, Farmer's Age, 271–94; Nordin and Scott, From Prairie Farmer to Entrepreneur, 122–26; Charles Post, "The Agricultural Revolution in the United States: The Development of Capitalism and the Adoption of the Reaper in the Antebellum US North," Science & Society 61, no. 2 (1997): 216–28.
52. Seventh Census, 1850, lxxviii; Population of the United States in 1860, 678–79.
53. Ibid., lxxii, lxxvii, lxxviii; Manufactures of the United States in 1860, 666–69, 676–77.
54. Manufactures of the United States in 1860, 729, 730.
55. Jill Lepore, These Truths: A History of the United States (New York: W.W. Norton, 2018), 168–72.

Jacob K. Friefeld | Homesteading and the Making of the Midwest

John Kurt had no interest in soldiering or city living. Born in Switzerland, Kurt spent his youth in the Swiss army before finding work in a cheese factory. In his early twenties he left the snow-capped mountains of his home in 1880 for the United States and soon found work in New York City. He just as quickly left the throngs of New York behind for Ohio and the Midwest. He bounced from one laborious job to another—bricklaying, sawmill work, and work on the railroad—before leaving Ohio to claim a 159-acre homestead on the plains near Chadron, Nebraska. Kurt joined nearly 250,000 other settlers who homesteaded in the territories of Nebraska, Kansas, and the Dakotas before the turn of the twentieth century.[1]

Homesteading has long been dismissed by scholars as irrelevant to the overall settling of the American Midwest and West.[2] Scholarship based on newly available data and reassessments of old studies demands that historians look at the Homestead Act anew and temper long relied upon anecdotes with more complete data sets.[3] Scholars have also begun to search for the borderlands that separate the Midwest from the West, paying particular attention to the place of the Great Plains in these internal borderlands.[4] This study speaks to new research on internal borderlands and begins the investigation of the Homestead Act's significance in the making of the Midwest and its role in midwestern consolidation and identity formation in the late nineteenth century.

The Midwest underwent two distinct settlement patterns. Settlers acquired land in the old Midwest of Ohio, Indiana, Illinois, Missouri, Michigan, Iowa, Wisconsin, and Minnesota largely through cash sales. The settlers, like John Kurt, in the new Midwest of Kansas, Nebraska, and the Dakotas, acquired their farms largely through the Homestead Act. While new and old midwestern settlement created distinct patterns, they resembled each other because the homesteaders in the new Midwest largely came from other midwestern territories. This allowed the old Midwest to replicate itself in these territories increasingly settled by

U.S. citizens.[5] New midwestern settlement also took on a more diverse and radical incarnation than it had in the old Midwest as it invited both white women and African Americans to claim homesteads. In this way, the Midwest spread and consolidated itself largely due to the Homestead Act of 1862.

Between the American Revolution and 1860, the United States added the midwestern states of Ohio, Indiana, Illinois, Missouri, Michigan, Iowa, Wisconsin, and Minnesota. The financial weakness of the U.S. federal government early in its history made certain that most of the territory that became the Midwest would be sold to create revenue. Thomas Jefferson envisioned an "Empire of Liberty" for the common (white) American in the lands of the Midwest, but early expansion privileged revenue over speedy settlement.[6]

The cash sale of public lands remained the focus of both raising government revenue and public domain disposal for the early national period until the passage of the Homestead Act in 1862. But before settlers could claim free homesteads, the Graduation Act of 1854 provided for the disposal of most of the remaining public land in the old Midwest. By the time of the Graduation Act, much of the unsold public land in these states had been on the market for over ten years for the regular price of $1.25 per acre. The Graduation Act provided for the reduced price for lands that had been on sale for more than ten years. Lands that had been for sale between ten to fifteen years were reduced in price to $1.00 per acre and continued decreasing in price at five-year intervals. Land that remained unsold after thirty years dropped to twelve and a half cents per acre.[7] This immediately and significantly dropped the price on over 27,000,000 acres of midwestern land and caused an instant land rush that gobbled up most of the remaining public land in the old Midwest. With the old Midwest settled, the United States stood poised to push on and expand the Midwest into Kansas, Nebraska, and the Dakotas.

In the South, the United States was fractured. The Civil War brought places like Fort Sumter and Bull Run to the lips of Americans everywhere. But this rupture also brought opportunity. For years Whigs, Free Soilers, and Republicans had tried to introduce legislation that offered cheap or free land to settlers in the territories adjacent to the old midwestern states, but southern lawmakers had blocked those attempts. With much of the South having seceded, the debate over and signing of the Homestead Act from 1860 to1862 marked the end of a long struggle by these northern advocates to pass a law allowing settlers to claim 160 acres of the public domain for only a small administration fee as long as they were over twenty-one years old, built improvements on their land, and resided on the land for five years.[8]

Passage of the Homestead Act created two different settlement patterns, one for the old Midwest and another for the new Midwest. In the old midwestern states, nearly all the land had been disposed of through the cash sale regime, which explains why these old midwestern states were homesteaded much less than the newer states. In Ohio, Indiana, and Illinois, homesteads accounted for only 1 percent of the state's total acreage, and only slightly more in Iowa, Michigan, Missouri, and Wisconsin (3 percent, 6 percent, 8 percent, and 9 percent respectively). Of the midwestern states that entered the union before 1861, only Minnesota broke single digits in percent of land homesteaded at 20 percent. (See Figure 1.)

The states that entered the Union in 1861 and later represent a stark contrast. At least a quarter of those states' land was settled through homesteading: 25 percent in Kansas, 41 percent in the Dakotas, and 45 percent in Nebraska.[9] Counting only homesteads claimed in each state after entering the Union, North Dakota and South Dakota boasted 39 percent and 32 percent of total acres homesteaded. This disparity between old and new midwestern settlement indicates two very different settlement patterns.[10]

Looking at homesteading's role in new farm formation for the period 1860–1900—the main period of consolidation for the Midwest before the Midwestern Moment, when it began articulating itself more

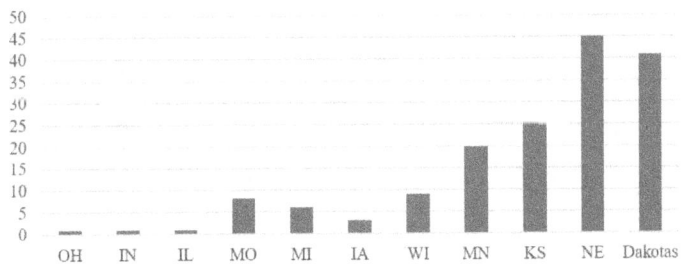

Figure 1. Percent of total state acreage homesteaded.[11]

fully as a region—the difference between the old and new Midwests becomes clear.[11] In order to find the number of new farms formed between 1860 and 1900, I subtracted the number of farms in 1860 for each state from the total farms in the states in 1900. For example, in 1860 Ohio contained 180,000 farms. In 1900, Ohio contained 277,000 farms. Subtracting 180,000 from 277,000 gives a total of 97,000 new farms created in Ohio from 1860 to 1900 (277,000 − 180,000 = 97,000). To figure what percentage of those 97,000 new Ohio farms were homesteads, I added all the homesteads in Ohio from 1868–1905. I used 1868–1905 rather than 1860–1900 because the first homesteads were proved up in 1868, and any homesteads that had been proved up in 1905 would have been new farms in 1900—homesteads filed but not yet proved up.[12] So, between 1868 and 1905, Ohioans proved up 108 homesteads. Divide homesteads (108) by new farms (97,000) to find that between 1860 and 1900, homesteads accounted for a paltry 0.1 percent of new farms in Ohio (108/97,000 = 0.0011).[13]

Repeating the above operation for all the midwestern states shows that in the new Midwest, 64.6 percent of new farms were homesteads, 47 percent in Kansas, 62.3 percent in Nebraska, and 96.5 percent in the Dakotas. The closest any old midwestern state comes to Kansas's 47 percent is Wisconsin at 24.8 percent. In Minnesota, the largest homesteading state in the old Midwest, homesteads accounted for only 13.1 percent of new farms. Combined with the data on homesteads as percent of total land claims, this data on farm formation shows there was a distinct settlement pattern in the new Midwest that relied heavily on homesteading. (See Figure 2.)

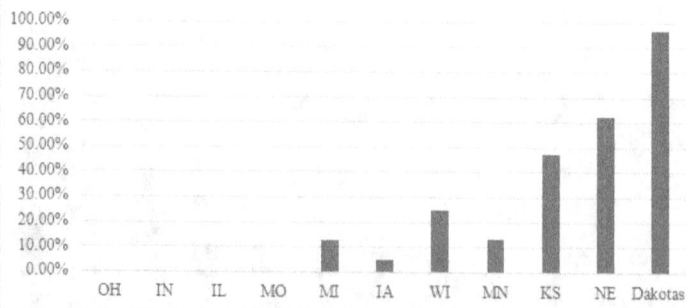

Figure 2. Homesteads as percent of new farms (1868–1900).[14]

While the old and new Midwests were settled in different ways, this does not mean the people who lived in each part of the Midwest were terribly dissimilar. It is difficult to tell who exactly settled the homesteads in the new Midwest due to a paucity of data. However, the largest study area of homesteaders ever assembled comes from the new Midwest. This study area encompasses 621 claimants in ten townships in central and western Nebraska.[14] Of these 621 claimants, 325 previously lived in the Midwest, 109 migrated from Europe, eighty-seven came from the U.S. Northeast, thirty came from the U.S. South, and two crossed the border from Canada.[15] The remaining sixty-eight homesteaders came from an unrecorded U.S. state (sixty-two) or an unrecorded foreign country (six). This means that Midwesterners accounted for 52 percent of the claimants with 17.6 percent coming from Europe, 14 percent coming from the Northeast, 4.8 percent from the South, and 0.3 percent from Canada.

These percentages are not entirely accurate because they include sixty-eight homesteaders whose origin data does not appear in their file. Leaving out the settlers with unknown origins changes the total number of homesteaders to 553. With this new total, accounting only for the homesteaders whose origins were recorded by their local land office, a majority (58.8 percent) came from other parts of the Midwest. Of the 111 immigrants with known origins, the majority, fifty-eight, came from Central European German-speaking areas with the next largest group, twenty-eight, coming from the British Isles. This German and British Isles settlement, perhaps ironically, made the new Midwest *even more* midwestern. In all the states of the old Midwest before the new midwestern states entered the union, the largest immigrant groups were those from German states and the British Isles.[16] (See Table 1.)

In short, the Homestead Act brought people from the old Midwest and immigrants from groups who lived in large numbers in the old Midwest into the new Midwest. This allowed the old Midwest to replicate and consolidate itself on free land in the territories of Kansas, Nebraska, and the Dakotas.

What differentiated this replication from the old Midwest was the diversity of the settlers. In particular, the new midwestern homesteaders included large numbers of white women and black people, two groups who had been mostly prevented from owning land in the old Midwest.

Table 1. Top Three Foreign Resident Populations in the Old Midwest by State in 1860[17]

Foreign Residents/State	IA	IL	IN	MI	MN	MO	OH	WI
Largest Foreign Resident Group	British Isles 42,725	British Isles 149,835	German 66,705	British Isles 61,826	British Isles 18,698	German 88,487	German 168,210	German 123,879
Second Largest Foreign Resident Group	German 36,555	German 130,804	British Isles 36,049	German 38,787	German 18,400	British Isles 56,003	British Isles 124,633	British Isles 63,431
Third Largest Foreign Resident Group	British America 8313	British America 20,132	British America 3166	British America 36,482	Scandinavia 11,782	France 5283	France 12,870	Scandinavia 23,265

In the wake of the American Revolution, free white men enjoyed the ability to acquire, hold, and bequeath land to future generations. Free women remained under the constraints of coverture. So, even if a woman acquired property, upon marriage she gave up many of the rights to that property. In the wake of the banking crisis of the 1830s, legislatures began passing an increasing number of married women's property acts to shield white women from their husband's debts. Women's rights activists advocated for an expansion of these laws, and between the 1840s and 1880s, legislatures passed still broader protections for women's property in marriage.[17] Achieving landownership, an important status in a still largely rural society, remained difficult for women.

The Homestead Act, passed in the midst of the liberalizing of women's property ownership, removed part of this barrier to owning land. The Homestead Act allowed settlement by any head-of-household over the age of twenty-one, thereby allowing women to claim land in the new Midwest in a way that had not been available to them before. However, the General Land Office (GLO) limited a married man and woman to owning a single homestead unless they had been single when they proved up their claims. If the woman married during the proving up period, the GLO assumed she would reside on her husband's claim and abandon her own.[18]

As the Homestead Act allowed them to settle, women took advantage of the opportunity. In the ten Nebraska townships in Custer and Dawes Counties, women accounted for sixty-four of the 621 homesteaders, about 10.3 percent. This is within the 7 to 18 percent range of women homesteaders that scholars suggest we should expect.[19] Testing this range, I chose two counties in each new midwestern state in which I investigated the prevalence of women homestead claims. I chose counties that were both heavily homesteaded and in different geographic locations in each state. From east to west, I examined Roberts County, SD (Northeast), Polk County, NE (East-central), Jewell County, KS (North-central), Bottineau County, ND (North-central), Sherman County, KS (Northwest), Dawes County, NE (Northwest), Fall River County, SD (Southwest), and McKenzie County, ND (West-central). For all but one county, I used Bureau of Land Management data. The only exception is Polk County, for which I used data that was generously shared by independent researcher Richard Pehrson. Women accounted for between 6.33 to 17.72 percent of claimants in these eight counties. (See Table 2.)

The counties with the fewest female homesteaders are those farthest east. In Roberts County, Polk County, and Jewell County, women only homesteaded at about a 6 to 7 percent rate. By the time homesteaders claimed land in Fall River and McKenzie counties, women accounted for more than 17 percent of the claimants. Before 1895, the GLO did not allow a married couple to both prove up homesteads even if they had been single when initially filing their claims. An 1895 decision changed this practice and allowed two applicants who married while in the process of settling their homesteads to prove up both claims.[20] This change in the law's implementation encouraged single women who might be looking to marry a local homesteader to claim land in her own name because she would be assured a chance to prove up even if she

Table 2. Successful Homesteads Claimed by Women in Eight New Midwestern Counties[21]

County	Women Claimants	Total Claimants	Women as Percent of Claimants
Jewell County (Eastern KS)	176	2670	6.59%
Sherman County (Western KS)	186	1579	11.78%
Polk County (Eastern NE)	61	964	6.33%
Dawes County (Western NE)	253	2151	11.76%
Bottineau County (Eastern ND)	459	3821	12.01%
McKenzie County (Western, ND)	818	4617	17.72%
Roberts County (Eastern, SD)	154	2223	6.93%
Fall River County (Western, SD)	404	2347	17.21%

married another claimant. Unsurprisingly, the two counties, Fall River and McKenzie, in which women claimed at more than a 17 percent rate were the only two counties examined in which the claimants all received patent after the 1895 rule change. The new Midwest welcomed women to hold land and made it easier for them to do so over time.

Similar to white women, the old Midwest was not accommodating to black settlers. After the Revolution, settlers moved into the Northwest Territory; among these settlers were free black Americans who established successful farms in the region. Laws limiting their rights and overt violence frustrated the hopes of many of these early free black farmers.[22] By 1868, slavery had been abolished and the Fourteenth Amendment had turned black Americans into citizens and potential homesteaders. After the Civil War, Radical Reconstruction that implemented army occupation and limited participation for former rebels promised to provide a space in the South where black people could gain access to security and opportunity. To help with the transition from slavery to freedom, Congress established the Freedmen's Bureau to, in part, help secure fair contracts between black laborers and southern landowners. Likewise, in 1866 Congress passed the Southern Homestead Act (SHA) in hopes of providing freedpeople the ability to own land. The SHA allowed claimants to homestead up to 80 acres (later 160 acres) in the five southern states with available public lands. Congress hoped the SHA might produce an independent, landowning, black yeomanry in the South. Unfortunately, poor timberland and white violence dashed these hopes and prevented black people from starting farms through the SHA.[23] Within this context of poor farmland and violence, many black southerners began to look to other public lands available for homesteading in the Midwest.

The community of Bliss near the Wheeler and Holt county line in Nebraska was one midwestern black homesteader community. The Blair, Dixon, and Stewart families arrived in Nebraska to settle around 1885 and started their community by claiming homesteads. A J. Stewart made his 160-acre claim of "prairie land" that was "most valuable for farming" in October 1884.[24] Stewart, along with his wife Irena Stewart and one of their seven children, identified a level piece of ground from which they stripped the prairie grass to provide a foundation for their sod house. They then cut sod for the walls, likely three feet wide at the base and closer to twelve inches near the roof.²⁵ The Stewart family home had two rooms and a board roof with sod laid over the top. Building a sod house required strenuous labor, but this process was cheap for the Stewarts and allowed them to save money for their first years of survival in the new Midwest. The Stewarts made the most of their dirt-floored sod home and added three beds, a stove, table, eight chairs, and a clock. Along with their sod home, the Stewarts added a 13-foot by 34-foot sod stable, granary, corn crib, and hen house. By 1888 they cultivated crops on sixty acres of their land and kept six horses, five head of cattle, and ten hogs.²⁶ Stewart proved up and took full ownership of his land in December 1889.

The Bliss community grew in two distinct claim periods. The first homesteaders proved up their claims from 1889 to 1892. Hector Bell Dixon, head of one of the prominent families in Bliss, filed his claim in 1885. He proved up in 1890. Dixon lived on his claim with his eight children. The family cultivated twenty-five acres of wheat, oats, rye, and corn. They also planted 420 trees, twenty of which were apple trees. When they proved up, the Dixons valued their land at $748 per acre. His brother, James Dixon, and Henry Blair, head of another prominent Bliss family, proved up the same year. John Lewis joined them as landowners in 1892 when he proved up on 160 acres. Lewis, his wife, and three children, cultivated sixty-eight acres, planted 8000 forest trees and eighty fruit trees, and built a barn, corn crib, granary, hen house, well, and hog house. They also built and lived in a sod house. Life in the early days of the Bliss settlement was probably difficult. But by the early 1900s, the community had achieved enough success to encourage a second generation of homesteaders.²⁷

The second patent period occurred from 1906 to 1911. The Blair family remained prominent during this time, led in 1900 by Susie Blair, Henry Blair's daughter, with her claim of 160 acres. She cultivated twenty-five acres and built a house and well. She then spent the winter months working off her land to earn money.²⁸ Two months after Susie Blair, Samuel D. Jones homesteaded in the Bliss community with his wife and two children. The family cultivated 102 acres and planted between fifty and seventy-five fruit trees.²⁹ William Blair, likely Susie's brother, also received a patent on 160 acres and was followed by Daniel Newman, Corneeleous Dixon, and Benjamin Jackson. In all, the Bliss community members claimed eleven homesteads and received patents for 2398.4 acres. The community grew to include at least fifty-six residents. The Bliss community formed cooperative relationships with the surrounding white settlers. In order to prove up on homesteads, homesteaders had to list four witnesses who could confirm they had been living and making improvements on the land. They also had to call two of these witnesses to testify on their behalf on the day they proved up. Members of the Bliss community relied on both their black and white neighbors to prove up and secure landownership in the Midwest. Susie Blair, for example, called both local black homesteader Samuel Jones and Nettie Scriven, a white woman, to witness for her.[30] The clearest example of cooperation across race is Benjamin Jackson. As the last homesteader to prove up in the Bliss community, Jackson could have called one of his more than fifty black neighbors or one of the other ten black homesteaders as witnesses. When it came time to prove up in 1910, he relied on a white neighbor, Frank Hawley, to witness for him. The second witness he called, T.P. Story, doesn't appear in the census in Wheeler or Holt counties, but the census taker listed the Story family in the area as white. Bliss homesteaders might have called white witnesses because these white neighbors' farms were closer to them than the earlier Bliss settlers. This witnessing pattern may speak to tensions between members of the Bliss community. Or it suggests that Bliss community members distrusted land office officials, and they felt compelled to choose white witnesses to secure their ownership of the land they had poured their lives and sweat into for five years. No matter which one of these scenarios, Bliss homesteaders felt that their white neighbors would give fair testimony.

Other black homesteaders replicated the successes of the Bliss community in different new midwestern locales. In Nicodemus, Kansas, black homesteaders began arriving in 1877. They claimed more than 13,000 acres of land and sent E.P. McCabe, a Nicodemus community leader, to serve as the state auditor after he won a statewide election in 1882.[31] Norvell Blair, the brother of the Bliss community's Henry Blair, moved from Illinois to Sully County, South Dakota, where his family homesteaded in the early 1880s. The Blairs encouraged other black settlers to homestead in the area, and soon black homesteaders had made twenty-nine claims on more than 5000 acres. Likewise, in Cherry County, Nebraska, black homesteaders built the community of DeWitty.

By 1915, DeWitty boasted 146 residents living on 29,402 homesteaded acres.[32] In these communities, black Americans, most of whom had family roots in the South, found security to build communities, educate their children, and farm in the new Midwest.[33]

Americans and immigrants, like Swiss-born John Kurt, who prospered on his homestead in Nebraska and married Maggie Maika, a woman who had claimed her own homestead in 1900, were part of the process of homesteading the new midwestern states.[34] Approximately 65 percent of the farms created in the region from 1868 to 1905 were established as a gift from the federal government. Homesteading helped settle Midwesterners in the new Midwest, thereby consolidating the Midwest from the East in Ohio to the West in Kansas, Nebraska, and the Dakotas. This settlement was also diverse and radical in that it extended its land to both black and white women as well as black men.

This analysis raises even more questions about homesteading and midwestern identity. For example, how did the fact that a majority of farms in the new Midwest grew as a result of a federal free land program affect assumptions about the relationship between the federal government and the citizenry? At the end of the nineteenth century, Midwesterners who had created homes and started families on free federal land undoubtedly wondered why price manipulations in distant markets made it harder for them to earn a living. But as freight prices rose and crop prices fell, these midwestern men and women again looked to federal policy as populism swept the new Midwest. What was the relationship between homesteaders and the populist movement in the Midwest? How did the radical assumption that both black people and white women deserved the opportunity to own land and build lives in the new Midwest affect the political assumptions of the region? Increasing urbanization, drought, and depression would threaten and scatter many of these homesteading communities in the twentieth century, but homesteading dramatically shaped the way in which people settled and consolidated the Midwest as a region before 1900.

Notes

This research was supported in part by National Park Service grant #P17ACOO181 and the University of Nebraska's Center for Great Plains Studies, which I gratefully acknowledge. All views expressed are

those of the author. I thank three research assistants—Jessica Carter, Crisanto Dubuc, and Katie Meegan—for their help.
1. *Compendium of History, Reminiscence and Biography of Western Nebraska* (Chicago: Alden Publishing Company, 1909), 1097-98.
2. Fred A. Shannon, *Farmer's Last Frontier: Agriculture, 1860-1897* (1945 repr. Farrar and Rinehart, 1973). Shannon was the most extreme critic of the Homestead Act.
3. Richard Edwards, Jacob K. Friefeld, and Rebecca S. Wingo, *Homesteading the Plains: Toward a New History* (Lincoln: University of Nebraska Press, 2017). Edwards, Friefeld, and Wingo challenge the scholarly consensus regarding homesteading.
4. Jon K. Lauck, ed. *The Interior Borderlands: Regional Identity in the Midwest and Great Plains* (Sioux Falls: The Center for Western Studies, 2019). Each essay in this volume is an important addition to the historiography on internal borderlands.
5. Native dispossession accompanied this process of settlement. For a discussion of the Homestead Act's role in dispossession see Edwards, Friefeld, and Wingo, *Homesteading the Plains*, 91-128.
6. Benjamin Horace Hibbard, *A History of the Public Land Policies* (New York: The Macmillan Company, 1924), 1-6.
7. Paul W. Gates, *History of Public Land Law Development* (Washington, DC: Public Land Law Review Commission, 1968), 185-86.
8. Richard Edwards, "Changing Perceptions of Homesteading as a Policy of Public Domain Disposal," in *Great Plains Quarterly* 29, no. 3 (Summer 2010): 181.
9. The Dakotas are considered together here due to 33,951 homesteads having proved up while the states were still considered Dakota Territory.
10. Homestead National Monument of America, "State by State Numbers," accessed 15 January 2019, https://www.nps.gov/home/learn/historyculture/statenumbers.htm
11. Jon K. Lauck, "Mapping the Contours of the Midwestern Moment" in Jon K. Lauck, ed., *The Midwestern Moment: The Forgotten World of Early-Twentieth-Century Midwestern Regionalism, 1880-1940* (Hastings, NE: Hastings College Press, 2017), ix-xv.
12. A proved-up homestead is a completed homestead that the claimant fully owns.
13. U.S. Department of the Interior, *Homesteads* (Washington, DC: Bureau of Land Management, 1962); Alan L. Olmstead and Paul W. Rhode, "Farms, By Region and State: 1850-1997." Table Da93-158 in *Historical Statistics of the United States, Earliest Times to the Present: Millennial Edition*, edited by Susan B. Carter, Scott Sigmund Gartner, Michael R. Haines, Alan L. Olmstead, Richard Sutch, and Gavin Wright (New York: Cambridge University Press, 2006).

14. For a discussion of this study area see Edwards, Friefeld, Wingo, *Homesteading the Plains: Toward a New History*, 67–72.
15. I include in the Midwest states both the old and new Midwests as discussed throughout this essay. I include Maryland and DC in the Northeast and West Virginia with the South.
16. Data on the foreign-born population of each state in the Midwest in 1860 from Joseph C.G. Kennedy, *Population of the United States in 1860 Census Compiled from the Original Returns of the Eighth Census* (Washington: Government Printing Office, 1864).
17. Carole Shammas, "Reassessing the Women's Property Acts," *Journal of Women's History* 6, no. 1 (Spring 1994): 11.
18. Edwards, Friefeld, and Wingo, *Homesteading the Plains*, 129–31.
19. Katherine Harris, *Long Vistas: Women and Families in Colorado Homesteads* (Niwot: University of Colorado Press, 1993); Sheryll Patterson-Black, "Women Homesteaders of the Great Plains Frontier," in *Frontiers: A Journal of Women Studies* 1, no. 2 (Winter 1972): 67–88; Susan A. Hallgarth, "Women Settlers on the Frontier: Unwed, Unreluctant, Unrepentant," in *Women's Studies Quarterly* 17, no. 3 (Fall–Winter 1989): 23–34; H. Elaine Lindgren, *Land in Her Own Name: Women as Homesteaders in North Dakota* (Norman: University of Oklahoma Press, 1996).
20. U.S. General Land Office, *Circular from the General Land Office Showing the Manner of Proceeding to Obtain Title to Public Lands under the Pre-Emption, Homestead, and Other Laws* (Washington, DC: Government Printing Office, 1895); for an explanation of the evolution of the implementation of the Homestead Act see Rhea Wick, "An Annotated Review of GLO Circulars, 1862–1904," in Edwards, Friefeld, and Wingo, *Homesteading the Plains*, 205–16.
21. This data was gathered by searching for all homesteads in each county and picking out the names that likely belonged to women. Bureau of Land Management General Land Office Records, accessed 5 March 2018–2 April 2018, https://glorecords.blm.gov/search/default.aspx.
22. Anna-Lisa Cox, *The Bone and Sinew of the Land: America's Forgotten Black Pioneers and the Struggle for Equality* (New York: Public Affairs, 2018).
23. Richard Edwards, "African Americans and the Southern Homestead Act," *Great Plains Quarterly*, 39, no. 2 (Spring 2019).
24. A.J. Stewart, Homestead Records: Neligh Land Office, Township 23N, Range 10W, Section 18, Fold3.com Digital Archive, accessed 18 January 2019, https://www.fold3.com/image/271428934.
25. David B. Danbom, *Sod Busting: How Families Made Farms on the 19th-Century Plains* (Baltimore: Johns Hopkins University Press, 2014), 34–35.
26. Stewart, Homestead Records.
27. Hector B. Dixon, Homestead Records: Neligh Land Office, Township 24 North, Range 12 W, Section 11, Fold3.com Digital Archive, accessed 18 January 2019, https://www.fold3.com/image/274575346; John S. Lewis,

Homestead Records: Neligh Land Office, Township 23 North, Range 9 West, Section 15, Fold3.com Digital Archive, accessed 18 January 2019, https://www.fold3.com/image/273034658.
28. Susie M. Blair, Homestead Records: O'Neill Land Office, Township 24N, Range 11W, Section 9, Fold3.com Digital Archive, accessed 11 May 2018, https://www.fold3.com/image/253/307963604.
29. Samuel D. Jones, Homestead Records: O'Neill Land Office, Township 24N, Range 12W, Section 12, Fold3.com Digital Archive, accessed 11 May 2018, https://www.fold3.com/image/253/307994880.
30. Susie M. Blair, Homestead Records; U.S. Census, Holt County, Nebraska, 1900.
31. Jacob K. Friefeld, Mikal Brotnov Eckstrom, and Richard Edwards, "African American Homesteader 'Colonies' in the Settling of the Great Plains," *Great Plains Quarterly* 39, no. 1 (Winter 2019): 14–15.
32. Ibid., 18–21.
33. Richard Edwards, Jacob K. Friefeld, and Mikal Brotnov Eckstrom, "'Canaan on the Prairie': New Evidence on the Number of African American Homesteaders in the Great Plains," *Great Plains Quarterly* 39, no. 3 (Summer 2019): 236. Edwards, Friefeld, and Eckstrom conclude that likely over 26,000 African Americans participated in homesteading in the Great Plains.
34. Maggie Kurt, Homestead Records: Alliance Land Office, Township 33N, Range 47W, Section 7, Fold3.com Digital Archive, accessed 18 January 2019, https://www.fold3.com/image/287418803.

Sara Egge

The Emergence of Midwestern Political Culture in Northwest Iowa

On April 17, 1884, the *Spencer Reporter* published the meeting minutes of the Board of Supervisors of Clay County, Iowa. The meeting minutes appeared prominently in the center of the page. Above the minutes was a six-month report of the Clay County Women's Christian Temperance Union (WCTU). To their left was the "Personal Mentions" section.[1] Arranging these news stories together was a regular practice for the editor of the *Spencer Reporter*. His weekly editions looked remarkably similar, with columns full of stories that illuminated the daily lives of the people who lived there. Only the dates changed, marking the passage of time. The *Spencer Reporter*, like most midwestern newspapers, captured the heart of community life. Editors printed an astounding range of stories in local newspapers, from mundane to extraordinary, which makes them the best source for understanding midwestern political culture. As Kathleen Neils Conzen noted, "Midwestern culture and identity grew to maturity alongside the popular press."[2] Newspapers were both essential economic boosters, "stimulating local settlement and investment," and central to politics, especially during campaign seasons.[3] But they were also formative in creating a "local ethos," one that "could weld strangers into a functioning community in competition with other communities while forging solid links to broader regional and national wholes."[4] Regional newspapers published before 1900 reveal how midwestern political culture emerged out of the imperative to build communities. As white settlers carved out farms, neighborhoods, and towns, they created more than just a new physical landscape. Midwestern political culture emerged out of a particular historical moment in which the process of settlement infused religious, ethnic, and gendered values with civic identity. In transforming a physical landscape, Midwesterners created a political culture that relied on religion, ethnicity, and gender to inform it. The specific confluence of these distinctions defined local communities.

The trio of stories in the *Spencer Reporter* outline how religious ideals, ethnic identities, and gendered notions created midwestern political culture. According to the Board of Supervisor's minutes, six male supervisors met in the county auditor's office on April 7 to discuss county business. James G. Dodd was the chairman of the Board of Supervisors. Born in Indiana to a mother from Ohio, Dodd was a Civil War veteran who had served in Company I, Iowa Second Calvary Regiment. By 1880, he was farming with his wife Elizabeth, born in New York, and their four children near Douglas in Clay County.[5] Serving with Dodd as supervisors were J.W. Fairbanks, James Goodwin, John P. Mills, and Theodore P. Bender.[6] All four of Dodd's colleagues were from states in the East, with Fairbanks from Massachusetts, Goodwin from Ohio, and Mills and Bender from Pennsylvania. Goodwin and Mills were farmers while Bender bought and sold livestock for a living.[7] The final member of the group was Henry B. Wood, a New Yorker by birth and lawyer by training, who was the county auditor.[8] The six men who composed the Board of Supervisors were ethnic Yankees, distinguished for their Protestant religious beliefs, ties to the Northeast, Anglo-Saxon heritage, and middle-class backgrounds. Yankees were often the first white settlers to move to the region after the Civil War, and they wholeheartedly supported communal institutions, volunteering countless hours in support of civic initiatives. Yankees celebrated civic pride, believing their vision for community righteous and moral. In turn, they cultivated high expectations for political engagement, particularly at the local level. Across the Midwest, Yankees like the six members of the Clay County Board of Supervisors were ubiquitous in matters of local governance.[9]

The meeting minutes reveal a county in the throes of settlement. The first five orders of business related to negotiating the appointment of public officials and the rates at which the county levied taxes. The minutes indicated that the settlement process in Clay County was far from over, as the Board approved both the resignation and appointment of public officials—a justice of the peace and constable, respectively—and agreed to investigate the "matter of refunds and rebates of taxes where there is any question as to the legality of the same."[10] Settlement was neither static nor brief, and negotiation marked the long-term efforts at local governance. Cooperation was also key when it came to infrastructure development, a top priority for local midwestern officials. Vast distances and poor transportation networks especially plagued Midwesterners. To that point, about half of the remaining motions considered by the Board of Supervisors dealt with roads and bridges. One motion came from George Runyan, a farmer and a fellow Yankee born in New York.[11] Runyan sought redress for damages sustained when officials took "earth, dirt, and gravel from his land to fix the highway west from the grade south of the Spencer bridge."[12] Another motion considered vacating a road "running in a zig zag or crooked course."[13] Two more motions revealed that the Board of Supervisors had taken bids to construct bridges in the county. Bridge construction and road maintenance were issues frequently discussed by officials. Iowa was known for its roads that were "as deep as they were wide."[14] By the 1880s, Iowans, like most Midwesterners, agitated for improvements, but roads remained a local concern until the early twentieth century. Grading, tiling, draining, and surfacing roads was a high cost born by taxpayers and carried out by locals at the expense of their time and equipment.[15]

While Yankees engaged in extensive infrastructure development during settlement, they spent even more time building institutions. Yankees believed wholeheartedly in civic engagement, and they fostered a strong commitment to shared communal institutions. Schools, churches, and other public places provided physical structures to hold the myriad community activities that Yankees agreed all Midwesterners should pursue.[16] These activities were collective and included farmers' associations, fraternal organizations, and a host of social, religious, and civic groups. Scholars Tom W. Rice and Marshall Arnett argue that in the 1880s, Midwesterners who engaged in building communal institutions were fostering above-average levels of social capital. These ethnic white Yankees labored and suffered, shared and celebrated together.[17] They were joiners who fostered personal connections that made for vibrant social cohesion.

While Yankee values profoundly shaped the Midwest, so too did the values of immigrants. European immigrants flooded the region after the Civil War, usually claiming land for farming and settling in rural enclaves. Most of these immigrants were Scandinavians and Germans, but in some places, other ethnic groups, like Czechs, Poles, or Belgians, to name only a few, held a majority.[18] The percentages of these groups varied across the region and fluctuated over time. In Clay County, less than 20 percent of the population was foreign-born, but in some townships, the percentage was much higher. Small enclaves of Germans, Danes, Swedes, and Norwegians had appeared in the County by 1890.[19] Like Yankees, immigrants sought to build communities in the Midwest, but they differed in how they understood community. For most immigrants, their first priority was to maintain their ethnic and religious identities. As a result, they avoided Yankee designs on the Midwest and often formed their own schools, churches, and public places. The ethnic tensions that brewed between Yankees and immigrants profoundly shaped midwestern political culture. Bonded together, yet indelibly split, these groups grew to live together in both conflict and cooperation.[20]

Even though Midwesterners understood civic engagement in many different ways, they unanimously prioritized infrastructure development. In doing so, they could relieve tensions and build some trust.[21] After roads and bridges often came schools and churches. They served significant social functions, bringing people together regularly and fostering order among newcomers.[22] For Yankees, schools and churches were twin pillars of morality. For immigrants, public and parochial schools promised a better life through education while churches served as the center of enclave activities.[23] Midwesterners often either raised funds to purchase or donated lands for churches, libraries, and other community structures. Since the 1790s, land survey legislation had set aside section 16 and, by about 1850, section 36 for school lands.[24] In April 1884, the Clay County Board of Supervisors signaled its support for schools as it considered two motions to sell school lands. In both cases, there were no bidders. The next motion tabled the matter until the June 1884 meeting.[25]

Of all the motions before the Board of Supervisors, the one requesting a permit to sell alcohol showcases the intricacies of midwestern political culture. David Painter, a druggist and native Iowan, made his second appearance before the Board and received a permit to "sell intoxicating liquors for medicinal, mechanical, sacramental and culinary purposes ... for one year."[26] The members of the Board had made Painter jump through a number of legal hoops to obtain the permit. He had to pay a bond, wait for Wood, the county auditor, to give "due and legal notice" to the public, and respond to any potential objections.[27]

Some time had passed since Painter first had approached the Board, but the minutes still reflect a strong sense of reluctance. That he could sell "intoxicating liquors" for a narrow set of purposes and only for a year was telling.[28] Painter faced resistance because he sought to sell alcohol in a predominantly Yankee county where most residents abstained from it.

Temperance was the most significant political issue in the Midwest in the late-nineteenth century. The health problems that came with inebriation were one thing. The threat to democracy drunkenness posed was another. For many Midwesterners, especially Yankees, sobriety was key to community development. Engaging in civic matters required a commitment to order, reason, and morality, so Yankees often endorsed prohibition as a matter of civic virtue. It put them in stark contrast with most immigrants, who considered alcohol consumption part of their cultural values. Temperance was a community decision because of local option laws in the Midwest, making it a volatile issue. Whether a town or county was wet or dry depended on the dominant ethnic, religious, and gendered values of the community. Individuals did not consider controversial matters like temperance solely on their political merits. Their politics stemmed directly from their identities, which made anticipating stances easy and changing minds nearly impossible. In the case of temperance, the ethnic and religious diversity of the Midwest meant that alcohol regulations varied tremendously. They were often strikingly different among towns in the same county and among counties in the same state. More often than not, they followed the ethnic and religious composition of the residents who lived there. Debates about proposed temperance legislation were therefore extended ethnic and religious fights. They were deeply personal and overtly political.[29]

The war over temperance had waged for years in Clay County by the time Painter applied for his permit. The settlement process kept temperance a hot-button issue as newcomers formed factions that battled for control of local governance. When a pro-saloon candidate became the mayor in 1881, pro-temperance factions fought back. They helped bury his campaign in 1883 when he lost as the incumbent in the race.[30] Pro-temperance Yankees maintained control of the county government, making it a surprise that Painter received his permit when he did. In addition, by 1884, Clay County had a robust chapter of the WCTU. In fact, directly above the Board of Supervisor's meeting minutes was a full report of the activities of the Clay County WCTU.[31] The WCTU was a hallmark of midwestern political culture. The first national WCTU convention occurred in 1874 in Ohio. The second president, Frances Willard, hailed from Wisconsin. By 1890, the WCTU was the biggest women's organization in the world. The WCTU agitated for a number of reforms, including sanitation, peace, health, and labor.[32] Among midwestern Yankee women, the WCTU was extremely popular. Yankee women often understood their temperance activism as intimately entwined with their ethnic identities and cultural values. Building the institutions that composed communities required the civic and moral vision that the WCTU espoused.

While the WCTU was popular in the Midwest, not every county had a WCTU as well organized as the one in Clay County. There were chapters at Spencer, Peterson, Greenville, Annieville, Pleasant Valley, and Barlow in addition to the Clay County union. In total, the WCTU held thirty-two mass meetings or lectures in the span of six months. They raised nineteen dollars at one social alone "for the purpose to carry on the temperance work in the county."[33] The secretary of the WCTU, Eva Gilchrist, added that subscriptions to the WCTU's official publication, *The Union Signal*, were up. Gilchrist had come to Iowa from Michigan. She was a Yankee, and her mother, Martha Janes, was the first female ordained minister in the Free Baptist church and an ardent temperance supporter and suffragist.[34] The religious, ethnic, and gender identities that converged in the Clay County WCTU reveal how midwestern political culture developed. Yankees joined collectively to build civic institutions that perpetuated a moral vision of the Midwest that often did not include immigrant cultural values. Their belief in civic engagement created a political landscape in which a narrowly defined Yankee standard of participation was paramount.

All Midwesterners enjoyed a robust social landscape into which people readily infused politics. Community institutions produced frequent opportunities for social connection. Community building not only included the creation of physical spaces but also the construction of the relationships that defined them. The final article in the *Spencer Reporter*, the "Personal Mentions" section, revealed the character of those relationships. It listed an assortment of local news, especially gossip, that kept readers up-to-date about the intimate lives of local residents. Articles like this one had many names, including "Local and Personal," "Around Home," and "Home and Family."[35] The information contained in this section reveals the familiarity with which Midwesterners understood each other. The "Personal Mentions" article, to the left of the meeting minutes of the Board of Supervisors, noted the visitors to Clay County. Some "put in a few days here" on business, like O.C. Ainsworth, a "well-known real estate man," while others, such as Dr. L.M. Van Buren "and lady" traveled to visit friends. Dr. Van Buren and "his lady," whom the editor of the *Spencer Reporter* never named, had been "spending the winter visiting among their old friends, who were very numerous."[36] That the staff of the *Spencer Reporter* kept close tabs on the visitors to Clay County and reported a striking number of details about them was not surprising. Most midwestern newspapers did so, which demonstrates that private travel plans were public business.

Other news contained in the "Personal Mentions" section reveals the nature of the midwestern social landscape. From intimate to mundane, the tidbits of gossip collected and shared on the pages of midwestern newspapers created complex patterns of sociability. Publicizing the trivial was a privilege midwestern newspapers did not afford all residents. Newsworthy items encountered silence when editors considered an individual's gender, ethnic, class, or racial identities inferior. Two examples from the *Spencer Reporter* showcase the nature of sociability. One local man called only "Mr. Miller" drove "quite a large herd of cattle through town this morning which he bought up in Minnesota."[37] Driving cattle was a routine affair, but the editors clearly believed it merited the "Personal Mention" column. "Mr. Miller" was undoubtedly well-known and privileged enough in the community that only a casual note was necessary for readers to recognize him. Other gossip included an item about Nellie McKay, "sister to Mrs. W.T. Bowen, of this city" who had "the misfortune to have her right wrist broken while skating at the new rink at Sanborn."[38] The *Spencer Reporter* did not indicate if Nellie was staying with Eva Bowen, her unnamed sister, or what course of action she had taken to address her injury. What the short piece revealed was how a detail about kinship brought attention to a girl with a broken wrist.

In both cases, the actual brief and the news it contained was less important than the fact of its inclusion. These bits of local gossip reinforced community identity through shared social experiences. They affirmed the privileged position that the Miller and Bowen families occupied. While Miller's common surname and lack of identifying details made him difficult identify, W.T. Bowen and Eva were Yankees.[39] Their inclusion confirmed the frequent and public role Yankees played in midwestern communities. More importantly, the prominence of the "Personal Mentions" column and its location next to the WCTU report and the meeting minutes of the Board of Supervisors also reveals how Midwesterners easily overlapped their political and social lives.[40] Readers of the *Spencer Reporter* could read about politics and gossip on the same page, revealing how effortlessly social connections shifted into politics. It was easy to form political convictions out of religious, ethnic, and gendered identities when they were the means by which Midwesterners came to distinguish themselves before 1900.

Midwestern political culture grew out of the political and social networks that developed as white Yankees and foreign-born immigrants settled the Midwest. The civic engagement that Yankees embraced encouraged people to become active citizens in political affairs. Immigrants also prioritized institution-building, but they did so while maintaining specific religious, ethnic, and gender identities. Civic participation became both the means to community development and the signal of belonging, the element that became the heartbeat of midwestern political culture. An appearance in a midwestern newspaper was one sign that a resident belonged to a community. It was both public and symbolic recognition of an individual's or group's personal and political connections to the institutions that defined the particular locale. Like the trio of articles in the *Spencer Reporter* indicated, therefore, belonging made midwestern political culture relational in that residents contributed as members of families, political organizations, or other associations.[41]

Settling the region and establishing a political culture was a fraught and contested process that many times silenced those who resisted Yankee visions of community. Some ethnic groups rebuffed pressure to assimilate and received scant attention in midwestern newspapers or county histories edited by Yankees. There was little mention in the *Spencer Reporter* about the German, Danish, Swedish, and Norwegian immigrants who by 1890 composed approximately 10 percent of the population of Clay County.[42] When they appeared, as they did in the *Spencer Reporter* in January 1886, it was to praise them for acting like Yankees. The editor commended local Swedes and Norwegians for building "well kept [sic.] farms, [with] their great big barns, grain stacks without number, large yards full of fat hogs and fine cattle."[43] He could not resist pointing out, however, that these Scandinavians were Lutherans who practiced "bundling," a "performance" in which engaged couples went to bed together on Sunday nights. The Yankee writer assured readers that "honor and modesty" are kept "spotless," and he noted that among Scandinavians, "illegitimate children are hardly known where this custom prevails."[44] But his assurances of morality revealed that Yankee ideas about belonging were fragile illusions. Settling the Midwest required pragmatic decisions to boost economic and infrastructure development by welcoming immigrants, but it also fostered ethnic diversity that made Yankees uneasy. Finally, Indigenous peoples appeared infrequently in sources about midwestern political culture. As Susan E. Gray argues, the "discursive technique for disappearing Indigenous people proved as effective as forcible bodily removal," one that saw Native Americans as irrelevant to the "business of white settlement after 1815."[45]

Belonging through civic engagement was paramount to Yankees, which is why they cultivated an impressive number of groups dedicated to community matters. These societies primarily emerged at the axis of religion, ethnicity, and gender. Women played an outsized role in midwestern political culture because the Yankee impulse for civic engagement encouraged gender inclusivity. Women often worked for community initiatives from within collective organizations segregated by gender, but by pursuing civic goals, they took on public leadership roles. Midwestern newspapers abounded with the civic work women undertook. The prominent placement of the WCTU in the *Spencer Reporter* showcases one such example. This group of female Protestant Yankees dedicated themselves to moral uplift through reform, and they gained influence through their work. Martha Janes, Eva Gilchrist's Yankee mother and a Free Baptist pastor, became the Clay County WCTU president in June 1884, and shortly thereafter she secured a front-page column in the *Clay County News*, another local newspaper. While the column existed for only a few months, she used it to champion both temperance and women's suffrage. She also articulated the Yankee vision of civic engagement as she defined the parameters of their work. Members of the WCTU were "responsible individuals" who characterized their community activism in promotion of temperance as necessary to "protect the home."[46] In addition to their advocacy for temperance, the Clay County WCTU passed resolutions in favor of woman suffrage.[47]

Alongside the WCTU, federated women's clubs also engaged actively in civic matters in the Midwest. The club movement emerged nationally in the 1860s among professional women. The structure encouraged exclusivity, and most women's clubs were small, composed of elite, educated women. In the Midwest, middle-class and educated Yankees typically joined the local federated women's club. These clubs offered "intellectual stimulation" and opportunities for "upward mobility."[48] On the surface, members studied various topics and presented the results of their research to each other. But clubs allowed women to become political actors as they learned about parliamentary procedure, public speaking, and fundraising.[49] Before 1900 in counties across the Midwest, federated women's clubs formed with a vision of civic activism. The Spencer Woman's Club, a group of "strong-minded women with a look toward the future," began meeting in 1894.[50] It joined the General Federation of Women's Clubs in 1896, and the following year the club formed a Village Improvement Committee. Local newspapers soon reported regularly on their activities. The Spencer Woman's Club built a public restroom for visitors to the county seat. They carried out a beautification program, planting trees and flowers at government buildings. They purchased an abandoned lot and turned it into the first public park. Eventually, they started the first garbage collection service and birth registration program in Clay County.[51]

Midwestern women in church organizations also engaged regularly in politics. Ladies' aid societies and female mission societies were fundamental to the growth of churches in the region. As the primary fundraisers, these groups raised huge sums to construct churches. Records from across the Midwest attest to the financial power women amassed by selling goods at bazaars, socials, and suppers. Female church organizations advertised often in midwestern newspapers, and invitations to these gatherings appeared frequently in columns like the "Personal Mentions" one. Ladies' aid societies purchased organs, furnaces, curtains, and pulpits, leaving parishioners with tangible evidence of their righteous devotion to their religious communities.[52] Politics often occurred in these lovingly adorned buildings, especially in Congregational and Methodist Churches composed mostly of Yankees. For example, in 1875, the members of the First Congregational Church's Ladies' Aid Society in Spencer held a bazaar to support a new church building. It is unclear how much they raised, but the First Congregational Church constructed its new church the following year and the bazaar became an annual affair. Political leaders regularly used the building for meetings. The Ladies' Aid Society was especially proud to host a number of pro-suffrage lecturers in this space.[53]

Midwesterners created a vibrant political culture by 1900. Settlement brought Yankees with a vision of community life that venerated participation. Civic engagement was paramount to them, and they struggled with people who sought to defy their designs for community. Diverse individuals participated in local affairs because of the imperative to construct infrastructures and institutions. Building communities rooted midwestern politics in place, and contributing to civic initiatives signaled belonging. Belonging was a powerful but disputed idea. Yankee collective associations composed of women, including the WCTU, federated women's clubs, and church organizations, played essential roles in forming midwestern political culture. The Yankee zeal for civic engagement encouraged gender inclusivity in remarkable ways. It also played out in a diverse cultural landscape in which residents approached politics from their religious, ethnic, and gendered identities. These factors made belonging both the most essential and contested element that defined midwestern political culture.

Notes

1. "County Legislation—Proceedings of the Board of Supervisors of Clay County at their April, 1884, Meeting," *Spencer Reporter,* 17 April 1884.
2. Kathleen Neils Conzen, "Pi-ing the Type: Jane Grey Swisshelm and the Contest of Midwestern Regionality," in Andrew R.L. Cayton and Susan E. Gray, eds., *The Identity of the American Midwest: Essays on Regional History* (Bloomington: Indiana University Press, 2001), 93.
3. Ibid.
4. Ibid.
5. James G. Dobb, 1880 United States Federal Census, Douglas, Clay County, Iowa, page 262C, Roll 333, Ancestry.com (Provo, UT: Ancestry.com

2013); Enrollment of Ex-Soldiers and Sailors, their Widows and Orphans, 1889, Records of the Adjutant General's Office, Kansas State Historical Society, Topeka, Kansas, *Kansas: Enrollment of Civil War Veterans, 1889*, Ancestry.com (Provo, UT: Ancestry.com, 2013).
6. J.W. Fairbanks, Microfilm of Iowa State Censuses, 1885, State Historical Society of Iowa, Ancestry.com (Provo: UT, Ancestry.com, 2007); John P. Mills, 1880 United States Federal Census, Gilletts Grove, Clay County, Iowa, page 222B, Roll 333, Ancestry (Provo, UT: Ancestry.com, 2010); Theodore Bender, 1880 United States Federal Census, Spencer, Clay County, Iowa, page 226C, roll 333, Ancestry.com (Provo, UT: Ancestry.com, 2010); James Goodwin, 1880 United States Federal Census, Summit, Clay County, Iowa, page 242A, roll 333, Ancestry.com (Provo, UT: Ancestry.com, 2010).
7. Ibid.
8. Henry B. Wood, United States Federal Census, Spencer, Clay County, Iowa, page 225A, roll 333, Ancestry.com (Provo, UT: Ancestry.com, 2010).
9. Susan E. Gray, *The Yankee West: Community Life on the Michigan Frontier* (Chapel Hill: University of North Carolina Press, 1996), 2–6.
10. "County Legislation," *Spencer Reporter*, 17 April 1884.
11. George Runyan, 1880 United States Federal Census, Spencer, Clay County, Iowa, page 228D, roll 333, Ancestry.com (Provo, UT: Ancestry.com, 2010).
12. "County Legislation," *Spencer Reporter*, 17 April 1884.
13. Ibid.
14. William H. Thompson, *Transportation in Iowa: A Historical Summary* ([Des Moines]: Iowa Department of Transportation, 1989), 69–72.
15. Ibid., 70.
16. Gray, *The Yankee West*, 2–6, 12; Richard Lyle Power, *Planting Corn Belt Culture: The Impress of the Upland Southerner and Yankee in the Old Northwest*, (Indianapolis: Indiana Historical Society, 1953), 6; William Labov, *Principles of Linguistic Change: Cognitive and Cultural Factors* 3 (2010), 216–18.
17. Tom W. Rice and Marshall Arnett, "Civic Culture and Socioeconomic Development in the United States: A View from the States, 1880s–1990s," *Social Science Journal* 38 (2001): 42–46; Andrew R.L. Cayton, Christian Zacher, and Richard Sisson, eds., *The American Midwest: An Interpretive Encyclopedia* (Bloomington: University of Indiana Press, 2006), 1724–26.
18. Robert P. Swierenga, "The Settlement of the Old Northwest: Ethnic Pluralism in a Feature-less Plain," *Journal of the Early Republic* 9 (Spring 1989): 73–105; 76–79; Andrew R.L. Cayton and Susan E. Gray, "The Story of the Midwest: An Introduction," *The Identity of the American Midwest*, 15; Frederick C. Luebke, "Ethnic Group Settlement on the Great Plains," *Western Historical Quarterly* 8 (October 1977): 412, 417, 427–28; Andrew R.L. Cayton and Peter Onuf, *The Midwest and the Nation: Rethinking the History of an American Region* (Bloomington: Indianan University Press,

1990), 27; John C. Hudson, "Migration to an American Frontier," *Annals of the Association of American Geographers* 66 (June 1976): 258.
19. Clay County, Iowa, "County-Level Results for 1890," Historical Census Browser, University of Virginia Library, http://mapserver.lib.virginia.edu/php/county.php.
20. Cayton and Gray, "The Story of the Midwest," 3; John Radzilowski, *Prairie Town: A History of Marshall, Minnesota* (Marshall, MN: Lyon County Historical Society, 1997), 116–17; Robert D. Putnam, Lewis M. Feldstein, and Don Cohen, *Better Together: Restoring the American Community* (New York: Simon and Schuster, 2003), 1–10.
21. Kenneth J. Arrow, "Gifts and Exchanges," *Philosophy and Public Affairs* 1 (Summer 1972): 357–62.
22. Thomas J. Morain, *Prairie Grass Roots: An Iowa Small Town in the Early Twentieth Century* (Ames: Iowa State University Press, 1988), 13–14.
23. Jon K. Lauck, *Prairie Republic: The Political Culture of Dakota Territory, 1879–1889* (Norman: University of Oklahoma Press, 2010), 60; Karl B. Raitz, "Ethnic Maps of North America," *Geographical Review* 68 (July 1978): 346; Robert P. Swierenga, "The Little White Church: Religion in Rural America," *Agricultural History* 71 (Autumn 1997): 417; Cayton and Onuf, *The Midwest and the Nation*, 49.
24. C. Albert White, *A History of the Rectangular Survey System* (Washington, DC: Bureau of Land Management, United States Department of the Interior, 1991), 110–12.
25. "County Legislation," *Spencer Reporter*, 17 April 1884.
26. Ibid.; David Painter, 1880 United States Federal Census, Spencer, Clay County, Iowa, page 225B, roll 333, Ancestry.com (Provo, UT: Ancestry.com, 2010).
27. Ibid.
28. Ibid.
29. Eileen L. McDonagh and H. Douglas Price, "Woman Suffrage in the Progressive Era: Patterns of Opposition and Support in Referenda Voting, 1910–1918," *The American Political Science Review* 79 (June 1985): 415 35; Samuel Gillespie and James E. Steele, *History of Clay County, Iowa from Its Earliest Settlements to 1909, Also Biographical Sketches of Many Prominent Citizens of the County as Well as Its Illustrious Dead* (Chicago: S.J. Clarke, 1909), 95; Cayton and Onuf, *The Midwest and the Nation*, 61, 88.
30. Gillespie and Steele, *History of Clay County*, 95.
31. "The following is a report of the Clay county Women's Christian Temperance Union," *Spencer Reporter*, 17 April 1884.
32. Genevieve G. McBride, *On Wisconsin Women: Working for Their Rights from Settlement to Suffrage* (Madison: University of Wisconsin Press, 1993), 80–93.
33. "The following is a report of the Clay county Women's Christian Temperance Union," *Spencer Reporter*, 17 April 1884.

34. "Mary Simmerson Cunningham Logan and John A. Logan, *The Part Taken by Women in American History* (Wilmington, DE: Perry-Nalle, 1912), 736; Frances E. Willard and Mary A. Livermore, eds., *A Woman of the Century: Fourteen Hundred-Seventy Biographical Sketches Accompanied by Portraits of Leading American Women in All Walks of Life* (Chicago: Charles Wells Moulton, 1893), 417; Gillespie and Steele, *History of Clay County*, 95; Marriage of Eva Sober to Malcolm M. Gilchrist, Film Number 141034, Ancestry.com, Iowa, Select Marriages Index, 1758–1996 (Provo, UT: Ancestry.com, 2014).
35. See, for examples of these articles, the "Home and Family" column in the *Spencer News-Herald* (Clay County, Iowa), the "Local and Personal" column in the *Press and Dakotan* (Yankton County, South Dakota), and the "Around Home" column of the *Lyon County Reporter* (Lyon County, Minnesota).
36. "Personal Mentions," *Spencer Reporter,* 17 April 1884.
37. Ibid.
38. "Personal Mentions," *Spencer Reporter,* 17 April 1884; W.T. Bowen, 1880 United States Federal Census, Lincoln, Winneshiek, Iowa, page 176C, roll 370, Ancestry.com (Provo, UT: Ancestry.com, 2010).
39. W.T. Bowen, 1880 United States Federal Census, Lincoln, Winneshiek, Iowa, page 176C, roll 370, Ancestry.com (Provo, UT: Ancestry.com, 2010).
40. Thomas Bender, *Community and Social Change in America* (New Brunswick, NJ: Rutgers University Press, 1978), 5–7; Kenneth P. Wilkinson, *The Community in Rural America* (New York: Greenwood, 1991), 2; Orville Vernon Burton, "Reaping What We Sow: Community and Rural History," *Agricultural History* 76 (Autumn 2002): 645.
41. Cayton and Onuf, *The Midwest and the Nation,* 55–56, 68–75, 85.
42. Clay County, Iowa, "County-Level Results for 1890," Historical Census Browser, University of Virginia Library, http://mapserver.lib.virginia.edu/php/county.php.
43. Ibid.
44. Ibid.
45. Susan E. Gray, "Native Americans and Midwestern History," in Jon K. Lauck, Gleaves Whitney, and Joseph Hogan, eds., *Finding a New Midwestern History* (Lincoln: University of Nebraska Press, 2018), 56.
46. "Is Woman's Ballot Necessary?" *Clay County News,* 19 June 1884; ["The following is a report ..."], *Clay County News,* 17 April 1884; "Minutes of the Second Annual Convention of the Clay County Women's Christian Temperance Union," *Clay County News,* 5 June 1884; "County Convention," *Clay County News,* 12 June 1884; ["The W.C.T.U. will meet ..."], *Clay County News,* 18 January 1884; Gillespie and Steele, *History of Clay County*, 95.
47. "The Ladies of Spencer," *Clay County News,* 11 January 1884.

48. Sara M. Evans, *Born for Liberty: A History of Women in America* (New York: Free Press, 1989), 139–40.
50. "History of Spencer Federated Woman's Club," loose paper in Spencer Woman's Club Minute Book, 1894–1901, Spencer Woman's Club Collection, Clay County Heritage Center, Spencer, Iowa.
51. "History of Spencer Federated Woman's Club," loose paper in Spencer Woman's Club Minute Book, 1894–1901, Spencer Woman's Club Collection, Clay County Heritage Center; Spencer Woman's Club Minute Book, 1894–1901, 10, 79; Spencer Woman's Club Scrapbook, 2, Spencer Woman's Club Collection, Clay County Heritage Center; Gillespie and Steele, *History of Clay County*, 175; "Spencer Woman's Club, Minute Book 1910–1915, Spencer Woman's Club Collection, Clay County Heritage Center; "Free Exhibition," *Spencer Herald*, 24 January 1912; "Farmers' Institute," *Spencer Herald*, 7 February 1912; "Garbage," *Spencer Herald*, 8 July 1914; "City Council Passes Garbage Ordinance," *Spencer News-Herald*, 22 March 1916; "What About Your Garbage?" *Spencer News-Herald*, 3 May 1916; "Birth Registration," *Spencer News*, 24 March 1914.
52. Patricia Bizzell, "Frances E. Willard, Phoebe Palmer, and the Ethos of the Methodist Woman Preacher," *Rhetoric Society Quarterly* 36 (Autumn 2006): 377–84; Judith Meyer, "Ethnicity, Theology, and Immigrant Church Expansion," *Geographical Review* 65 (April 1975): 180–92.
53. "First Congregational Church Spencer, Iowa," folder 5, box 1, Church History Collection, Clay County Heritage Society; Gillespie and Steele, *History of Clay County*, 196; "Suffragette Here Sunday," *Spencer News-Herald*, 12 April 1916; "Clay County Women Organize Suff Club," *Spencer News-Herald*, 19 April 1916.

Lisa Payne Ossian | The "I Too" Temperance Movement

A Reevaluation of Midwestern Women's Political Action at the Turn of the Last Century

"I am woman, hear me roar
In numbers too big to ignore"
—Helen Reddy, "I Am Woman" (1972)

Mrs. Albert G. Ossian, president of a local Women's Christian Temperance Union, delivered a short talk at the annual reception for the school faculty in Stanton, Iowa, on November 7, 1929. Mrs. Ossian (or Bessie) welcomed the teachers and explained the "Scientific Temperance Instruction" that the WCTU followed for school essay and poster contests. Another WCTU member, Mrs. Marie Ossian, then served the two-course luncheon. Three teenagers from the young people's branch (Misses Elva, Florence, and Marveline) passed the plates while the forty-five members of this local chapter entertained their guests with renditions of pop songs.

Thus continued a long tradition of local, state, and national participation of the WCTU in 1929, almost a decade since the passage of the Eighteenth Amendment. Prohibition voices continued to support their cause in a variety of community social events as well as public speeches and political debates during the next three years, but the trend of the temperance tide was turning terribly quickly after the stock market crash, more than Mrs. Ossian or any other Prohibition leader could have imagined.[1]

In 1930 this author's step-great-grandmother (Mrs. Albert Ossian) and other local residents still deeply believed in the Eighteenth Amendment, that Prohibition would continue until certainly their grandchildren or great-grandchildren came of age. Yet three years into the thirties this delightful promise or dreadful experiment suddenly ended with the ratification of the Twenty-first Amendment. In 1920 repeal had not seemed probable much less possible. An amendment to the Constitution of the United States implied constancy; no amendment had ever faced repeal consideration.

I began an essay about Prohibition's demise in *The Depression Dilemmas of Iowa, 1929–1933* with this scenario, but near publication, I received a phone call from another of Bessie's great-granddaughters, who had read my article within *The Social History of Alcohol and Drugs* and asked if I would like a copy of Bessie's memoir. Of course.

As Bessie Norling Anderson Ossian would confess in her fifteen-page memoir titled "The Autobiography of Betty 'Bessie' Norling, Wife of Axel Victor Anderson and Albert G. Ossian," her midwestern childhood was never ideal. Within the Christian Orphans' Home records, she recalls that the four Norling children were admitted on July 14, 1894, because their mother had died and their father was "a drunkard." "We heard later that he had written for us," Bessie added a poignant note, "but the Home Board found that he still drank so did not let us go to him. No doubt he didn't care a lot, or he would have made a man of himself. I could never really forgive him as I often felt it was because of his drink that Mother went to an early grave." Bessie then stated her vow: "I still have a horror for a drinking man. I never would consider keeping company with any man who liked liquor. And the two I married were sober in that respect."

Upon reading Bessie's words, my previous evaluation of her as a rather moralistic woman imposing the temperance curriculum on local teachers changed dramatically. I now envisioned her as a young girl, deeply hurting from her alcoholic father's abandonment, and as a grown woman, sincerely promising to only marry a non-drinking man. I too have been hurt, she seemed to say to other WCTU members, by a father's neglect due to alcohol. Therefore, I believe a reexamination is needed of midwestern women's protests within the temperance movement, the first and largest wave of women's political representation in this country.

The WCTU of Iowa had organized in November 1874, the same month as the national organization, and continued with strong membership numbers for each year until the 1930s. The union described its methods as evangelistic, educational, preventative, social, and legal. The members promoted abstinence of all alcohol with various watchwords such as *agitate, educate,* and *organize* along with inspirations of love, loyalty, and light. And the dues remained a dollar a year with a badge of knotted white ribbon as membership symbol; the union listed 60,000 Iowa women as paid members. Its official publication became *The Iowa Champion,* its songbook gleaned from The Loyal Temperance Legion, and its current motto rang with the phrase, "The Eighteenth Amendment forever!"[2]

In Iowa and Kansas (the two strongest Prohibition states following Maine), the dilemma of prohibition did not easily resolve itself. Many devoted activists and rather average citizens continued their cause with a combination of social, moral, or economic reasoning. Some of the energy, organization, funding, and passion had perhaps declined since 1920 while fears were only increasing that neither the legal nor social benefits of Prohibition would be revealed. Still, we great-grandchildren should remember that the consumption of liquor and other intoxicating beverages had decreased during the years of Prohibition and after. As historian K. Austin Kerr reminds readers in her history of the Anti-Saloon League, "The conventional wisdom overlooks one simple yet highly significant fact: prohibition worked."[3]

Although the temperance movement at the turn of the last century has been typically viewed as a failed moralistic experiment, midwestern women created the largest women's political movement, passing two Constitutional amendments aimed at increasing women's political representation and decreasing men's domestic violence. Midwestern women, in numbers too big to ignore, publicly announced accounts of male violence and neglect due to alcohol as they formed an original "I Too" movement of the last century. But as theorist Catherine Murdock points out in her book titled *Domesticating Drink*, "Temperance has not merited the same concern for historians of gender as other reforms."[4]

"Perhaps because of my roots in a rural, poor community," as Carol Mattingly, another gender historian, explains her interest in temperance women's rhetoric, "I find it easy to understand and appreciate temperance women. I do not see them as conservative and complicit in their own oppression, charges often leveled against them. Instead, temperance women seem much like women I knew during childhood—strong, sensible women who recognized the real circumstances of their existence and strove, pragmatically, to improve life for themselves and for others."[5]

Temperance women presented their rhetorical arguments consistently and familiarly to ever-increasing audiences. Improving family and nation remained their overall goal.

This perspective, however, has not been reflected but severely distorted in the common lore. The textbook history of Prohibition examines the story from a northern, urban, youthful male perspective. But for older midwestern rural women, the Prohibition era could not strut with a boastful tale of pushing the envelope and breaking the rules, or proclaim a proud pronouncement of personal liberty and dodging daring criminals, nor look back with a wistful nostalgia of glamorous speakeasies and slippery moonshiners. From an older midwestern woman's point of view, the personalities, issues, and events of Prohibition become necessarily more poignant, even tragic. Yes, midwestern women could embody the trailblazer spirit with its independent, adventurous streak, but the story of temperance certainly demanded a strong work ethic and community relatedness, also pioneering qualities.

Religion and immigration should also be reexamined during the temperance era. Immigrants from Norway and Sweden settled eagerly in the Midwest to purchase farmland, but many Scandinavians also fled rampant rates of alcoholism, leaving countries that would eventually enact strong prohibition laws. Nordic culture and Lutheranism had not cultivated fond memories of a drinking culture, such as the memories of Germans, Irish, and Italians of beer gardens, whiskey wakes, or wine dinners. And during the Great War, German American culture, particularly midwestern brewers, received a virulent backlash. All things German—especially beer—could not be tolerated during wartime's patriotic rationing of food. Sacrificing Americans, those proud patriots partaking in "Wheatless Wednesdays," would leave no room for grain to be utilized in alcoholic brewing or distilling.

The era, the issues, and the geography of temperance present many layers, not simple dualities of either/or nor right/wrong. One should not dismiss the Midwest as prim and proper but rather Midwesterners embraced complex family- and community-minded ideals with traditional religious commitments. By 1910, over 50 percent of Americans still lived on farms or in communities under two thousand residents. Some Midwesterners did defy "dry" expectations, such as German Catholic immigrants in Carroll County, Iowa, who would never be persuaded of state or national prohibition. But in most Midwest regions, the "wets" were certainly outnumbered by the "drys," the Methodists, Lutherans, and Baptists.[6]

To succinctly examine congressional districts over the last century reveals our nation's massive population and corresponding political shift. In 1910 Iowa had eleven congressional districts as did California. Kansas had eight districts. In other words, Iowa and Kansas possessed twenty-three electoral votes in 1910 compared to California's thirteen. Today, however, Iowa and Kansas claim only four congressional districts for a total of twelve electoral votes while California has fifty-five electoral votes. The political balance has certainly shifted further west. No longer do midwestern votes and numbers roar.

This "common lore" of Prohibition focuses on the urban northwest and portrays New York City, despite its urban diversity, as representative of the entire United States. "Whether in the form of buying bootleg liquor, drinking in nightclubs, or supporting political efforts to undermine the reach of the dry law," contends Michael Lerner in *Dry Manhattan*, "Americans in many parts of the United States vigorously resisted Prohibition, their rebellion against the Eighteenth Amendment growing more pronounced as the years went by."[7] Lerner's argument lacks regional or gender analysis. Prohibition could and did work for many Americans as they accepted local laws and the Constitution. "Though it failed as social policy," he insists, "Prohibition has fascinated Americans for generations, especially in the realm of popular culture. The flappers, jazz, speakeasies, and gangsters of the era." Lerner only imagines "The Dry Crusade" as an ugly, controlling group while many contemporaries saw it as a mission, a religiously motivated journey, "a Noble Experiment."[8]

Common lore believes Prohibition was suddenly pulled on Americans by a small but determined group of rural Midwesterners. Temperance was not a suddenly created movement but existed in three waves: the first wave from Maine's prohibition law in 1846 until 1873; the second with WCTU formation in 1874 until the Great War in 1914; and the final wave until 1919. In 1847 Iowa and six other states held local option elections for communities and counties to abolish the saloon. Iowa voted "dry" in 1855, but its legislature overturned the law and would not submit it to a citizens' vote. In 1866 Kansas passed its famous "local option and prohibitory law." By 1879 Kansas passed a constitutional prohibitory amendment bill, and the following year adopted statewide prohibition under constitutional authority with 8000 votes "to spare." In 1880 the Iowa legislature adopted a prohibitory bill, and two years later the electorate voted statewide prohibition by a nearly 30,000 majority. When its state supreme court declared the law "null and void" due to liquor interests, Iowa simmered in "an uproar" for four years until Prohibition forces finally closed the saloons.[9]

Still, saloons survived with a hundred operations reported just in Sioux City, Iowa. Although Kansas had been an officially dry state since 1880, many still considered their local law "a joke, the state a drinker's paradise, and the local politicians hand in glove with liquor vendors and saloonkeepers."[10] And Kansas remains popularly known for the most violent of Prohibition protests. In 1890, the small town of Medicine Lodge held seven saloons despite their state prohibition laws, and periodically, the WCTU picketed them in the manner of the former "Crusaders" with kneeling and praying women.

Carrie Nation herself had participated and even composed songs to go along with their praying protests. But at age fifty-three, Nation along with another WCTU follower walked into a Medicine Lodge drugstore selling illegal liquor, and with her sledge hammer smashed a keg of whiskey to "smithereens." "No one dared confront her formidable, flailing rage," comments historian Behr. Although she was destroying private property, saloons were legally deemed "illicit property." Later, Nation's followers used hatchets and other terrifying weapons, but as her "hatchetations" grew increasingly violent and numerous, these Plains women's actions and beliefs became a national joke by the early 1900s.[11]

Not simply "a revolt from the village," temperance development emerged from a rather complex scenario. The midwestern region—era, landscape, economics, politics, religions, families—created a strong, multifaceted temperance movement. Historian John Miller notes that "the values, industry, character, and spirit of the Midwest around the turn of the twentieth century" could "inspire and nurture." At the turn of the century, the Midwest became "a region rife with conflict and creativity," comments another regional historian Michael Steiner. "Between and 1920, during an era of midwestern economic, political, and cultural dominance—or a Midwestern Moment, if you will," notes Steiner, "the region's population exploded from twenty-two million to thirty-five million, outstripping the population of the New England and Mid-Atlantic states combined and coming to constitute a third or more of the nation's inhabitants." As historian Jon Lauck strongly advocates, "In the broader culture, the Midwest is often relegated to the role of 'flyover country.' But it was not always thus."[12]

A few historians have adopted this reevaluating slant. As journalist Daniel Okrent notes, "Temperance had meant moderation, both in quantity and variety. But even a group as powerful, wealthy, and self-interested as the United States Brewers' Association met its match in the foe who would engage it for nearly half a century—women. Specifically, women of Protestant, Anglo-Saxon stock, most of them living in the small cities and towns of the Northeast and Midwest."[13] Or as historian Murdock states, "Male drinking triggered a formation of separatist women's groups that worked for prohibition laws to control men's alcohol abuse." As Murdock emphasizes, the American temperance movement became "the longest, most popular social cause of the nineteenth century." Temperance women wanted to be considered "respectable."[14]

Current Prohibition's lore ignores the absolute ugliness of saloons in the nineteenth century. The public house had become a male-only social and political establishment, energetic in its traditions and enthusiasms, but many saloons in the last century would only now be described as dreary, dank, dark, dull, dirty, and dangerous places that could easily lead to male neglect and financial waste of households' resources. The saloon represented domestic violence against women and children as well as places of prostitution and venereal disease. As Iowa writer Bryce T. Bauer has portrayed in *Gentlemen Bootleggers* about Templeton moonshining in north-central Iowa, saloons in the nineteenth century were "places far more primitive and debauched." "Often they were foul dens," Bauer continues, "the domain of men and harlots only."[15] Other historians such as Edward Behr simply described "the squalor of the taverns" while Norman H. Clark labeled this drinking environment of money, politics, and masculinity as "the saloon nexus."[16] As Clark goes on to explain, "Drinking is more than rebellion and individualism and freedom."[17]

Female temperance members, both passionate and cautious, began to exclaim that "I Too" have been hurt by male violence exacerbated by drink. And if alcohol—intoxicating liquors—could be abolished, then this violence might be tempered as well, or so the temperance logic predicted. The litany of sexual abuses connected with the saloon were extensive: white slavery, prostitution, venereal disease, rape. Murdock emphasizes WCTU members' beliefs: "Only by closing saloons could such crime be stopped."[18]

In hindsight, this "saloon as evil" perspective perhaps seems naive. "They [WCTU] had expected to be greeted, when the great day came," writes historian Herbert Asbury, "by a covey of angels bearing gifts of peace, happiness, prosperity, and salvation, which they had been assured would be theirs when the rum demon had been scotched." The reality, accepts Asbury, would be quite different. "Instead they were met by a horde of bootleggers, moonshiners, rumrunners, hijackers, gangsters, racketeers, trigger men, venal judges, corrupt police, crooked politicians, and speakeasy operators, all bearing the twin symbols of the Eighteenth Amendment—the tommy gun and the poisoned cup."[19] Particularly in Chicago, this "saloon nexus" of masculine profiteers grew even more violent and coordinated than anyone who opposed their wet worldview could have imagined.

But challenging "the saloon" offered a symbol for further discussion of societal change. "By the mid-nineteenth century," theorist Mattingly explores, "many women recognized that the temperance issue offered an ideal vehicle for speaking about women's concerns." Temperance reform, many activists came to believe, meant an expanded definition of women's social and legal rights. Women realized their absolute need for the franchise, to vote for lawmakers if they were ever to be powerful agents for societal change. Therefore, temperance necessitated suffrage. "Unlike later New Women," analyzes Mattingly, "temperance women venerated women's connection with motherhood and the home, and they cherished their religious associations; at the same time, they argued for dress reform, for women's right to earn their own living and to be independent of men, and to women's right to equality generally."[20]

At the first national convention of the Woman's Christian Temperance Union in Cleveland, Ohio (1874), Annie Wittenmyer (from Iowa) would be elected the union's first president. Initially the WCTU did not emphasize militant or even political action, and during Wittenmyer's five-year presidency, the WCTU expanded to become the largest women's organization in the United States. When Frances Willard became WCTU's second president, she provided the motto "Do Everything" along with the energy and enthusiasm to grow the organization even further. Willard remained clever, consistent, contemporary, caring, and charming—almost a cult figure. And WCTU's numbers kept growing: 158,477 in 1901 compared to the National American Woman's Suffrage Association at 8,981. By 1919 the WCTU had reached 346,638 members. With these dramatic numerical contrasts, some historians believe the WCTU, not the NAWSA, earned the most responsibility for suffrage within the Nineteenth Amendment.[21]

"Using the motto 'Do Everything,'" as historian W.J. Rorabaugh explains, "WCTU members specialized in whatever reform was closest to their hearts."[22] But some of the Iowa WCTU members wanted to break away from the national organization, feeling uncomfortable with emerging suffrage partisan issues. Mary Aldrich, Iowa's WCTU president in 1878, tried to call for further unity and reminded members of their crucial need for suffrage. "Despite efforts at amelioration," writes Mattingly, "J. Ellen Foster and the official Iowa delegation finally walked out of the national convention in 1889 and began a separate Nonpartisan Woman's Christian Temperance Union. Although no other states made such a strong show of opposition, many others found it necessary to pacify local and state members on this issue."[23]

Political action certainly expanded after the Nineteenth Amendment. In 1924 Marie C. Brehm ran for vice president on the National Prohibition Party, which counted 57,222 votes. "More than world peace, child labor reform, infant maternal health, or the equal rights amendment," Murdock comments, "Prohibition provided women a distinct and respected public voice."[24] During the presidential election of 1928, Mary Roberts, the Maine state superintendent of WCTU from Waterboro, wrote to Lou Hoover. "It appears to be left for me to discover you—to lead us on to victory," as Roberts inquired of the possible first lady's political action. "Will you lead us on? We must win, for our life-long ideals are at stake and every woman has her own especial work to perform, I believe. You yours, I mine."

"Yet, there comes stealing over me a pent-up emotion," Roberts continued, "that you alone may ignite that patriotic fire in our women's being, which will achieve utilitarian and ultimate success. I am an idealist, trying patiently to be very practical. Will you help me to help Mr. Hoover, give me a cue? We need to be so wise and tactful." Lou and her husband Herbert Hoover, both Iowans and Quakers, appeared to be ideal Prohibition representatives, but organized women began to worry their work may come undone although repeal of the Eighteenth Amendment seemed far-fetched.

"You will not see any message from me during the campaign," Lou Hoover wrote back a week later. "It seems to me (and to many of my friends) that it is very much better that I should not be expressing my opinion on any phases of the present election problems, as so many might misconstrue my motives, if not even misquote my statements." Her writing style on Prohibition appears passive for such a dedicated woman, usually direct in manners and strong with actions.

Still, her husband's campaign came first. "So I hope you understand how much I would like to help in a practical way to make the campaign a success," concluded Lou, "and why I think it advisable that I take no active part in it, in the way of writing or 'speechmaking' or otherwise."[25] Even without Lou's endorsement, temperance women's organizations continued to further Herbert Hoover's candidacy in 1928 and 1932 with outstanding numbers of support and the corresponding votes.

Ida B. Wise was a catchy name for Iowa's WCTU president, and she well remembered her first childhood impression of the local saloon with "the well-worn stone steps and its evil odor." Now lobbying at the June 1932 Republican Convention in Chicago, Wise was further disgusted when delegates failed to support the Prohibition plank. "I am heartbroken tonight over it all," she began with a voice breaking from "fatigue and honest sorrow." "I love my country. I have always had a real obsession for my country. That's why I have worked so hard for prohibition in order to make it a better country."[26]

Another long supporter of temperance and Hoover's presidency, Clara Burdette began campaigning for him in a motor car tour from Fargo, North Dakota, to Maine. Burdette wrote her assessment of the midwestern political climate to the president in July. "The sum total of my conclusion is that women of every type desire to be as loyal to you as ever," Burdette emphasized, "but they are praying you will not leave them as uncertain concerning your attitude on this controversial issue as has the plank in the platform of our Republican Party." Her letter's conclusion was certainly direct: "The women of this country are dry. They do not make as much noise about it as the anti-drys do but their votes will count in November."²⁷

Eleanor Roosevelt also faced political dilemmas within presidential campaigns. "I happen to be personally absolutely dry and to believe in the Eighteenth Amendment and the strict living up to the spirit of the law," Roosevelt proclaimed earlier to the National Woman's Democratic Law Enforcement League in January 1928, "but I disagree with those who consider this question the question of vital importance today and I also think that there is a great deal of muddled thinking, especially on the part of certain groups of women, as to the manner to obtain temperance and enforcement of the Eighteenth Amendment."²⁸

During the 1932 campaign, Roosevelt continually appeared to choose party over personal principle, stating, "I myself do not drink anything with alcoholic content, but that is purely an individual thing." Although Eleanor Roosevelt is an icon to the second and third wave of the women's movement, many organizers from the first wave of temperance felt betrayed by the new first lady, that she acquiesced to her husband and the Democratic Party. "In placing party loyalty and individualism before her support of the Eighteenth Amendment," feminist Murdock concludes, "Roosevelt contributed to the dismantlement of womanhood as a public and political force."²⁹ As biographers have now revealed but not known by contemporaries during the campaign, Eleanor herself had been emotionally hurt by her alcoholic father, but she kept that pain to herself, never proclaiming "I too."

Societal and legal injustices, issues of physical abuse, and the generally unequal treatment of women escalated as components of women's voiced temperance concerns. Women were not destined to be passive victims of inebriate men, and temperance appealed to women across all socioeconomic, racial, religious, regional, and national identities in a fashion that was accessible and motivational.³⁰ WCTU members and their supports decided to persist.

Other parallels reflected in temperance rhetoric emphasized a woman's right to her own body, equal pay for equal work, and the imperative for women to focus on their own needs. In Iowa at the end of the nineteenth century, Marion Dunham called for the right for married women to control their own bodies, stating aloud that rape could occur within a marriage, a horrific crime she believed alcohol exacerbated. "The wife must be conceded the right to retain as full control over her body after marriage as before," Dunham proclaimed, "a right now denied both by law and custom, and because of which the foulest outrages have been perpetrated through the ages."[31]

The temperance movement deliberately developed a particular linguistic tactic, essential for unity, with its chosen style of the movement's phrasing—to use the singular "woman." "Woman as universal," writes Murdock in *Domesticating Drink*. This phrasing strategy was also utilized by the three largest organizations representing women at the turn of the century: Woman's Christian Temperance Union, Woman's National Committee for Law Enforcement, and the National American Woman Suffrage Association. During this first wave of feminism, constructing "the woman movement" appealed to "womankind," not just some women.[32]

The numerous midwestern women within this "Midwestern Moment" refused to be ignored as they seemed to say: "I Too" have witnessed violent events, and "I Too" desire change. "The persistence and skill with which the architects of Prohibition pleaded their cause over most of a century, winning state after state until an overwhelming majority in Congress voted for the Eighteenth Amendment, was a textbook example of successful lobbying," writes Behr.[33] But temperance in its third wave became Prohibition, a much more combative movement—hatchetations aside—turning away from moral suasion, the "Do Everything" philosophy of bettering women's lives—legally, politically, and socially—with voices and stories. The third wave contrasted sharply with its rapidly rising style of the Anti-Saloon League, a single-issue national lobbying entity led exclusively by men.

Collective memory surrounding Prohibition sneeringly asks what this "tragic experiment" accomplished. "While the temperance movement is often seen as a failed movement," notes Mattingly, "temperance women, through their rhetorical acumen, created effective change for women, both politically and personally." The list of temperance achievements, Mattingly states, is actually quite impressive: changed local and state laws raising the age of consent, improved property and legal rights for women, passed two Constitutional amendments, and demonstrated the need to become publicly active and provided instruction in how to do so with an inclusive model of rhetorical precision.

And the temperance movement's original goal of limiting alcohol remained intact and achieved remarkable success through political persuasion and educational presentations. "The most important legacy of prohibition in the United States concerned a dramatic change in drinking habits," comments Rorabaugh. "The raunchy all-male saloon did disappear for good, and per capita consumption of alcohol was reduced for a very long time."[34]

As Murdock points out, federal and state prohibition laws had reduced consumption by almost a third. Society turned away from "Demon Rum" with perhaps "a cocktail metamorphosis" by domesticating drinking in personal and public arenas. "Prohibitionists and suffragists," concludes Murdock, "often one and the same, sought to eliminate male excess—abusive drinking, political corruption, domestic violence—through Prohibition and suffrage reforms."[35]

The central irony of repeal in 1933, writes Charles River Editors, is that in many parts of the country "the Twenty-first Amendment made it harder, not easier, to get a drink." "Repeal," agrees Okrent, "replaced the almost-anything-goes ethos with a series of state-by-state codes, regulations, and enforcement procedures. Now there were closing hours and age limits and Sunday blue laws, as well as a collection of geographic proscriptions that kept bars or package stores distant from schools, churches, or hospitals." The aftermath of Prohibition provided more regulatory laws, remaking America's private and public spaces more sane and safe.[36]

In this new century, the twisted pink ribbon demonstrating breast cancer awareness is proudly displayed and widely recognized by American women and men but is seldom remembered for its historical precedent—the WCTU twisted white ribbon. The #MeToo Movement of 2017 could, and should, look back a century, realizing that its passion and success are due to its historic roots in the temperance women with their printed words, vocalized issues, and consistent arguments of women's rights (albeit without the hashtag) that echo to us today.

> I Too have been injured and alone, wounded by alcohol.
> I Too have watched my father drink away our family's money.
> I Too have bruises from drunken anger.
> I Too have tried to stop my husband's attacks on my body.

I Too have witnessed prostitutes trapped in saloons.
I Too have seen young girls victimized by the evils of alcohol.
I Too have a right to my own body.
I Too have a right to an equal wage and my own money.
I Too have experienced the corruption of my community by the liquor interests.
I Too have been hurt and deserve recognition.
I Too need a vote to create change.[37]

Temperance women reinvigorated a battle against alcohol twenty years after the Civil War which lasted until the end of the Great War that would indeed change the tenor of our society. She was Woman. Remember her roars. In numbers too big to ignore. Perhaps temperance women won their overall war after all.

Notes

1. *Council Bluffs Nonpareil*, 10 November 1929, 1.
2. Nodaway Valley Historical Museum (Clarinda, Iowa), Page County Women, Temperance folder, *The Iowa Champion*.
3. K. Austin Kerr, *Organized for Prohibition: A New History of the Anti-Saloon League* (New Haven, CT: Yale University Press, 1985), 276.
4. Carol Mattingly, *Well-Tempered Women: Nineteenth-Century Temperance Rhetoric* (Carbondale: Southern Illinois University Press, 1998), 115.
5. Mattingly, *Well-Tempered Women*, 1.
6. Elizabeth Johanneck, *Twin Cities Prohibition: Minnesota's Blind Pigs & Bootleggers* (Charleston, SC: The History Press, 2011), 9, 25, and 65; and W.J. Rorabaugh, *Prohibition: A Concise History* (New York: Oxford University Press, 2018), 40, 50, and 62.
7. Michael A. Lerner, *Dry Manhattan: Prohibition in New York City* (Cambridge: Harvard University Press, 2007), 2.
8. Lerner, *Dry Manhattan*, 2.
9. Herbert Hoover Presidential Library Archives, Fred G. Clark Papers, American Economic Foundation, "The Crusaders Program for 1938," 99–100, 13, 15, 16, 17, 18, and 19.
10. Herbert Asbury, *The Great Illusion: An Informal History of Prohibition* (Mineola, New York: Dover Publications, Inc., 2018. Originally published by Doubleday & Company, 1950.), 90 and 113.
11. Edward Behr, *Prohibition: Thirteen Years That Changed America* (New York: Arcade Publishing, 1996), 42.
12. Jon K. Lauck, ed., *The Midwestern Moment: The Forgotten World of Early Twentieth Century Midwestern Regionalism, 1880–1940* (Hastings, NE: Hastings College Press, 2017), 120, 134, 156, 207, 209, and 247.

13. Daniel Okrent, *Last Call: The Rise and Fall of Prohibition* (New York: Scribner, 2010), 3, 9, and 12.
14. Catherine Gilbert Murdock, *Domesticating Drink: Women, Men, and Alcohol in America, 1870–1940* (Baltimore: John Hopkins University Press, 1998), 4, 6, and 11.
15. Bryce T. Bauer, *Gentlemen Bootleggers: The True Story of Templeton Rye, Prohibition, and a Small Town in Cahoots* (Chicago: Chicago Review Press, 2014), 12.
16. Behr, *Prohibition*, 10; and Norman H. Clark, *Deliver Us from Evil: An Interpretation of American Prohibition* (New York: W.W. Norton & Company, 1976), 67.
17. Clark, *Deliver Us from Evil*, 224–25.
18. Murdock, *Domesticating Drink*, 79.
19. Asbury, *The Great Illusion*, 117 and 137.
20. Mattingly, *Well-Tempered Women*, 13 and 52.
21. James D. Ivy, "Wittenmyer, Annie Turner" and "Woman's Christian Temperance Union (WCTU) United States" in Jack S. Blocker Jr., David M. Fahey, and Ian R. Tyrrell, eds., *Alcohol and Temperance in Modern History. An International Encyclopedia* (Santa Barbara, California: ABC Clio, 2003), Volume II: 674 and 679; and Mattingly, *Well-Tempered Women*, 188.
22. Rorabaugh, *Prohibition: A Concise History*, 110.
23. Mattingly, *Well-Tempered Women*, 171 and 172.
24. Murdock, *Domesticating Drink*, 114.
25. Hoover Presidential Library, Lou Hoover Subject File, Box 91, Folder: Campaign of 1928.
26. Ossian, *The Depression Dilemmas of Iowa, 1929–1933*, 146–47.
27. Hoover Presidential Library, Lou Hoover Subject File, Box 71, Folder: Mrs. Clara Burdette.
28. Murdock, *Domesticating Drink*, 130.
29. Ibid., 131.
30. Mattingly, *Well-Tempered Women*, 97, 123, and 163.
31. Ibid., 37.
32. Murdock, *Domesticating Drink*, 120.
33. Behr, *Prohibition*, 4.
34. Rorabaugh, *Prohibition: A Concise History*, 110.
35. Murdock, *Domesticating Drink*, 94, 128, and 159.
36. Gustavo Vazquez-Lozano and Charles River Editors, *The Prohibition Era in the United States: The History and Legacy of America's Ban on Alcohol and Its Repeal* (Lexington, Kentucky: Charles River Editors, 2019), no page numbers listed in pamphlet; and Okrent, 374.
37. Author's composition of "I Too" imagined imagery.

C.A. Norling | "To improve the musical taste, capacity and voices of our people"

The Rise of Public Art-Music Interests Amidst the Rise and Fall of the Iowa State Normal Academy of Music, 1867–1871

Following the Civil War, America's musical landscape was abuzz with enthusiastic audiences and eager musicians. The eminent touring soprano Clara Louise Kellogg recalled that "the end of the war had made the nation a little drunk with excitement" for public entertainment and, as a result, her immediate postwar concerts in Chicago were exceptionally well attended.[1] A similar trend likewise occurred in the nearby state of Iowa where, in the decade following the end of the war, press discourse surrounding the founding and operation of a musical academy in Iowa City incited noticeable public interest in music education. Whereas, prior to the war, local newspapers showed little regard for ideals of collective musical taste amidst their deliberations of territorial necessities and nascent statehood, by the late 1860s, Iowa City's newspapers turned their attentions toward statewide awareness for art-music repertories. Though recreational and sacred music was unquestionably integral for the region's antebellum pioneers, the five academic sessions held by the Iowa State Normal Academy of Music between 1867 and 1871 marked a noticeable shift in the musical lives of the local population.[2]

This chapter uses Iowa City's Normal Academy of Music as a case study of a formative period in the establishment of a midwestern cultural identity through music. Using contemporaneous press coverage and extant operational documentation, it chronicles the academy's rise to public prominence and subsequent fall from institutional favor, and it highlights the associated outpouring of community interest in music instruction that was considered a common good by the local population. Though the academy's faculty, curriculum, and repertory betrayed adherence to the traditions of New England—not unlike the construction of early midwestern settlements and infrastructures— its significance within the Midwest arose from an investment in community music engagement and the subsequent public discourse that surrounded it. From its origins in local singing-school conventions to its presentation of community concerts and offering of statewide scholarships, the academy displayed socially concerned impulses behind the presentation of its predominantly art-music repertory, a sentiment echoed in the press and seemingly shared by the wider public. This study reveals that midwestern identities were often formed at the local level and that watershed moments for the region's social composition, though perhaps brief in their own time, resonated far beyond their initial occasion and immediate location. Furthermore, the period's expansion of press discourse proved to be an important catalyst for changes in the region's civic musical culture. As such, the case of the Iowa State Normal Academy of Music represents a singular contribution to the formation of a midwestern cultural identity, one that illuminates the formative processes that were integral to both the region's burgeoning musical self-awareness and its continued notions of musical tastes and repertories.

The academy's story begins with the 1839 arrival of early Iowa pioneer Robert Hutchinson. A native of New Hampshire, Hutchinson was born into a family of amateur and professional musicians. His father was both a farmer and a noted local musician, and his brother Jacob was member of Brigham Young's Nauvoo Band.[3] Most notably, however, Robert Hutchinson was related to the famous Hutchinson Family Singers, with whom he attended church as a child. Staunch reformers and abolitionists, the sibling singers achieved unrivaled prominence in the decades leading to the Civil War, touring widely with their popular songs often derived from sacred music.[4] In his published memoirs, baritone John twice recalled meetings with Robert during performance tours in Iowa. "In my boyhood [Robert] sang with me in the choir at Milford," wrote John, later adding, "He pre-empted Iowa City."[5] Upon his arrival, Iowa City was still very much an incipient western settlement, and Hutchinson's background in construction placed him in local demand.[6] In 1842, Hutchinson joined a group of fellow settlers in the establishment and erection of a local Presbyterian church, and when Iowa City was incorporated in 1853, Hutchinson served as its first marshal for a period of two years.[7] Hutchinson later purchased controlling shares in the Mechanic's Academy, an important regional vocational school.[8] After nearly thirty years in Iowa City, Hutchinson served as president of the State Historical Society of Iowa from 1867 to 1868, and remained affiliated with the Historical Society until his death in 1887.[9]

Throughout the 1860s, Hutchinson's financial gains from limestone quarries and real estate investments positioned him as a leader in the community and allowed him to pursue musical improvements for Iowa City. Hutchinson ran the committee to "provide music" for the inaugural meeting of a local Old Settler's association in 1866 and, more significantly, served on organizational committees for the area's largest music conventions.[10] Beginning in the 1840s, music conventions, or "singing-school conventions," flourished throughout the United States and typically consisted of multi-week courses in singing and general musical literacy.[11] Stemming in part from a renewed interest in rural sacred-music training brought about by the Second Great Awakening, the northeastern singing-school model favored a practice-based curriculum that encouraged church-music cultivation and widespread musical appreciation through direct musical participation.[12] Such methods were adopted and widely staged by the eminent hymnist and pedagogue Lowell Mason of Boston and afforded educators an opportunity for group instruction and performance on a larger scale, a practice standardized in Mason's *Manual of the Boston Academy of Music* (1836). Believing in both the societal importance of music and the superiority of European repertory, Mason sought a codified form of education to elevate musical tastes. As musicologist Michael Broyles noted, "Mason saw that art music could be very much a part of everyday life ... enjoyed, not only by the cultivated few but by the many."[13]

Mason's own methods, informed by and focused upon his protestant ideals of morality, retained the decidedly religious underpinnings of their church-revival origins but ultimately adhered to the musical practices of Europe. Unlike the contemporaneous southern singing schools that widely adopted the American shape-note tradition (a musical training system that utilizes shaped notes with corresponding pitches and that came to be known as "Sacred Harp"), Mason retained the notation systems of Europe and outwardly rejected the shape-note method as a product of seemingly inferior folk traditions, a judgment grounded in class-based perceptions of aesthetic merit.[14] Indeed, Mason even published the accounts of his European travels in order to "influence ... [the] improvement and universal diffusion" of music.[15] Though also successfully utilized in his Boston Academy of Music and the public-school systems of New England, Mason's ideas were primarily disseminated through the substantial proliferation of his instructional songbooks that was linked to the national expansion of singing schools.[16] For the Midwest, these temporary singing schools, largely run by traveling New England-trained educators, offered local residents exposure to both church music and the now-canonic choral works of continental Europe. What is more, Mason's singing-school model undoubtedly offered the economically growing region the trappings of northeastern societal wealth and supposed cultural prominence.

Though similar events were held almost annually in Iowa City beginning in 1858, the conventions of 1866, overseen by Hutchinson, garnered much acclaim and sparked local interest in community musical endeavors.[17] In February 1866, Iowa City's *Weekly Republican* announced a forthcoming two-week convention to "improve the musical taste, capacity and voices of our people."[18] Taught by Chicago-based composer J.F. Fargo, the event saw 160 attendees, a noted record for both Iowa City and the course's instructor. The press claimed that the convention's final concert was "remarkably successful ... the best ever heard from unprofessional singers."[19] On October 3, it was announced that, "[a]fter much correspondence," the subsequent two-week musical convention would be run by Henry Southwick Perkins, a former pupil of Mason in Boston.[20] Much like the previous event, this convention was likewise dubbed a triumph, and Perkins was said to have "sustain[ed] his Eastern reputation as a skillful teacher and thorough drillmaster."[21] His notoriety as both an educator and compiler of school songbooks seemingly made the prospect of Perkins's continued Iowa service advantageous to the growing interest in local musical training.[22] At the close of the two-week session, the organizing committee published their gratitude for the efforts of Perkins and the faculty in a unanimous resolution signed "Robert Hutchinson, Chairman." Regarding the convention's entire faculty, Hutchinson wrote: "[W]e can but earnestly hope that this [convention] may be only the prelude to their permanent ... residence in our City."²³

Following the popular singing conventions, demand for improvements to civic musical instruction spread rapidly in Iowa City, and the establishment of a permanent teaching institution was a persistent topic of public discussion. It was suggested that the conventions managed by Perkins had the ability to "awaken among [Iowa's] people interest in the cultivation of music and the development of correct musical taste."²⁴ In October, 1866, the *Republican* reported that a "Musical Academy [is] close at hand ... a present pressing necessity."²⁵ "Here is a time held for a competent man," the same newspaper later claimed, adding that "[o]ur people are much inclined to musical cultivation ... [and w]e hope our people will give all the encouragement possible, for it is absolutely necessary to render complete our educational facilities."²⁶ In response to the post-convention enthusiasm, Hutchinson and the convention's executive committee founded the Iowa State Normal Academy of Music to "give complete courses of instruction in the science of music— both vocal and instrumental."²⁷ Additionally, the new academy would continue holding regular public concerts and performances of large vocal works from the European repertory as established by the conventions throughout its existence. Hutchinson was elected as the institution's first president, Perkins was subsequently installed as its director, and a faculty of primarily Bostonian music educators was hired for private lessons and class instruction.²⁸

Though not a complete normal school in itself, the academy was established in conjunction with the Normal Department of the University of Iowa and was intended to bolster the state's primary-school education, musical and otherwise. The growing interest in normal education during the post-war years was a connection of great importance to the incorporators who sought not only the instructional advancement of their students but the proliferation of standardized musical instruction across the state of Iowa. Sparked by an early-nineteenth century demand for competent primary-school educators, the normal movement began with the 1839 establishment of the Normal School in Lexington, Massachusetts, an institution that emphasized "instruction in the art of teaching" and, more specifically, trained future educators "[t]o teach thoroughly the principals of the several branches studied, so that the pupils have a clear and full understanding of them."[29] By mid-century, the success of the early normal system brought about its expansion and, following the war, normal schools proliferated in the North's postbellum economic upsurge. Reportedly, some 23,000 students were enrolled in the nation's seventy normal programs in 1875.[30]

The westward spread of normal school education in the 1850s established numerous midwestern normal schools that adopted notably egalitarian connotations. As historian Jurgen Herbst stated with no uncertainty, "The midwestern state normal schools ... were democracy's institutions."[31] Formed in what were then some of the nation's newest states—Ypsilanti, Michigan in 1853; Normal, Illinois in 1857; Winona, Minnesota in 1858; Emporia, Kansas in 1864; and the department at the University of Iowa as early as 1856—these teacher-training institutions represent one of the first attempts to codify the region's educational capacities.[32] The midwestern normal schools were, in short, founded for the perceived betterment the region's inhabitants, and, in the absence of an educational infrastructure, were often the only source of systematic teacher training. In his 1867 defense of the normal school system, Richard Edwards, then president of the Illinois State Normal University, asserted that the "good [the normal school] does is diffused throughout the common schools taught by its graduates and pupils to the remotest nooks of the state," adding that there was "no more legitimate expenditure a state can make in the interest of the masses."[33] The University of Iowa's Normal Department, for example, took their task seriously and, upon admission, required all students to sign the following statement: "We ... hereby declare that it is our intention to engage in the business of Teaching in the schools of Iowa, that our object in resorting to the Normal Department of the University, is the better to prepare ourselves for the discharge of this important duty."[34]

In Iowa City, the establishment of a Normal Academy of Music in connection with the Normal Department's general-education offerings incited noticeable fanfare. A December 1866 article in the *Republican* titled "Prof. Perkins Returns to Iowa" voiced local excitement for the famed teacher's permanent relocation and his intent to "labor ... in the cause of Musical culture."[35] In the following March, a writer for Iowa City's *State Press* was "glad to know that we are all to have a genuine musical treat which will drive from our memories the jarring discords which have gone before."[36] What is more, the academy's partnership with the University brought widespread awareness to the new institution and likely contributed to its enrollment. Though catalogs and allocation records indicate that the University's Normal Department "employ[ed] a competent teacher of vocal music" as early as 1860, the establishment of the academy offered the opportunity for a robust course of musical offerings.[37] Facilities in the University's Old Chapel building were allocated to the academy and, in addition to overseeing music courses and summer sessions, Perkins was tasked with organizing music for commencement ceremonies, directing the chapel choir, and providing weekly vocal lessons for upwards of seventy-five students throughout a given school year.[38] Courses in music theory, education, and performance were advertised in the University's catalogue as credits that would "afford peculiar advantages to students."[39]

Unquestionably Hutchinson's largest musical undertaking, the academy opened its first official session in August of 1867. The nearly six-week summer session offered intensive instruction in music theory, choral singing, and solo performance to 105 attendees,[40] an experience with a noticeable financial commitment. In addition to the session's flat-rate fee of $20 (currently equivalent to nearly $350), students could elect to pay for further training in areas of their own interest, including $1 individual lessons in voice, piano, organ, violin, or cello.[41] Though much of the academy's pedagogical material was either composed, arranged, or compiled by American musicians and music educators, very little, if any, of the music was distinctly midwestern in subject or musical content. Rather, their songbooks contained a mixture of domestic, patriotic tunes, art-music excerpts, and arrangements of English folksongs that served to incite national pride and reverence for foreign music within routine musical training. For example, the academy's primary songbook, Perkins' own *The Nightingale* (1860), features three- and four-part arrangements of patriotic songs such as "My Native Hills," "Red, White, and Blue," "Our Country's Flag," and "Hail Columbia," alongside selections from Vincenzo Bellini's *Il puritani* and Giuseppe Verdi's *Il trovatore*, and melodies by Wolfgang Amadeus Mozart set to new, English texts.[42]

Despite the transatlantic origins of its instructional materials, however, the academy's public performances were dominated by large

Figure 1. Faculty and students of the Iowa State Normal Academy of Music on the steps of the Old Capitol Building in Iowa City circa 1870. (Henry Southwick Perkins seated at center.) Isaac A. Wetherby Collection. PA60a, Folder 2, No. 4. "Iowa Normal Academy of Music." Special Collections, State Historical Society of Iowa, Iowa City.

European choral works that highlighted both the curriculum's Christian underpinnings and adherence to European repertories. For Perkins and members the academy's board, the alleged cultural cachet of European repertory was both in keeping with the aesthetic ideals of Mason in Boston and a testament to the social aspirations of a community eager to tout its post-war growth. As such, the inaugural session ended with what was billed as Iowa's first public performance of Franz Joseph Haydn's oratorio *The Creation*, a daring undertaking that featured a substantial student chorus and solo performances by the academy's vocal faculty.[43] The size and scope of the 1868 session were nearly identical to those of the previous year, and the session closed with a performance of Felix Mendelssohn's cantata *Hymn of Praise* (*Lobgesang*, Op. 52).[44] Attendance reports show a marked increase in academy participants for the 1869 session; a total enrollment of some 142 students took part in the culminating performance of Georg Friederich Handel's English-language oratorio *Messiah*.[45] In 1870, the academy, which expanded its course offerings to include "physical exercises," enrolled 128 students and gave a performance of Mozart's *Twelfth Mass* (now commonly attributed to, among others, Mozart contemporary Wenzel Müller), during which Perkins was gifted a "fine gold tipped baton" by members of the community.[46] The session of 1871 was equally well-enrolled and concluded with Mendelssohn's *Elijah*, a challenging mid-century oratorio that the *Republican* reported was "seldom attempted out of the large cities."[47]

Beyond the attention associated with its initial establishment, the academy's local musical activities were of continued discussion in the press, and its public musical concerts were of perennial interest. Each of the academy's summer sessions mounted at least two large-scale community concerts that were ideal outlets for addressing the perceived expansion of local musical awareness, and for which tickets were widely sold. Following a mid-session concert in September, 1867, the *State Press* reported that the academy was a "fixed fact" in Iowa City and that it would bring "great improvement in the musical taste of our people."[48] The final concert of the 1868 session—an event so well attended that it was "crowded both inside and out"—was given exorbitant praise for its musicality, and Perkins was warmly thanked in the local press for "the untold amount of good he is doing for the cause of music in our midst."[49] The performance of the *Twelfth Mass* in 1870 was said have "surpassed any previous effort" by the academy and it received a lengthy review in the *State Press*. With a chorus of seventy-five students, the work was "nobly rendered," and it was asserted that the academy's continued work "commands the attention, confidence, and respect of the [local] people."[50] Amidst the rumors of the academy's closure in September of 1871, it was suggested that any loss of the academy's "superior educational advantages" would be greatly lamented "should the institution be removed to some other section of the State."[51] Regarding the increased local interest in musical training that surrounded these concerts, Perkins wrote that "[i]t is a very natural sequence that these public educational efforts should find the proper elements in which to propagate in these Western States," and that, in this endeavor, "Iowa is not a whit behind."[52] Similarly, at the close of the 1870 session, the academy's committee directly acknowledged their northeastern cultural models when they published that the academy's curriculum offered "advantages scarcely to be met with *even* in the older Institutions of the East."[53] In addition to holding public concerts, Perkins further sought to increase local art-music literacy with the establishment of a public "Reading Room" that was intended to hold "all of the principal music papers published in the United States ... for free use."⁵⁴

Likewise, as stipulated by the incorporators from the beginning, scholarships were awarded to students for each session. In order to increase the financial accessibility and far-reaching influence of an otherwise expensive training program, the scholarships were funded largely by local investors, known as "scholarship subscribers," and were advertised throughout the institution's existence. Despite the initial promise of some seventy-five scholarships, the inaugural session included only thirty-five to forty scholarship holders.⁵⁵ An advertisement for the academy's 1868 summer session in the *Daily Iowa State Register* of Des Moines listed the scholarship rate at one half of the regular tuition costs.⁵⁶ Prior to the session in 1870, the *University Reporter* announced the academy's new "liberal plan," an expansion of scholarship awards to two full-scholarship offerings for students, "either ladies or gentlemen," in each of the state's counties.⁵⁷ Further notices appeared in local newspapers throughout much of the state promising "free tuition" and specifically calling for the participation of local educators.⁵⁸

In 1871, however, despite public support, positive concert reviews, and a steady enrollment, the University's trustees severed ties with the academy. The academy's fall was largely caused by the University's academic transitions and was a byproduct of the unification and expansion of the "Academical Department." In the opening years of the 1870s, the Normal Department's independent teacher-training activities were slashed drastically and were gradually enveloped into the course offerings of the University's academic degree programs, a plan that left little room for musical instruction.⁵⁹ Education historian James Fraser posited that this very moment was "the beginning of the formal engagement by American colleges and universities in teacher education" and that it was incited by "university desires for academic respectability."⁶⁰ "In keeping pace with the academical department in its growth and development," then Normal Department principal S.N. Fellows called for the "transferring [of] all elementary normal training to such normal schools as may be established throughout the state, reserving only to the University the *higher* normal work."⁶¹ At the start of the 1871 school year, advanced normal training was offered to "only such members of the Junior and Senior classes of the Academical Department as intend to become teachers" and, by the following year, "the Normal and Academical Departments [had] in main coalesced" and "the only facilities [then] furnished to those preparing to teach ... [were] those of the Academical Department."[62] In short, amidst the University's academic restructuring of the early 1870s, music courses were no longer listed among other degree requirements and, thus, the Normal Academy of Music was left without a departmental home, more a result of shifting educational priorities than instructional deficiencies. The University ultimately "put its hand to the plow and looked back," remembered Perkins, adding that this seemingly regressive decision signaled that there was "very little affinity between politics and music."[63]

Though Perkins focused most of his disappointment toward the responsible University officials, it is likely that two additional factors influenced the academy's closure. First, evidence suggests the continuing presence of internal struggles between Perkins and O.C. Isbell, a local music teacher and an initial member of the academy's trustees. In August 1870, the Board of Directors reprinted that Isbell, "although not a member of the Board, used every unfair and deceptive means in his power to disorganize and break up the Normal Academy of Music." The academy's board ultimately "condemn[ed], in the most emphatic terms, the action and conduct of the said O.C. Isbell," adding that he was "a dishonorable man, disposed to rule or ruin, and unworthy of the confidence and patronage of the people."[64] Isbell, previously listed as the University's "Instructor of Instrumental Music," likely resented the new position of Perkins and the transferal of the University's music instruction to the academy.[65] In a pseudonymous letter published in the press, Perkins claimed that Isbell sought to gain control of the academy and, when his plans failed, spread "falsehoods" accusing Perkins of mismanaging scholarship funds. "[Isbell] is advised ... not longer to embarrass or retard the rapid progress which our music school has thus far made," wrote Perkins, evoking the recognizable, progressive rhetoric surrounding the academy's public successes.[66] Second, it is entirely possible that academy's aforementioned scholarship program became simply too expensive to be financially sustainable. Though nothing suggests any substantial loss of local scholarship investors, the concurrence of the University's abandonment of normal training with both the tension among academy leadership and the expansion of financial aid doubtlessly contributed to the academy's early demise.

Despite its brief existence, the Iowa State Normal Academy of Music and the figures involved in its activities incited lingering enthusiasm for art-music and music education in the region. All told, the academy enrolled a total of 610 students in its five academic sessions and even more in its year-round offerings, many of whom attended on generous scholarships and went on to become performers and educators.[67] For example, after the completion of the 1870 summer session, Robert Hutchinson's niece, Nellie V. Hutchinson, operated her own local studio of keyboard and vocal students.[68] Famed soprano Harriet Hope Glenn maintained an international career as a soloist and vocal coach after her studies at the academy.[69] Likewise, pianist L.A. Phelps found international success following his work with Perkins in Iowa and settled in Chicago where he taught collegiate voice lessons.[70] In honor of their accomplishments, Perkins asserted in the press that Glenn and Phelps were "'representatives,' not only of Iowa, but of the 'State Normal Academy of Music.'"[71] Perkins resided in the Midwest for the remainder of his career and, after the management of the academy in Iowa City and some two hundred musical conventions statewide, relocated to Chicago.[72] His efforts to expand the region's music education infrastructure continued as he founded the Chicago College of Music and oversaw music academies in Kansas, Wisconsin, and Illinois. His ultimate influence in the region is evident in his significant contributions to music education organizations. A charter member of the still-influential Music Teachers National Association, Perkins did much to link Iowa's music educators with annual music conventions and, later, served as the founding president of the Illinois State Music Teachers Association.[73] For his contributions to the region's musical education, the now-defunct Western College of Iowa bestowed Perkins with an honorary doctorate in 1887.[74] Though musical activities continued at the University of Iowa into the twentieth century, the University lacked a lasting, institutionally recognized music department until the current School of Music was organized by Philip Greely Clapp following his 1919 arrival from Boston.[75]

Hailing the perceived development of Iowa's musical cultures in the nineteenth century, the Iowa Federation of Music Clubs published this statement in 1938: "Here in a new state is an eager throng which will learn all the East can teach and then courageously venture into paths of its own."[76] Despite its unabashedly coastal allegiances, the statement encapsulates the historical processes that occurred. Largely adherent to Bostonian musical tastes and educational practices, the academy captured the region's burgeoning interests in musical training, and its public visibility had lasting influences on Iowa's musical and cultural identity. Though antebellum Iowa City's need for permanent improvements to civic infrastructure outweighed any demand for musical education, its postwar importation of northeastern musical practices provoked a dramatic increase in civic musical awareness. However, that these events were often considered harbingers of Iowa's purported cultural progress also suggests significant implications for the study of the region. As historians and musicologists continue to define the region's cultural identities, subsequent attention to midwestern musical life will undoubtedly contend with its loyalty to the musical cultures of New England and Europe. Coastal origins and international influences notwithstanding, the Iowa Normal Academy of Music reflects the social ambitions of some of the state's pioneering figures who, without the cultural infrastructures of the eastern seaboard, sought to establish a framework for the creation and consumption of art-music in the Midwest. Indeed, rather than relying on pre-established musical institutions, the academy's founders benefited greatly from the density and necessary interconnectedness of a midwestern civic culture that promoted music as a form of so-called social and communal "cultivation." Perkins himself later recalled these self-starting impulses when he described the events surrounding the academy's operations as "keeping with the young, thriving, go-ahead state of Iowa."[77] Ultimately, it was perhaps the community's mutual impulses, then, that stimulated the early public recognition of what they believed could be a shared midwestern musical selfhood.

Notes

Research such as this benefits greatly from the work of numerous archivists and librarians. I would like to thank, among others, Katie Buehner and Dr. Amy McBeth of the University of Iowa's Rita Benton Music Library, David McCartney of the University of Iowa's Special

244   "To improve the musical taste, capacity and voices of our people"

Collections and Archives, and Mary Bennett and Dr. Hang Nguyen of the State Historical Society of Iowa for their dedication to historical education, organization, and preservation. My gratitude is also owed to Drs. Marian Wilson Kimber, Trevor Harvey, and Sarah Suhadolnik for their comments and words of encouragement.

1. Clara Louise Kellogg, "A Singer's Story," *The Saturday Evening Post*, 23 August 1913.
2. This chapter does not purport to claim that art-music repertories were the lone form of musical activity in the region at the time. For example, Iowa City's musical citizens supported a local music store as early as 1854. *Legislative Reporter* (Iowa City, Iowa), 23 December 1854.
3. Perley Derby, *The Hutchinson Family: Or the Descendants of Bernard Hutchinson of Cowlam, England* (Salem: Essex Institute Press, 1870), 56, 83; Stephen C. Eubanks, "A History of the Nauvoo Brass Band," *Journal of Band Research* 51, no. 2 (2016): 48.
4. Scott Gac, *Singing for Freedom: The Hutchinson Family Singers and the Nineteenth-Century Cultures of Reform* (New Haven: Yale University Press, 2007), 98.
5. John Wallace Hutchinson, *Story of the Hutchinson's (Tribe of Jesse) Vol. 2*, Charles Mann, ed. (New York: Da Capo Press, 1977), 93.
6. Hutchinson's first house in Iowa City is still extant and is now the home of the University of Iowa Press. Dating to 1843, the building stands at 119 Park Road and is in close proximity to Hutchinson's initial limestone quarry, which is approximately situated at what is now 141 North Riverside Drive. Margaret Keyes, *Nineteenth-Century Home Architecture of Iowa City* (Iowa City: University of Iowa Press, 1993), 13–15.
7. Though the original church succumbed to a fire in the late 1840s, the subsequent building, completed in 1856, still stands at 26 E Market Street. *History of Johnson County, Iowa: 1836–1882* (Evansville, IN: Unigraphic Inc., 1973), 676; Jacob Van Der Zee, *100 Years of Presbyterianism in Iowa City, Iowa: 1840–1940* (Iowa City: The First Presbyterian Church, 1940), 12.
8. Benjamin F. Shambaugh, *Biographies and Portraits of the Progressive Men of Iowa: Volume 11* (Des Moines: Conaway & Shaw, 1899), 55.
9. *Tenth Biennial Report of the Board of Directors of Historical Society of State of Iowa, To the Governor* (Des Moines: R.P Clarkson, 1875), 14.
10. Roger Moninger, *Proceedings of the Johnson County Old Settler's Association* (Iowa City: Johnson County Historical Society, 1925), 9.
11. Edward B. Birge, *History of Public School Music in the United States* (Washington: Music Educator's National Conference, 1966), 26.
12. James R. Goff, *Close Harmony: A History of Southern Gospel* (Chapel Hill: University of North Carolina Press, 2002), 35–37.

13. Michael Broyles, "Lowell Mason on European Church Music and Transatlantic Cultural Identification: A Reconsideration," *Journal of the American Musicological Society* 38, no. 2 (1985): 330.
14. Goff, *Close Harmony*, 35.
15. Lowell Mason, *Musical Letters from Abroad: Including Detailed Accounts of the Birmingham, Norwich, and Dusseldorf Musical Festivals of 1852* (New York: Mason Brothers, 1854), iv.
16. Indeed, each of Mason's publications were unusually popular in his lifetime, many having sold between ten thousand and five hundred thousand copies each. Hutchinson himself owned a copy of Mason's *Boston Glee Book* (Boston: Oliver Ditson, 1838), a volume now held in the University of Iowa School of Music's nineteenth-century songbook collection. Carol A. Pemberton, *Lowell Mason: His Life and Works* (Ann Arbor: UMI Research Press, 1986), 173.
17. Conventions were held in Iowa City in 1858 and 1860, and annually between 1862 and 1865. Henry Southwick Perkins, "Music Conventions," *Annals of Iowa* 1871, no. 1 (1871): 448.
18. "Musical Convantion," [sic] *Iowa City Republican*, 7 February 1866.
19. "The Musical Convention," *Iowa City Republican*, 21 February 1866.
20. "Musical Convention," *Iowa City Republican*, 3 October 1866.
21. "The Musical Convention," *Iowa City Republican*, 14 November 1866.
22. Prior to his work with the convention of 1866, Perkins briefly taught public-school singing in central Illinois and served as the principal of the Northern New York Academy of Music. Henry Southwick Perkins, "Reminiscences of Early Days in School Music," *School Music* 40 (1908): 8.
23. *Iowa City Republican*, 21 November 1866.
24. "The Musical Convention," *Iowa City Republican*, 22 January 1868.
25. "Musical Convention and Academy," *Iowa City Republican*, 31 October 1866.
26. "The Concert," *Iowa City Republican*, 21 November 1866.
27. Henry Southwick Perkins, "The Iowa State Normal Academy of Music, at Iowa City [part 1]," *Annals of Iowa* 1872, no. 1 (1872). 62.
28. Ibid., 62, 64, 65, 77.
29. Letter from Cyrus Peirce to Henry Barnard, 1 January 1841, in Arthur Norton, ed., *The First State Normal School in America: The Journals of Cyrus Peirce and Mary Swift* (Cambridge: University of Cambridge Press, 1926), 1.
30. Charles A. Harper, *A Century of Public Teacher Education: The Story of Teacher Colleges and How they Evolved from Normal Schools* (Westport, CT: Greenwood Press, 1939), 72.
31. Jurgen Herbst, *And Sadly Teach: Teacher Education and Professionalization in American Culture* (Madison: University of Wisconsin Press, 1989), 109.
32. Harper, *A Century of Public Teacher Education*, 86–96.

33. Quoted in William Phelps, "Normal Department," *The Minnesota Teacher and Journal of Education* 2, no. 2 (1868), 58.
34. *Catalogue of the Iowa State University at Iowa City for the Year 1861–62* (Davenport: Luse, Lane & Co., 1862), 13.
35. "Prof. Perkins Returns to Iowa," *Iowa City Republican*, 26 December 1866.
36. *State Press* (Iowa City, IA), 13 March 1867.
37. Board of Trustees, Record Book A, Records of State University of Iowa Board of Trustees and Board of Regents, 1847–1909, University Archives, The University of Iowa Libraries, Iowa City.
38. James Senior Stinehart, "History of the State University of Iowa: Musical Activity to 1915" (MA thesis, University of Iowa, 1941), 10.
39. *Catalogue of the State University of Iowa for the Year 1866–67* (Davenport: Lush, Lane & Co., 1866), 47.
40. Henry Southwick Perkins, "The Iowa State Normal Academy of Music, at Iowa City [part 2]," *Annals of Iowa 1872*, no. 2 (1872): 145.
41. *State Press* (Iowa City, IA), 8 July 1868.
42. Henry Southwick Perkins, *The Nightingale: A Choice Collection of Songs, Chants and Hymns, Designed for the Use of Juvenile Classes, Public Schools, and Seminaries; Containing Also a Complete and Concise System of Elementary Instruction* (Boston: Oliver Ditson, 1860). Fittingly, the copy held by the University of Iowa's Special Collections features a penciled annotation to the title of Perkins' "My Native Hills" that reads "My Native Hills [in Iowa]."
43. Tickets for the concert were sold to the public at rates of fifty and seventy-five cents. *State Press* (Iowa City, IA), 11 September 1867.
44. Despite offering lessons in instrumental performance, it is unlikely that the academy trained enough musicians to support the full orchestrations of the chosen repertory. Rather, it is plausible to assume that the concert's organist, A.T. Smith, provided much of the orchestral accompaniment in reduction. In a conversation with Arthur Scoleri of R. Karstens Organ Works, it was noted that the concert's 1868 venue, Trinity Episcopal Church, was then equipped with a newly built, single-manual organ from William A. Johnson of Massachusetts, a statement corroborated by period press reports of the church's "grand Organ Concert" of 1866. The organ and the church building (formerly located at the corner of Dubuque and Burlington Streets) are no longer extant. "The Concert," *State Press* (Iowa City, IA), 16 September 1868; "Iowa City Church Directory," *State Press* (Iowa City, Iowa), 19 September 1866.
45. Perkins, "The Iowa State Normal Academy of Music, at Iowa City [part 1]," 69–70.
46. Raymond Comstock, "Contributions of the Orsen Perkins Family to Nineteenth Century American Music Education" (PhD diss., University of Iowa, 1970), 85; "The Academy of Music," *State Press*, 21 September 1870.

47. "Close of the Academy of Music," *Iowa City Republican*, 20 September 1871.
48. *State Press* (Iowa City, IA), 4 September 1867.
49. "The Concert," *State Press* (Iowa City, IA), 16 September 1868.
50. "The Academy of Music," *State Press* (Iowa City, IA), 21 September 1870.
51. *Daily Evening Press* (Iowa City, IA), 4 September 1871.
52. Perkins, "Musical Conventions," 447.
53. "The Academy of Music," *State Press* (Iowa City, IA), 21 September 1870.
54. *Iowa City Republican*, 22 January 1868
55. Perkins, "The Iowa State Normal Academy of Music, at Iowa City [part 1]," 64, 66.
56. "Iowa State Normal Academy of Music," *Daily Iowa State Register*, 1 August 1867.
57. "Special Musical Convention," *University Reporter* (Iowa City, IA), 1 June 1870.
58. For examples, see *Iowa Voter* (Knoxville, IA), 8 June 1871; *Daily Journal* (Sioux City, IA), 8 July 1871; *Republican* (Toledo, IA), 13 July 1871.
59. Rather than continuing to house disparate academic departments, the University consolidated its academic programs into a larger "Academical Department." *Catalogue of the Iowa State University at Iowa City for the Year 1870-71* (Davenport: Griggs, Watson, & Day, 1871), 26.
60. James W. Fraser, *Preparing America's Teachers: A History* (New York: Teacher's College Press, 2007), 139.
61. *Report of the President of the State University of Iowa to the Board of Regents*, 20 December 1871 (Des Moines: G.W. Edwards, 1872), 121.
62. *Catalogue of the Iowa State University at Iowa City for the Year 1871-72* (Davenport: Gazette Book and Job Steam Printing, 1872), 44, and *Catalogue of the Iowa State University at Iowa City for the Year 1872-73* (Davenport: Gazette Book and Job Steam Printing, 1873), 46.
63. Perkins, "The Iowa State Normal Academy of Music, at Iowa City [part 1]," 63.
64. "Academy of Music," *State Press* (Iowa City, Iowa), 17 August 1870.
65. *Catalogue of the Iowa State University at Iowa City for the Year 1862-63* (Davenport: Luse, Lane & Co., 1863), 3.
66. "Editor of Press," *State Press* (Iowa City, IA), 28 April 1869.
67. Perkins, "The Iowa State Normal Academy of Music, at Iowa City [part 2]," 145.
68. *Daily Evening Press* (Iowa City, IA), 13 September 1871.
69. "An Iowa Woman Becomes A Famous Star of the Opera," *The Postville Herald* (Postville, IA), 15 February 1934.
70. William Smythe Babcock Mathews, *A Hundred Years of Music in America: An Account of Musical Effort in America* (Chicago: G.L. Howe, 1900), 216.
71. "Our London Letter," *Daily Press* (Iowa City, IA), 7 June 1876.
72. Perkins, "Musical Conventions," 446-50.

73. Homer Ulrich, *A Centennial History of the Music Teachers National Association* (Cincinnati: Music Teacher's National Association, 1976), 123.
74. Comstock, "Contributions of the Orsen Perkins Family to Nineteenth Century American Music Education," 43.
75. Charles Edward Calmer, "Philip Greely Clapp: The Later Years (1909–54)" (PhD diss., University of Iowa, 1992), 93.
76. "Prelude" in Helen Smith Ristvedt, Lewis Bolton, and Myra Cobb Ousley, eds., *Musical Iowana, 1838–1938* (Des Moines: Iowa Federation of Music Clubs, 1938), 9.
77. Perkins, "The Iowa State Normal Academy of Music at Iowa City [part 1]," 63.

Christa Adams | Creating a Site of Midwestern Cosmopolitanism

Heterotopia, East Asian Art, and the Cleveland Museum of Art, 1914–1916

Cleveland, Ohio, and the Cleveland Museum of Art do not immediately come to mind when considering the prevalence of Asian art and antiquities in museums in the United States. One might first think of the Museum of Fine Arts, in Boston, New York City's Metropolitan Museum of Art, The Art Institute of Chicago, or the Freer and Sackler Galleries located on the Mall in Washington, DC. The curators at the Museum of Fine Arts and the Metropolitan Museum of Art, starting in the early and middle nineteenth century, acquired, cataloged, and displayed some of the finest examples of East Asian art and antiquities available outside of China and Japan. By the turn of the twentieth century, Charles Lang Freer, Detroit railroad industrialist, determined that the best home for his extensive collection of East Asian art and artifacts would be a national museum, to be associated with the venerable Smithsonian Institution in Washington, DC.[1] The development of such fine, urban art museums on the eastern coast of the United States is perhaps unsurprising, given the relative wealth and perceived sophistication of these large urban centers. Coastal cities, like Boston and New York, also were important economic centers in the burgeoning global trade of the late nineteenth and early twentieth centuries.[2] The relative cosmopolitanism of these port cities resulted in the popularization of Chinese export goods among regional consumers. Yet smaller museums also emerged in the late nineteenth and early twentieth centuries in cities throughout the midwestern United States; of these, the new art museum in Cleveland, incorporated in 1913, with its peculiar emphasis upon building a strong and varied collection of Oriental art, serves as an excellent case study of the myriad ways that art objects and antiquities from diverse global sources augmented and served a homegrown civilizing mission. The staff working at Cleveland's newly christened art museum focused upon the acquisition, study, and display of Asian antiquities and *objets d'art*. These pieces, in the minds of both curators and the museum's first director, Frederic Allen Whiting, proved instrumental in the successful realization of the goals of the "civilizing mission" directed at the lower-class urban denizens of the city of Cleveland, which entailed exposing museum visitors to fine examples of art and craft from global points of origin.[3] The polyglot displays that emerged at the museum, including Asian art objects, as well as those gleaned from European sources, are representative of what Beth Lord identified as a *heterotopia*, "in which contingent fragments of a large number of historical series become evident."[4] The public presentation of these East Asian art objects and antiquities, in hybrid displays, enhanced and strengthened the prestige of the museum, and by default, the city at large, situating it as a unique midwestern heterotopia.

Local advocacy for the construction of a museum began in the late nineteenth century, as a by-product of the emergence of wealthy and "highly independent [urban] nonprofit associations" in the northern United States.[5] Construction commenced in 1913, and in December of that year, Whiting was appointed the first director of the new Cleveland Museum of Art.[6] Whiting's background in the burgeoning Arts and Crafts movement informed his strategies for building a comprehensive collection of high-quality art objects and antiquities from around the world. J. Arthur MacLean, first curator of Oriental art at the museum, assisted Whiting in this endeavor. Whiting emphasized acquiring objects of both aesthetic and historical appeal; in this way, industrially employed Clevelanders who visited the museum could expect to encounter examples of fine craftsmanship. MacLean focused more on the nascent historical-civilizational pedigree attached to art objects and antiquities. Taken together, their respective visions guided the early processes of acquisition at the Cleveland Museum of Art, where art objects and antiquities from around the world were acquired for collective display and public consumption. These activities likewise reflected broader regional philanthropic trends, suggesting that the emergence of the Cleveland Museum of Art was a facet of the "Midwestern Moment" of the late nineteenth and early twentieth centuries.[7] Far from being a region bereft of culture and diversity,[8] the Midwest was poised, at the turn of the twentieth century, to lead the nation in museum construction and other civically oriented philanthropic efforts.

Of particular interest here, however, is the emphasis that Whiting and MacLean placed on building a strong Asian art collection, alongside examples of European and American art, in the relatively small, urban, midwestern Cleveland Museum of Art. This focus on cultural pluralism and diversity in Cleveland reflects the "tumultuous" nature of American society in the late nineteenth and early twentieth centuries, whereby the Midwest emerged as a "raucous cultural battleground" that bred both "conflict and creativity."[9] Whiting, acting in line with these trends, suggested that there were two types of museums. One type comprised the large institutions, like those at Boston and New York, that possessed "rich ... collections" of "Oriental" and "Egyptian" art, respectively.[10] He also discussed smaller museums, like those located in "Pittsburgh, Buffalo, Chicago, Toledo, St. Louis, Cincinnati, and Indianapolis," that possessed "permanent collections of varying importance" but attracted the public "largely through a continuous series of temporary exhibitions of works by modern artists."[11] Whiting sought to realize a "happy medium" between these polarities in Cleveland.[12] As Evan H. Turner indicates, Whiting "clearly viewed Cleveland as belonging to the second group of museums," but he likely "yearned to associate it with the first."[13] As such, Whiting, in his tenure as director, sought to produce, in Cleveland, an institution with a "distinct individuality among museums throughout the world," suggesting that he and his team "should, at the outset, determine some branch of art which is not adequately represented in any American Museum, selecting if possible a field in which a sufficient collection could be secured without too large an expenditure of time and money."[14] Asian art thus served as the new museum's distinguishing field, referencing the importance of cultural pluralism while aiding in the development of Cleveland's own "regionalist ... identity."[15]

While Whiting primarily concerned himself with the quality and value of new acquisitions, he was keenly aware of the cultural cachet that a fine Asian art collection would entrench in Cleveland. Writing to Denman Ross, a trustee at Boston's Museum of Fine Arts, Whiting elaborated upon the important role that Asian art objects and antiquities might play in Cleveland's new museum. Whiting suggested that "the most likely field for the important department which will give the Museum its individual character is China."[16] MacLean tended to support this view. In his tenure as curator of Oriental art he regularly published celebratory missives in the museum's *Bulletin* introducing readers to newly acquired art objects and antiquities from Asia. He believed that Cleveland's museum needed to be a "well balanced one," and that this balance could be achieved through working to "interest the people of Cleveland in Oriental things as well as Oxidental [sic] things."[17] MacLean believed that "magnificent pieces" of Asian art could help Clevelanders "become impressed with the importance of this foreign art, and on account of the object being first class, large, and therefore impressive, they would find little difficulty in accepting the importance and excellence of the art about which they know so little."[18] These ideals gained further support and legitimacy from Langdon Warner, who served as a museum adjunct and, ultimately, leader of the museum's 1916 "Oriental Expedition."

The rapid urbanization, industrialization, and population growth of midwestern cities like Cleveland reflected the rising global power of the United States. The United States in the early twentieth century surpassed longtime leaders Britain and Germany in industrial production. Despite these industrial achievements, many American elites felt a distinct sense of cultural inferiority. This sense became particularly acute when Americans juxtaposed the relatively short history of their nation with the historical pedigrees of European nation-states.[19] Measuring themselves against the achievements of Britain, France, and Germany, these Euro-American leaders could boast of industrial and technological superiority, while simultaneously perceiving their own nation as lacking in cultural greatness when compared with European civilizations. As previously discussed, elites in cities like Boston and New York collected objects and antiquities from around the world to represent and bolster the cultural sophistication of their cities. Yet some cultural leaders and their wealthy benefactors looked to East Asia for examples of greatness.[20] This trend, quite evident among the founders and leaders of the Cleveland Museum of Art, is less well-documented in the scholarship. Cleveland's museum building program illustrates this trend, showing how Asian nations like China, Japan, and Korea were, along with their European counterparts, sources of cultural capital and inspiration for American collectors. Elements of this case study can be employed to evaluate the collecting habits of elites and benefactors in other midwestern American cities developing in this period, and can likewise serve to contrast the region with other, less philanthropically and civically inclined regions like the American South.[21]

The wealthy Detroit industrialist and self-taught art connoisseur Charles Lang Freer, long a proponent of the civilizational greatness of East Asian nations, inspired the founders and first director of the Cleveland Museum of Art to look to Asia for tangible representations of cultural success. Freer was born on February 25, 1854, in Kingston, New York, one of six children from an impoverished family.[22] After forgoing public education, Freer began to work for Frank J. Hecker, owner of a rail-car production facility, where he steadily rose through the company ranks until, in 1884, he was made vice president of Hecker's Peninsular Car Company, located in Detroit, Michigan.[23] The operation was successful enough that, by 1899, Freer retired from business as a self-made millionaire.[24] Perhaps as a result of leisure time, or out of a desire to create a notion of aesthetic distinction, Freer developed an interest in the accumulation of artwork. Although he initially collected prints and oil paintings, his tastes soon turned to Asian artwork from Japan, China, and Korea.

Between 1894 and 1911, Freer made five separate trips to Asia where he acquired art objects and antiquities of unsurpassed quality.[25] During this period, Freer immersed himself in the study of Asian art and history. He purchased catalogs, guidebooks, and other texts, and consulted with Ernest Fenollosa and W.H. Holmes, two of the most distinguished contemporary American scholars of Asian art. Freer also engaged the services of "native expert[s]" whose educational background Freer deemed superior to even those of the most educated American historians of Asian art.[26] Freer counseled Whiting to focus his initial acquisition efforts on Asian art objects and antiquities. He suggested that through the methods of acquisition, appropriation, and display of Asian art, Cleveland could tangibly illustrate its own arrival as a bastion of industry *and* culture in the Midwest. Asian art objects and antiquities, aesthetically pleasing and historically significant, would prove instrumental in the realization of the city's civilizing and educational missions, and outward projection of civilizational success. Freer praised Whiting's plans to purchase fine examples of Chinese and Japanese artwork, indicating that a relatively small museum, like that in Cleveland, could with proper planning and a thoughtful program of acquisition rival the collections of museums located in larger, wealthier cities. Freer stated "that smaller Museums can be made more valuable artistically and educationally because such institutions can specialize, can obtain finer exhibits, take better care of them, learn more about their nature and place, and offer the people education worth while [sic]."[27] Freer indicated that a museum located in a city like Cleveland did have the potential to become great if issues related to the collection and specialization were tackled early on. The educational potential of the objects acquired was rivaled only by their cultural, social, and historical value, which, when displayed publicly, would, according to Freer, enhance the "civilization" of the United States itself.[28] Freer's arguments here paralleled those of the midwestern author Hamlin Garland, who championed the cause of public education in the arts. Hamlin believed that public access to art education would result in the cultural development and social uplift of the Midwest.[29] In the context of Cleveland, East Asian art objects and antiquities proved to be instrumental tools utilized by local elites to educate and assimilate the city's working-class citizenry, collectively ushering them toward a more modern, cosmopolitan existence.[30] Simultaneously, the collective, superior historical and civilizational pedigree of these objects could be co-opted by the city of Cleveland through display in its newly constructed art museum.[31]

Some of the Cleveland Museum of Art's earliest acquisitions were of fine pieces of artwork from China. In 1915, the museum acquired a stone Buddhist "votive" carving. The object was profiled in the April 1915 edition of the *Bulletin of the Cleveland Museum of Art* as a headlining piece and important new acquisition. According to the *Bulletin*, the carving dated to the fifth century CE, and featured a reclining Bodhisattva Avalokiteśvara surrounded by other Bodhisattva figures and symbolic Buddhist imagery.[32] Of greater interest was the nature of the *Bulletin*'s description, in which the anonymous author (likely curator of Oriental art J. Arthur MacLean) waxed poetic on both the great age of the object at hand and its cultural significance. The author stated that the new "accession" was welcome "not wholly because it is unique in date, but because it reveals a true religious and artistic spirit ... and ... stands as an example of Buddhist art comparable in every respect to similar expressions of the early art of Western civilization."³³ Although an ancient, foreign object, its intrinsic meaning "may be intelligible" to the viewer, who, if "receptive," could expect "to receive the message of this so-called pagan art so long delayed."³⁴ The "receptive," cultured viewer, then, might expect to find a "rich reward" after spending time "contemplate[ing] this carving," despite its great age and perceived cultural distance.³⁵ MacLean indicated that Clevelanders could appreciate this foreign object as a beautiful piece of artwork, rather than as an "idol" or element of a foreign form of religious worship.³⁶ He invited readers to be mindful of the great age of the object, and to consider how artistically and socially advanced a region must be to sustain the production of such a fine piece of sculpture that illuminated the "true religious and artistic spirit" of the time.³⁷ MacLean thus believed that viewers in early-twentieth-century Cleveland, Ohio, could still have a meaningful experience of a foreign religious object, here a Chinese Buddhist sculpture, because it was produced in a place with a sophisticated existent social hierarchy, by individuals, not unlike themselves, who were "full of love and joy and hope."³⁸ The relative scarcity of the votive would lend prestige to the new museum in Cleveland.³⁹ Additionally, the "delicacy" and style of the carving hinted at the growing importance of stylistic influences that were systematized in the succeeding Tang dynasty, considered a high point in medieval Chinese artistic production.⁴⁰ The statue's presence in Cleveland would also contribute "materially to [the] long line of study" of such objects "which is yet to besiege us" in the United States.⁴¹ Here the author makes reference to the growing interest among both scholars and members of the public in the arts and antiquities of nascent East Asian nations. To create a fine, well-curated collection of these sorts of objects would make Cleveland a front-runner among American art museums; further, the objects themselves, because of their antiquity and intrinsic historical pedigrees, would become a part of the city at large.

Langdon Warner, collecting on behalf of the museum abroad in 1915 and 1916, lobbied for the purchase of rare bronzes, desirable because they were examples of "the finest specimens of bronze casting in the world."⁴² Warner recommended acquiring examples of Tang dynasty paintings, sculpture, and ceramics, which referenced China's "Golden Age," and were "comparable to the similar art of the West which we love and revere."⁴³ According to Warner, it was essential that Americans become the first to "recognize the importance of the art and history of that other half of the world, which was so powerful in its day and is on the road to become so again."[44] Warner's focus here upon the prior power of China is representative of his respect for the region; in the Ming and Qing dynasties, China was one of the wealthiest nations on Earth. Further, Warner's contention that China, transitioning from an ancient imperial system of rule to one of democratic governance, sheds light on his belief that China was not mired in civilizational stasis. Warner's beliefs about China help to complicate existing postcolonial arguments about "Western" views of the so-called "East." This idea nuances existent arguments that suggest that foreigners, through consumption of art objects and antiquities, inherently imposed their own conceptions of how a given region became more civilizationally sophisticated (in effect, creating and providing a history for a given region).[45] This sort of action was not necessary in the case of China, since it was a culturally dynamic, sophisticated, influential empire for centuries. Describing China in a letter to Whiting, Warner delighted in his good fortune, since he was in "this vastest of countries and oldest of nations" where "six thousand years of history is in the making."[46] For Warner, China's prior power was symbolically manifested in the fine art objects and antiquities produced in earlier historical periods; these finely crafted, aesthetically pleasing objects were physical proxies for that civilizational sophistication. His further contention that China would again *become* powerful and internationally significant hints at a fascinating, largely unexplored facet of what motivated foreigners to engage in cultural appropriation of Asian material culture in the early twentieth century. Because China was once culturally sophisticated and powerful (evidenced by the record of masterfully produced art objects and antiquities), it would likely, in the future, occupy that space again.[47] Americans broadly, and Clevelanders specifically, living in a relatively new nation could, through acquisition, distinguish themselves by acquiring and displaying elements of formerly superior East Asian states. To Warner, Asian antiquities, and in particular those from China, were plentiful and relatively inexpensive to purchase as a result of recent political shifts in the region; this combination was fortuitous for collectors like Warner and the Cleveland Museum of Art, since these items were available, reasonably priced, and, yet, imbued with incredible cultural significance. When acquired and placed on display in

Cleveland, these objects would form the basis of a "glorious collection ... in which any individual might take pride."[48]

Other early acquisitions included a carved marble head, a vase from the Qianlong period (1735–1796), and a "Buddhist Trinity," described in an edition of the *Bulletin* by curator of Oriental art J. Arthur MacLean as being a "masterpiece" capable of "enlighten[ing]" the population as a result of the "universal[ity]" of its design.[49] MacLean hoped that this Cleveland-centered "enlightenment" might trigger a sense of affinity with China, so that any "seeming strangeness may become a thing of the past."[50] While potentially "strange" in nature, with contact and education, this "seeming strangeness" would be eliminated;[51] even as these objects were integrated into the fabric of the museum, their pedigrees were *sympathetically appropriated* by the museum on behalf of the population of the city of Cleveland. Through the display of these objects in dedicated Oriental art galleries at the museum, the objects' intangible pedigrees were effectively transferred to the site of display. Michael Taussig, in *Mimesis and Alterity*, describes the phenomenon as such, indicating that the "notion of the *copy* [here the galleries at the Cleveland Museum of Art] ... affect[ed] the original to such a degree that the *representation* shares in or acquires the properties of the *represented*."[52] The Oriental galleries at the Cleveland Museum of Art, as copies or representations, nonetheless participated in the historical pedigree of the objects displayed; this occurred to the degree that the museum effectively became a part of that pedigree and history of display and use. In this way, the museum could claim ownership of the pieces displayed along with their attendant cachet while simultaneously becoming an intrinsic part of the evolving historical experience of the objects themselves. This is akin to traditional Chinese beliefs regarding connoisseurship, where individual owners might, in the case of scroll paintings, add their own chop or name to the painting, conveying a sense of ownership and participation in the ever-evolving provenance of a given piece. Chinese scholar-collectors thus sought to "study, preserve, and transmit" both ideas and objects from the past, so that they might continue to be engaged with and enjoyed by members of future generations.[53] The museum's galleries, functioning as faithful facsimiles (or copies) of sites of display or use from the regions of origin, nonetheless permitted the displayed objects to exert and/or reflect some elements of their original purpose; thus their pedigrees were preserved, and transferred through display to the museum.⁵⁴ The museum, then, could claim control over the cultural "power" of these objects, since the museum provided the facsimile that permitted the objects to continue to retain, exert, or reflect some element of their original cultural purpose and/or value.

Through the acquisition of art objects and antiquities from China and Japan, the founders and staff of the Cleveland Museum of Art sought to transfer a cachet or pedigree from the ancient, culturally superior "Orient" to the upstart, technologically advanced but culturally inferior midwestern United States. By possessing and displaying these art objects and antiquities in Cleveland, the director, curators, and trustees of the Cleveland Museum of Art ensured that the city would be both technologically advanced and culturally relevant; ultimately, physical objects from East Asia were central to the realization of these aspirations. This is not to say that the museum would function as a purely didactic institution; although public education and edification were certainly goals, the processes of collection, appropriation, and display enacted at the Cleveland Museum of Art might also be understood within the context of a broader discourse. Specifically, through the act of acquiring and placing on display art objects and antiquities from China, Japan, and Korea, together in the context of their own galleries and at times alongside unrelated pieces from other regions and eras, the director, curators, and trustees at the museum were participating in the production of an instructive heterotopia. One notable example of this occurred in 1915, when a Chinese carved marble Buddha statue, acquired as part of the Worcester R. Warner Collection, was placed on display in the museum's Garden Court alongside carved artifacts from the ancient Near East and Classical carvings.⁵⁵ Additionally, in its Inaugural Exhibition in 1916, the museum administration set aside five of fifteen galleries for the display of art objects and antiquities from the "Orient."⁵⁶ This initial system of display placed Asian art objects and antiquities front and center at Cleveland's new museum. Conversely, when the Metropolitan Museum of Art moved to its current location adjacent to Central Park in 1880, of twelve galleries only one was set aside for "Chinese and Japanese Art Objects," which were displayed together in one room on the north end of the museum's upper level.⁵⁷ Beth Lord's concept of a heterotopia was more apparent in Cleveland, as Asian art objects and antiquities were regularly placed on display, at times in galleries adjacent to similar pieces produced in different regions. Following the Inaugural Exhibition, which ended in September 1916, museum officials retooled the galleries. Gallery X now displayed "a selection of textiles from the Near and Far Eastern countries ... being an extension of the textile exhibit in the Print Room on the ground floor," where, presumably, "Western" textiles were displayed.[58] As Lord notes, this kind of instructive heterotopia, though "constituent of multiple, discontinuous historical series," could nonetheless "contribute to progress" in a non-teleological sense, as it destabilized collective beliefs in "fixed" historical events and regional affiliations.[59] Lord's assessment, when viewed in the context of the Cleveland Museum of Art, supports the idea that Asian art objects and antiquities could contribute equally, alongside pieces from Europe, to the formation of a new culturally distinctive entity. The new museum in Cleveland can thus function as a prime example of a midwestern heterotopia, since it provided a counterpoint to the staid, didactic methods of display employed by curators at New York's Metropolitan Museum of Art and the Museum of Fine Arts, Boston. By placing greater emphasis on the arts of Asia in the museum's formative period, the director and curators were unwittingly engaging in the formation of a new discourse that presented Asia as an important center of aesthetic and productive inspiration and power.[60]

The Cleveland Museum of Art thus became a site of cultural tension and, simultaneously, a space that welcomed ethnic difference as a result of their *sympathetic appropriation* of important art objects and antiquities from East Asian nations, where objects were acquired to enhance the prestige and cultural capital of Cleveland, while simultaneously being celebrated for representing the civilizational successes of their places of origin. Maya R. Jasanoff, in *Edge of Empire*, discusses a similar concept, suggesting that, in spite of the clear relationships between processes of collection, cultural appropriation, and power, "real people in the real world do not necessarily experience other cultures in a confrontational or monolithic way."[61] The actions of collectors certainly did serve to shore up and legitimize the power of the appropriating entity (in this case, the Cleveland Museum of Art on behalf of the city and region). However, as Jasanoff indicates, collecting is simultaneously an informal activity, engaged in by individual actors beyond more formal channels of state-directed cultural appropriation.[62] Certainly individual collectors and benefactors were motivated by a desire to distinguish themselves culturally; the fact that this distinction was realized via the medium of emulating the actions of their collecting peers in the "Orient" speaks to a certain unusual openness or willingness to both appropriate and be distinguished via the process of appropriation.[63] In this way, collecting, as an act of sympathetic appropriation, serves to both "reinvent" the collector and allow the collector to exhibit an appreciation in, and "accommodat[ion]" of, in this case, East Asian art objects and antiquities.[64]

Visitors to the new Cleveland Museum of Art in its formative years could experience culture, refinement, and social uplift. Objects and antiquities from East Asia, far from representing the further materialization of American culture, could serve as spiritualized or representative proxies for the various periods and regions that they were products of. Their collective, intangible pedigrees would, through transference of ownership to the museum, serve to enhance the cultural cachet and level of distinction of the city of Cleveland, and all of those who resided within its bounds, distinguishing it from counterparts on the East Coast. In this way, Asian art figured prominently in the cultural "renaissance" of the city of Cleveland, a site of midwestern heterotopia in action.

Notes

1. Linda Merrill, "The Washington Building," in Thomas Lawton and Linda Merrill, eds., *Freer: A Legacy of Art* (Washington, DC: Freer Gallery, Smithsonian Institution, 1993), 235.
2. Craig Clunas, "Introduction," in Craig Clunas, ed., *Chinese Export Art and Design* (London: Victoria and Albert Museum, 1987), 18–20.
3. Nancy Einreinhofer, *The American Art Museum: Elitism and Democracy* (London: Leicester University Press, 1997), 32–33.
4. Beth Lord, "Foucault's Museum: difference, representation and genealogy," *Museum and Society* 4 (2006): 10.
5. Kathleen D. McCarthy, *American Creed: Philanthropy and the Rise of Civil Society, 1700–1865* (Chicago: The University of Chicago Press, 2003), 78.
6. Evan H. Turner, "Prologue: to 1917," in Evan H. Turner, ed., *Object Lessons: Cleveland Creates an Art Museum* (Cleveland: Cleveland Museum of Art, 1991), 4.
7. Jon K. Lauck, "Introduction: Mapping the Contours of the Midwestern Moment," in Jon K. Lauck, ed., *The Midwestern Moment* (Hastings, NE: Hastings College Press, 2017), x–xi.

8. See Jon K. Lauck, *From Warm Center to Ragged Edge: The Erosion of Midwestern Literary and Historical Regionalism, 1920–1965* (Iowa City: The University of Iowa Press, 2017), 13.
9. Michael C. Steiner, "The Midwestern Mind of Jane Addams: Cultural Pluralism and the Rural Roots of an Urban Idea," in Jon K. Lauck, ed., *The Midwestern Moment* (Hastings, NE: Hastings College Press, 2017), 208–09.
10. Frederic Allen Whiting quoted in Turner, "Prologue," 4.
11. Ibid., 5.
12. Ibid.
13. Turner, "Prologue," 5.
14. Frederic Allen Whiting, quoted in Turner, "Prologue," 5.
15. For more on philanthropy and midwestern identity formation, see Michael J. Pfeifer, "A Symphonic Midwest: The Minneapolis Symphony Orchestra and Regionalist Identity, 1903–1922," in Jon K. Lauck, ed., *The Midwestern Moment* (Hastings, NE: Hastings College Press, 2017), 101.
16. Frederic Allen Whiting to Denman Ross, letter, 20 May 1914, The Cleveland Museum of Art Archives, Records of the Director's Office: Frederic Allen Whiting, box 12, folder 131.
17. J. Arthur MacLean to Denman Ross, letter, 3 April 1915, The Cleveland Museum of Art Archives, Records of the Director's Office: Frederic Allen Whiting, box 12, folder 131.
18. Ibid.
19. For more see Warren Cohen, *East Asian Art and American Culture* (New York: Columbia University Press, 1992).
20. Consider here the beliefs of Charles Lang Freer, discussed below.
21. See McCarthy, 78–79.
22. Linda Merrill, "Acquired Taste," in Thomas Lawton and Linda Merrill, *Freer: A Legacy of Art* (Washington, DC: Smithsonian Institution, 1993), 13.
23. Ibid., 14.
24. Ibid.
25. For more on philanthropy and midwestern identity formation, see Michael J. Pfeifer, "A Symphonic Midwest: The Minneapolis Symphony Orchestra and Regionalist Identity, 1903–1922," in Jon K. Lauck, ed., *The Midwestern Moment* (Hastings, NE: Hastings College Press, 2017), 101.
26. Frederic Allen Whiting to Denman Ross, letter, 20 May 1914, The Cleveland Museum of Art Archives, Records of the Director's Office: Frederic Allen Whiting, box 12, folder 131.
27. Frederic Allen Whiting to Charles Lang Freer, letter, 29 May 1914, The Cleveland Museum of Art Archives, Records of the Director's Office: Frederic Allen Whiting, box 9, folder 108.

28. Charles Lang Freer to K.T. Wong, letter, 7 March 1918, The Charles Lang Freer Papers, Freer Gallery of Art and Arthur M. Sackler Gallery Archives, Smithsonian Institution, Washington, DC.
29. For more see Keith Newlin, *Hamlin Garland: A Life* (Lincoln: University of Nebraska Press, 2008), 202. Garland emphasized the value of public education in the arts, suggesting that this collective endeavor might aid in strengthening the "developing culture of the Midwest."
30. J. Arthur MacLean to Mrs. Henry S. (Mary) Upson, letter, 29 December 1914, The Cleveland Museum of Art Archives, Records of the Director's Office: Frederic Allen Whiting, box 8, folder 84. MacLean gushes over the value of Charles Lang Freer's collection of Asian art, and also indicates that "it has always been my contention that China, next to Egypt, was the most interesting of all nations."
31. Ibid.
32. M. (likely J. Arthur MacLean), *The Bulletin of the Cleveland Museum of Art* 2, no. 1 (April 1915): 1. Avalokiteśvara is a *bodhisattva*, or "enlightened being" that, upon realizing final Nirvana chooses continued rebirth, in an effort to assist in bringing all sentient beings to a point of enlightenment or spiritual realization. This choice is indicative of the great compassion of the bodhisattva for all beings trapped within the cycle of life, death, and rebirth known as *samsara*.
33. Ibid.
34. Ibid.
35. Ibid.
36. Ibid.
37. Ibid.
38. Ibid.
39. Ibid.
40. Ibid.
41. Ibid.
42. Langdon Warner to Frederic Allen Whiting, letter, October, 1915, The Cleveland Museum of Art Archives, Records of the Director's Office: Frederic Allen Whiting, box 14, folder 146a. 1.
43. Ibid., 2.
44. Langdon Warner, memo, October 1915, The Cleveland Museum of Art Archives, Records of the Director's Office: Frederic Allen Whiting, box 14, folder 146a.
45. Bernard S. Cohn, *Colonialism and Its Forms of Knowledge: The British in India* (Princeton: Princeton University Press, 1996), 3.
46. Langdon Warner to Frederic Allen Whiting, letter, 2 April 1916, The Cleveland Museum of Art Archives, Records of the Director's Office: Frederic Allen Whiting, box 14, folder 146.
47. Andre Gunder Frank deals with similar issues in *ReOrient: Global Economy in the Asian Age* (Berkeley: University of California Press, 1998), xxiv–xxv.

Frank argues that "Eurocentric social theory" caused scholars to overlook the contributions of Asians in the early modern period.
48. Langdon Warner to Frederic Allen Whiting, letter, October, 1915, The Cleveland Museum of Art Archives, Records of the Director's Office: Frederic Allen Whiting, box 14, folder 146a. 5.
49. J. Arthur MacLean, "A Buddhist Trinity," *Bulletin of the Cleveland Museum of Art* 1, no. 3 (November 1914): 2–3.
50. Ibid.
51. Ibid.
52. Michael Taussig, *Mimesis and Alterity* (New York: Routledge, 1993), 47–48.
53. Michel Beurdeley, *The Chinese Collector Through the Centuries: From the Han to the 20th Century* (Rutland, VT: Charles E. Tuttle Company, 1966), 15.
54. Ibid.
55. *Handbook of the Museum: A Description of the Museum Its Collections and Its Work* (Cleveland: Cleveland Museum of Art Press, 1928), 5 and 63.
56. Fred W. Lowrie, *The Cleveland Museum of Art: Catalogue of the Inaugural Exhibition June 6–September 20, 1916* (Cleveland: The Roger Williams Press, 1916), Contents and Maps.
57. Winifred E. Howe, *A History of the Metropolitan Museum of Art* (New York: Arno Press, 1974), 194–95.
58. "Wade Textiles and Oriental Arms," *The Bulletin of the Cleveland Museum of Art* 3, no. 4 (October 1916): 2.
59. Ibid.
60. Ibid.
61. Maya R. Jasanoff, *Edge of Empire: Lives, Culture, and Conquest in the East 1750–1850* (New York: Vintage Books, 2005), 7.
62. Jasanoff, *Edge*, 8.
63. Ibid., 10–11.
64. Ibid.

Joshua Jeffers

Colonizing the
Indigenous Past

Settler-Colonial Place
Making and the Ancient
Landscape of the Early
Midwest, 1775–1840

In her book *Firsting and Lasting: Writing Indians Out of Existence in New England,* historian Jean M. O'Brien argues that New Englanders "created a narrative of Indian extinction" that discursively eliminated Native Americans from the New England landscape and "appropriate[d] the category 'indigenous' away from Indians and for themselves."[1] In a "stark break with the past," New Englanders replaced Native peoples by writing them out of local histories and denying their existence in the present. When looking at Euro-American communities in the early Midwest, we see many of the elements that O'Brien describes in New England: commemorative monuments, historical celebrations, and intense local interest in amateur archaeology and "pioneer history." For New Englanders, O'Brien argues, this was about whitewashing the history of New England but also claiming modernity and denying it to Indians. But an element that is largely absent from New England but absolutely essential to understanding this process in the early Midwest is the presence of extensive earthen architecture apparently constructed in ancient times.[2]

During the late eighteenth century, the region that becomes the Midwest was known simply as the West or the Western Country, and, more specifically, during the last decade of the eighteenth century and first decade of the nineteenth this typically meant the "Ohio Country," roughly the area hemmed in by the Ohio River, Lake Erie, and the Maumee-Great Miami corridor. This area saw some of the most intense homesteading during this early period and in many ways marks the beginning of a process of landscape transformation and, as I will attempt to show, place-making and regional identity formation that ultimately extends throughout the Old Northwest and beyond the Mississippi River. Thus while it is certainly possible to find similar themes and processes throughout the early Midwest during this period, which in many ways is precisely my point, this essay will focus on Ohio. While local Natives and traders had long been aware of the curious earthen mounds and complexes that covered the region, it was the intense surveying and homesteading especially following the 1795 Treaty of Greenville that brought what locals would come to refer to generically as "the Mounds" into the popular consciousness. The discovery of these "vast remains of ancient fortifications, embankments, stone walls, [and] earthen mounds" prompted conflicting emotions for many Americans. They represented evidence of large-scale civilizations, which puts the lie to the idea that the region was some sort of primeval wilderness or virgin landscape, but they might also "prove that this country was formerly inhabited by a race of men very different from the present American Indians."[3] Early Euro-American migrants frequently noted with wonder and excitement the evidence of ancient societies that was all around them. "The Western Country," wrote one early traveler, is "covered with mounds, barrows, mausolea, and tumuli as thick as the autumnal leaves that strew the brooks in Vallambrosa."[4] "You cannot ride twenty miles in any direction without finding some of the mounds, or vestiges of the ramparts," wrote another.[5] Early Circleville resident and Mound enthusiast Caleb Atwater characterized the region as "indeed nothing but one vast cemetery of the beings of past ages."[6] The mythology that emerged around this landscape and the "race of men" who built it offered a compelling historical context in which to situate an emergent settler society. While antiquarians wrote of a landscape "reposing in the stillness of death, once the scene of a busy and crouded [sic] population; those temples, now devoted to the idolaters of silence, once resounded with shouts of war or songs of peace," boosters cited the earthworks as proof of the fertility and "healthfulness" of their locations.[7] "Wherever we find the traces of former population," wrote geographer Daniel Blowe, "we are sure to find land of an excellent quality."[8] But regardless of the myriad ways that observers and commentators interpreted these earthworks, the Mounds became symbolically associated with this region and structured how Americans conceptualized it historically and even geographically. "The most numerous, as well as the most considerable of these remains," observed American writer, state supreme court justice, and early resident of Pittsburgh Hugh Henry Brackenridge, "are found precisely in the part of the country where traces of a numerous population might be looked for, to wit, from the mouth of the Ohio (on the east side of the Mississippi) to the Illinois river, and on the west side from the St. Francis to the Missouri. I am perfectly satisfied that cities similar to those of *ancient Mexico*, of several hundred thousand souls, have existed in this part of the country ... The principal city and center of population was between the Ohio, Mississippi, Missouri, and Illinois."[9]

Figure 1. Extant Mound sites, c. 1891.[10]

This architecture was indeed ubiquitous with thousands of sites across the region, and as the Euro-American population expanded westward during the late eighteenth and early nineteenth centuries, revealing the extensiveness of the built landscape and piquing American imaginations, the region came to symbolize both new beginnings *and* an ancient heritage. Writings about these complexes and their supposed builders located in the early midwestern landscape an ancient historical legacy that informed local identity and shaped how Americans thought about the region and situated it as part of the new nation. Stories about the Mounds and their supposed builders offered Americans a way to contextualize settler expansion in a broader historical tradition, and observers consistently filtered their understanding of the early Midwest through the lens of the ancient landscape and the ancient people that they believed created it. In the process, commentators gave the early Midwest a regional distinctiveness while also helping to validate a policy of Indian removal through claims to the ancient past. The stories that Euro-Americans told themselves about the ancient history of this landscape contributed to what many saw as a richer and more satisfying *national* narrative. Rather than simply purifying the landscape of Indians "in a stark break with the past," however, Moundbuilder[11] literature offered a rapprochement between an ancient, glorious past and a providential future. While not writing Indians out of existence, writers cast them as the descendants of barbarians and Euro-Americans as redeemers of the land. This colonization of the indigenous past domesticated the landscape and enabled Euro-Americans to assert an indigeneity grounded in the ancient history of the landscape.[12]

This essay contends that the presence of ancient moundscapes shaped Americans' perceptions of the early Midwest and that interpretations of the Mounds and the supposed builders not only established regional distinctiveness but also informed national processes of place-making and identity formation. The creation of Moundbuilder "mythstories" served to colonize the ancient history of the landscape and cast Euro-American immigrants as the rightful heirs. Native peoples became interlopers, a historical abomination, that Euro-American settlement rectified, and the casting of white immigrants as the redeemers of ancient indigenous populations came to serve as a powerful and convenient narrative structure for framing the national ideology of Indian removal and settler-colonial expansionism. Moreover, this literature offers insight into how settler-colonial societies employ historical knowledge in the process of place-making. In creating an ancient heritage for the landscape and situating themselves as modern redeemers of ancient "Americans," American migrants, boosters, antiquarians, and intellectuals helped to frame local identity and national ideology not only in terms of an inevitably vanishing Indian, but also in terms of placing Euro-American conquest and Native American removal within a larger historical context that, like the "vanishing Indian," served to validate and rationalize those processes.

As settler-colonial theorists Patrick Wolfe, Lorenzo Veracini, and others have argued, settler societies are characterized by dissonant impulses to eliminate indigenous populations while at the same time demarcating a new indigeneity. In other words, settler colonialism operates on both affirming and repudiating impulses that serve to root the immigrant population in the conquered landscape, and this process of place-making directly shapes identity formation through the creation of histories, origin stories, and local lore, what historian Walter L. Hixon refers to as "a collective usable past."[13] Since migrants are "settling" a conquered landscape, the collective history that emerges is particularly susceptible to validating, celebratory, and otherwise satisfying narratives that ultimately *become* the indigenous past for the immigrant population. This colonization of the past is an intellectual process of historical appropriation and reinvention that I argue directly informs place-making and regional identity formation in what becomes the Midwest. Tales of ancient, non-Indian civilizations helped to transform a supposedly history-less wilderness of savage debauchery into an ancient realm of high civilization, a sort of pre-America, that was destroyed, like its Roman counterpart, by "savage hordes." This indigenous past thus made American settlers into indigenous actors reclaiming the landscape, while simultaneously appropriating the history of recent conquest into a reflexive, self-indigenizing narrative. In this way, regional and national distinctiveness became mutually constitutive. If the country's colonial heritage and national origins are tied to the East Coast, the soul of the landscape and the ancient heritage of the nation were in the "Western Country."

Few phenomena worked on the early American imagination like the architectural remnants of the so-called Moundbuilders. "No objects in the state of Ohio seem to have more forcibly arrested the attention of travelers, nor employed a greater number of pens," observed Ohio resident, physician, and historian Daniel Drake in 1815, "than its antiquities."[14] Nearly all commentators were struck by the extensiveness and peculiarity of the earthen architecture. The geographer Daniel Blowe, for example, described "a wall from four to seven feet high extend[ing] from the Great to the Little Scioto, a distance of seven miles."[15] Mounds were "to be found in almost every cornfield" and "on almost all the rivers of the West," wrote H.H. Brackenridge.[16] Though traders, such as George Croghan, had mentioned the Mounds in personal correspondence as early as the 1760s, the first published description of an earthwork was in 1775 by the *Royal American Magazine*, a short-lived periodical published in Boston, which gave the dimensions and a simple drawing of the complex at Circleville. Though early commentaries were simply descriptive, they laid out the basic assumptions that would come to characterize Moundbuilder mythology: they were constructed by "a martial race of mankind" and "the present Indians were not the builders."[17]

Over the next decade, the Mounds and their supposed builders became a literary trope and topic of legitimate inquiry among the nation's intelligentsia, even making it into political satire. In a column titled "American Antiquities" that ran in 1786 and 1787, the Hartford Wits[18] related a mock epic poem supposedly found among recently discovered ruins, embedded with "utensils more curious and elegant than those of Palmyra or Herculaneum." Through these manuscripts, Anarch, "a prophetic bard" who, "by his magic invocations, caused the years of futurity to pass before him," relates ancient epic battles between chaos and order, which the Wits used to highlight and criticize what they saw as the threats posed by Anti-Federalism, the public debt, and the popular discontent of the Shays and other uprisings.[19] By combining images of ancient epic battles and contemporary politics, the authors employ the ancient landscape as a vehicle for interrogating and propagating contemporary ideology, integrating America's ancient past, political present, and what the authors saw as threats to America's future into a single story. Moreover, they employ the landscape of the early Midwest as a place of ancient wisdom that the nation would be wise to heed and respect. This interweaving of national politics and the national landscape proved appealing to many Americans who sought a validating national heritage on par with that of the Old World. Then, in 1788, the *American Magazine* began publication of a series of letters between Noah Webster and Yale president Ezra Stiles in which they debated who actually built these complexes.[20]

Assuming from the start that ancestors of Native Americans could not have engineered the earthworks, Webster queries,

> What will the public say of the following opinions, that the Southern Indians [i.e. Aztecs, Mayas] ... are descended from the Carthaginians or other Mediterranean nations, who found their way to the continent at a very early period, and spread themselves over North as well as South America—that these nations had become more civilized, than the present northern Indians—that at a late period of time, perhaps four or five centuries ago, the Siberian Tartars found their way to the North West parts of this country, and pushed their settlement till they met the southern and more ancient settlers—that, accustomed to a colder climate and more active and hardy life, were the Goths and Vandals of North America, and drove the more ancient settlers from their territory—that in the contest between these different tribes or races of men, were constituted the numerous fortifications discovered on the Ohio, the northern lomes, and in all parts of the western territory.[21]

In other words, the large, apparently more advanced civilizations of Central America were actually of Mediterranean origin and built the Mounds during years or even generations of raids and conflict with less advanced northern peoples who originated in Siberia and were the ancestors of contemporary Native Americans. The obvious parallel with the fall of the Roman Empire suggests that for many, the ancient history of the western landscape was more than simply an interesting puzzle. It held the potential to at once establish a racial connection between the recent and ancient history of North America and to alienate Native peoples from the history of the land.

Thus by the time homesteading began in earnest after 1795, Moundbuilder mythology was already heavily associated with this region, and theorizing about the "ancient inhabitants of America" had become a "favourite theme of speculation" among both leading intellectuals and local antiquarians.[22] In 1820, for example, Daniel Blowe referred to "the great interest excited of late, regarding '*Western Country,*'" a region that "abounds with the vestiges of an immense ancient population; and the curious antiquary can no where in the western country find a richer field for his researches."[23] At the local level, interaction with the Mounds tended to manifest in three ways: living among them, collecting and displaying their contents, and theorizing about their builders. While some migrants viewed them as convenient places to carve out storage cellars and harvest raw materials or simply as agricultural impediments, others, like the founders of Marietta and Circleville, Ohio, saw them as sources of contemplation and local pride as well as unique, identifiable features that put these towns on the mental map of the new nation. In other words, they became part of the early identities of these towns by offering something that eastern regions could not. Wealthy Americans, for example, could ape the neoclassicism then popular in Europe and take a Grand Tour of sorts, visiting the ruins, reflecting on ancient civilizations, and collecting and displaying "curiosities." While the Mounds did not offer the same level of architecture as the ruins in Italy and Greece, they served well the dissonant impulses of the young nation to both expand and settle, to emulate and annihilate Natives, and to reject and embrace their Old World heritage.

At Marietta and Circleville, town planners, while destroying parts of the complexes, incorporated others into the layout of the towns. Indeed, Circleville, founded in 1810, takes its name from the circular mound in which it was enclosed, though concentric streets proved problematic and the town was "squared" in the late 1830s. In Marietta, efforts to maintain the earthen architecture proved more enduring. Founded at the confluence of the Ohio and Muskingum Rivers by the New England–based Ohio Company in 1788, the preplanned grid of streets sat astride two large square complexes and several mounds.

Joshua Jeffers 273

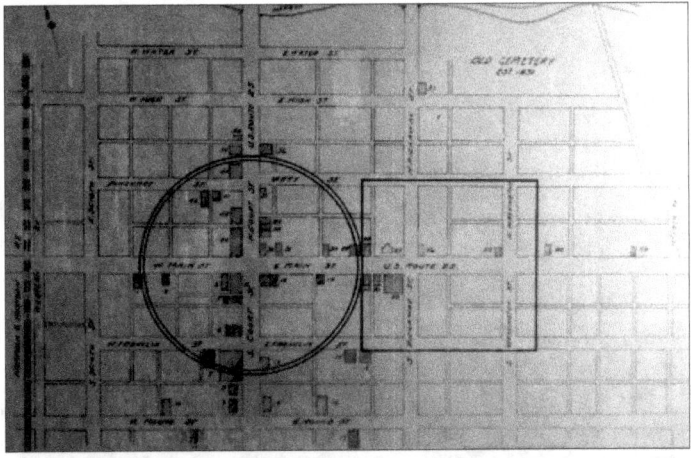

Figure 2. Circleville before and after "squaring."[24]

After cutting down old-growth trees that "remained on the walls and mounds," some containing nearly 500 rings, and seeing "other trees in a growing state [that] were, from their appearance, much older," Ohio Company associates altered the planned town grid to preserve more of the earthworks.[25] They also, like their own stockade, Campus Martius, assigned them Latin names, which included *Quadranaou* and *Capitolium*, the two largest mounds, and the *Sacra Via*, a walled pathway leading to the river. This broad avenue descended from the larger of the

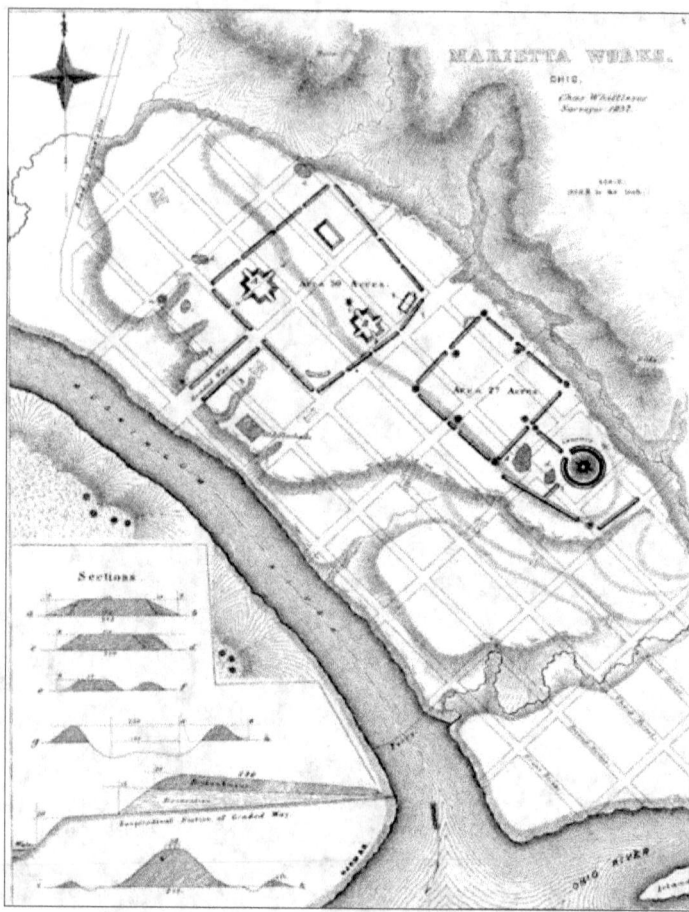

Figure 3. Marietta streets overlaying earthworks, 1837.[27]

two square enclosures, referred to as "the Town" by early inhabitants, by a perfect grade to the lower terrace of the Muskingum. Such engineering feats combined with such antiquity appealed to Mariettans who saw themselves as the bringers of civilization and the leaders of an expanding new empire. As historian Andrew Cayton has written, "Mariettans felt a primitive nobility exuding from its remnants," and observers imagined the grand rituals, bravery, and prestige of these forebears passing on to them.[26] Interspersed among streets named for national heroes, the earthworks offered a veneer of the majestic, the ancient, and the romantic to the "Jamestown of the Old Northwest," pulling the ancient landscape into the history and memory of this new founding. In perhaps the clearest example of an integration of local identity and national history, the large Conus mound situated at the center of "Mound cemetery" in Marietta would soon overlook the highest concentration of Revolutionary War officers of any cemetery in the country.

As new towns sprang up at Athens, Newark, Chillicothe, Portsmouth, and dozens of other locales, each with its own complement of mounds and earthworks, antiquarians and amateur archaeologists quite literally began bringing their backyards into their parlors and sorting "collection[s] of objects in Natural History" (a euphemism for skulls, bones, and mummies) into boxes, shelves, and mantelpiece museums.[28] The practice of collecting and displaying "artifacts," "antiquities," or "natural curiosities" as they were variously called was widespread and highly respected with many local antiquarians gaining "transient but dazzling fame."[29] Moundbuilder artifacts became synapses linking the fetishization of "the Moundbuilders"—the collecting of remains and artifacts, their display in cabinets and on mantelpieces, and their reinvention as private property to buy and sell—and the local process of place-making and regional identity formation. These artifacts and the stories that went with them, observes archaeologist Curtis M. Hinsley, "served as icons of belonging, enmeshed and embroiled in the dynamics of community and regional growth."[30]

Collectors combined to form "scientific and literary" societies for the comparison, display, and discussion of their finds. In 1818, for example, Cincinnati's *Western Spy* advertised a "recently instituted society for the collection, proscription, exhibition and illustration of natural and artificial curiosities, particularly those of the *Western Country*, [intended for] the establishment of a permanent Museum, on a scale so comprehensive as to receive specimens of everything curious which they may be able to procure."[31] Some of these societies developed into state or national organizations, such as the American Antiquarian Society, formed in Boston in 1812, and the Historical and Philosophical Society of Ohio, founded in 1831, which had as one of its stated goals to learn all they could about the "labors of a race now extinct," but the general tendency was centripetal, toward local pride and jealousy of outside meddling.[32] Sale of a collection to outsiders, except under

Figure 4. Grave Creek Mound, c. 1838.

severe financial stress, often brought harsh admonishment and potential ostracism. During the 1850s, for example, Ohio residents became furious over the sale of Edwin H. Davis's collection to the Blackmore Museum in England and subsequently guarded their personal collections fiercely.[33] Nevertheless, extensive networks of exchange, both of ideas and artifacts, did emerge. Circleville resident and founding member of the American Antiquarian Society Caleb Atwater wrote that he "receive[s], by every mail specimens of minerals, and drawings of ancient works, accompanied by descriptions of them; specimens of something either curious or valuable relative to the natural history or antiquities of the country. The objects themselves are numerous all over this great secondary region."[34] Such societies provided an outlet for interested antiquarians to exchange ideas, but they also quickly developed into voyeuristic institutions that helped promote the collection and display of remains and artifacts. They also tended to let fantasy take them where it may. In his 1806 travel narrative, for example, the British writer Thomas Ashe, known for his exaggeration and misrepresentation, described two "curious relics," which he had not seen but had heard descriptions of from a "learned doctor," one of which was "a green spherical stone, twelve inches in diameter, divided into twelve sides ... and distinguished by characteristic engravings."³⁵ Ashe insinuated to his readers that this was the philosopher's stone.

Certainly by the 1820s, the collecting and displaying of artifacts had become a bona fide intellectual pursuit and a widely practiced local custom. Museums and private exhibits sprouted up in numerous western towns to become, in some cases, rather lucrative local businesses with extensive collections. One author described two such museums in Cincinnati, "one of which contains a great variety of western antiquities, many skulls of Indians, and more that an hundred [sic] remains of what has been dug out of the aboriginal mounds." Perhaps the most famous of such displays was at the Grave Creek mound near present-day Wheeling, West Virginia, in which A.B. Tomlinson, nephew to the owner, sunk shafts and discovered burial chambers. Tomlinson expanded one chamber and in 1838 opened a museum inside the mound where tourists, for a fee, could be lowered into the mound to gawk at exposed remains.³⁶ Tomlinson also extracted hundreds of ivory beads and sea shells as well as copper jewelry, which he displayed in his mound-top "open-air museum."

In this way, the process of place-making became intertwined with the collecting and displaying of antiquities and helped to establish a strong sense of regional distinctiveness. According to literary scholar Susan Stewart, acts of collecting—finding, selecting, ordering, displaying—establishes control over environment, objects, and history. The process may be especially prominent, she argues, under conditions of pioneering, exploration, and settlement, when claims to locale, landscape, and property are tenuous, and thus may involve "intentional ignoring of proprieties of native history." Thus, the formation of American communal and individual identities came to involve digging, collecting, and displaying aboriginal "relics," and these activities played a central role in creating "an index of civic respect and belonging" in which Americans contextualized their past and domesticated the western landscape as uniquely American.³⁷ Like stuffed animals, security blankets, and other "transitional objects" that serve as existential bridges, the fetishization of "relics" embodied a point of connection between the physical colonization of landscape and the intellectual colonization of the past, which becomes a central element of both place-making and identity formation in the early Midwest.³⁸

Beginning in the 1820s there was a concerted effort by local leaders, boosters, and antiquarians to record the reminiscences of the aging frontier generation and give the region its own distinctive historical and literary culture.[39] This local history movement expanded on and solidified characteristics associated with the region like agricultural fertility, homesteading, and Indian fighting. But it also witnessed the fluorescence of theorizing about the "Moundbuilders," and through the lens of these ancient peoples and the ancient landscape, Americans situated the western landscape, the recent history of conquest, and, by extension, the nation in a new historical context. This theorizing tended to contain three primary elements: blanket denial of any connection to Native Americans, a link to ancient Greece and Rome, and attempts to square the existence of people in the Americas with the biblical story. American writers were quite resourceful in drawing from historical explanations of where Indians had come from in order to "prove" that "the Moundbuilders" fit biblical accounts of human history. One popular interpretation was that they were part of the so-called Lost Tribes of Israel. This version derives from earlier efforts by clergymen to reconcile the existence of indigenous peoples in the Americas with biblical stories, such as the great flood and the single creation described in Genesis. A typical expression of this view is Caleb Atwater's *Description of Antiquities Discovered in the State of Ohio and other Western States* published by the American Antiquarian Society in 1820.

Atwater, whom one historian refers to as "the first major figure in the intellectual and cultural history of Ohio," was the postmaster at Circleville and a leading figure in the local history movement.[40] Atwater proclaims the "Antideluvian" origins of the cultural act of mound-building, citing, among others, Virgil, who "speaks of tumuli being as ancient as they were sacred, even in his time."[41] Having established the antiquity of mound-building, Atwater turns to the "high places" of the Jews. After their expulsion, he writes, did these lost tribes "forget to raise afterwards, similar monuments and places of worship? They did not ... high places, of various altitudes and dimensions, were raised on every high hill, and under every green tree, throughout the land of Palestine, and all the east." "Let the reader examine similar piles of stones on the waters of the Licking, near Newark, in the [Ohio] counties of Perry, Pickaway and Ross," writes Atwater, "and then ask himself, Whether those who raised our monuments, were not originally from Asia ... examine the loftiest mounds, and compare them with those described as being in Palestine." Thus it was ancient Jews who built the mounds where "great national affairs were transacted ... kings crowned and deposed ... peace concluded and war declared. [Where] they celebrated anniversaries of great national events, and buried the illustrious dead. The Jews, on many great occasions," writes Atwater, "assembled at Gilgal, [which] signifies 'a heap.' Here was a pile of stones, which were brought from the bed of the river Jordan, and piled up on the spot where they encamped for the first night after they crossed that river, on their entrance into 'the promised land.'"[42] The idea of connecting the western landscape to such sacred moments in the Christian past would prove especially satisfying for many Americans, and antiquarians wrote sprawling accounts of Hebrew migrations to America for which they give dates, described routes traveled, and even specified which groups were responsible for certain earthworks.[43]

As Atwater observed, there is certainly no shortage of Old World examples of earthen tombs, mysterious sepulchers, and ancient tumuli. From none other than Herodotus comes the details of the burial of a Scythian king that included "rais[ing] a vast mound above the grave ... and seeking to make it as tall as possible."[44] The *Iliad* similarly relates that Achilles heaped a great mound over the remains of his friend Patroclus and how Hector, who slayed Patroclus, was eventually interred in a mound. Alexander the Great supposedly spent a great deal of money to build a proper burial mound for his friend Hephaestion, and the Roman Emperor Julian, who was killed near the Tigris River in 363, was interred in a "huge tumulus." Such examples provided a direct link in the minds of Euro-Americans from the ancient societies of the Old World to the ancient history and landscape of the early midwestern landscape. Confronting the hitherto, in the minds of Euro-Americans, timeless and tradition-free western landscape, the potential for connection with the Old World opened the floodgates of speculation and conjecture. Antiquarians offered theories of ancient migrations and visitations that brought virtually anyone from the ancient world who had ever been suspected of building a mound of earth. In this way, an entire cottage industry of theorization, romanticization, and a sort of necrophilic voyeurism informed the creation of the ancient past and regional distinctiveness of the early Midwest.

Easily the most persistent and broadly shared feature of Moundbuilder mythology was that they were not constructed by descendants of Indians. Reverend David Jones captured the refrain of most, writing in 1774 that "the present Indian inhabitants were not the builders, and can give no satisfactory account who were."[45] The most popular travel manual of the day, Zadoc Cramer's *Navigator*, which went through twelve editions between 1801 and 1825, told readers that "this country must have been thickly settled centuries ago, perhaps with a people much better acquainted with the arts than any of the Aborigines of N. America ever did or do now pretend to boast."[46] While a spate of early observers, including Thomas Jefferson, would not rule out that ancestors to Native Americans had built the Mounds, for most it was a foregone conclusion that they had not. As Atwater put it, "the foundation on which [this claim] rests is so frail, that I certainly should not trouble myself or my reader to refute it," and for many the earthworks were constructed by "a different people who have been destroyed by ... the present race of Indians."[47] As early as 1795, Jacob Bailey described a struggle between "the Moundbuilders" and "fierce savages," who "burst, like an impetuous torrent, upon their polished and more effeminate neighbors, [destroying] all their monuments of industry, art, and refinement," even giving dates—between 795 and 995 CE.[48] In 1803 Thomas Rodney similarly confided to his journal that "these mounds ... were not [built by] the present race of Indians but a different people who have been destroyed by [them]."[49] "It is a natural inference," wrote Timothy Flint, editor of the *Western Monthly Review* in Cincinnati, "that the country must have been antecedently inhabited by a more civilized and more powerful people."[50] "We can only account for the ultimate fate of those who were [the builders]," William Henry Harrison told the Ohio Historical Society, "by supposing that they were entirely extirpated ... Their departure, (if they did depart) must have been a matter of necessity. For no people, in any stage of civilization, would willingly have abandoned *such a country*; endeared to them as it must have been ... Unless, like the descendants of Abraham, they had fled from the face of a tyrant and the oppressions of unfeeling task-masters ... preferring, like the devoted Numantians, to be buried under the ruins of their own walls [rather than face] an ignominious fight."⁵¹ Though it is never clearly explained how such a backward society eliminated such an advanced one, the idea that these local monuments were built by "lazy Indians" was hardly satisfying, and this school of thought offered Americans a tidy perspective on both the past and the present.⁵² As one author put it, only the United States had such a "perfect union of the past and present; the rigor of a nation just born walking over the hallowed ashes of a race whose history is too early for a record, and surrounded by the living forms of a people hovering between the two."⁵³

The work that did perhaps the most to solidify the image of the early Midwest as a site of ancient conquest and the historical soul of the nation is Josiah Priest's *American Antiquities and Discoveries in the West*. Peddled door-to-door, the book sold tens of thousands of copies and became an archaeological classic among laymen. In an overtly nationalist tone, Priest expanded the horizons of America's pre-contact history in ways that hit all the right chords. "Ancient millions of mankind had their seats of empire in America," he proclaimed,

> [and] it yet remains for America to awake her story from its oblivious sleep, and tell the tale of her Antiquities—the traits of nations, coeval, perhaps, with the eldest works of man this side of the flood. The mounds have their origin in the dark night of time beyond even the history of Egypt itself ... [and] armies, equal to those of Cyrus, of Alexander the Great, or of Tamerlane the powerful, might have flourished their trumpets, and marched to battle, over these extensive plains.

But, he assured his readers, "abundant evidence can be procured to show that [the Mounds] are *not of Indian* origin." Based on a description by Josephus of a Roman "camp," he credited Romans with the earthworks at Marietta, no doubt a tempting notion for many Mariettans. Priest located explorers for Alexander the Great in South America, had Egyptians interring mummies in the Limestone caves of Kentucky, and placed "Hindoos" and Welshmen in the Mississippi Valley, prompting one reviewer to characterize the book as "a sort of curiosity-shop of archaeological fragments, whose materials are gathered without the exercise of much discrimination, and disposed without much system or classification, and apparently without inquiry into their authenticity."[54] Despite his wide-ranging efforts to place America at the center of ancient history, it is the early midwestern landscape that Priest presents as the linkage between the ancient past and a providential future. It is here that he locates the epic battles between Indians and Moundbuilders, but also the resting place of Noah's Ark and artifacts like "Triune cup," which was discovered in a mound in Cincinnati and supposedly contained "an allusion to the Trinity of the Godhead."[55]

Pulling from such works, literary artists pushed romanticization of "the Moundbuilders" to new levels. Sarah J. Hale's poem "The Genius of Oblivion," for example, situated "the Moundbuilders" as the progeny of star-crossed lovers who fled the Phoenician city of Tyre and crossed the Atlantic.[56] William Cullen Bryant, perhaps the most well-known Moundbuilder poet, characterized the American landscape as a "mighty sepulcher ... ancient as the sun," and in 1832 published "The Prairies," which played on popular fantasies surrounding the Mounds, evoking a simultaneous nostalgia and anticipation of those ancient empires and epic battles. His Moundbuilders clearly preceded the Indians, who would later massacre them, and they lived in a great agricultural paradise, where they employed bison as draft animals and erected great mounds as tombs, platforms for worship, and fortification.[57] Similarly, in *Behemoth: A Legend of the Mound-Builders,* Cornelius Mathews, a heavily nationalistic novelist, sought to supply America with a literary tradition on par with Greece's *Iliad* and Rome's *Aeneid*. He tells the tale of a Moundbuilder hero named Bokulla who devises a way to trap and kill the monster mammoth that terrorized "the Moundbuilders" and had prompted them to build their earthworks. Mathews had dozens of contemporaries, such as Daniel Pierce Thompson, who published a melodrama titled "Centeola; or, The Maid of the Mounds," which, like Hale, used Moundbuilder myth as a background for American romance. Perhaps the most influential of these romances was written around 1809 by the Reverend Solomon Spaulding. Though it wasn't published until years later, it circulated for decades in manuscript form to great effect. Titled *Manuscript Found,* this work was supposedly a translation of twenty-eight rolls of parchment found stone-covered in an artificial cave at the top of a mound near Conneaut, Ohio. Spaulding's tale has fair-skinned "Moundbuilders" inhabiting mighty cities where they work iron, keep livestock, including the domesticated mammoth, and compose literature.[58]

By 1840, the conviction that the ancestors of Native Americans had annihilated the more advanced "Moundbuilders" had only hardened among most, honed by the nation's religious and imperial impulses and the ideological ecumenism of Jacksonian democracy. At the time of contact, proclaimed Alexander Bradford in 1841, "the continent was inhabited by savage hordes [who had exterminated the Moundbuilders]"; thus "the time had arrived when a new race, and the Christian religion, were appointed to take possession of this soil."[59] Through such juxtaposition, Moundbuilder literature placed the early Midwest at the heart of an ancient heritage that helped to define the region as both distinctive *and* distinctly American and fed the twin ideologies of Indian removal and Manifest Destiny. As Andrew Jackson put it in his second annual message to Congress,

> In the monuments and fortresses of an unknown people, spread over the extensive regions of the West, we behold the memorials of a once powerful race, which was exterminated or has disappeared to make room for the existing savage tribes ... [and] the tribes which occupied the countries now constituting the Eastern States were annihilated or have melted away to make room for the whites.[60]

In his rationalization of removal, Jackson *claims* the "Moundbuilders," making them part of America's national narrative and identity and offering a way for Americans to come to terms with both Indian policy and the settler-colonial impulse to domesticate the landscape and its history. Thus by the 1830s the "monuments and fortresses" of the early Midwest, rather than testaments to ancient indigenous populations, had become evidence of an inevitable process connecting the national future to an ancient past. In the face of what one scholar has characterized as "an awesome burden of evidence to the contrary," this narrative had become the standard popular understanding of America's pre-contact history, and these fantasies became deeply embedded in both local and national identity as part of an emergent

284   Colonizing the Indigenous Past

ideology of American settler nationalism.[61] As the fantasies became ever more extravagant, detailed, and non-Indian, they allowed Americans to express the history of the land in a way that was, from their perspective, exciting and satisfying, but also edifying and validating. Whether coins supposedly found in the Mounds "engraved with *unknown characters, and yet having the year expressed by Arabian figures* [Arabic numerals]" *proved* that the builders were of Old World origin or that supposedly discovered iron implements meant that the "Moundbuilders" had advanced beyond Stone Age technology, these stories were at the heart of the process that transformed the "Western Country" from wilderness to homeland and Euro-American immigrants from pioneers to indigenes.[62] As nature and architecture, fantasy and memory, omens from a distant past and harbingers of a glorious future, in a sort of historical imperialism, Moundbuilder mythology enabled Americans to claim the continent's ancient history and situate the present and future as the fulfillment of that ancient legacy.

Notes

1. Jean M. O'Brien, *Firsting and Lasting: Writing Indians Out of Existence in New England* (Minneapolis: University of Minnesota Press, 2010), xv, xxii, xxiii, xxvi.
2. O'Brien mentions a literature on the possibility of a race of people who existed prior to contemporary Natives that emerges relatively late in New England, and she suggests that this may have been a bit of regional competitiveness in response to "Moundbuilder" literature, which focused on the Old Northwest. Ibid, 87, 233.
3. Daniel Blowe, *A Geographical, Historical, Commercial, and Agricultural View of the United States of America; Forming a Complete Emigrant's Directory through every part of the Republic* (London: Edwards & Knibb, 1820), 523.
4. Thomas Ashe, cited in *The Port Folio* vol. 1 (1809), 160.
5. Thaddeus Harris, *Journal of a Tour into the Territory Northwest of the Allegheny Mountains* (Boston: Manning & Loring, 1805), 148.
6. Caleb Atwater, "Preface," *Archaeologia Americana: Transactions and Collections of the American Antiquarian Society*, Volume 1 (United States: American Antiquarian Society, 1820), 5.
7. Hugh Henry Brackenridge, *Views of Louisiana; Containing Geographical, Statistical and Historical Notices of that Vast and Important Portion of America* (Baltimore: Schaeffer & Maund, 1817), 174.
8. Blowe, *A Geographical...*, 535.
9. H.H. Brackenridge, "On the Population and Tumuli of the Aborigines of North America. In a Letter from H.H. Brackenridge, Esq. to Thomas

Jefferson" *Transactions of the American Philosophical Society*, New Series, Vol. 1 (1818), 151–59, 154, 155–56.
10. Adapted from Cyrus Thomas, *Catalogue of Prehistoric Works...* (Washington, DC, 1891).
11. In our current parlance "Moundbuilders" is a popular term used to refer to a variety of different North American cultures living throughout the Great Lakes and Ohio and Mississippi Valleys from roughly 3500 BCE to 1600 CE. The accumulation of archaeological evidence over the past century has shown that this architecture was constructed by many different indigenous cultures in the Americas, in different ways, and for different reasons. The study of these cultures remains a source of debate and inquiry, but since the late nineteenth century scholarly consensus has been that the earthen architecture was constructed by cultures indigenous to America. Over the past century or so our understanding of these societies has deepened enormously as archaeologists have interpreted elements of material culture to identify societal evolution and cultural change and more recently employed radio-carbon dating, GIS (Geographical Information Systems), and archaeobotanical analyses. From this evidence we know that at least some of the societies living in this region during the fifteenth and sixteenth centuries constructed earthen architecture and were ancestors to some of the Native societies living in this region during the eighteenth century. While one-to-one correlations are beyond the current evidence, it seems clear that at least some of the Native societies living in this region during the eighteenth century, Shawnees for example, were descended from pre-contact societies, such as the culture archaeologists refer to as Fort Ancient, who the evidence suggests introduced corn-based agriculture to the Ohio Valley and constructed Serpent Mound. So while it is currently not possible to draw more detailed conclusions about the very distant past, the idea that the Indians living in the early Midwest were just recent migrants with no more right to the land than the (mainly Scotch-Irish and German) immigrants that displaced them is indeed quite flawed. See, Penelope Drooker, *View from Madisonville: Protohistoric Western Fort Ancient Interaction Patterns*, Memoirs of the Museum of Anthropology, No. 31 (Ann Arbor: University of Michigan, 1997); David Brose et al., eds., *Societies in Eclipse: Archaeology of the Eastern Woodlands Indians, 1400–1700* (Washington, DC: Smithsonian Press, 2001); A. Martin Byers, *The Real Mound Builders of North America: A Critical Realist Prehistory of the Eastern Woodlands, 200 BC–1450 AD* (Lanham, MD: Lexington Books, 2018); Elliot M. Abrams and AnnCorinne Freter, eds., *The Emergence of the Moundbuilders: The Archaeology of Tribal Societies in Southeastern Ohio* (Athens, OH: Ohio University Press, 2005); Bradley Lepper, *Ohio Archaeology: An Illustrated Chronicle Of Ohio's Ancient American Indian Cultures* (Wilmington, OH: Orange Frazer, 2005). During the late eighteenth and early nineteenth centuries, however, the term "Moundbuilders" referred to a single culture,

typically of Old World origin, that, it was believed, built the earthen architecture.
12. O'Brien, *Firsting and Lasting*, xxvi.
13. Patrick Wolfe, "Settler Colonialism and the Elimination of the Native," *Journal of Genocide Research* 8, no. 4 (December 2006): 387–409; Lorenzo Veracini, *Settler Colonialism: A Theoretical Overview* (New York: Palgrave Macmillan, 2010); Walter L. Hixon, *American Settler Colonialism: A History* (New York: Palgrave Macmillan, 2013), 11.
14. Daniel Drake, *Natural and Statistical View, or Picture of Cincinnati and the Miami Country, Illustrated by Maps* (Cincinnati: Looker and Wallage, 1815), 199.
15. Blowe, *A Geographical...*, 533.
16. Brackenridge, "On the Population," 153.
17. "A Plan of an Old Fort and Intrenchment in the Shawanese country, taken on horse back, by computation only" and "Letter to the Editor," *Royal American Magazine for January 1775* (Boston, 1775): 29–30, American Periodicals Series 1; David Jones, *A Journal of Two Visits ... in the Years 1772 and 1773...* (New Jersey, 1774), Early American Imprints, Series 1, no. 13356 (filmed), 41.
18. The Hartford Wits, David Humphreys, Joel Barlow, John Trumbull, and Lemuel Hopkins emerged from a literary society at Yale College and satirized society and politics during the 1780s, in particular their dissatisfaction with the Articles of Confederation and what they saw as the dangers of Anti-Federalism.
19. *The Anarchiad: A New England poem*. New Haven, 1861. 125pp. Sabin Americana, originally published in *The New Haven Gazette and Connecticut Magazine* 1786-87, vi, 11.
20. Ezra Stiles, *American Magazine* (March 1788), 246–47; (April 1788), 291–94; Noah Webster, *American Magazine* (December 1787), 15–19; (January 1788), 87–93; (February 1788), 146–56; (July 1788), 537–41.
21. Noah Webster, "Letter 1," *The American Museum, or, Universal Magazine, Containing, Essays on Agriculture ...* Jul–Dec 1790; 8, 1; American Periodicals Series pg. 11.
22. Brackenridge, "On the Population...," 151.
23. Blowe, *A Geographical...*," 6, 534.
24. Adapted from Henry Howe, *Historical Collections*, 2 vols., (1902).
25. Manasseh Cutler, cited in Martin Andrews et al., *History of Marietta and Washington County...* (1902), 15.
26. Andrew R.L. Cayton, *The Frontier Republic: Ideology and Politics in the Ohio Country, 1780–1825* (Kent, OH: Kent State University Press, 1986), 29; Gordon Sayre, "The Mound Builders and the Imagination of American Antiquity in Jefferson, Bartram, and Chateaubriand," *Early American Literature*, Vol. 33 (1998), 225–249, 230.

27. Ephraim Squire and Edwin Davis, *Ancient Monuments of the Mississippi Valley* (New York: Bartlett & Welford, 7 Astor House, 1848), 73.
28. Timothy Flint, *Letters from America Containing Observations on the Climate and Agriculture of the Western States, the Manners of the People, the Prospects of Emigrants, &c. &c.* (Edinburgh: W. & C. Tait, Prince's Street, 1822), 113.
29. Robert Silverberg, *Mound Builders of Ancient America* (Greenwich: New York Graphic Society, 1968), 53.
30. Curtis M. Hinsley, "Digging for Identity" in Devon A. Mihesuah (ed.), *Repatriation Reader: Who Owns American Indian Remains?* (Lincoln, 2000), 48.
31. *Western Spy and Literary Cadet*, Sept., 26, 1818.
32. Benjamin Tappan, "Address Delivered Before the Society, December 22, 1832," *Journal of the Historical and Philosophical Society of Ohio*, Part I (1838), 1:19–20.
33. Marshall McKusick, *The Davenport Conspiracy Revisited* (Ames: Iowa State University Press, 1991); Henry Shapiro, "The Western Academy of Natural Sciences of Cincinnati and the Structure of Science in the Ohio Valley, 1810–1850," in Alexandra Oleson and Sanford C. Brown, eds., *The Pursuit of Knowledge in the Early American Republic: American Scientific and Learned Societies from Colonial Times to the Civil War* (Baltimore: Johns Hopkins University Press, 1976), 219–47.
34. Atwater, *Transactions and Collections*, 1, 5.
35. Thomas Ashe, *Travels in America, performed in 1806...* (1808), cited in *Port Folio* 1, ser. 3 (Jan. June, 1809), 160.
36. Tomlinson, "Letter to J.S. Williams," *American Pioneer* 2.5 (May, 1843), 201.
37. Susan Stewart, *On Longing: Narratives of the Miniature, the Gigantic, the Souvenir, the Collection* (Baltimore: Johns Hopkins Press, 1984), 153.
38. D.W. Winnicott, "Transitional Objects and Transitional Phenomena," in *Playing and Reality* (London, 1971), 1–25; Eviatar Zerubavel, *Time Maps: Collective Memory and the Social Shape of the Past* (Chicago: The University of Chicago Press, 2003), 43.
39. Terry Barnhart, "'A Common Feeling:' Regional Identity and Historical Consciousness in the Old Northwest, 1820–1860," *Michigan Historical Review*, Vol. 29, No. 1 (Spring, 2003), 39–70, 42.
40. Terry Barnhart, "James McBride: Historian and Archaeologist of the Miami Valley," *Ohio History* winter/spring Vol. 103 (1994), 23–40, 29.
41. Caleb Atwater, *Description of Antiquities Discovered in the State of Ohio and other Western States* (1820), 164–65.
42. Atwater, *Description of Antiquities...*, 196, 206–7.
43. Silverberg, *Mound Builders*, 53.
44. Herodotus, Book IV, Chap. 71.
45. Jones, *A Journal of Two Visits*, 41.

46. Zadoc Cramer, *The Navigator; containing directions for navigating the Monongahela, Allegheny, Ohio and Mississippi Rivers;...* 8th edition (Pittsburgh, 1814), 216.
47. Atwater, *Description of Antiquities...*, 196, 206–7; Dwight L. Smith and Ray Swick (eds.), *A Journey through the West* (Athens, 1997), 124.
48. Jacob Bailey, *Collections of the Massachusetts Historical Society*, IV (1795), cited in Curtis Dahl, "Mound Builders, Mormons, and William Cullen Bryant," *New England Quarterly*, vol. 34, no. 2, 184.
49. Smith and Swick (eds.), *A Journey through the West*, 124.
50. Timothy Flint, *Letters from America*, 101.
51. William Henry Harrison, *Discourse on the Aborigines of the Valley of the Ohio* (1838), 8, 47; Numatians were a second-century BCE Celtiberian society who burned their walled city rather than have it fall to the invading Romans.
52. James H. McCulloh, *Researches on America* (Baltimore, 1817), 203.
53. Cited by Brian W. Dippie in *The Vanishing Indian: White Attitudes and U.S. Indian Policy* (Middletown, CT: Wesleyan University Press, 1982), 17; as "American Antiquities," *Western Monthly Rev.* (March 1828), 1:656, but I believe this citation to be an error.
54. Josiah Priest, *American Antiquities, and Discoveries in the West*. 3rd ed., rev. (Albany, 1833), 38, 42–45, 111–13, 54; Samuel Haven, "Archaeology of the United States" *Smithsonian Contributions to Knowledge*, no. 8 (1856), 41.
55. Priest, *American Antiquities*, 224–25, 227, 51.
56. Silverberg, *Mound Builders*, 85–86.
57. William Cullen Bryant, *Poems* (1832); Silverberg, *Mound Builders*, 87.
58. *The "Manuscript Found." Or "Manuscript Story," of the Late Rev. Solomon Spaulding* (Lamoni, Iowa, 1885).
59. Alexander Bradford, *American Antiquities and Researches into the Origin and History of the Red Race* (Boston, 1841), 435.
60. James Richardson (ed.), *A Compilation of the Messages and Papers of the Presidents* v. 2, 521.
61. Dippie, *The Vanishing American*, 17–18.
62. McCulloh, *Researches*, 208, fn; "Tomlinson Letter to J.S. Williams," *American Pioneer* (May 1843), 200; Robert Levering, "Extraordinary Coincidence; or, Supposed Discovery of the First Inhabitants of America," *American Pioneer* (September 1843), 410; C. Morris, "The Extinct Races of America," *The National Quarterly Review* 24 (December 1871): 121–44, 128.

Michael Leonard Cox | Isaac Walker and the Complexities of Midwestern Native American Identity

This chapter examines aspects of the life of a Wyandot man at a transitional point in his peoples' history and the history of the early-nineteenth-century Midwest. Isaac Walker came of age among the Ohio Wyandots in the years after the War of 1812, a time of intensive American settlement and growing marginalization of Native Americans in the Midwest. As indigenous people in the Midwest ceased to be a military threat after the war, pressure began to build to push Native Americans to leave their midwestern homelands, eventually culminating in Indian removal in the 1830s and 1840s. In the chronological lurch, however, Native Americans in the Midwest worked to build new lives for themselves among the growing settler populations and to forge futures in their homelands. In many ways, Isaac Walker's life serves as a microcosm of one approach indigenous people took to ensure their futures by blurring the lines between "Indian" and "white" to produce a unique, pliable identity. Isaac Walker's story exemplifies identity formation and expression at a liminal moment in the history of his people and of the region they occupied. While stories of multicultural individuals such as Walker's exist in other regions, the unique confluence of peoples, cultures, and historical moments that made up the early-nineteenth-century Midwest provided the milieu to generate a story like Isaac Walker's at the very moment of American midwestern historical formation.[1]

Walker's family occupied a critical place in the Wyandot community. His father, William Sr., was an adopted Wyandot who had been a captive from a large Virginia family. William Sr. had taken various positions on the U.S. government payroll, serving for a time as an Indian agent, interpreter, and postmaster. Isaac's mother, Catherine, was the daughter of Isaac Rankin, a British trader affiliated with the Hudson's Bay Company, and Catherine Montour, member of a prominent mixed-ancestry Iroquoian family.[2] Isaac Walker was born near Detroit in 1794, growing up largely on his father's land near Brownstown and in the Wyandot communities straddling the international boundary. During the War of 1812, Isaac, along with his father, older brother, and uncle, escaped capture by the British and joined the Americans at Detroit, while the British destroyed his father's property.[3] Documented details of his education are scant, but Isaac definitely attended Joseph Badger's school at the Lower Sandusky mission established by the Presbyterians from 1809 to 1811, when the school closed as the War of 1812 loomed.[4] Though Isaac Walker, according to the nascent blood quantum standards of his day, was likely no more than one-eighth Wyandot, he and his siblings successfully asserted that they were one-fourth Wyandot, a contention that gained import among the Wyandots in the 1820s and 1830s, when blood fractions began to matter to both Wyandots and whites.[5] Regardless, their mother's membership in the nation (and Big Turtle clan identity, which she passed on to her children), and the acceptance of their father as an adoptee, made Isaac and his siblings members of the nation and recognized as such by the Wyandot people.

Walker's life as a member of the Wyandot nation reveals the complicated nature of his personal identity as well as his economic activities and interests. Isaac Walker made a substantial portion of his living by working for the United States government, usually as an interpreter. Walker, along with his father William, brother William, and a handful of other men, held distinct advantages in a community where very few spoke English with any level of fluency. Isaac and his father, in particular, appear to have attained the greatest favor of the United States by the latter 1810s, especially since they not only were bilingual, but literate as well.[6] The Walkers also seem to have been preferred interlocutors by the Wyandot leadership, who put great trust and reliance in the two men. Isaac was involved in the efforts to complete the 1817 Treaty of Fort Meigs, which extinguished Ohio indigenous claims to the lands secured them by the Treaty of Greenville, excluding small reservations scattered throughout northwest Ohio.[7] The Wyandots held the largest of these reservations, called the Grand Reserve, which encompassed the Sandusky River valley, including the principal Wyandot town of Upper Sandusky. Isaac Walker and his father played a significant role in negotiating the treaty and in the bargaining that took place regarding the size and location of the reserved lands. While some observers criticized the Walkers for allegedly inhibiting the treaty and encouraging the Wyandot leaders to reject it, the family emerged from the negotiations, if anything, with a stronger position in the community and with the United States government.[8] To formally conclude the treaty, Isaac conducted a party of signatory chiefs from the Wyandot, Seneca, and Delaware nations to Washington, DC, in 1817, demonstrating the young man's important role in fostering the cooperation necessary to enact the diplomatic agreement.[9]

No matter the turnover in chiefs, Indian agents, or federal administrations, Isaac Walker and his kin remained important players in the local-level operations of the U.S. government on the Grand Reserve, making their livings in significant ways through the American colonial apparatus. They had the specialized knowledge, business connections, and historical precedent necessary to both the Wyandot leaders and the government agents assigned to the Reserve. Throughout the 1820s, Isaac was consistently employed as an interpreter for various councils and whenever his father was unavailable. Following the death of William Walker Sr. in 1823, Isaac seemed poised to take his place as the full-time government interpreter.[10] However, the U.S. Indian agent at Upper Sandusky chose to split the interpreter's pay and duties between Isaac Walker and Robert Armstrong, another sometime government interpreter of white ancestry, in an effort to appease both prominent men (and their large and powerful families). Isaac Walker complained about the arrangement, citing the lack of a living wage (he made $240 in 1824, for example, only half of the $480 provided for the Wyandot interpreter) and the fact that his proximity to the agency, three miles closer than Armstrong, caused him to bear the bulk of the interpreting duties.[11]

In addition to his duties with the Indian agency in the 1820s, Walker also co-owned and operated the family inn/store at the southern edge of the Grand Reserve. Isaac's father had built the store, called the "Walker Place," with the approval of the Wyandot council. The store served as a primary source of American consumer goods on the Reserve, as well as an inn for the ever-growing traffic on the roadways established near the Grand Reserve. Upon William Walker Sr.'s death, the store passed in equal shares to his widow and Isaac, his eldest child living in Ohio. Isaac devoted significant time and money to improving both the business and surrounding farmland throughout the 1820s. Isaac believed that he had just claim to own the business and land through inheritance. He asserted that his father had been

> permitted and requested to remain at this place by the Chiefs of the Wyandot Nation in full council (but not recorded) [Prior to Treaty of Fort Meigs in 1817] ... and at the treaty of Fort Meigs the Chiefs in full council renewed this consent for the said deceased and family to remain on the premices [sic] they then occupied at Upper Sandusky— where the old fort stood and to have the use and hold it as Indian property: and it should be considered as property belonging to said family as much as was made use of and said family should enjoy every privilege that belonged to any person in the Nation.[12]

He built an addition onto the house to accommodate his family and more customers, while also enclosing a significant amount of land in fences to accommodate more crops and livestock.[13] While hard numbers about the volume of business or amount of cash coming into Isaac's hands do not seem to exist, the profit must have been enough to offset the deficiency of his interpreter's pay, as well as to provide for the support of his family, his mother, and younger siblings. Additionally, the symbolic importance of Walker as a conduit of American economic consumerism on the Reserve cannot be ignored. In place of the defunct government trading houses that had gouged Wyandot customers before the War of 1812, the stores operated by men like Isaac Walker served as major source of manufactured goods and an outlet for indigenous cash acquired from annuities and off-reservation employment.[14]

In addition to his role as a proprietor of the family store, Walker was also a frequent customer at off-reservation general stores operated by white men who settled on the boundaries of the Grand Reserve. The ledger for one such store, located on Tymochtee Creek just outside the Grand Reserve, provides clues to the consumption patterns of Wyandots like Isaac Walker who were more adapted to Euro-American economics and culture. In many ways, a cursory overview of the Tymochtee ledger conforms to what one might suspect. The primary reservation community contact with the store was through more acculturated individuals such as William Walker Jr., Isaac Walker, George Wright, and Francis Driver, nearly all of whom were usually grouped with the more adaptive circles of the Wyandot community.[15]

Isaac Walker was the most frequently noted Wyandot client in the Tymochtee store, with twenty-nine separate ledger entries from November 1824 to December 1828. Walker's purchases ran the gamut from basic household items (a butter tub, snuff, tea, and the like) to manufactured goods like gloves, shoes, and a new saddle. He also bought some relatively expensive luxury items, such as Nankin grapes for $6.50 (Nankin is a small town in northcentral Ohio) and a pair of lambskin gloves for $2.50. Interestingly, the ledger records only two instances of Walker's purchase of unfinished fabric of any kind (most Wyandot consumers were buying fabric for use in home production of clothes), and one of those specifically notes that his mother, Catherine, made the purchase on his account. Walker was married for the entire period in question to Rebecca, a local white woman discussed below. Cultural difference does not seem incredibly important here, as it is unlikely that his wife lacked the skills to make clothes. One is tempted to speculate that perhaps the family demonstrated their affluence by buying manufactured clothes, or perhaps purchased clothes from a local tailor, though there is no concrete evidence to scaffold this assertion. Whatever the cause, Isaac Walker's purchasing patterns are distinctly different from others in the Tymochtee ledger, even those of his own siblings, and may be indicative of the adaptive tendencies he demonstrated in other aspects of his life.[16]

Along with his political and economic role and standing in the community, Walker became intimately involved with the various cultural and social activities on the Reserve, particularly the various missionaries who visited the Wyandots in the early nineteenth century. In his youth at the Lower Sandusky mission, Isaac appears to have served as an interpreter as well as a student.[17] He made note in those early years that Christianity had a marked effect on the few Wyandots who attended, though he does not seem to have devoted himself to Christianity.[18] After the War of 1812 Walker's mother, Catherine, was one of the first and most devout adherents to the Methodist mission established at Upper Sandusky, and Isaac, though apparently skeptical of the motives of the Methodists at first, became an interpreter, an adherent, and a founding member of the Methodist Missionary Society formed in 1828.[19] By that time, several Wyandot leaders, as well as a significant percentage of the general population, affiliated with the Methodist mission, and Walker took a leading role as an interpreter for the Methodist preachers. In summing up Isaac's relationship with the Methodists, James B. Finley, the longtime missionary, wrote in Isaac's obituary that he was "often employed in interpreting the Gospel to the wanderers of his own nation, when his own heart became filled with its important truths."[20] Additional evidence of his religious interpretation and skill also comes from Mononcue, a chief on the tribal council and an early convert to Methodism, who asserted that after receiving a Bible from a Methodist minister, he "took [it] to Br. Isaac Walker, and got him to read it to me."[21] Though active in the church, Isaac Walker was not a full member until ten days before his death, when he "obtained the pardon of his sins; after which he manifested an unshaken confidence in God to the last moment."[22]

While Walker was a strong presence in a variety of ways on the Grand Reserve, he also bridged the gap to the surrounding white world in personal and political ways. On June 28, 1822, Isaac Walker married Rebecca Hamlin, a white widow with two young daughters from her first marriage. The couple had one son, Isaiah, born in July 1826, whose later economic interests and identity became a major focus of lawsuits surrounding Isaac's property rights.[23] Walker's marriage outside of the Wyandot community was not unique, as many of the progeny of adoptees chose to marry spouses from the local white community, and there seems to have been little overt stigma against such marriages, either from the Wyandots or white Ohioans.[24] In a very personal way, Walker's marriage reflects the permeable, in some ways unimportant, distinctions between Indian and white worlds drawn by successive generations of scholars.[25]

Perhaps there is no greater evidence of Walker's assertion of a new kind of identity than his exercise of the franchise, which was reserved to white male citizens. In 1820, the State of Ohio created Crawford County, which included, at least nominally, the territory encompassed by the Grand Reserve. In 1821, all thirteen eligible men in Crawford Township, Crawford County, assembled to hold the first election for local offices. Among them was Isaac Walker, the only member of the Walker family (including his father), indeed the only member of the Wyandot nation, to vote in the election. Due to the exceedingly small number of voters, every one of the thirteen voters was able to hold an elected office. Isaac became the constable. He participated in all subsequent elections held in the township until his death.[26] Though I have uncovered few details about the elections themselves or the subsequent exercise of his political duties, there is no evidence that either local whites or the Wyandot Nation challenged or questioned Walker's political duality at the time. He was both an important figure in the Wyandot community and one in the local white political world, a unique position only he occupied.

Isaac Walker died of an unknown illness in May 1829. He was thirty-four years old. His early death was not unusual on the Grand Reserve, or in other indigenous communities in the region, as a variety of ailments disproportionately struck Native Americans in comparison to surrounding populations. With his death, of course, the story of Isaac Walker's life might seem to be over.[27] However, an ongoing debate about Isaac Walker's identity had only begun. By the fall of 1829, his widow sought some resolution of her property rights from Isaac's estate, appealing to Indian Agent John McElvain to inquire with the Office of Indian Affairs about the matter. McElvain asked the War Department to determine whether she had a valid claim, "she having no Indian blood in her." McElvain asked if she was entitled to a portion of the land should the Walkers decide to divide one for her, whether she had the power to sell the land to a white man, and whether said white man "would ... be permitted to live on the Indian reservation without leave from the proper authority [United States government]." Most importantly, as the history turned out, McElvain asked whether, in the event Rebecca Walker should remarry, her husband would be permitted to live on the property with her.[28] A month later, McElvain again asked for the Commissioner of Indian Affairs to render assistance as Joseph Chaffee, a white man and new husband of Rebecca Walker, had moved to the Grand Reserve. As her new husband, Chaffee sought to establish both his legal presence on Isaac's former lands and control of Rebecca's stake in the inheritance.[29] The Wyandot chiefs asked McElvain to remove Chaffee, a man who McElvain argued "is that kind of a man, that will take no advice."[30] The War Department refused to take any side in the dispute between the Walkers and Rebecca (and Joseph Chaffee, by extension), as it was "a case of individual right" that must be settled by legal means.[31]

It is important to note that Isaac had left a will, to be executed by John Carey of Crawford County. An examination of the will (two extant copies, one a rough draft and one an official copy) provides an interesting insight into Isaac's life and, to some extent, his identity. Other than order of information, the draft will differs little from the final copy. Walker wished that his debts be paid from his estate as soon as convenient. The bulk of his personal property (furniture, carriage, traveling trunk, etc.) was to go to his widow, aside from a few items each given to his younger brothers Matthew and Joel, and his sister Nancy Garrett. His share of the improved farmland on the reservation was to be divided equally between two entities: (1) his mother Catherine and two minor brothers Matthew and Joel, and (2) his widow Rebecca and minor son Isaiah. In the event of a sale of the Grand Reserve (a strong possibility in light of the push for Indian Removal by the Jacksonian Democrats at the time of his death), the proceeds he would be entitled to should be divided accordingly. He did include the provision that his wife could "continue to reside here [in the Walker family household]." Despite this proviso, Isaac Walker seems to have prepared for the event that either Rebecca or his family (or both perhaps) would wish to sever their cohabitation by authorizing the executor of the will to appropriate enough money to buy two eighty-acre lots off-Reservation to be the property of Rebecca forever. He also asked the executor to locate one section of land on the Reservation (due Isaac by the 1817 treaty), with the consent of the chiefs, for the use of his son Isaiah. Finally, as a codicil to the will, Isaac asked the executor to set aside $700 to be used by his wife at any time she chose, and to take the remainder of his money and put it in an interest-yielding bank account, the interest to be used by Rebecca. Technically, according to the will, all other property, and the actual balance of the aforementioned account, would be for the use of his son Isaiah.[32] For example, the executor Carey had been paid the monies owed Isaac for services to the government to go toward the estate established for his son.[33]

In the years following Isaac's death, relations between the Walker family and Joseph Chaffee seem to have soured rapidly. William Walker Jr. told former missionary James B. Finley that the Walker family had engaged in lawsuits against both John Carey and Chaffee regarding Isaac's property.[34] Another example is an 1831 newspaper announcement filed by George Garrett, an adopted Wyandot and husband of Isaac's sister

Nancy, who had apparently given Chaffee a "note of hand" for $190 on November 18, 1829. Garrett warned readers that, should Chaffee attempt to sell the note, Garrett refused to pay "unless compelled by law."[35]

As the question surrounding Isaac Walker's estate and Chaffee's claims lingered, the Wyandot Council interceded in the Isaac Walker affair directly in 1833. Noting provisions in the treaties signed in 1817 and 1818, they gave John Carey permission to locate a 640-acre section of land for the use and possession of Isaiah Walker, the only child of Isaac. It is important to note that this land was specifically for *Isaiah's* use and possession, not Chaffee's.[36] Chaffee wrote the War Department in his capacity as Isaiah Walker's guardian to clarify whether the aforementioned land would be deeded to Isaiah. If so, Chaffee would enter the land and improve it "for the benefit of the heir."[37] The Office of Indian Affairs informed Chaffee that Isaac Walker's name was not on the 1817 treaty at all.[38]

By 1834, a lawsuit initiated in Crawford County wound its way to the Ohio Supreme Court, where Walker's complicated identity had to be hashed out legally. While the lawsuit was ostensibly about a lease agreement, the crux of the matter was the identity of Isaac Walker. As noted, Isaac's widow had married Joseph Chaffee. By standard American law, Chaffee had acquired control of Rebecca's property, which included Isaac's half interest in the Walker Place. He chose to lease the property for a year's term, but the lessee, the aforementioned George Garrett, failed to pay on the grounds that the land was Wyandot land and not subject to Chaffee's control or ownership. Chaffee sought to define his rights in court.[39]

The heart of the argument about the case was whether Isaac Walker had the ability to will property to his wife, and whether that property was transferable to her non-Wyandot husband. Chaffee's lawyer, relying on standard American property rights, rested his claim on the argument that "Isaac claimed to be a citizen of the United States, and exercised the privilege of voting at elections, though he also received his dividend of the annuities secured by the treaties, to be paid to the Wyandot nation of Indians, as one of the nation." Isaac had expended "a large sum of money in improving" his inherited land, and the plaintiff claimed that his widow and young son (and Chaffee by extension) had a right to that property and the improvements thereon.[40]

The defense, conversely, argued that while under normal statutes the plaintiff should win, the fact that Walker was a Wyandot, living as a Wyandot on Wyandot land, precluded the white plaintiff from winning the case. Based on the existing federal laws, particularly the Indian Trade and Intercourse Act of 1802, non-Indians could not possess, rent, lease, or use indigenous lands without federal approval by treaty. The defense ultimately argued that "assuming that Isaac Walker was one of the Wyandot tribe, subject to the usages and laws of the Indians, we conclude that his last will must be carried into effect according to the laws and usages of the sovereign power, whose citizen and subject he was." According to this logic, Walker's will was subject to the rules of *his* nation, the Wyandot Nation, who did not allow non-Wyandots to own land or property on the Grand Reserve, which was also in accord with federal law. The judgment of the state Supreme Court concurred with the defense, ruling that Walker inherited his property rights from his father, an adopted member of the Wyandot Nation, and that the plaintiff, not being a member of the tribe in line of succession, did not possess title to the land. Though the court did not decide whether Isaac Walker was legally a Wyandot or a white man, his property rights were based on his status as a Wyandot citizen.[41]

Despite the finding against his rights in the court case, Chaffee continued to press both his claim and the question of Isaiah's lands. Again writing as Isaiah's guardian, Chaffee wrote the War Department to assure them that Isaac Walker was indeed listed on the 1817 treaty, but by his Wyandot name, not his English name. He enclosed a certificate from the Wyandot chiefs clarifying that Isaac was listed on the treaty. Chaffee wished for the president to produce a deed for Isaiah to the 640 acres in question (which Chaffee would of course control until Isaiah reached adulthood).[42] The War Department asked Indian Agent Purdy McElvain to investigate the claims and determine their validity.[43] The Wyandot Council confirmed that Isaac Walker, listed by his Wyandot name, was on the 1817 treaty lists, and that they approved the land selected by John Carey on Isaiah's behalf. The chiefs, Isaac's brother William, and Joseph Chaffee all signed the communication.[44] Despite the assertions and actions of the Wyandot Council, the Walker family, and Chaffee, however, the War Department determined that the chiefs had no power to grant Isaiah Walker land individually. According to the treaty of 1817, the entire Grand Reserve had been granted to the chiefs by patent in fee simple "for the use of the persons mentioned in the Schedule annexed to the treaty of whom Isaac Walker was one." This meant that chiefs held a "trust grant," which meant the lands were "for the equal and common use of the persons named in the Schedule." Not only did Isaiah Walker (through his father) not have a right to individual land ownership, none of the Wyandots did. The only entity the Wyandots could convey land to would be the United States government.[45] As for Isaac Walker's property rights, the Wyandot tribal council, seemingly at the urging of Isaac's brother William, passed a resolution in the 1830s that secured title to his buildings, physical property, and land rights to his young son, as well as recognizing his son as a Wyandot citizen. Isaac Walker's descendants continued to live their Wyandot identities after removal to Kansas and later Oklahoma, where his kin became leading figures within and without the Wyandotte community.[46]

The story of Isaac Walker's life, and the subsequent legal wrangling about his identity, provide us with a glimpse into the complexities of identity and race in the early-nineteenth-century Midwest. The product of generations of intermixing of peoples and cultures, Isaac Walker forged a unique identity that drew upon both his indigenous and white ancestry and cultures, both blending and shifting this identity to suit his interests. He made his living, cast his ballots, bought and sold his goods, and married across the boundaries between Indian and white society. This was made possible because of the time period and geographic location he occupied. Indeed, his story is a story of what was made possible through the contact of cultures in the Midwest in the first decades of the nineteenth century and reveals the nuances of personal identity some Native Americans could express in this space and place. Walker's story can also be read as a microcosm of the broader transitions of the nineteenth-century Midwest, where indigenous visibility began to fade and be marginalized, giving way to the increasing dominance of Euro-American peoples and cultures.

Notes

1. There are several examples of the blurring of racial identities among midwestern Native Americans in this era. For a few examples, see Donald H. Gaff, "Three Men from Three Rivers: Navigating between Native and American Indian Identity in the Old Northwest Territory," in Daniel P. Barr,

ed., *The Boundaries Between Us: Native and Newcomers along the Frontiers of the Old Northwest Territory, 1750–1850* (Kent, OH: Kent State University Press, 2006), 143–60; Bradley J. Birzer, "Jean Baptiste Richardville: Miami Metis," in R. David Edmunds, ed., *Enduring Nations: Native Americans in the Midwest* (Urbana: University of Illinois Press, 2008), 94–108; and Susan Sleeper-Smith, "Resistance to Removal: The 'White Indian,' Frances Slocum," in ibid., 109–23.

2. For a biography of William Walker Sr., see "Text on Life of William Walker snr. By William Walker jnr.," 21 March 1860, Wisconsin State Historical Society, Lyman C. Draper Collection (hereafter Draper Collection), roll 57, 11 U 12 and 11 U 14. For biographical information on Catherine Walker, see "Notes by Lyman C. Draper, Gov. Walker's Parents & Means of Ind'n. Information," ibid., 11 U 102.

3. Ibid., 11 U 14. Also see "A List of William Walker's Property Destroyed by the British Troops in the War of 1812," William Walker Papers, Kansas City Kansas Public Library (hereafter WWP, KCKPL).

4. "Notes by Lyman C. Draper of an interview with William and Mrs. Walker at Wyandott," July 1868, Draper Collection, 11 U 72. For more on the Badger mission and school, see Michael Leonard Cox, "Wendats, Presbyterians, and the Origins of Protestant Christianity on the Sandusky River," in Thomas Peace and Kathryn Magee Labelle, eds., *From Huronia to Wendakes: Adversity, Migrations, and Resilience, 1650–1900* (Norman: University of Oklahoma Press, 2016), 111–43.

5. Catherine Walker, Isaac's mother, was usually considered one-half Wyandot, but in genealogical terms had more white ancestry. For more on the Wyandot and perceptions of race and identity in this period (and references to other studies of the Wyandot in this era), see Michael Leonard Cox, "The Ohio Wyandots: Religion and Society on the Sandusky River, 1795–1843" (PhD diss., University of California, Riverside, 2016).

6. Maureen Konkle presents an interesting consideration of Native American literacy as a tool of both critique of American policy and evidence of cultural change over time, rather than cultural corruption or inauthenticity. See Konkle, *Writing Indian Nations: Native Intellectuals and the Politics of Historiography, 1827–1863* (Chapel Hill: University of North Carolina Press, 2004).

7. "Foot of the Rapids (Fort Meigs), 1817," Clarke Historical Library, Central Michigan University, accessed 13 February 2019, https://www.cmich.edu/library/clarke/ResearchResources/Native_American_Material/Treaty_Rights/Text_of_Michigan_Related_Treaties/Pages/Foot-of-the-Rapids-(Fort-Meigs),-1817.aspx.

8. For examples of the Walker family involvement with the treaty process, see William Walker to Lewis Cass, 27 May 1817, Letters Sent and Received, Michigan Superintendency, Indian Affairs (hereafter LSRMS), M1, roll 3, National Archives and Records Administration (NARA); Paul D. Butler

and Solomon Smith to Cass, 30 May 1817 (copy), John Johnston Papers, Ohio Historical Society, roll 1. Cass had asked Butler and Smith to "have an eye on the proceedings in the Indian Country and particularly upon the conduct of Walker." Cass to Duncan McArthur, 13 June 1817, LSRMS, M1, roll 3, NARA; Johnston to Cass, 12 June 1817, Ibid.; and Cass to Walker, 7 June 1817, ibid.

9. This tour is referenced in many publications. See for example H. Bigelow and Orville L. Holley, *The American Monthly Magazine and Critical Review*, Vol. 2 (New York: D. Fanshaw, 1817), 139.

10. Notably in William Walker's will, he provided property and proceeds for all of his children except Isaac. Isaac only received a horse "as his full share of my estate, as it is intended that he, shall, be provided for out of my wife's Tract of land near honey creek." "Last will and testament of William Walker," 10 March 1823, WWP, KCKPL.

11. Isaac Walker to Lewis Cass, 1 November 1823, LSRMS, M1, roll 13, NARA.

12. For his part, Isaac maintained that his father's property, other than physical improvements, had all gone to paying his debts. Isaac claimed that only his labor had provided for his mother and four youngest siblings, which led him to assert that he should have title over the property. "Statement of Isaac Walker taking charge of the family after the death of his father WW Sr.," 20 July 1825, WWP, KCKPL.

13. John McElvain to Thomas McKenney, 4 October 1829, Letters Received by the Office of Indian Affairs, Piqua Agency (hereafter LROIA, PA), M234, reel 669, NARA.

14. One likely (though limited) ledger from the Walker store is "Store Ledger," Mildred Willis Papers, Oklahoma Historical Society.

15. "General Store Ledgers, Tymochtee, Ohio (Wyandot County), 1824–32," Center for Archival Collections, Bowling Green State University (hereafter BGSU), MMS-1131.

16. Ibid.

17. Isaac and the other Walker children proved invaluable to the mission school, as they could "speak both the English and Wyandot language very well." "Religious Intelligence," *A New Series of the Evangelical Intelligencer; for 1809. Published under the Patronage of the General Assembly of the Presbyterian Church in the United States of America*, III (Philadelphia: William P. Farrand, 1809), 379–80.

18. David Elliott, *The Life of the Rev. Elisha Macurdy* (Philadelphia: William S. Martien, 1848), 124.

19. "Register of the Missionary Society at Upper Sandusky," John Stewart United Methodist Church, Upper Sandusky, Ohio, Center for Archival Collections, BGSU, MS-466.

20. James B. Finley, *History of the Wyandott Mission* (Cincinnati: Wright and Swormstedt, 1840), 416.

21. "A Sketch of the Life of Ma-nuncu," *The Methodist Magazine*, Vol. X (New York: Bangs and Emory, 1827), 470.
22. Finley, *History of the Wyandott Mission*, 417.
23. The couple also had a son, William, who died in infancy. For Rebecca's genealogy, see John Joseph May, *Danforth Genealogy* (Boston: Charles H. Pope, 1902), 129.
24. Intermarriages were frequently recorded in marriage records in several Ohio counties. "Marriage record files," author's possession.
25. Fay A. Yarbrough, in her discussion of Cherokee mores on race in the first half of the nineteenth century, notes that in Cherokee society at this time, racial definitions were used to define which potential partners would be suitable or unsuitable for marriage. Yarbrough convincingly argues that the Cherokee (and by extension other Native Americans) forged their own racialized notions in the process, particularly tri-racial systems of definition. Fay A. Yarbrough, *Race and the Cherokee Nation: Sovereignty in the Nineteenth Century* (Philadelphia: University of Pennsylvania Press, 2008), 4–9.
26. Nevin O. Winter, *A History of Northwest Ohio: A Narrative Account of Its Historical Progress and Development form the First European Exploration of the Maumee and Sandusky Valleys and the Adjacent Shores of Lake Erie, down to the Present Time* (Chicago: The Lewis Publishing Company, 1917), 646.
27. Isaac Walker left a number of ventures in progress at the time of his death. For example, he had purchased a windmill from near Piqua, Ohio. See John Johnston to William Walker, 24 July 1829, WWP, KCKPL.
28. John McElvain to Thomas McKenney, 4 October 1829, LROIA, PA, M234, reel 669, NARA. McElvain had requested the opinion of Michigan Territorial Governor (and local Superintendent of Indian Affairs) Lewis Cass on the case, but he refused to commit to one.
29. Chaffee opened one of the first taverns at Tymochtee, the location of the general store mentioned earlier. Winter, *A History of Northwest Ohio*, 645.
30. John McElvain to Thomas McKenney, 21 November 1829, LROIA, PA, M234, reel 669, NARA.
31. Thomas McKenney to John McElvain, 24 November 1829, Letters Sent, Office of Indian Affairs (hereafter LSIOA), M21, reel 6, NARA.
32. "Draft of the Will of Isaac Walker," 19 May 1829, WWP, KCKPL; and "Last Will and Testament of Isaac Walker," 16 October 1829, ibid.
33. John McElvain to Thomas McKenney, 6 February 1830, LROIA, PA, M234, reel 669, NARA.
34. William Walker to James B. Finley, 22 April 1831, James B. Finley Papers, Archives of Ohio United Methodism, Ohio Wesleyan University.
35. "Caution," in *Marion Phoenix*, 23 April 1831. Also published in the 30 April, 7 May, 14 May, and 21 May 1831 editions.
36. "Statement of Wyandot Chiefs (copy)," 22 March 1833, Letters Received by the Office of Indian Affairs, Ohio Agency (hereafter LROIA, OA)

M234, reel 601, NARA. The proposed section was in the northwest corner of the reservation, and abutted with Chaffee's own land just outside the Grand Reserve.
37. Joseph Chaffee to Lewis Cass, 22 March 1833, LROIA, OA, M234, reel 601, NARA.
38. Elbert Herring to Joseph Chaffee, 6 April 1833, LSOIA, M21, reel 10, NARA.
39. "Chaffee v. Garrett," in Charles Hammond, *Cases Decided in the Supreme Court of Ohio in Bank*, Vol. VI (Cincinnati: Robert Clarke & Co., 1872), 421–26. For lower court references to the case, see "Joseph Chaffee vs. George Garrett," in *Supreme Court Journal*, 12–13, Crawford County Court Records, reel 11, BGSU.
40. "Chaffee v. Garrett."
41. Ibid.
42. Joseph Chaffee to Lewis Cass, 22 March 1835, Letters Received by the Office of Indian Affairs, Ohio Agency Emigration and Ohio Agency Reserves (hereafter LROIA, OAE/OAR), M234, reel 603, NARA.
43. Elbert Herring to Purdy McElvain, 2 April 1835, LSOIA, M21, reel 15, NARA; and Elbert Herring to Joseph Chaffee, 2 April 1835, ibid.
44. Wyandot Chiefs to Lewis Cass, 30 April 1835, LROIA, OAE/OAR, M234, reel 603, NARA. Purdy McElvain confirmed the facts in McElvain to Elbert Herring, 14 May 1835, LROIA, OAE/OAR, M234, reel 603, NARA.
45. Elbert Herring to Purdy McElvain, 27 August 1835, LSOIA, M21, reel 17, NARA. Chaffee continued to press his claims for compensation despite the Ohio Supreme Court ruling. Joseph Chaffee to J.M. Porter, 17 April 1843, LROIA, OA, M234, reel 602, NARA. The department told Chaffee once again that it was a private matter between himself and the Walkers. T. Hartley Crawford to Joseph Chaffee, 26 April 1843, LSOIA, M21, reel 33, NARA. Chaffee grew exasperated, as the Walkers continued to refuse to do anything, with most of the family gone to Kansas by 1843. Chaffee asked for more guidance for where to go, exclaiming, "I must have relief from some source, either from the Dept. or from Congress." Joseph Chaffee to T.H. Crawford, 9 October 1843, LROIA, OA, M234, reel 602, NARA. His claims were only ever partially met.
46. For example, his grandson became a key source of ethnographic and traditional information about the Wyandotte in the early twentieth century. Bertrand N.O. Walker (Hen-Toh), *Tales of the Bark Lodges* (Jackson: University of Mississippi Press, 1995 [1919]).

Eric Michael Rhodes | Midwestern "Mobocracy"

The Emergence of Labor Politics and Racial Exclusion in Cincinnati and the Lower Old Northwest, 1829–1836

During her stay in the 1820s, Englishwoman Frances Trollope was shocked by the behavior of the workers whom she encountered in Cincinnati.[1] There, the everyman was as prideful as any European elite. Yet they disdained the markers of that continent's aristocracy. Cincinnatians "quoted that phrase of mischievous sophistry, 'all men are born free and equal.'"[2] They revered the name of Thomas Jefferson.[3] One of Trollope's white[4] domestic workers accused her of treating those in her employ "as bad as if we was Negurs."[5] When she asked if Cincinnati should pass a law restricting the construction of reeking pork slaughterhouses, a local replied: "No, no ... that may do very well for your tyrannical country, where a rich man's nose is more thought of than a poor man's mouth; but hogs be profitable produce here, and we be too free for such a law as that."[6]

In the popular imagination, the Midwest of the United States has often been associated with Jeffersonian, Puritan notions of "hard work."[7] Around the time of Trollope's residence, a free labor ideology developed in Cincinnati. It arose in step with the ongoing Market Revolution. Yet observers considered Cincinnati the capital of a region defined as much by its industry and fierce egalitarianism as its racial prejudice. Because the southern extent of the Old Northwest was the section of the United States where the interests of white laborers found their most radical expression, a particular strand of populism emerged around Cincinnati. Matthew Stanley's *The Loyal West* contends that the "tendency toward ... social conservatism and racialized populism" has been a consistent facet of the Midwest's social identity since the Civil War.[8] However, the region displayed these characteristics as early as the 1820s. The clash between an early form of free labor ideology, migration, and changing economic circumstances catalyzed this tendency.[9] By the 1830s, the future "Lower Middle West" was emerging as a region defined—paradoxically—by both freedom and exclusion, and by a conservative political consensus on economics and race.[10] Cincinnati's white "mobocrats" promoted this consensus, and they left an indelible mark on the region's identity.[11]

In his seminal *Frontier Republic*, Andrew Cayton shows that Jeffersonian settlers—and their prerogatives of democratic rights, meritocracy, localism, independence, and liberty—clashed with Federalist settlers who prioritized the creation of a national, pluralistic, and complex society in the Ohio country of the Early Republic.[12] The melding of Jeffersonian notions of liberty and Federalist economic conceptions produced a strong egalitarianism among Ohio's white settlers, with respect to both economics and politics.[13] By the late 1820s, this synthesis between the "conflicting revolutionary visions of the American future" became a feature of the Old Northwest's identity.[14] Jeffersonian and Federalist principles found a compromise in "hard work."

Jacksonian Cincinnati was, according to John Fairfield, "an expanding city of economic opportunity, egalitarian democracy and cultural ambition." It "exemplified free labor values" more than any other city in the nation by the late 1820s.[15] Individuals in the Old Northwest, with their "ambition to get forward," dedicated themselves to vocations and—according to their "right to rise" through hard work within a supposedly egalitarian (Jeffersonian) economy—aspired to ascend the social ladder conceptualized and justified by the Federalists.[16] As the nation entered the Second Party System, Cincinnatians combined a Whiggish faith in meritocratic opportunity (and the social order which it justified) with the Democratic principles of egalitarian republicanism and the interests of independent "small producers" or farmers and urban machinists.[17] This early form of free labor ideology emphasized "freedom, independence, and self-reliance."[18] Yet this philosophy was distinct from the one championed by the Republican party in the 1850s.[19] As we shall see, early free labor adherents in the lower Old Northwest had an ambivalent relationship to black people and to slavery.

The Market Revolution gave rise to the free labor consensus, which accommodated Federalist notions of the national economy with Jefferson's meritocracy. The "Queen City of the West" was perfectly poised to grow apace with the national market and became a major port city by the Jacksonian Era. Visitors to Cincinnati in the early 1830s were stunned by Cincinnati's exploding population. "Thirty years ago," wrote Frenchman Gustave de Beaumont in 1831, "the banks of the Ohio were a desert."[20] In the early 1800s, Cincinnati had been a small trading outpost. But by 1830, it was the nation's eighth most populous city with around 24,000 residents.[21] "I don't think that there is a city in the world," said Beaumont, "that has experienced such prodigious growth."[22]

The foundation of this growth lay in Cincinnati's geography. Sitting on the Ohio River, an outpost between the "Slave Power" and the "Money Power," it became a hub of steamboat traffic.[23] Before the State of Ohio became "fly-over country," it was "steam-through" country: boats carried raw cotton from Louisiana to Lowell, while finished consumer goods steamed in the other direction. Most of the ham and bacon made in "Porkopolis" ultimately landed on the tables of enslaved African Americans in the South.[24] Jacksonian Cincinnati benefited both from the country's growing industrial might and from slavery's capitalism.[25] Cincinnati was the perfect expression of market society, stitching together the nation's two economic poles. It was a "frontier city," as intimately tied to the East as it was the West, and to the North as to the South.[26] According to Beaumont and his travel partner Alexis de Tocqueville, Cincinnati's position on the Ohio made it "the *entrepôt* of the Mississippi and of New England and of the North and the South of America."[27] This geography would eventually contribute to the maturation of a nascent lower midwestern identity.

The lower Old Northwest was developing a character distinct from other regions of the United States. Cincinnati stood apart from the eastern cities from which European visitors to Ohio had embarked. The city embraced the ideology of free labor with exceptional zeal. Visiting Cincinnati in 1836, the economic philosopher Michel Chevalier remarked that "the useful occupied all thoughts" of the city's "industrious, sober, frugal" population. "Cincinnatians," he continued, "have taken [Benjamin] Franklin as their patron saint, and they have adopted *Poor Richard's Almanack* as a fifth gospel."[28] The doctrine of hard work appealed to both the wage-earning and merchant classes of Cincinnati. Many laborers imagined that they could climb the social ladder and enter the owning class through sheer determination. Capitalists and their managers justified their increasing wealth *vis* the growing class of poor laborers by claiming they had worked hard for their station.[29] Work was the way in which citizens could become self-sufficient and independent—two essential tenets of free labor ideology.

Hard work went hand in glove with democracy for Cincinnatians. The opposite of hard work was leisure, which Cincinnatians abhorred. Cincinnati was, Chevalier noted, well-suited for "work-loving people, but not for those who are enamored of pleasure and relaxation."[30] To a greater extent than in the neighboring Northeast and South, Chevalier reported, Cincinnatians considered "leisure ... the stepping stone to aristocracy."[31] "Aristocracy" in this sense stood for undeserved power—economic or political. Cincinnatians thought that no one should be permitted wealth or power without having worked for them. To allow for this would not be in keeping with free labor meritocracy, and thus would be immoral. The immorality of privilege was inherent to Europe and the East of the United States, the thinking went, and Cincinnatians defined themselves against each.[32] In Cincinnati, "hemmed in by the laborious habits of the country, by political notions, and by religion," wrote Chevalier,

> a man [of leisure] must either resign himself to the same mode of life with the mass [of Cincinnatians], or seek a soil less unfriendly to his tastes in the great cities of New York, Philadelphia, or New Orleans, or even in Europe.[33]

The national market allowed many lower Old Northwesterners to view their society in egalitarian terms—another facet of free labor ideology. In Cincinnati and much of the North, work was shifting away from the "long-term, paternalistic obligations of apprenticeship or the legal subjugation of indentured servitude" toward what Chevalier called "republican industry."[34] The systems of patronage and *noblesse oblige* with which visitors from the East were so familiar did not seem to exist in Cincinnati.[35] Instead, lower Old Northwestern worker-citizens asserted their independence through the new market for wage labor. In this sense, "republican industry" espoused both economic and political liberty.[36]

To the surprise of European visitors, domestic work under "republican industry" took on a radically different meaning in the lower Old Northwest than in parts of the country settled before Ohio. French nobleman Theodore Pavie warned his compatriots never to call a hired Cincinnatian "by the name of 'waiter' or 'servant,' because she will leave your house that day, that hour, that instant!"[37] To her surprise, Frances Trollope learned that Cincinnati's women preferred dangerous, wage-paying factory jobs to working as maids. Notwithstanding that the latter was better remunerated, "they think," Trollope wrote, "their equality ... compromised" by domestic work.[38] When Trollope proposed to pay her maid "by the year," the retort came: "You be a downright Englisher sure enough! ... You must just give me a dollar and a half a week."[39] This offer, Trollope accepted "with all dutiful submission."[40] Wages meant independence from patronage, and the pride which came with this independence made Cincinnati's workers fiercely egalitarian. They often assumed the rhetoric of the War of Independence in discussing economic relations.[41] Workers would never again be subjects of a king or queen—nor of an eastern elite.

Cincinnatians' confidence in the nascent ideal of free labor grew apace with the size of their pocketbooks. Lower Old Northwesterners zealously promoted the idea that citizens could reap the rewards of hard work within the parameters of what was thought to be a meritocratic economy. During the 1820s, those eager to take advantage of the new market economy poured into this city which loudest proclaimed the gospel of free labor. Immigrants came from New England, the middle states, the South, and northern European countries—particularly Ireland—to "get forward."[42]

Many poor southern whites migrated to Cincinnati in pursuit of the dream of free labor. Alexis de Tocqueville wrote that while hard work was honored among Ohio's whites, it was disgraced in Kentucky and deprived the South of an enterprising spirit.[43] Slave society idealized the leisure afforded the planter class. There, menial labor and domestic work was to be done by enslaved African Americans, not free whites.[44] As a result, explained Tocqueville, Covington and Newport did not receive many migrants and remained far less urbanized than Cincinnati.[45] Aspiring whites came north to gain independence and work their way up the social ladder. But arriving on "free soil," they remained wedded to the racist dispensation of the Slave Power. In fact, white workers on the Ohio side of "slavery's borderland" insisted that part of what made them free laborers was *not* being slaves.[46] To take again the example of domestic work, in Cincinnati it was a dishonorable vocation because it was not only *not* paid in wages; it was the type of work reserved for black people a few miles away. Trollope's "help" promised to bring her "mother's slave, Phillis ... from t'other side the water, to help [her] clean."⁴⁷ Her maid eventually quit because she felt herself above such domestic work. Free whites in Cincinnati would not stoop to the social level associated with non-citizens.⁴⁸

Of course, black Southerners also saw the appeal of Cincinnati's culture of free labor. But reaping the rewards of hard work was hardest for these migrants. White Ohioans reasoned that African Americans—particularly freed slaves—were incapable of being independent and self-sufficient, and therefore, of partaking in free labor. They would instead become dependents of the state, living undeservedly on the fruits of the hard work of white Cincinnatians.⁴⁹ The supposed natural dependency of black people undermined societal virtue, "replacing it with self-interested vice," leading eventually to societal collapse.⁵⁰ Many white Cincinnatians feared that after statehood in 1803, as city father Daniel Drake put it, "we should be degraded by the free negroes of other states, and infested with their run-away slaves."⁵¹

To discourage black migration, the Ohio legislature passed the Black Laws of 1804 and 1807.⁵² Many whites feared that black migrants would bring their "immoral," "lazy" ways to Ohio. Others worried that the state would be accused of harboring escaped "property," thereby risking discord with their economic partners in the South.⁵³ Still others feared that black migrants would compete with whites for jobs.⁵⁴ Under the Black Laws, African Americans wishing to settle in Ohio had to find two white sponsors to guarantee a "surety" of five hundred dollars.⁵⁵ They also had to register with local overseers of the poor, who would ensure that they were not becoming dependents of the state.⁵⁶ Black migrants had to carry proof of their freedom at all times.⁵⁷ If black people failed to meet any of these requirements, they could be sent out of the state. Ohio's Black Laws were the first such statutes in the United States and in what would become the Midwest.⁵⁸

During his visit, Tocqueville asked one prominent Cincinnatian about what he called these "very severe laws against blacks."⁵⁹ "We are trying to discourage them in every possible way," came the reply. In 1808, for example, one city ordinance attempted to discourage black

Cincinnatians from continuing in their "idle lives and vicious habits."[60] Laws weren't the only barriers to black people, but white Cincinnatians "annoy them in a thousand ways."[61] For example, whites sometimes refused to pay their black laborers, and African Americans could not bring legal suit against them.[62] Black workers in Cincinnati were all too aware that they could not obtain the ideal of free labor as easily as whites. But despite these significant legal and cultural barriers, free blacks and escaped slaves continued to seek a better life in Cincinnati throughout the first decades of the 1800s.

Black migrants settled predominantly in the neighborhoods of Bucktown (First Ward) and Little Africa (Fourth Ward), and on the waterfront.[63] White landlords built ramshackle tenements in each quarter to house the new laborers.[64] Daniel Drake remarked that black work was limited to "laborious occupations," as black people were "prone to the performance of light and menial drudgery."[65] Thus, these poor, black communities became easy and identifiable targets for white scorn. "Petty thefts" were attributed to black residential areas in Cincinnati.[66]

Cincinnati, the first major Old Northwestern city to which large numbers of African Americans migrated, was thoroughly segregated. White landlords profited from the concentrations of low-rent, black tenement housing, which required little in the way of maintenance because their residents had little geographic choice.[67] In 1829, the city council officially segregated its schools along the lines of race.[68] Churches, too, were segregated.[69]

This segregation concretized the racial hierarchy of the day. Protestant whites and Englishmen predominated over the Germans; the Irish came next.[70] Black people were last in the pecking order. Black workers, wrote English observer E.S. Abdy, knew that "the free Negro labored under disadvantages unknown either to the slave or the white worker" because of Ohio's racial caste system.[71] Still, they came. However, by the late 1820s, free labor was losing credibility among sectors of Cincinnati's working class.

White wage earners felt increasingly left behind as the growth of the new market economy accelerated.[72] While the Market Revolution was not yet complete, factories were quickly replacing shops.[73] The artisan system—in which apprentices studied with master craftsmen, who in turn became journeymen and eventually masters with their own shops—was under assault, as factory owners increasingly employed new technologies and unskilled workers.[74] Journeymen, whose masters had leveraged their shops into factories, suffered diminished future prospects. Unskilled laborers, toiling away in factories, had not risen above the rank of worker, despite their hard work.

Interestingly, things weren't as bad for white workers in Cincinnati as they were in other parts of the country. Cincinnati's artisans had reason to feel threatened by changes in the economy and rising labor competition, but the everyman's economic conditions appeared relatively good to contemporary visitors. In an interview with a local, Tocqueville reported that in Cincinnati "the price of labor is so high (*one third more than in New England*) and the cost of living so low, that in two or three years [laborers] can put by some capital."[75]

Still, the white working class could not help but worry that their prospects of "getting forward" were under threat. While back East, white workers formed unions to oppose diminishing returns, in slavery's borderland they made migrant workers into scapegoats.[76] As Cincinnati's black population doubled in size from 1825 to 1829 (to ten percent of the city at large), white workers became doubly convinced that competition from free blacks was at the root of their diminished prospects.[77] Newspapers of the time echoed the popular sentiment: black people were of "an idle, intemperate and dissolute race ... a burden on the resources of the State and to the energies of the laboring class of citizens."[78] Paradoxically, then, black people were at once both lazy and an economic threat.

Black labor was seen as an affront to the social order of the capital of the Old Northwest. Free blacks were not supposed to partake of free labor ideology, with which white Cincinnatians identified. And when they did, white Cincinnatians thought it was at the expense of their economic progress. Whites thought free labor was reserved for them, Ohio's "true citizens": the Black Codes had institutionalized this common view. This whites-only version of free labor led Tocqueville to theorize that "the prejudice of race appears to be stronger in the states that have abolished slavery than in those where it still exists; and nowhere is it so intolerant as in those states where servitude has never been known."[79]

White working-class Cincinnatians sought a political solution to the problem of undeserving blacks. And the voice of the white worker could be heard loud and clear in Jacksonian Cincinnati. Visitors and locals alike proclaimed the Old Northwest to be the most democratic section of the country—another facet of emergent midwestern identity.[80] "Republican principles, established without restriction" ruled Cincinnati, and the average citizen could "march through the plentitude of his liberty without restriction on his interests and passions."[81] Because Ohio's constitution was written at the zenith of Jeffersonian democracy, it empowered the white everyman. Under it, white men, regardless of property-holding status, were entitled to the right to vote. The frequency and breadth of elections in Ohio were shocking to visitors.[82] The will of the electorate—all male and all white—was manifest to the greatest degree.

Some of Cincinnati's elites, primarily Whigs, worried that there was *too much* democracy in Ohio.[83] The masses, according to the Europeans who interviewed them, were not sufficiently enlightened to govern. Future Supreme Court Justice and Cincinnatian Salmon P. Chase complained to Tocqueville that many of those elected to local government were "absolutely unworthy to occupy the position to which they have been elevated."[84] Instead of valuing political experience and wisdom in their candidates, white worker-voters preferred those who had successfully climbed the social ladder and had the common touch.[85] Another lawyer told Tocqueville that former Congressman and General William Henry Harrison had lost a recent local election to a political outsider who had made his living selling cakes in the street.[86] The merchants responsible for bringing riches to Cincinnati and those who could project a hard-working, free labor ethos often won office.[87] Politicians won Cincinnati's electorate, explained Chase, "by base flattery of its passions, by drinking with it."[88] While New Englanders were judicious in their vote, "in the West, candidates have to go out to harangue [their] followers in the streets and drink with them in the taverns."[89] At best, Ohio had the most mediocre politicians in the nation.[90] At worst, Ohio had a propensity for electing opportunistic demagogues who could seize power by appealing to the basest impulses of their supporters.[91]

The Whigs whom Tocqueville interviewed cited Cincinnati's strong support of President Andrew Jackson, a Democrat, as evidence that democracy had run amok in the Old Northwest.[92] Even though he filled his cabinet with his cronies, Jackson's anti-corruption platform appealed to lower Old Northwestern farmers and urban laborers who viewed the East as morally bankrupt.[93] These "small producers" hated taxes, and worried that the central government and the banks would exercise tyranny over them.[94] Suffrage in Ohio was so broad, claimed Tocqueville's interviewees, that the passions of working-class "Jackson men" decided elections.

Yet Jackson was not the enemy of Whiggish capitalism his critics made him out to be. Harry Watson's neat dichotomy, between "sober and hardworking" Whigs—who wanted to conserve the market order—on the one hand and the reactionary Democrats—who opposed it—on the other, somewhat broke down in the Cincinnati of the 1830s.[95] While it was true enough that the reactions of urban artisans to the nation's first capitalist depression—the Panic of 1819—gave rise to Jackson, Old Hickory's life story as a self-made man fit well into the "right to rise" narrative to which many Ohio Democrats adhered.[96] Further, Jackson himself associated with and moved in elite circles of upper middle-class businessmen.[97] The white everyman in Cincinnati knew that his destiny was tied up in the national market; he wanted to advance from the menial labor he was doing in service of the market to owning a piece of it. He wanted a market in which he could "get forward"; in which he would profit from his labor given his "right to rise." Jackson men in Cincinnati adhered to a version of free labor ideology which idealized a market that served them.

Both Whigs and Democrats upheld what Johnathan Glickstein has called "*herrenvolk* democracy."[98] Under it, Ohio's white laborers benefited from a native "system of egalitarianism" under which they could exercise their political will. But this egalitarianism was limited to white men, the only eligible voters in Cincinnati. And though Watson writes that voting for Jackson allowed the white working-class electorate to vent their frustrations while "blunting their potentially disruptive consequences" (and further that "ethno-cultural conflict" did not override class animosities), this was not the case in Cincinnati.[99] And this points to the emergence of a uniquely midwestern identity.

As we have seen, images of the region we now call the Midwest as politically populist and economically egalitarian date to the white settlement of Ohio in the Early Republic period. These settlers of the

Old Northwest carried with them an Anglo conception of liberty for insider whites predicated on the suppression of outsiders. Because the Old Northwest was settled during the emergence of free labor ideology, the region was marked by the promise of free citizenship for whites to the exclusion and subjugation of non-white non-citizens. This intellectual framework was all the more acutely felt in the lower reaches of the Old Northwest, where slavery's exploitation was close at hand.[100]

Channeling their energies as an economically disaffected and politically empowered bloc, white residents of working-class wards in Cincinnati launched a political campaign to limit the growth—and eventually, the existence—of the city's black population, who represented a challenge to the region's whites-only free labor consensus.[101] In 1827, a petition emerged from white artisans and unskilled laborers living in the First Ward complaining that black-occupied tenements in their neighborhood were a nuisance.[102] When it became clear that city council would not remove the renters—many councilmen were merchants who profited from the labor of black Cincinnatians—white citizens submitted another petition demanding restriction of black migration to Cincinnati.[103] The council set up a committee to examine the matter.

The Supreme Court of Ohio decided against a suit claiming that the Black Laws were unconstitutional in 1829.[104] Calls from white workers to banish black people from Cincinnati increased in the wake of the decision, and whites made banishment an issue in the local elections that year.[105] White workers of the Third Ward—between Little Africa and Bucktown—declared that they would not vote for any candidate "but such as will put in force the laws of the state relative to black and mulatto persons."[106] That April, pro-Black Laws candidates rode this wave of reactionary fervor into office.[107] The overseers of the poor published a declaration soon after the elections calling for all black citizens to put up their bonds or leave the state. Further, they introduced a limitation on white employers' hiring of black laborers without proof of surety.[108] But this was not enough to placate whites. By the end of the summer, frustrated that not all of Cincinnati's black population had left, white laborers took the law into their own hands.

The *Western Star* reported on August 29th that riots had broken out in Cincinnati. White workers, according to the *Star*:

animated by the prospect of high wages, which the sudden removal of fifteen hundred laborers from the city, might occasion, thinking the law not rapid enough in its movements, in getting rid of the blacks, during three several nights made the most violent assaults, in great numbers upon the blacks ... throwing stones, demolishing houses, doing every other act of riotous violence.[109]

Scholars estimate that by the time the dust had settled, around half of Cincinnati's black population had fled to Canada.[110] Cincinnati's black population did not rise above six percent again until after the end of the Civil War.[111] According to Nikki Taylor, this was one of the first recorded incidents of mob violence intended not only to intimidate its target but to expel an entire population.[112] The documentary record shows that the Cincinnati riot of 1829 was perhaps the first incident of urban mob violence intended to drive out blacks in the nation's history.[113] E.S. Abdy certainly thought so: "Brutal and ungrateful as the whole Union has shewn [sic] itself to [black] people, not one State had dared, till lately, to push its hatred so far, as to expel them by violence."[114] Segregation enforced by violence had debuted as a feature of the Lower Middle West.

The free labor consensus which emerged in the 1850s—wholly opposed to the Slave Power—had not yet developed, and a certain ambivalence toward, if not an acquiescence to, slavery took hold in Ohio. Wrote Abdy, the riots of 1829 were an effort to "break up an asylum, which the fugitives from Kentucky ... are sure to find there, on crossing the river."[115] This accommodationist strain of free labor ideology was native to the lower reaches of Ohio, Illinois, and Indiana.[116] If slavery kept black people from impinging on the fruits of their labor, many white lower Old Northwesterners thought it a safeguard and completely compatible with their vision of (whites-only) free labor.[117]

Other lower Old Northwesterners sought to profit by actively participating in slavery's capitalism. This was not lost on William Wells Brown when he fled from the man who had enslaved him. Fleeing the docks at Cincinnati, he ran for the woods "knowing well that [he] could not travel, even in the State of Ohio ... without danger of being arrested."[118] The Quaker who eventually gave him shelter warned Wells when they met on the road north of Cincinnati that he was "in a very pro-slavery neighborhood."[119] Brown had good reason to fret. Denizens of such Ohio neighborhoods would sell around 375,000 African Americans back into slavery during the antebellum period.[120] While the practice was illegal according to Ohio law, it was far from rigidly enforced.[121] One southern Ohio newspaper reported that a magistrate capitulated to a Kentucky slave owner who had come across the river in search of an enslaved man named Tom.[122] Despite protestations from some citizens, the slave catchers took him away. That night, in Cincinnati, "stimulated with even the faint prospect of escape, or perhaps predetermined on liberty or death, [Tom] threw himself from the window which is upwards of fifty feet from the pavement."[123] Tom could not find liberty in Ohio, where many citizens opposed the existence of free black life and sought to profit from slavery.

Exclusionary and pro-slavery opinions were not by any means limited to the working classes in Jacksonian Cincinnati. The Colonization Society, composed of elites, thought white citizens could not coexist with black people because of the latter's fundamentally lazy and immoral character. The Society advocated the banishment of black Cincinnatians "back to Africa."[124] Their publications in the newspapers served as racist fodder, whipping up anti-black sentiment in a white citizenry who already saw black migrants as an economic threat.

Many elites accommodated slavery as a political and economic necessity. Cincinnati's merchants—having proven themselves morally worthy by working hard, according to reigning free labor ideology—won most of the votes of white working men, who aspired to their station. Historian Richard Wade made the distinction more precise: Cincinnati's "urban affairs were managed not merely by merchants, but usually by the most successful ones."[125] The most successful merchants in Cincinnati during the Jacksonian Era were those who traded with the South. Without selling manufactured goods to slaveholders and marketing their pork as food for enslaved African Americans, these Cincinnati elites would have lost their political and economic station.[126] If Cincinnati became known as a haven for runaways, it would hurt the commercial ties and the comity with southern slaveholders which gave rise to Cincinnati's merchant class.[127]

Given Ohio's radical republicanism and wide suffrage, no businessman could win office in the 1830s without appealing to the sentiments of white workers. This meant taking seriously the latter's zeal to restrict black migrants' access to the city's labor market by either banishment or enslavement. Cincinnati businessmen therefore had a vested interest in the maintenance of both Ohio's Black Laws and slavery. One could not hope to reach the zenith of economic or political power in Jacksonian Cincinnati without implicating oneself in the politics of free labor, slavery's capitalism, and racial banishment.

White Cincinnatians defined themselves at once by their *ties to* and their *separation from* the South. Cincinnati's merchant class owed its wealth to the existence of slavery. But the expansion of slave society north of the Ohio would be ruinous to the free labor ideology which justified its power. In other words, Ohio did not exist without Kentucky. Lower Old Northwestern identity was born of the geographic and economic interstice between free labor and slavery.[128]

Therefore, a politics of compromise on slavery emerged in the lower stretches of the Old Northwest.[129] White Cincinnatians had to seek a middle ground between freedom and unfreedom because they saw themselves as a product of each. Daniel Drake explained to English visitor Harriet Martineau that "the hills of Western Virginia and Kentucky cast their morning shadows on the plains of Ohio, Indiana, Illinois, and Missouri."[130] If lower Old Northwesterners failed to forge a common identity with their neighbors to the south, continued Drake, the cost would be no less than civil war:

> Thus connected by nature in the great valley, we must live in the bonds of companionship or imbrue our hands in each other's blood. We have no middle destiny.[131]

The ideal of political "moderation" as a way to keep the peace thus took on its importance among the lower Old Northwest's ruling commercial elite as the national market grew. This moderation did not split the difference between slavery and complete freedom for African Americans, however. Rather, because of the centrality of slavery to Cincinnati's economy and its proximity to Kentucky, merchants tried to limit the parameters of the debate to the interests of slaveholders on one extreme and those of the white free laborer on the other. However, a vocal segment of the population refused to partake in this compromise. They called for the abolition of slavery and the elimination of Ohio's Black Laws. This affront to commercial elites and the regional identity they had attempted to promote would not be tolerated.

In 1835, James Birney and some associates from the fledgling Ohio Anti-Slavery Society dared to establish an abolitionist newspaper in Cincinnati. *The Philanthropist* excoriated Cincinnati's business elite, insisting that they were "more interested in keeping up the Slavery of the South, than they [were] in maintaining the Liberty of the North."[132] Birney attacked the supposed free labor values of Cincinnati, in which businessmen sincerely believed: "You have ARISTOCRACY: we, the PEOPLE—you have INDOLENCE: we, ACTIVITY—you have WEALTH: we, PRINCIPLE—you have the spirit of OPPRESSION: we, of LIBERTY."[133]

This rhetoric exposed the hypocrisy of Ohio's accommodationist consensus and its celebration of white free labor, anti-sectionalism, and black exclusion.[134] Businessmen feared that Birney's abolitionists would "sever the golden chain" endearing Cincinnati's businessmen to their slaveholding partners.[135] The "Yankee" abolitionists threatened to disturb the delicate consensus they had made with the Slave Power.[136] Abolitionism was "unfair to the South" and "prejudicial to our quiet and prosperity," the merchants claimed.[137] The newspapers, owned by and mouthpieces for wealthy businessmen, began publishing articles advocating the removal of abolitionists "peaceably if it could, forcibly if it must."[138] Over the course of 1836, Cincinnati's businessmen, politicians, and citizens of note held meetings to plot the eradication of the abolitionist scourge.[139] Cincinnati, these elites determined, could not be seen to tolerate abolitionism.

When Birney seemed unfazed, the elite turned to mob violence. Middle-class agitators enlisted the help of Kentucky slaveholders and white working men to drive the "Yankees" out.[140] This mob of "moderates" swore they would tar and feather Birney in an act of republican revenge, for he was impinging on *their* rights as free citizens.[141] That summer, "well-dressed" mobs destroyed *The Philanthropist*'s printing press, ran the abolitionists out of town, and once again attacked black households.[142]

Harriet Martineau unequivocally blamed the commercial elite for the anti-abolitionist violence. It was "chiefly merchants" who encouraged the riot, owing to the "gold-dust which [blinded] them." Here were self-described republicans and free laborers advocating violence against those who would question their hypocrisy, she wrote. "Let them not," she continued, "boast of their liberality ... till such can be roused from their delusion."[143]

The exclusionary impulse and this reactionary strain of populism were so strong in Cincinnati that the nation took note.[144] As destructive as the violence stemming from jealous whites was to Cincinnati's black population, it inspired the cause for black human rights within and without the city. In response to the brutality of 1829, Cincinnati's first abolitionist group formed at the Lane Seminary.[145] The riots of 1836 galvanized many Ohioans, such as Salmon P. Chase, who had before been antislavery yet suspicious of abolitionism.[146] They organized against rule by "mobocrats."[147] Disturbed by the violence against black Cincinnatians, the free black citizens of Philadelphia organized the first national convention for civil rights in 1830.[148] Yet Cincinnati had not seen the last of "mobocracy."[149] When a black boy beat a white boy in a street fight, the whites of the "Queen City of Mobs" again attacked their black neighbors in 1841.[150]

Jacksonian Cincinnati, widely understood as the Old Northwest's most important city at the time, was the crucible of the Midwest's "tendency toward ... conservatism and racialized populism."[151] There, a free labor ideology which championed citizens' "right to rise" economically and politically, through hard work, left its mark. Yet white, male citizens—operating under *herrenvolk* democracy—excluded those whom they deemed unworthy of "rising" from partaking in this ideology.[152] When their opportunity to "get forward" was threatened by abolitionism and economic panic, Cincinnati's citizens scapegoated easily identifiable, socially inferior "others."[153] The Lower Middle West's propensity for reactionary populism and racial conservatism—from the Copperhead movement to "racialized labor violence to sundown towns to lynching"—emerged as early as the 1820s.[154] Ever since, African Americans in the region have faced "a southern racial code, northern segregation and discrimination, and western frontier mob violence."[155] The legacy of conservative "moderation" and reactionary populism which began forming as early as the reign of Cincinnati's "mobocracy" has had a profound impact on midwestern identity.[156]

As the oldest section of the settled Midwest, we should look to the lower Old Northwest for the roots of the Lower Middle West's identity, if not midwestern identity at large. Southwestern Ohio displayed "what would become quintessential midwestern characteristics" before any other part of the larger region: a respect for humble hard work, political egalitarianism and moderation, and racial banishment.[157] Cincinnati was the Midwest's chief frontier city, and on the banks of the Ohio economic, political, and cultural forces came to bear on interactions between its residents which would shape the larger region's identity.[158] In Jacksonian Cincinnati, the "messiness, occasional beauty, and terrible violence" wrought by the uneasy compromise between Federalist and Jacksonian philosophies in the context of racial politics, economic upheaval, and migration were on full display.[159]

As a frontier and border region, neither East not West nor North nor South, slavery's former borderland has, over time, displayed both of the characteristics described in this Civil Rights-era adage:

> In the South, the white man doesn't care how close you get, as long as you don't get too high. In the North, he doesn't care how high you get, as long as you don't get too close.[160]

Notes

Thanks to the staff at the Beinecke, Herman B. Wells, and William T. Young libraries, and to David Lincove of the Ohio State University Libraries, as well as to Scott Sanders and Robert Fogarty. This chapter benefited tremendously from the comments of Margaret Breidenbaugh, Andrew Offenburger, Kevin McGruder, Kelly Mill, Matthew Salafia, Matthew Stanley, and Lindsay Schakenbach Regele. I couldn't have written it without Kelly's unwavering support and encouragement. Thanks to my advisors Steve Conn and Nishani Frazier. Any and all errors of fact and interpretation are my own. Note on translations: All quotes from titles appearing in the French language were translated by the author.

1. Frances Trollope, *Domestic Manners of the Americans* (Barre, MA: Imprint Society, 1969).
2. Ibid., 55.
3. Ibid.

4. I refer to "whites" in this chapter without making ethnic distinctions. Even the Irish are referred to as "white." Matthew Jacobson writes that it was the crucible of the Great Migration of the 1920s when "whiteness was consolidated" into the category of "Caucasian"—a mixture of "Celts, Slavs, Hebrews, Iberics, and Saracens." But large numbers of black migrants came to Cincinnati in the 1820s, and it is not illogical to surmise that this might have "consolidated whiteness" to a considerable degree *vis* such an identifiable "other." I will hew to Nikki Taylor's use of the term "white," which Richard Wade employed in reference to the Jacksonian-era Irish in the context of Cincinnati as early as 1954. While Taylor acknowledges that during the 1820s the Irish were seen as the social analogues of free blacks, she includes an important qualifier: non-black migrants often assimilated into citizenship by shedding their accents, and their children had an even better chance of gaining whiteness than they, even as early as the 1820s. The larger point however is not about who was white necessarily but that the Irish people who partook in violence against blacks set an example that would be followed by whites, many of whom who had Irish ancestors, in future campaigns of anti-black vigilantism. See Matthew Jacobson, *Whiteness of a Different Color: European Immigrants and the Alchemy of Race* (Cambridge: Harvard University Press, 2003), 8; Nikki Taylor, *Frontiers of Freedom: Cincinnati's Black Community, 1802–1868* (Athens: Ohio University Press, 2005), 27; Richard Wade, "The Negro in Cincinnati, 1800–1830," *The Journal of Negro History* 39, no. 1 (1954): 43–57.
5. Trollope, *Domestic Manners*, 43.
6. Ibid, 82; Andrew Cayton, *The Frontier Republic: Ideology and Politics in the Ohio Country, 1780–1825* (Kent: Kent State University Press, 1986), xi.
7. R. Douglas Hurt, "Ohio: Gateway to the Midwest," in James Madison, ed., *Heartland: Comparative Histories of the Midwestern States* (Bloomington: Indiana University Press, 1988), 206; James Shortridge, "Images of the Midwest," in Andrew Cayton, Richard Sisson, and Chris Zacher, eds., *The American Midwest: An Interpretive Encyclopedia* (Bloomington: Indiana University Press, 2007), 58; James Shortridge, *The Middle West: Its Meaning in American Culture* (Lawrence: University Press of Kansas, 1994), 2.
8. Matthew Stanley, *The Loyal West: Civil War and Reunion in Middle America* (Urbana: University of Illinois Press, 2017), 10.
9. Hurt writes that Ohio politics have always been characterized by job-oriented, bread-and-butter politics. See Hurt, "Ohio," 220.
10. Stanley, *Loyal West*, 10; Hurt, "Ohio," 206.
11. Patrick Folk, "'The Queen City of Mobs': Riots and Community Reactions in Cincinnati, 1788–1848" (PhD diss., University of Toledo, 1978), 159.
12. Cayton, *Frontier Republic*, x–xi.
13. Ibid.
14. Ibid.

15. James Shortridge, "Cincinnati, Ohio," in Andrew Cayton, Richard Sisson, and Chris Zacher, eds., *The American Midwest: An Interpretive Encyclopedia* (Bloomington: Indiana University Press, 2007), 1154.
16. Kelly Arehart, "Chapter 8: The Market Revolution," in Jane Green, ed., *American Yawp* (Stanford: Stanford University Press, 2018).
17. Jonathan Glickstein, *Concepts of Free Labor in Ante-Bellum America* (New Haven: Yale University Press, 1992), 261–62; William Holmes, "Populism: In Search of Context," *Agricultural History* 64, no. 4 (1990): 42.
18. Leah Glaser, "Contextual Essay," A Guide to Primary Sources for U.S. History, 2005.
19. Eric Foner theorized in 1970 that "free labor" was a philosophy championing "the superiority of an open ... northern society in which work was both honored and rewarded and which damned as backward the slave-based society of the South." See Richard Sewell, "Free Soil, Free Labor, Free Men: The Ideology of the Republican Party Before the Civil War by Eric Foner," *Journal of American History* 57, no. 3 (December 1970): 716. On pages 9 and 11–15 of *Free Soil, Free Labor, Free Men: The Ideology of the Republican Party before the Civil War* (New York: Oxford University Press, 1970), Foner offers his conception of the free labor ideology, which became the standard interpretation in subsequent years.
20. Gustave de Beaumont, *Lettres d'Amérique, 1831–1832*, André Jardin and George Pierson, eds. (Paris: Presses universitaires de France, 1973), 193.
21. Boston University Department of Physics, "Cincinnati Population History," http://physics.bu.edu/~redner/projects/population/cities/cincinnati.html.
22. Beaumont, *Lettres*, 193.
23. The Slave Power thesis, deployed by Republicans during the 1850s, held that a cabal of rich slaveowners was attempting to undermine U.S. democracy for their own gain. President Andrew Jackson's supporters perceived a "Money Power" of elites and bankers trying to do the same. I refer to them here because versions of each gained wide currency in Jackson-era Cincinnati. For an excellent discussion of each and a validation of the Republicans who coined the former term, see Leonard Richards, *The Slave Power: The Free North and Southern Domination, 1780–1860* (Baton Rouge: Louisiana State University Press, 2009).
24. Robert Gioielli, "Cincinnati, the Miami Valley and the Ecology of Slavery" (Lecture, September, 2017); Robert Gioielli, "Rethinking Porkopolis: Cincinnati's Environmental History, Through Pigs" (Museum Exhibition, 27 November 2016).
25. On "slavery's capitalism," see Edward Baptist, *The Half Has Never Been Told: Slavery and the Making of American Capitalism* (New York: Basic Books, 2016); Sven Beckert and Seth Rockman, eds., *Slavery's Capitalism: A New History of American Economic Development* (Philadelphia: University of Pennsylvania Press, 2016).

26. Daniel Aaron, *Cincinnati, Queen City of the West: 1819–1838* (Columbus: Ohio State University Press, 1992); Adam Arenson, Barbara Berglund, and Jay Gitlin, eds., *Frontier Cities: Encounters at the Crossroads of Empire* (Philadelphia: University of Pennsylvania Press, 2013); Richard Wade, *The Urban Frontier: The Rise of Western Cities, 1790–1830* (Cambridge: Harvard University Press, 1959).
27. Alexis de Tocqueville, *Tome V: Voyages En Sicile et Aux Etats-Unis Dans Les Oeuvres Complètes* (Paris: Gallimard, 1961), 265, 284.
28. Michel Chevalier, *Lettres sur l'Amérique du Nord*, Tome II (Brussels: Société belge de librairie, 1838), 56, 65.
29. Arehart, "The Market Revolution."
30. Chevalier, *Lettres*, 72.
31. Ibid.
32. Edward Watts contends that Old Northwesterners saw themselves as colonized by the Northeast, and that they insisted on their distinctiveness *vis* the East Coast and Europe. Edward Watts, *An American Colony: Regionalism and the Roots of Midwestern Culture* (Athens: Ohio University Press, 2002), xi.
33. Ibid., 73.
34. Arehart, "The Market Revolution."
35. Andrew Cayton writes that Ohio settlers, "having explicitly rejected an *ancien régime* that rested on patronage and deference," preferred a society in which "relatively open competition of talents among white males would be the primary path to wealth and success." See Cayton, *Frontier Republic*, x.
36. Economic and political authority were anathema to most white Cincinnatians. Andrew Cayton writes that Ohio settlers "saw their defiance of authority as an assertion of local and individual prerogatives, their birthrights as freeborn Americans." See Cayton, *Frontier Republic*, xi.
37. Theodore Pavie, *Souvenirs Atlantiques: Voyage Aux États-Unis* (Paris: Roret, 1833), 66–67.
38. Trollope, *Domestic Manners*, 42.
39. Ibid.
40. Ibid.
41. Matthew Salafia, *Slavery's Borderland: Freedom and Bondage along the Ohio River* (Philadelphia: University of Pennsylvania Press, 2013), 71.
42. In 1825, around twenty-one percent of Cincinnati's population was foreign born. Black people outnumbered foreign immigrants in that year. The majority of foreign-born immigrants were Irish at the time—in 1830, only five percent of the population had been born in Germany. See Nancy Bertaux, "Structural Economic Change and Occupational Decline among Black Workers in Nineteenth-Century Cincinnati," in Henry Louis Taylor, ed., *Race and the City: Work, Community, and Protest in Cincinnati, 1820–1970* (Urbana: University of Illinois Press, 1993),

129–30; "German," Cincinnati: A City of Immigrants, http://www.cincinnati-cityofimmigrants.com/german/.
43. Tocqueville, *Voyages*, 131.
44. Salafia, *Slavery's Borderland*, 49.
45. Tocqueville, *Voyages*, 131.
46. Salafia, *Slavery's Borderland*.
47. Trollope, *Domestic Manners*, 42.
48. Chevalier, *Lettres*, 61.
49. Salafia, *Slavery's Borderland*, 85.
50. Ibid., 84.
51. Daniel Drake quoted in Taylor, *Frontiers of Freedom*, 33.
52. Ohio History Central, "Black Laws of 1807," http://www.ohiohistorycentral.org/w/Black_Laws_of_1807.
53. Taylor, *Frontiers of Freedom*, 33.
54. "Black Laws of 1807."
55. Ibid.
56. Salafia, *Slavery's Borderland*, 85.
57. Ibid.
58. Taylor, *Frontiers of Freedom*, 32.
59. George Pierson, *Tocqueville in America* (Oxford: Oxford University Press, 1938), 360.
60. Wade, *Urban Frontier*, 46.
61. Pierson, *Tocqueville*, 360.
62. Ibid.
63. Folk, "Queen City," 44.
64. Taylor, *Frontiers of Freedom*, 38.
65. Wade, *Urban Frontier*, 45.
66. Taylor, *Frontiers of Freedom*, 24.
67. Folk, "Queen City," 44; Taylor, *Frontiers of Freedom*, 38.
68. Paul Finkelman, "The Strange Career of Race Discrimination in Antebellum Ohio," *Case Western Reserve Law Review* 55, no. 2 (January 2004): 373; 390.
69. Taylor, *Frontiers of Freedom*, 39–40.
70. Ibid., 24.
71. E.S. Abdy paraphrased in Aaron, *Cincinnati*, 304.
72. Harry Watson, *Liberty and Power: The Politics of Jacksonian America* (New York: Hill and Wang, 2006), 8.
73. Arehart, "The Market Revolution"; Taylor, *Frontiers of Freedom*, 17; 52.
74. Taylor, *Frontiers of Freedom*, 53.
75. Alexis de Tocqueville, *Journey to America*, trans. J.P. Mayer (Garden City, NY: Doubleday, 1971), 83. Emphasis in original.
76. Hurt, "Ohio," 211.
77. Folk, "Queen City," 44.
78. Taylor, *Frontiers of Freedom*, 52.
79. Tocqueville quoted in Taylor, *Frontiers of Freedom*, 28.

80. The observations by travel writers are corroborated by Cayton, *Frontier Republic*, x: Ohio had "the fullest possible expression of democratic rights."
81. Beaumont, *Lettres*, 193–94.
82. Tocqueville, *Voyages*, 126.
83. Cayton, *Frontier Republic*, xi.
84. Pierson, *Tocqueville*, 355.
85. Cayton, *Frontier Republic*, x: "From the beginning of settlement in the Ohio Country in the early 1780s, it was clear that there would be no deference to traditional leaders and established authority."
86. Tocqueville, *Journey*, 88.
87. Ibid.
88. Pierson, *Tocqueville*, 355.
89. Ibid., 358.
90. Beaumont, *Lettres*, 194.
91. Tocqueville, *Voyages*, 132.
92. Tocqueville, *Journey*, 90.
93. Daniel Feller, "Andrew Jackson: Domestic Affairs," The Miller Center, https://millercenter.org/president/jackson/domestic-affairs.
94. Sean Wilentz, *Andrew Jackson: The 7th President* (New York: Times Books, 2005), 5.
95. Watson, *Liberty*, 200.
96. Charles Sellers, *The Market Revolution: Jacksonian America, 1815–1846* (New York: Oxford University Press, 1991).
97. Glickstein, *Free Labor*, 304.
98. Ibid., 13.
99. Watson, *Liberty*, 13.
100. Aziz Rana muses on American conceptions of liberty, within which I place early Cincinnati's brand of free labor ideology, thus: "The earliest projections of American power were the product of a specific approach to collective freedom held by Anglo settlers. These colonists saw their own internal account of liberty as necessitating external modes of supervision and control. This account of freedom, which emphasized continuous popular mobilization and direct control by insiders over the sites of political and economic decision making, provided generations of Americans with a basic vision of social possibility. However, the promise of such liberty was historically linked to practices of subordination. Many settlers believed that the preservation and enhancement of their own democratic institutions required Indian dispossession and the coercive use of dependent groups, most prominently slaves, in order to ensure that they themselves had access to property and did not have to engage in menial but essential forms of work. This fact embodies the two faces of American freedom: our long-standing difficulty in imagining liberty without suppression and free citizenship without the control of subject communities." Perhaps it is the force with which Rana's characteristically American insider/outsider liberty is felt in

what we today call the Midwest that allows politicians to refer to the region as "middle America" or "real America." See Aziz Rana, *The Two Faces of American Freedom* (Cambridge, MA: Harvard University Press, 2010), 3.
101. Sellers, *Market Revolution*, 386–89.
102. Taylor, *Frontiers of Freedom*, 54.
103. Ibid., 57.
104. Folk, "Queen City," 45.
105. Taylor, *Frontiers of Freedom*, 55.
106. Folk, "Queen City," 53.
107. Taylor, *Frontiers of Freedom*, 55.
108. Folk, "Queen City," 44–45.
109. "Riot," *The Western Star*, 29 August 1829.
110. Taylor, *Frontiers of Freedom*, 50.
111. Folk, "Queen City," 56.
112. Taylor, *Frontiers of Freedom*, 50.
113. Folk, "Queen City."
114. E.S. Abdy, *Journal of a Residence and Tour in the United States of North America from April, 1833, to October, 1834* (London: John Murray, 1835), 381–82.
115. Ibid.
116. Stanley, *Loyal West*, 22.
117. Aaron, *Cincinnati*, 302: "Many citizens from the middle states, who opposed slavery because it seemed to jeopardize the status of free labor, had no great dislike for the institution in the South. They simply did not relish the prospect of competing against cheap black labor in the free states"; Stanley, *Loyal West*, 23: There was a "symbiosis between racial exclusion and racial slavery" in the lower Old Northwest.
118. William Wells Brown, "The Escape of a Fugitive Slave: The Memoir of William Wells Brown," in Emily Foster, ed., *The Ohio Frontier: An Anthology of Early Writings* (Lexington: University Press of Kentucky, 1996), 176.
119. Ibid., 179.
120. Christopher Phillips, *The Rivers Ran Backward: The Civil War and the Remaking of the American Middle Border* (New York: Oxford University Press, 2016), 74.
121. Ibid.
122. Emily Foster, ed., "The Capture of a Fugitive Slave: A Newspaper Report," in *The Ohio Frontier: An Anthology of Early Writings* (Lexington: University Press of Kentucky, 1996), 176–82.
123. Ibid., 175.
124. Wade, "Negro in Cincinnati," 54.
125. Wade, *Urban Frontier*, 78.
126. John Hudson and Lawrence Brown, "Geography," in Andrew Cayton, Richard Sisson, and Chris Zacher, eds., *The American Midwest: An*

Interpretive Encyclopedia (Bloomington: Indiana University Press, 2007), 131; Salafia, *Slavery's Borderland*, 2.
127. Salafia, *Slavery's Borderland*, 155.
128. In this sense, Cincinnati was a "frontier city" as defined in Arenson, Berglund, and Gitlin in *Frontier Cities*.
129. Stanley, *Loyal West*, 4.
130. Harriet Martineau, *Retrospect of Western Travel, Volume II* (London: Saunders and Otley, 1838), 43.
131. Ibid.
132. Folk, "Queen City," 130.
133. Aaron, *Cincinnati*, 301.
134. Hurt, "Ohio," 206.
135. Aaron, *Cincinnati*, 300.
136. Many white Cincinnatians considered abolitionists "Yankees." See Stanley, *Loyal West*, 6.
137. Folk, "Queen City," 121.
138. Ibid., 108.
139. Ibid.
140. Ibid., 76; Stanley, *Loyal West*, 23.
141. Folk, "Queen City," 141.
142. Ibid.
143. Harriet Martineau, *Society in America* (London: Saunders and Otley, 1837), 148.
144. I use the phrase "reactionary populism" to refer to demagogic appeals to *herrenvolk* economics and politics. It is a bit of a misnomer: these appeals should be understood as "pseudo-populism." See Frank, Thomas, "Forget Trump—Populism Is the Cure, Not the Disease," *The Guardian*, 23 May 2018.
145. Folk, "Queen City," 60.
146. Ibid., 158.
147. Contemporary critics of this kind of distinctly lower Old Northwestern reactionary populism and vigilantism by whites warned against "mobocracy." See ibid.
148. Bridget Ford, *Bonds of Union: Religion, Race, and Politics in a Civil War Borderland* (Chapel Hill: The University of North Carolina Press, 2016), 325 n. 23.
149. Ibid., 159.
150. "Riots and Mobs, Confusion and Blood Shed," *Cincinnati Daily Gazette*, 6 October 1841; Folk, "Queen City," 205–84.
151. Stanley, *Loyal West*, 10.
152. As both Ford and Aaron point out, the Irish were not considered white until they assimilated and were the victims of much nativist violence at the hands of Anglo-Saxon Protestants from the 1830s onward. However, many Irish

people soon became vigilantes themselves, targeting black Midwesterners and others. See Aaron, *Cincinnati*; Ford, *Bonds of Union*.
153. This chapter traces the "mobocratic" elements of midwestern identity. Of course, thousands of freedom-seeking African Americans, along with abolitionists such as John Rankin, John Brown and Harriet Beecher Stowe, also contributed to the region's identity. So too did the likes of Eugene V. Debs. But at every turn, racial liberals and economic radicals had to contend with the racial conservatism and reactionary populism native to the lower Old Northwest. See, for example, Folk, "Queen City," 63.
154. From the dust jacket of Stanley, *Loyal West*.
155. Hurt, "Ohio," 212; Taylor, *Frontiers of Freedom*, 5.
156. Hurt writes that Ohioans, perhaps distinct from other Midwesterners, feared above all the dissolution of the Union. He suggests that this contributed to the state's traditional political conservatism. See Hurt, "Ohio," 208; Some readers might argue that Cincinnati was not representative of the region because it was an urban—not rural—space. However, white rural communities in the lower Old Northwest—having adopted the reactionary and exclusionary strain of free labor ideology discussed in this chapter—rioted against blacks, became Copperheads, lynched "others," created "sundown towns," etc. in the decades after 1836. See auut studio, *Map of White Supremacy Mob Violence*, 2016, http://www.monroeworktoday.org/explore/; James Loewen, *Sundown Towns: A Hidden Dimension of American Racism* (New York: Simon & Schuster, 2006); Stanley, *Loyal West*.
157. Gregory Rose, "Images of the Midwest," in Andrew Cayton, Richard Sisson, and Chris Zacher, eds., *The American Midwest: An Interpretive Encyclopedia* (Bloomington: Indiana University Press, 2007): "Before long, the valley displayed, arguably for the first time anywhere, what would become quintessential midwestern characteristics."
158. Introduction to Arenson, Berglund, and Gitlin, *Frontier Cities*.
159. Arenson, Berglund, and Gitlin, *Frontier Cities*, 4.
160. Hurt, "Ohio," 206; Whet Moser, "Martin Luther King in Chicago: Somebody Nobody Sent," *Chicago Magazine*, 16 January 2012.

Brie Swenson Arnold | African American Migration to Cedar Rapids, Iowa, and the Making of the Midwest, 1860–1900

When Joseph Bowlin arrived in Cedar Rapids, Iowa, in the early 1860s, he surely took in his new surroundings, surveying the bustling development that unfolded from the railroad depot and steamboat landing.[1] Founded in the 1840s, Cedar Rapids was, "as cities and towns in the middle west are spoken of," not a new town.[2] Bowlin would have seen grain mills that were the precursor of the factories that would make Cedar Rapids famous as well as churches, homes, and businesses.[3] The city's big-enough-yet-still-growing size spelled opportunity for Bowlin's own barbering business.[4] Yet he must have long weighed the merits of settling here, a city with no other black residents located in a state that barred black settlement.[5]

But he, and soon many other African Americans, decided to make Cedar Rapids—"model city of the Middle West"—home.[6] The experiences of Bowlin and other founding members of Cedar Rapids's black community offer a window into late-nineteenth-century black migration to the Midwest and its influence on the development of the region and its identity.[7] Between the Civil War and the close of the nineteenth century, thousands of African Americans left southern and northeastern places in favor of midwestern ones. As important studies by Leslie A. Schwalm, Michael P. Johnson, Jack S. Blocker, and others have shown, the Midwest was the region to which the majority of postwar black migrants relocated.[8] This migration and the arrival of significant numbers of African Americans in places where few to no black people had previously lived was a significant turning point in migrants' lives, the development of midwestern places like Cedar Rapids, and the emergence of the broader region. The fact that the Midwest grew rapidly and came to be thought of as a distinct region during the precise period in which African Americans first migrated there in substantial numbers merits greater consideration.[9]

Bowlin and others who migrated in the wake of slavery and civil war perceived the burgeoning region and its communities as best positioned to fulfill their goals and desires for expanded political, legal, and economic opportunities. Once in the region, they embraced those possibilities, built up midwestern communities and institutions, and initiated activism that pressed the still-malleable region to become one that more fully embraced ideals of equity, tolerance, and pluralism. Recovering the stories of specific individuals who settled in places like Cedar Rapids allows us to examine what drew late-nineteenth-century African Americans to the Midwest and which qualities were associated with the region at the time. Further, examining the actions and experiences of African Americans once established in the region illuminates the ways in which expanded black presence and activism further shaped the region and its characteristics. Late-nineteenth-century African Americans in places like Cedar Rapids fundamentally contributed to the making of the Midwest, steadily pressing to make pluralism, tolerance, and equity more central to the region's laws, practices, values, and identity.

Though African Americans had long been present and influential in places that came to be thought of as the Midwest, the Civil War was a turning point in black settlement in and influence on the region. Groundbreaking work by Schwalm and others has highlighted how the war and the demise of slavery triggered migration to midwestern places previously defined by black exclusion.[10] In the decades before the war, midwestern states and territories banned slavery but enacted laws aimed at prohibiting black settlement. Free from slavery but not white supremacy, anti-black racism manifested in the antebellum Midwest in laws, attitudes, and a "general Negrophobia."[11] Still, black communities emerged, with perhaps 65,000 African Americans, out of a total regional population of some eight million, living in midwestern states by 1860.[12]

The onset of the Civil War and the gradual collapse of slavery sparked by black self-liberation and Union military presence triggered significant wartime relocation of African Americans to midwestern places.[13] During as after the war, almost all migrants were former slaves. One of Cedar Rapids's earliest black settlers, Ellen Taylor, was enslaved in Virginia and Mississippi for some forty years before she arrived in Cedar Rapids in 1865.[14] One of Taylor's postwar Cedar Rapids neighbors, Laura Raspberry, spent more than fifty years in bondage in Mississippi before freedom came.[15] Andrew Ford, later a pastor at Cedar Rapids's African Methodist Episcopal (AME) church, was enslaved by descendants of George Washington at Mount Vernon for the first two decades of his life.[16]

Ford, Taylor, and other later-day Cedar Rapidians utilized the chaos of war to liberate themselves from slavery and relocate to midwestern places. George Howard made his way out of Missouri slavery by escaping into Iowa during the war.[17] Ellen Taylor escaped midway through the war and became part of a group of "contraband" slaves confiscated in Missouri by Union troops from Iowa, who facilitated her relocation to the Cedar Rapids area.[18] Encounters with midwestern soldiers often played a role in former slaves' migration to the region.[19] William Ousley, who settled in Cedar Rapids in the 1880s, liberated himself from slavery in Kentucky in 1862 and encountered soldiers from the 13th Wisconsin—who aided him in moving to Wisconsin during the war.[20] In 1861, Andrew Ford fled to Union lines in Alexandria, Virginia, where he made the acquaintance of soldiers who offered him a job in Michigan. Soon after relocating, Ford enlisted in Michigan's First Colored Regiment, later called the 102nd U.S. Colored Troops (USCT).[21] Soon after arriving in Iowa, George Howard enlisted in Iowa's all-black regiment, the 60th USCT.[22]

The fact that midwestern states like Iowa, which had only 1069 black people in total in 1860, were now raising black regiments highlights the shift in black migration to the region—a process that would continue throughout the rest of the century.[23] As historian Saje Mathieu explains, this became the first "in what historians increasingly understand as a three-pronged Great Migration that spanned nearly a century—1865–1896, 1910–1940, and 1940–1970."[24] As with many of their twentieth-century counterparts, late-nineteenth-century migrants predominantly chose the Midwest. Historian Michael P. Johnson estimates that more than 80,000 African Americans left the South in the 1860s alone, 97 percent of whom settled in the Midwest.[25]

Across the region, black communities expanded or were established for the first time. Though no black people lived in Cedar Rapids before the war, a community of about twenty, including Joseph Bowlin and Ellen Taylor, was established by 1865.[26] Bowlin, Taylor, and almost all other migrants settled there with multiple family members.²⁷ Bowlin arrived on his own but soon sent for his wife, daughter, and brother-in-law.²⁸ Ellen Taylor was joined by her husband, Johnson, and their children.²⁹ Laura Raspberry arrived with her son William, the youngest of the nineteen children she bore while enslaved, and William's wife and children.³⁰ Families, notes historian Anna-Lisa Cox, provided "a ready-made community" that built up black midwestern settlement.³¹ Former slaves Thomas and Anna Oliphant and their five Iowa-born children became some of Cedar Rapids's earliest black settlers after moving from a smaller Iowa town.³² After interracial couple George and Emily Scott moved to Cedar Rapids with their daughter, they may have convinced William Ousley's family to do so also.³³ By 1870, a community of at least fifty and likely closer to 100 African Americans was established in Cedar Rapids; by the 1890s, Iowa's leading black newspaper the *Iowa State Bystander* reported that "about 300 colored citizens" lived there.³⁴ While here, as elsewhere in the Midwest, African Americans were small in number, Iowa and other late-nineteenth-century midwestern states had the nation's highest percentage changes in black population.³⁵

Such growth was part of the broader population, economic, and political growth that characterized the postwar Midwest. As Jack S. Blocker explains, the region was "entering [its] peak years of wealth and national influence, emerging economically and politically from the shadow of the older states to the east."³⁶ The Civil War, Clarence Lang and others have observed, "accelerated the Midwest's industrial development, fueled the subsequent diversity of its economy and people, and fed its urban growth."³⁷ Proximity to water, rail, and agricultural resources merged with massive native-born and European immigration to grow quickly many midwestern cities, including Cedar Rapids—which swelled from a town of 1500 when Bowlin arrived to a full-fledged city of over 25,000 by 1900.³⁸ Most everyone was originally from elsewhere, with high rates of immigrants, their first-generation children, and native-born Americans originally from eastern and southern states settling in late-nineteenth-century Cedar Rapids.³⁹ Migration made it and other midwestern locales more ethnically, racially, and religiously diverse than other parts of the country at the time, something scholars assert distinguishes the Midwest and perhaps contributed to a "basis for racial liberalism" there.⁴⁰

Southern African American newspapers provide additional clues as to how the Midwest's distinctiveness and attractiveness to migrants were viewed in the late nineteenth century. The *Semi-Weekly Louisianian* explained that while "older" southern and northeastern states were "losing members," "the growing States" of the Midwest—including Iowa— were "gaining" population.[41] Iowa, another article reported, was one of the nation's most populous states.[42] More people meant more political representation; in 1870, only seven of the nation's thirty-seven states added congressional representation—five of which were midwestern states, including Iowa.[43] Importantly, Iowa's representatives tended to be Republicans, who more often supported black rights.[44] South Carolina's *The Leader* noted Iowa was at the forefront of political movements for "Equal Rights," "Equal Laws," and "Suffrage ... without regard to Color," as exemplified by its late 1860s enactments of black male suffrage and school desegregation.[45] The *Louisianian* viewed midwestern states as much stronger supporters of "universal education" than "different parts of the United States," namely the South.[46] The Midwest also diverged from the South in terms of its more diversified economy and new economic opportunities, which papers emphasized.[47] In Iowa, observed the *Louisianian*, "rich lands can be bought" and "employment can be had, for men and women" in towns, which could lay "the foundation of ... riches and prosperity."[48]

The expanding presence, activism, and community-building of African Americans in the Midwest further contributed to distinguishing the emerging region, as they steadily pressed to make tolerance, pluralism, and equity more central to the region's practices, laws, and values.[49] The arrival of black men and women in midwestern places contributed to altering some white Midwesterners' views and actions toward African Americans. While prejudice and white supremacy certainly remained, Nicole Etcheson and others have observed that the Civil War prompted many white Midwesterners to see themselves as different from white southerners, which made change possible.[50] For example, while black people were prohibited from settling in antebellum Cedar Rapids, by 1864 the *Cedar Valley Times* reported there was "a fixed determination on the part of the people to sustain Mr. Bowlin" and "his family" here, especially after a few "envious drunken rowdies" vandalized his barber shop.[51] Dozens of other whites denounced the "gross outrage" and a collection to "[make] up the loss he [Bowlin] sustained" was "met with a generous response."[52]

African Americans actively pressed whites to make inclusion and equal rights more central to Iowa's laws, values, and everyday practices. Their movement to the state resulted in rescinding exclusion by 1864.[53] After the war, new and longtime black Iowans utilized conventions, circulars, and petitions to appeal to "every true, honest, liberty-loving citizen of Iowa" to expand "equal rights."[54] In 1865, men of the 60th USCT—George Howard's regiment—petitioned the legislature, arguing it was "the duty of Iowa" to grant black men the vote.[55] Delegates at a "Colored Convention" in Des Moines asked for white Iowans' "sympathy and aid in securing ... rights and privileges" like black male suffrage and "the rights of our children to be admitted into the public schools of the State"—appeals that contributed to the achievement of both goals by 1868.[56] African Americans in Cedar Rapids exercised those new rights. Men, including Joseph Bowlin and William Ousley, were politically active—signing petitions, speaking out against excessive taxation, leading political meetings, and surely casting ballots.[57] The Bowlin, Oliphant, Ousley, and Raspberry children attended Cedar Rapids's integrated primary schools alongside the children of their white native-born and immigrant neighbors, which was also the case for brothers Luther and William Lowery and other African Americans who graduated from high school and college in Cedar Rapids.[58]

Black Midwesterners pressed for expanded rights and opportunities in additional ways, establishing businesses, homes, and institutions in predominantly white communities while simultaneously building a black "community within a community."[59] Just a few years after arriving in Cedar Rapids, Joseph "Bowlen's [sic] Barber Shop" was so successful he expanded into newer accommodations and hired other black and German immigrant barbers.[60] By 1870, Bowlin owned $3650 in real estate and personal property, a substantial change from the $50 he claimed a decade prior and far above the less-than-$200 average yearly income of a wage laborer.[61] Other black-owned barber and beauty shops, carpet-cleaning businesses, and restaurants were also established in Cedar Rapids. Marshall Perkins owned and operated a successful restaurant for nearly forty years, alongside his German-American wife Louisa, their three children, and their interracial staff.[62] Through their family and their business, the Perkinses cultivated tolerance—and economic opportunities. In addition to the restaurant, they owned a hotel and a home valued at $5000.[63] African Americans who settled in smaller midwestern towns and cities were often more able to acquire property— particularly ownership of a family home, which other Cedar Rapids families further evidence.[64] The Lowery brothers' parents, Thomas and Mary, saved the means to build a "large two-story house of nine rooms," while the Oliphant, Raspberry, Taylor, and other families managed to purchase more modest homes.[65] In general, black Midwesterners tended to own more property and be better off economically than their southern counterparts.[66]

Families like the Bowlins, Perkinses, Lowerys, Oliphants, and Raspberrys also built up important community institutions—including the churches, charity groups, women's clubs, and fraternal lodges that were "the core of midwestern towns."[67] Such institutions, explains Paula M. Nelson, "helped society function and reinforced the moral values and direction" of midwestern communities.[68] Joseph Bowlin played a fundamental role in raising the $1500 needed to build Cedar Rapids's first black church, the AME church where the Perkinses, Oliphants, Raspberrys, Fords, and others were important members and leaders.[69] Cedar Rapids's AME members organized literary societies, fundraisers, social events, and civil rights activities—including Emancipation Day celebrations, protests against racial discrimination in employment, and lawsuits against segregation.[70]

Such protests and lawsuits were necessary because racial discrimination, particularly in employment and public accommodation, remained widespread in Cedar Rapids and across the Midwest. Michael C. Steiner explains that during its formative years the Midwest was "coming to grips with ... diversity," sorting out the extent to which it would embrace pluralism, tolerance, and equality.[71] Other scholars add that while many midwestern states experimented with more liberal civil rights laws after the Civil War, the region's heritage of white supremacy was not easily undone and its "black and white residents became deeply and often antagonistically engaged in a process of redefining the meanings and implications of freedom and citizenship."[72] While African Americans worked for equal rights and treatment, their white neighbors "struggled to defend their own racial prerogatives"—especially in employment.⁷³ Most black men in Cedar Rapids, including Thomas Oliphant and William Raspberry, were relegated to low-paying, less-steady jobs as day laborers, teamsters, porters, and janitors.⁷⁴ Black women, like Thomas and Anna Oliphant's eldest daughter Emma, were almost always consigned to laundry and domestic work.⁷⁵ When Emma instead sought employment at a garment factory, the white women workers—many of whom were her neighbors and former schoolmates—fiercely objected.⁷⁶ Despite vigorous challenges to "the color line" in employment led by those like Emma Oliphant and William Raspberry, better-paying professional, clerical, and manufacturing jobs remained off limits to African Americans in Cedar Rapids and across the Midwest.

Racially discriminatory exclusion from public places was also widespread. As an 1883 *Cedar Rapids Evening Gazette* article explained, while in some situations blacks were "furnished accommodations," in others "they [were] debarred."⁷⁷ The uneven and unequal nature of exclusion from public places, explains historian Millington W. Bergeson-Lockwood, was "that much more painful and humiliating" for midwestern and northeastern African Americans because they "enjoyed relatively free exercise of their rights" in voting and education.⁷⁸ Legal cases initiated by black Midwesterners indicate they were commonly charged different rates, relegated to inferior accommodations, or barred entirely from hotels, taverns, restaurants, race tracks, soda fountains, and many "other places of public entertainment and amusement."⁷⁹ Such inequities prompted black Cedar Rapidians to organize an interracial Civil Rights Club, likely the city's first civil rights organization.⁸⁰ At its 1883 founding meeting at the AME church, black speakers explained that "equity is all we ask"—to be charged the "same rates" and accorded "equal" accommodations.⁸¹ Joseph Bowlin, who helped lead the meeting, surely experienced such discrimination while navigating daily life in Cedar Rapids. We know he was particularly moved to further action after being turned away from a roller-skating rink in 1884 "on the sole ground that he is a colored man."⁸² His subsequent lawsuit resulted in a precedent-setting case in which the Iowa Supreme Court sided with the roller rink—part of the national turn away from the civil rights gains of the postwar era and toward the legal sanctioning of segregation unfolding in the 1880s.⁸³ While black Midwesterners maintained many legal and political rights late-nineteenth-century black Southerners did not, social and economic equality remained elusive in midwestern communities. As a speaker at the Cedar Rapids Civil Rights Club meeting explained, "the continued development" and "social equality" of "the colored people of the city" were still contested questions.[84] Though Bowlin and others continued to take action to push Cedar Rapids and the broader Midwest toward being the tolerant, equitable, and accepting-of-its-diversity place they envisioned it could be, white Midwesterners widely continued to draw their own regionally distinct color line.

In many ways, late-nineteenth-century African Americans who migrated to midwestern places like Cedar Rapids made the Midwest by developing its communities, institutions, and values and pressing it to become the region that could "[push] the American republic closer to its own ideals."[85] While the Bowlins, Taylors, Fords, Raspberrys, Ouseleys, Oliphants, Perkinses, and others could attest to the ways racism in Cedar Rapids and the broader Midwest continually circumscribed their goals, rights, and desires, they also leveraged the region's possibilities and influenced its character. Uncovering their stories allows historians to more fully explore what drew African Americans to the Midwest, which opportunities and limitations they encountered once there, and how midwestern distinctiveness was viewed and shaped by many peoples—including the thousands of black people who created the region, too.

Notes

The author thanks Jon Lauck, Marvin Bergman, David Brodnax, Derek Buckaloo, and Annette Atkins for their feedback on this essay

1. Luther A. Brewer, *History of Linn County Iowa* (Cedar Rapids: Torch Press, 1911), 264–65, 431.
2. Ibid., 307.
3. Ibid., 64, 369. In the late nineteenth century, Cedar Rapids became home to Quaker Oats and Sinclair's (later Wilson's), some of the world's largest cereal and meatpacking plants. "Our Greatest Home Industry," *Cedar Rapids Evening Gazette*, 1 January 1901; "3,000 Barrel Mill," *Cedar Rapids Evening Gazette*, 18 October 1899; "History of Sinclair and Co.," Brucemore Historic Site, http://www.brucemore.org/history/people/sinclair/.
4. "Bath Rooms," *Cedar Rapids Times*, 10 September 1868; "TJ Dudley," *Cedar Valley Times*, 15 May 1862; "Business Directory of the City of Cedar Rapids," *Cedar Valley Times*, 26 December 1867.
5. On early black population: "A Gross Outrage," *Cedar Valley Times*, 3 March 1864; Brewer, *History of Linn County*, 332; Leola Nelson Bergmann, *The*

Negro in Iowa (Iowa City: State Historical Society of Iowa, 1948; reprint 1969); Willis Goudy, "Selected Demographics: Iowa's African-American Residents, 1840–2000," in Bill Silag, ed., *Outside In: African-American History in Iowa, 1838–2000* (Des Moines: State Historical Society of Iowa, 2001), 41. On black exclusion laws: *The Statute Laws of the Territory of Iowa* (Dubuque: Russell and Reeves, 1839; reprint, 1900), 69–70; *Acts, Resolutions, and Memorials Passed at the Regular Session of the Third General Assembly of the State of Iowa* (Iowa City: Palmer and Paul, State Printers, 1851), 172–73; Leslie A. Schwalm, *Emancipation's Diaspora: Race and Reconstruction in the Upper Midwest* (Chapel Hill: University of North Carolina Press, 2009); Robert R. Dykstra, *Bright Radical Star: Black Freedom and White Supremacy on the Hawkeye Frontier* (Ames: Iowa State University Press, 1997); Eugene H. Berwanger, *The Frontier Against Slavery: Western Anti-Negro Prejudice and the Slavery Extension Controversy* (Chicago: University of Illinois Press, 1967). *Census Returns of the Different Counties of the State of Iowa for the Year 1856* (Iowa City: Crum & Boye, 1857), 237, and *Census Returns of the Different Counties of the State of Iowa for the Year 1862* (Des Moines: FW Palmer, 1863), 32, https://www.iowadatacenter.org/Publications/iowa1856.pdf

6. "Cedar Rapids: A Model City of the Middle West" (Chicago: Chicago and North Western Railway, 1907), Collections of the State Historical Society of Iowa, Iowa City. Newspapers used in this study, including the *Iowa State Bystander* and the *Cedar Rapids Evening Gazette*, also commonly used the term "middle west" by the 1890s. On Cedar Rapids as a representative midwestern city: Brie Swenson Arnold, "An Opportunity to Challenge the 'Color Line': Gender, Race, Ethnicity, and Women's Labor Activism in Late Nineteenth-Century Cedar Rapids, Iowa," *Annals of Iowa* 74, no. 2 (Spring 2015): 104–05.

7. For works on the little-studied African American history of Cedar Rapids, see: Arnold, "An Opportunity to Challenge"; *Outside In*; Schwalm, *Emancipation's Diaspora*, 144; Eric A. Smith, *Oak Hill: A Portrait of Black Life in Cedar Rapids, Iowa* (Los Angeles: Amen-Ra Theological Seminary Press, 2006); Connie Hillsman and Bev Taylor, "African American Footprints of Cedar Rapids," http://africanamericanfootprints.blogspot.com/.

8. Janet Thomas Greenwood, *First Fruits of Freedom: The Migration of Former Slaves and Their Search for Equality in Worcester, Massachusetts, 1862–1900* (Chapel Hill: University of North Carolina Press, 2009), 5–6; Schwalm, *Emancipation's Diaspora*; Michael P. Johnson, "Out of Egypt: The Migration of Former Slaves to the Midwest during the 1860s in Comparative Perspective," in *Crossing Boundaries: Comparative History of Black People in Diaspora* (Bloomington: Indiana University Press, 1999); Jack S. Blocker, *A Little More Freedom: African Americans Enter the Urban Midwest, 1860–1930* (Columbus: Ohio State University Press, 2008); Nell Irvin Painter, *Exodusters: Black Migration to Kansas after Reconstruction* (New York:

Knopf, 1977); V. Jacque Voegeli, *Free But Not Equal: The Midwest and the Negro during the Civil War* (Chicago: University of Chicago Press, 1967); James L. Hill, "Migration of Blacks to Iowa, 1820–1860," *The Journal of Negro History* 66, no. 4 (Winter 1981–1982): 289–303.
9. On emergence of the Midwest as a region: Jon K. Lauck, *The Lost Region: Toward a Revival of Midwestern Identity* (Iowa City: University of Iowa Press, 2013); Michael C. Steiner, "The Birth of the Midwest and the Rise of Regional Theory," in Jon K. Lauck, Gleaves Whitney, and Joseph Hogan, eds., *Finding a New Midwestern History* (Lincoln: University of Nebraska Press, 2018), 3, 7–9; Lauck, "Introduction" to *The Midwestern Moment: The Forgotten World of Early Twentieth-Century Midwestern Regionalism, 1880–1940* (Hastings, NE: Hastings College Press, 2017). On the more-studied twentieth-century migration of African Americans to the Midwest: James R. Grossman, *Land of Hope: Chicago, Black Southerners, and the Great Migration* (Chicago: University of Chicago Press, 1989); Joe William Trotter Jr., *Black Milwaukee: The Making of an Industrial Proletariat, 1915–1945* (Urbana: University of Illinois Press, 1985); Kimberly L. Phillips, *Alabama North: African-American Migrants, Community, and Working-Class Activism in Cleveland, 1915–1945* (Urbana: University of Illinois Press, 1999); Isabel Wilkerson, *The Warmth of Other Suns: The Epic Story of America's Great Migration* (New York: Random House, 2010); Ira Berlin, "The Passage to the North," in *The Making of African America: The Four Great Migrations* (New York: Viking Books, 2010); Jeffrey Helgeson, "Politics in the Promised Land: How the Great Migration Shaped the American Midwest," in Lauck, Whitney, and Hogan, ed., *Finding a New Midwestern History*, 111–26. On invisibility of and need for further studies about African Americans in midwestern history: Lauck, *The Lost Region*, "Introduction"; Doug Kiel, "Untaming the Mild Frontier: In Search of New Midwestern Histories," *Middle West Review* 1, no. 1 (Spring 2014): 9–38; various essays in Andrew R.L. Cayton and Susan E. Gray, eds., *The Identity of the American Midwest: Essays on Regional History* (Bloomington: Indiana University Press, 2001); Pamela J. Edwards, "'Are There Any Black People in Iowa?': The African American Historical Museum and Cultural Center of Iowa," *History News* 58, no. 3 (Summer 2003): 18–21.
10. Schwalm, *Emancipation's Diaspora*, 3. Also Hill, "Migration of Blacks to Iowa"; Johnson, "Out of Egypt"; Blocker, *A Little More Freedom*, 16–17; Stephen A. Vincent, *Southern Seed, Northern Soil: African-American Farm Communities in the Midwest, 1765–1900* (Bloomington: Indiana University Press, 1999), xii; Clarence Lang, "Locating the Civil Rights Movement: An Essay on the Deep South, Midwest, and Border South in Black Freedom Studies," *Journal of Social History* 47, no. 2 (Winter 2013): 379.
11. Hill, "Migration of Blacks to Iowa," 290–91.
12. Includes present-day midwestern states that were states or territories in 1860: Ohio, Indiana, Illinois, Iowa, Wisconsin, Michigan, Minnesota,

Kansas (a state in 1861), and Nebraska and Dakota Territories. Estimates based on figures in: Anna-Lisa Cox, *The Bone and Sinew of the Land: America's Forgotten Black Pioneers and the Struggle for Equality* (New York: Public Affairs, 2018), 3; Schwalm, *Emancipation's Diaspora*, 45; Kansas Historical Society, "African Americans in Kansas," https://www.kshs.org/kansapedia/african-americans-in-kansas/17878; *Population of the United States in 1860; Compiled from the Original Returns of the Eighth Census* (Washington: Government Printing office, 1864), https://www.census.gov/library/publications/1864/dec/1860a.html.

13. Schwalm, *Emancipation's Diaspora*, Chapter 3.
14. Federal census (1900); "Death of Mrs. Ellen Taylor," *Cedar Rapids Evening Gazette*, 31 July 1909; Oak Hill Cemetery Association, "African American History at Oak Hill Cemetery," http://www.oakhillcemeterycr.com/wp-content/uploads/2015/08/African-American_2009-tour.pdf; "African American Footprints of Cedar Rapids."
15. Federal Census (1880 and 1900); "Mrs. Laura Raspberry," *Cedar Rapids Evening Gazette*, 17 February 1904.
16. Federal Census (1900); "Funeral for Andrew Ford," *Cedar Rapids Republican*, 2 January 1929, Collections of the African American Museum of Iowa; Pamela Nosek, "Combat Zone: African Americans in the Civil War—Part 2," *Iowa Griot: Newsletter of the African American Museum of Iowa* 2, no. 4; Scott E. Casper, *Sarah Johnson's Mount Vernon* (New York: Macmillan, 2009); "George Washington's Slaves," *Washington Post*, 21 February 2008; "John Augustine Washington III," *Mount Vernon Digital Encyclopedia*, http://www.mountvernon.org/digital-encyclopedia.
17. *Roster and Record of Iowa Soldiers in the War of the Rebellion*, Vol. 5 (Des Moines: State Printer, 1911), 1630; National Archives, *Consolidated Lists of Civil War Draft Registration Records (Provost Marshal General's Bureau; Consolidated Enrollment Lists, 1863–1865)*, Record Group 110.
18. Federal Census (1900); "African American History at Oak Hill Cemetery"; "Death of Mrs. Ellen Taylor."
19. Schwalm, *Emancipation's Diaspora*, Chapter 3; Hill, "Migration of Blacks to Iowa," 296–97.
20. Federal Census (1880); "William Ousley Personal War Sketch," *Personal War Sketches*, GAR Post 235 Records, Box 166, RG 99, State Historical Society of Iowa, Des Moines; "13th Infantry," *E.B. Quiner's Military History of Wisconsin* (Chicago: 1866); William Ousley, 18th USCT Company Descriptive Book, National Archives, *Compiled Military Service Records of Volunteer Union Soldiers Who Served with the United States Colored Troops*, Microfilm Serial M1822, Roll 76, accessed via Ancestry.com.
21 Casper, *Sarah Johnson's Mount Vernon*, 98; "Funeral for Andrew Ford"; Nosek; Detroit Historical Society, "First Michigan Colored Regiment," in *Encyclopedia of Detroit*, http://detroithistorical.org/learn/encyclopedia-of-detroit/first-michigan-colored-regiment; National Park Service, "102nd

Regiment, United States Colored Infantry," https://www.nps.gov/civilwar/search-battle-units-detail.htm?battleUnitCode=UUS0102RI00C.
22. *Roster and Record*, 1630; *Consolidated Lists*, Record Group 110; David Brodnax Sr., "'Will They Fight? Ask the Enemy': Iowa's African American Regiment in the Civil War," *Annals of Iowa* 66, no. 3 (Summer/Fall 2007): 266-92.
23. Goudy, "Selected Demographics," 41.
24. Saje Mathieu, "The African American Great Migration Reconsidered," *OAH Magazine of History* 23, no. 4 (October 2009): 20.
25. Johnson, "Out of Egypt," 229, 239. Also Berlin, "The Passage to the North," 134; William Cohen, *At Freedom's Edge: Black Mobility and the Southern White Quest for Racial Control, 1861-1915* (Baton Rouge: Louisiana State University Press, 1991), 87-91.
26. *Census Returns of the Different Counties of the State of Iowa ... 1865* (Des Moines: F.W. Palmer, 1865), 32, https://www.iowadatacenter.org/Publications/historical; *The Census of Iowa ... 1867* (Des Moines: F.W. Palmer, 1867), 37, https://www.iowadatacenter.org/Publications/iowa1867.pdf
27. Based on my database of adult black men and women living in the city in the late nineteenth century compiled using Cedar Rapids city directories, federal and state censuses, and the *Iowa State Bystander*. On family migration: Johnson, "Out of Egypt," 233.
28. "The People Will Sustain Him," *Cedar Valley Times*, 10 March 1864; "Bath Rooms"; Federal Census (1860, 1870, and 1880); Walter Bowlin and Mary Stratton Marriage Record, Cedar Rapids, 1885.
29. "Death of Mrs. Ellen Taylor"; Federal Census (1900); "African American History at Oak Hill Cemetery."
30. Federal Census (1880 and 1900).
31. Anna-Lisa Cox, *A Stronger Kinship: One Town's Extraordinary Story of Hope and Faith* (New York: Little, Brown and Company, 2006), 66.
32. Federal Census (1870 and 1880).
33. Federal Census (1860, 1870, 1880, 1900, and 1920); Winnie Phillips and Charles Gomer Marriage Record, Cedar Rapids, 1882; Davenport (Iowa) City Directories, 1867-1868; Cedar Rapids City Directories, 1870-1900; Iowa State Census (1885); "Marriages, Births, and Deaths," *Cedar Rapids Evening Gazette*, 21 April 1886; George Scott and Emily Allard Marriage Record, Cedar Rapids, 1886; National Archives, *Civil War Pension Index: General Index to Pension Files, 1861-1934*; Rock Island (Illinois) City Directories, 1882-1885; "The Colored Citizens," *The Daily Argus* (Rock Island, Ill.), 3 March 1876; Laura Maud Ousley and Boston Clay Marriage Record, Davenport, Iowa, 1936.
34. Goudy, "Selected Demographics," 41; Bergmann, *The Negro in Iowa*, 34; Smith, *Oak Hill*, 41; *Census of Iowa ... 1895* (Des Moines: F.R. Conaway, 1896), 127, https://ia600402.us.archive.org/5/items/

cu31924011106386/cu31924011106386.pdf; "A Visit to the White City," *Iowa State Bystander*, 21 April 1899; Cedar Rapids City Directories, 1867–1900. My research has found more black residents of Cedar Rapids than listed in census totals. On underenumeration of African Americans: Dernoral Davis, "Toward a Socio-Historical and Demographic Portrait of Twentieth-Century African-Americans," in Alferdteen Harrison, ed., *Black Exodus: The Great Migration from the American South* (Jackson: University Press of Mississippi, 1991), 2–3; Cox, *The Bone and Sinew*, xviii.

35. Goudy, "Selected Demographics," 41; Allan Johnston, "Being Free: Black Migration and the Civil War," *Australasian Journal of American Studies* 6, no. 1 (July 1987): 16. There was significant variety in the total number and the proportional-to-the-overall-population percentage of African Americans in midwestern places, but it typically ranged from less than 1 percent to 10 percent of the population. Cox, *A Stronger Kinship*, 6, 219; Schwalm, *Emancipation's Diaspora*, 2; Blocker, *A Little More Freedom*. Even in places associated with significant black migration, like Chicago, African Americans comprised only about 1 percent of the overall population in this period (Blocker, *A Little More Freedom*, 99).

36. Blocker, *A Little More Freedom*, 25.

37. Lang, "Locating the Civil Rights Movement," 379. Also see Lauck, *The Lost Region*, 7, 14, 19; Cayton and Gray, *The Identity of the American Midwest*, 16; Nicole Etcheson, "First Cousins: The Civil War's Impact on Midwestern Identity," in *Finding a New Midwestern History*, 39–52.

38. Jon Teaford, "The Development of Midwestern Cities," in *Finding a New Midwestern History*, 211–24; State Data Center of Iowa, "Total Population for Iowa's Incorporated Places: 1850–2000," http://data.iowadatacenter.org/datatables/PlacesAll/plpopulation18502000.pdf.

39. *Census of Iowa ... 1895*, 330, 334–35; Arnold, "An Opportunity to Challenge," 104–06; Pam Stek, "The 1898 American Cereal Company Strike in Cedar Rapids: Gender, Ethnicity, and Labor in Late Nineteenth-Century Iowa," *Annals of Iowa* 74, no. 2 (Spring 2015), 142–76.

40. Lang, "Locating the Civil Rights Movement," 386; also 375, 381, 385. Jon Gjerde, "Middleness and the Middle West," in *The Identity of the American Midwest*, 187; R. Douglas Hurt, "Midwestern Distinctiveness," in *The Identity of the American Midwest*, 169; Steiner, "The Midwestern Mind of Jane Addams, Cultural Pluralism and the Rural Roots of an Urban Ideal," in Lauck, ed., *The Midwestern Moment*; Lauck, *The Lost Region*, 7, 17; Dorothy Schwieder, *Iowa: The Middle Land* (Ames: Iowa State University Press, 1996), 83; James H. Madison, "State History in Regional Perspective," in Annette Atkins and Deborah L. Miller, eds., *The State We're In: Reflections on Minnesota History* (St. Paul: Minnesota Historical Society Press, 2010), 18–24; Mark Vinz, "Our Midwests," *Studies in Midwestern History* 1, no. 3 (April 2015), 26; James R. Shortridge, *The Middle West: Its Meaning in American Culture* (Lawrence: University of Kansas Press,

1989), 1, 100; Cayton, "The Anti-Region: Place and Identity in the History of the American Midwest," in *The Identity of the American Midwest*, 144–45.
41. "The New Congressional Apportionment," *Semi-Weekly Louisianian* (New Orleans), 30 November 1871.
42. "The Nation: Official Figures," *Semi-Weekly Louisianian*, 3 December 1871.
43. "The New Congressional Apportionment."
44. "Hon. George W. McCrary, of Iowa," *New National Era*, 15 September 1870; "The Mass Meeting," *The Leader* (Charleston, SC), 28 October 1865.
45. "Young Iowa," *The Leader* (Charleston, SC), 28 October 1865. "Gen. Grant on Impartial Suffrage in Iowa," *Charleston* (SC) *Advocate*, 28 November 1865; *Clark v. Board of Directors*, 24 Iowa 266 (1868); G. Galin Berrier, "The Negro Suffrage in Issue in Iowa—1865–1868," *Annals of Iowa* 39, no. 4 (Spring 1968): 241–61; Stephen J. Frese, "From Emancipation to Equality: Alexander Clark's Stand for Civil Rights in Iowa," *The History Teacher* 40, no. 1 (Nov. 2006): 81–110.
46. "Compulsory Education," *Semi-Weekly Louisianian*, 15 October 1871. Cox, *A Stronger Kinship*, 72–73; Hurt, 168; Kenneth Winkle, "'The Great Body of the Republic': Abraham Lincoln and the Idea of a Middle West," in *The Identity of the American Midwest*, 119.
47. Lang, "Locating the Civil Rights Movement," 374; Dorothy Schwieder, "Afterword," in *Outside In*, 562; Schwieder, *The Middle Land*, x–xii; Schwalm, *Emancipation's Diaspora*, 137; "The Nation—Official Figures," *Semi-Weekly Louisianian*, 3 December 1871; "In the States of Iowa and Indiana," *Semi-Weekly Louisianian*, 5 October 1871; "Miscellaneous News," *The Republican* (Maryville, TN), 30 May 1874; "Ninth Census of the United States," *The New National Era*, 20 June 1872; "Our Colored Citizens; Facts and Figures Showing His Rapid Advance," *Huntsville* (AL) *Gazette*, 17 March 1888.
48. "Colonization Schemes; What the Government Should Do—An Experimental Emmigration [sic] Bureau," *Weekly Louisianian*, 6 October 1877.
49. On Midwest as pluralistic, tolerant, democratic: Lauck, *The Lost Region*, 7, 17; Steiner, "The Midwestern Mind of Jane Addams"; Schwieder, *The Middle Land*, 83.
50. Etcheson, "First Cousins," in *Finding a New Midwestern History*, 40–41, 47. Also Cayton and Gray, *The Identity of the American Midwest*, 15–16; Blocker, *A Little More Freedom*, 15.
51. "The People Will Sustain Him," *Cedar Valley Times*; "A Gross Outrage," *Cedar Valley Times*.
52. Ibid.
53. State Library of Iowa, "Did Iowa ever pass a 'black exclusion' law?" https://www.statelibraryofiowa.org/services/collections/law-library/HistoricalFAQ/Q20.

54. *Proceedings of the Iowa State Colored Convention* (Muscatine, IA: Daily Journal Printing House, 1868), 9–10, http://coloredconventions.org/items/show/567.
55. *Muscatine Journal*, 6 November 1865, in Edwin S. Redkey, ed., *A Grand Army of Black Men: Letters from African-American Soldiers in the Union Army* (New York: Cambridge University Press, 1992), 293–95.
56. *Proceedings of the Iowa State Colored Convention*, 9, 7. At the time, only a handful of states (and none in the Midwest) allowed black male suffrage (Schwalm, *Emancipation's Diaspora*, 177).
57. "No Taxation," *Cedar Rapids Times*, 4 May 1871; "The Colored Citizens," *The Daily Argus* (Rock Island, Illinois), 3 March 1876; "The Civil Rights Club," *Cedar Rapids Evening Gazette*, 18 October 1883.
58. "Our Schools," *Cedar Rapids Evening Gazette*, 29 September 1885; "Monroe School," *Cedar Rapids Evening Gazette*, 22 October 1898; "A Visit to the White City"; "Commencement Exercises," *Coe College Cosmos*, 1 June 1902.
59. Greenwood, *First Fruits of Freedom*, 130.
60. Cedar Rapids City Directory, 1867 and 1876; "Bath Rooms"; "Most All of His Old Customers," *Weekly Times* (Cedar Rapids), 3 February 1876; Federal Census (1870).
61. Federal Census (1860 and 1870); "Real Estate Transfers," *Cedar Rapids Evening Gazette*, 15 September 1886; Cox, *A Stronger Kinship*, 85.
62. Cedar Rapids City Directories, 1884–1926; Marshall and Louisa Perkins Marriage Record, Linn County, Iowa, 1886; Federal Census (1900, 1910, 1920, and 1930); "Group portrait ... of [Marshall's] Lunch Room Restaurant," Collections of the African American Museum of Iowa; Arnold, "An Opportunity to Challenge," 114; "Blacks Continue to Suffer Most Prejudice," *Cedar Rapids Gazette*, 14 December 1975; *Outside In*, 202–03.
63. Federal Census (1900, 1910, 1920, and 1930); "Marshall Hotel to Open this Evening," *Cedar Rapids Evening Gazette*, 22 November 1913.
64. Blocker, *A Little More Freedom*, 49, 81, 215.
65. "A Visit to the White City"; Federal Census (1880, 1900, and 1910).
66. Cox, *The Bone and Sinew*, 206; Lang, "Locating the Civil Rights Movement," 380.
67. Paula M. Nelson, "Civic Life in a Midwestern Community," in *Finding a New Midwestern History*, 97.
68. Ibid.
69. "C.R. AME Church Marks 125 Years," *Cedar Rapids Gazette*, 20 July 1996.
70. Arnold, "An Opportunity to Challenge," 125–28; "C.R. AME Church Marks 125 Years"; "The Civil Rights Club"; "Color Line," *Cedar Rapids Evening Gazette*, 4 September 1897; "The Supreme Court; Decision in the Case of Jos. Bowlin vs. Lyon & Benjamin," *Cedar Rapids Evening Gazette*, 12 December 1885.

71. Steiner, "The Midwestern Mind of Jane Addams," 207. Also Cayton and Gray, *The Identity of the American Midwest*, 18.
72. Schwalm, *Emancipation's Diaspora*, 3. Also Etcheson, "First Cousins," in *Finding a New Midwestern History*, 40–41; Kathryn Schumaker, "Race, Place, and Belonging in the Midwest," *Middle West Review* 4, no. 2 (Spring 2018): 121–27; Cayton and Gray, *The Identity of the American Midwest*, 15–16; Blocker, *A Little More Freedom*, 15; Nicole Etcheson, "Barbecued Kentuckians and Six-Foot Texas Rangers: The Construction of Midwestern Identity," in *The Identity of the American Midwest*, 78–90.
73. Schwalm, *Emancipation's Diaspora*, 5. Arnold, "An Opportunity to Challenge"; Schwalm, *Emancipation's Diaspora*, 138; Blocker, *A Little More Freedom*, 44; Desmond King and Stephen Tuck, "De-Centering the South: America's Nationwide White Supremacist Order after Reconstruction," *Past & Present* 194, no. 1 (February 2007): 225.
74. Cedar Rapids City Directories, 1877, 1880, 1884, 1890, 1893, 1894, 1895, 1898; Federal Census (1880 and 1900).
75. Arnold, "An Opportunity to Challenge," 110–18.
76. Arnold, "An Opportunity to Challenge"; "Color Line"; "Threatened to Strike," *Cedar Rapids Evening Gazette*, 2 September 1897.
77. "The Civil Rights Club."
78. Millington W. Bergeson-Lockwood, "'We Do Not Care Particularly about the Skating Rinks': African American Challenges to Racial Discrimination in Places of Public Amusement in Nineteenth-Century Boston," *Journal of the Civil War Era* 5, no. 2 (June 2015): 257, 261.
79. Valeria W. Weaver, "The Failure of Civil Rights 1875–1883 and Its Repercussions," *Journal of Negro History* 54, no. 4 (October 1969): 371, 374, 378, and 379.
80. "The Civil Rights Club"; "AME Church Marks 125 Years."
81. "The Civil Rights Club."
82. E.C. Ebersole, *Reports of Cases in Law and Equity Determined in the Supreme Court of the State of Iowa* Vol. IX (New York: Banks and Brothers Law Publishers, 1886), 536–37; "The Supreme Court; Decision in the Case of Jos. Bowlin vs. Lyon & Benjamin."
83. Schwalm, *Emancipation's Diaspora*, 207; Tuck and King, "De-Centering the South," 239; Weaver, "Failure of Civil Rights."
84. "The Civil Rights Club."
85. Lauck, *The Lost Region*, 18.

David C. Miller | "Blood and Iron" and the Formation of German American Identity in the Midwest

Recollections of a Union Veteran

"Speeches and parliamentary votes will not settle the great questions of our times," Bismarck told the Prussian Diet. Vital political issues are decided by "blood and iron."[1] The President-Minister's words may sound unduly bellicose to American ears, but Germans had little difficulty in associating "iron" with military struggle and "blood" with historical tradition and ethnic heritage. Spoken in 1862 when Prussia was poised to unify the German states through armed force, these words led friend and foe alike to grasp the far-reaching implications.

To a far greater extent than the struggle for mastery in Germany, the American Civil War became a unification struggle capable of giving new direction to how people thought about nationhood, citizenship, and political liberties. Europeans who immigrated to America did not remain aloof. German-speaking recruits represented the single largest ethnic contingent participating in the "War between the States."[2] However, historians debate the extent to which the war altered German Americans' perceptions of themselves, the country, and their European heritage.[3]

For Union veteran Carl Diedrich Humke (1841–1928),[4] vivid war memories were essential to subsequent efforts to make sense of the tragic upheaval and comprehend its impact on his life. Humke's *Erinnerungen*[5] (recollections) reveal as much about his frame of mind at the time of composition as they do about the earlier "blood and iron" experiences that were critically important to his full maturation.[6] Because nearly three-fourths of the manuscript cover the war years, his recollections offer testimony about how he maintained strong identification with German culture while embracing the Union cause as an enlisted man in the ethnically mixed Sixteenth Iowa Infantry.

German by birth and upbringing, Carl Humke became an American citizen-soldier who subsequently married and settled in western Illinois where he achieved personal contentment and patrimonial success. The mature Humke came to regard himself as German and American, Westphalian and Midwesterner, Christian and citizen, farmer and family man. His inner identity—intrinsic to his deeper sense of self—was essentially composite in nature, the product of varied experiences within specific historical and geographic contexts.[7]

Focusing on a single life—no matter how significant—presents numerous interpretive challenges. Humke was not necessarily typical of Germans who immigrated at mid-century,[8] but he shared much in common with those who descended from peasant-farmers. His memoir, intended for family and friends, delineates the author's gradual integration into the upper Midwest before, during and after the terrible war provoked by secession. Yet the document also indicates how neither Humke nor many other German-speaking immigrants during the nineteenth century sought full immersion into mainstream Anglo-American society. Social integration entailed what Germans call *Anpassungen*—making selective accommodations—and realizing limited forms of cultural amalgamation.[9]

Faithful adherence to spoken dialects generally persisted among immigrant families as did interest in maintaining their diverse traditions. Nineteenth-century Germans, in fact, differed not only from each other but also from other ethnic groups and most notably in their social composition, wide geographic distribution, and high numbers.[10] Approximately six million German-speaking peoples came to America between the 1820s and the years immediately following the First World War. Nearly half of them would inhabit the more populous eastern seaboard. Most of the others, Carl Humke included, settled within the bustling "German Triangle"[11] of the Midwest where factors of demography, climate, and industrial technology were decisive in shaping attitudes, habits of mind, and what might be called ethnic thinking.[12]

Regional and sub-regional variations were always present. Significant generational differences between earlier immigrants ("grays") and later ones ("greens") complicated matters further.[13] Given such remarkable heterogeneity, no nationwide German American identity probably emerged. But making this observation need not imply other self-identifications were unimportant, repressed, or eliminated.[14] No less than other immigrants, Germans such as Humke respected their folkways, while adapting to changing circumstances and striving to maintain deeply rooted ties to family and religion.[15]

Although Humke devoted extensive portions of his recollections to wartime service, he did not minimize the importance of subsequent years when describing life with Hannah and their children. Admittedly, there remain deeply personal boundaries that historical explanation cannot easily trespass.[16] But the written account affords readers valuable insights into ethnicity, immigration, and assimilation as well as individual and group identity formation. His well-crafted narrative has wider application to understanding the historical development of the "Corn Belt" and greater Midwest.

Humke never marginalized his bicultural heritage. If anything, he affirmed it when assembling his memoir.[17] Throughout the recollections he repeatedly affirmed older attachments, while referencing new commitments. Four stand out: his continued adherence to the German cultural inheritance; becoming a disciplined soldier loyal to the Union army and its cause; identifying with German and old stock contemporaries who resided in the upper Midwest; and settling permanently in Illinois where he married and prospered as an enterprising farmer.

As will become evident, Humke's wartime experiences were more catalytic than cathartic. They did much to strengthen his character by fusing together those qualities that defined the man. His remarkable army service, which included incarceration in Andersonville's notorious prisoner-of-war camp, made his personal achievements before and especially after the war seem more significant and satisfying.[18]

Family, Friends, and Adopted Country

German American families assiduously cultivated their traditions through participation in local churches, fraternal organizations, beer gardens, sporting clubs, and social associations of all types.[19] Active involvement with *Deutschtum*, however, was always more than a favored option. It was essential to realizing successful migration and settlement. Carl Humke's relations with family and friends during his first years in America illustrate how this was so.

Born in the Gorspen district of the municipality of Petershagen (situated within the Prussian province of Westphalia), Humke was a villager descending from small landed proprietors rather than tenants or laborers. In his memoir he briefly described his early schooling and Protestant religious instruction,[20] while alluding to the challenges his family faced after the death of his father in 1849. The reader learns about his older brother and two sisters who had immigrated to the Unites States only a few years before 1857, the year Humke made the decision to cross the Atlantic.

Humke participated in the second great wave of German immigration[21] that began during the late 1840s. Accompanied by friend and fellow Westphalian Kristen Dörmann, he sailed from Bremen to New Orleans in a voyage that required seven weeks. Conforming to the common "chain migration" pattern, the two youths eventually joined other family members farming not far from Saint Louis. Acquiring land and becoming independent had been two powerful pull factors.[22] In fact, Humke humorously recalled that his decision to go to America derived in no small measure from Westphalia having "more farm-children [*Bauernkinder*] than farms." Yet he readily acknowledged restlessness and personal ambition as factors.[23]

His first years (1857–1861) in the country were challenging but made less difficult owing to his family's support and his own youthful ambition. Soon after leaving Saint Louis, he found work as a hired hand near Red Bud, Illinois, where his sister Mina and her husband farmed.[24] Not satisfied, he considered "it only appropriate that I find a place where I could learn to speak English. I wanted to work for an American, but I also wanted to visit [brother] Conrat [sic] in Warsaw, 175 miles [north] from Saint Louis, and then go [to Iowa] and see my sister Lisette."

Only after his monetary situation had improved did he travel to Warsaw [Illinois] and then to Iowa where not far from Davenport he worked as a hired hand outside the small town of Lowden. Encouraged by Lisette's generous husband Carl Penningroth,[25] Humke, who in 1860 was nineteen, briefly attended a "state-supported" grammar school to improve his speaking and writing skills. Becoming conversant in English proved advantageous because he soon began finding acceptance among old stock "Americans."[26]

His changing fortunes coincided with secession of the Lower South and the likelihood of civil war [Bürgerkrieg]. Although aware of the seriousness of the impending struggle, he did not explain why he enlisted in the army. Receiving steady income was an immediate consideration.[27] Perhaps a sense of duty also motivated him. Whatever the reasons, Humke, his friend Dörmann, and several acquaintances who spoke the dialect known as Low German agreed they must support the Union by volunteering.[28] After harvest (October 1861) he and the others signed three-year army enlistments. They began training in Davenport[29] as part of the Sixteenth Regiment Iowa Volunteer Infantry, remembered as the "German Regiment" because of the inclusion of large numbers of immigrant soldiers.[30] Humke became attached to Company B, one of three companies heavily composed of recruits who came from Prussia and the small duchy of Holstein.

Humke's military experiences proved eventful. Embedded within his well-structured narrative are descriptions of tactical innovations implemented in the western theater.[31] Critically important to formation of his outlook, however, were two noteworthy features of his wartime service: first, in having enlisted in an ethnically mixed Iowa regiment, and second, in fighting in the generally successful campaigns of the western theater. Such circumstances, especially when combined with his fluency in English, apparently lessened the frequency of antagonistic encounters with native-born Americans and reduced the degree of estrangement commonly experienced in the east where the "damned Dutch" were routinely derided in the popular press.[32]

Camaraderie, as distinct from close fraternization, was also generally present within the Sixteenth Iowa Infantry Regiment. Fighting alongside enlisted men who were both old stock and German, Humke never saw himself as part of an auxiliary force attached to the Union army.[33] In contrast to frustrated German recruits from Pennsylvania and New York, the foreign-born inhabitants of distressed border states, or many of the discontented soldiers of the Eighty-second Illinois Infantry (which also fought in the east and was led by Friedrich Hecker), he enjoyed tolerably good relations with Anglo-Americans during and especially after the war.

Humke's attitudes toward class differences, however, were likely conflicted when he first arrived in America and remained so at the time of enlistment. Over the years his perspective on social distinctions and matters of ethnicity broadened somewhat. As regarded denominational life, his views became almost latitudinarian. Nevertheless, when later writing about the war he did not hesitate to identify national origins of soldiers and civilians. Typically, he called most English-speaking soldiers "Americans." He mentioned the "kleine scotitishmann" [sic] who was General John McArthur, a native of Scotland. Those hailing from Ireland were recognized to be Irish when there was little doubt. Interestingly, the Irish were not scorned by him. His closest associates in Company B of the Iowa Sixteenth Infantry Regiment were described by him as *Plattdeutsche* or "Low Germans" from Westphalia and neighboring states. But more often they were identified as Germans who, not surprisingly, preferred to talk in their hard-sounding dialect.[34]

Despite the terrible sufferings of war, he offered fair appraisals of old stock and German commanding officers.[35] He also wrote honestly about enlisted men. "Although the soldiers were occasionally cocky," he admitted, "it could happen that in the very next battle, they would perform well and still have a blue bean [a bullet] tear its way between their ribs."[36] He wrote how a few "were rather dim-witted, of course, but most were able and strong men; although they should not be compared with a Prussian officer and especially when it concerns going into battle." After the war his respect for ex-soldiers apparently deepened. Indeed, he remained generally sympathetic toward most combatants—including "boys" or *Jungen* who had dishonored themselves.[37]

"Damned Dutchman" and "Damned Yankee"

Wartime service invariably brought out the incipient northerner in Humke. Campaigning in the south and personally confronting that section's stark differences tended to reaffirm his loyalty to the army and its cause. Being shot at by Confederates also proved highly persuasive. Later in life Humke seemed unable to forget the harsh workings of the slave system. Nor was he inclined to minimize other anachronistic features of the Old South, which had struck him as having constituted almost a world apart from Iowa and Illinois.

His opinions of the slave system and its countless victims, furthermore, were entirely in keeping with the many negative reactions of old stock and German soldiers who campaigned in the Lower South. Indeed, many of the Iowa regiment's German-born enlisted men descended from peasant-farmers.[38] They remembered their own family histories and how they had remained bound for generations by feudal obligations and humiliating restrictions imposed by impartible inheritance laws. This explains in part why sympathy for ex-slaves was widespread and commonly mixed with expressions of pity.[39]

Not surprisingly, Humke's most memorable passages recounted dramatic interventions made by soldiers to protect fleeing slaves from vindictive masters.[40] Yet he never fully elaborated on his antislavery sentiments. Although his opposition to the slave system was sincere, he wrote that he did not believe at the time that it was practical for thousands of former slaves and their families to pack up and leave plantations in their efforts to follow the still advancing armies.[41] Because former slaves traveling alongside Union armies on the march faced terrible risks, commanding officers often discouraged attempts to relocate. As a tradition-bound German who valued hearth and home, Humke, too, remained convinced that the newly freed peoples were better off by simply staying put.

His attitudes were likely complicated by lingering racial assumptions.[42] Although he did not employ racist vocabularies (in English or German) or offer stereotypical characterizations found in so many published letters and diaries, his retrospective account, nevertheless, revealed a fundamental inability to comprehend the former slaves' extreme desperation to escape their condition of servitude.[43] The psychological distance separating humane Union soldiers such as Humke from ex-slaves remained immense. In the upper Midwest, where African Americans were few, the racial chasm would long persist.

Less uncertain is how military discipline and the constant rigors of camp life helped maintain regimental morale, which doubtlessly reinforced Humke's powerful desire for final victory. Marching and fighting almost continuously in hostile territory for two and a half years encouraged something equally basic—namely, adoption of a vindictive north-versus-south attitude. When combined with the brutal application of what was already called the "hard hand of war," making direct contact with the Old South brought into focus what was essentially a northern sectional perspective.[44] After settling permanently in Illinois, he began to resemble others who were identifiably "Middle Western" in orientation.

Humke made additional observations that revealed as much about himself as about fellow soldiers in the Iowa regiments. Dangerous encounters with Confederates—described as "die Grauen" ["the Grays"] with its connotations of dread and terribleness—led him to reconsider basic commonalities among northern enlisted men.[45] Despite persistent Nativist attitudes, the doltish behavior of too many young infantrymen, and the inevitable tensions bred by the language barrier, he came to appreciate how many native-born soldiers in the western theater of operations—if not openly democratic—were at least meritocratic. Those serving in the ranks were able to set aside their occasional cockiness and express genuine respect for those who behaved responsibly by minimizing selfish ambitions and doing their duty. Although not without social prejudices of their own, European-born soldiers also displayed—especially in moments of adversity—an appealing social egalitarianism that was probably more readily appreciated within frontier settlements of the upper Midwest than in the urban east.

Union soldiers fighting alongside each other in locally recruited company units, furthermore, have left voluminous testimonies indicating how the army promoted patriotic sentiments and sought to foster a healthy solidarity capable of downplaying class and ethnic differences.[46] German publishers regularly seconded these calls for unity and cooperation. While the results of such efforts remain difficult to gauge, they were not necessarily inconsequential.[47]

Although a "damned Dutchman" in the eyes of many old stock Americans, Humke came to regard himself as one of those *verdammten Yankees* of whom angry southern men and women incessantly complained and northerners could proudly invoke. Significant, too, was his consistent employment of *wir*, the first-person plural, when describing success on and off the battlefield. Promotion to corporal in early 1863 prior to the long siege of Vicksburg apparently reinforced devotion to duty—indeed, it remained a source of personal satisfaction that he did not fail to mention several times in his recollections. Favorable conditions encountered in Illinois after the war further sustained his self-confidence and contributed to formation of a fundamentally positive outlook.[48]

Obviously, Humke was not unaffected by the *Schmelztiegel* (literally "melting pan" or "crucible") phenomenon.[49] But the assimilative experience was more complex than commonly acknowledged by later writers. Humke, though a dedicated Union soldier, continuously referenced his membership in the older *Deutschtum* and never stopped doing so. Not unlike old-stock Americans of both north and south who identified with local and regional *mores*, he remained a product of Westphalia, and hence, *Deutsch*. He was what Frederick C. Luebke described as a "stomach German"[50]—that is, someone who perpetuated German ways of life, maintained the old-world diet, and spoke a mix of dialect and American colloquial English.

Strength in Numbers: Group Identifications
Humke's membership in the ethnically mixed Sixteenth Iowa Regiment complicated rather than undermined his commitment to the Union. His continued dedication was not without certain qualifications. As might be expected, strategic success played a significant role in sustaining his loyalty to the national cause.[51] Because victory on western battlefields in 1862 and 1863 tended to obviate overt criticism of foreign-born soldiers, he and presumably many others came to appreciate how success helped guarantee freedom to speak the German language and enjoy customary life without persistent fears of harassment from military and civilian authorities. Even before the traumatic imprisonment at Andersonville, Humke realized—and perhaps to a greater extent than others—how supporting the Union cause did not conflict with his personal liberty to be German.[52]

Old-stock soldiers who embraced the cause of national reunification (or, for that matter, those who fought for the Confederacy) also recognized how the great struggle might safeguard related political interests. Winning could advance personal objectives.[53] None of this, however, could be taken for granted by most German soldiers and civilians.[54] Disillusionment, as mentioned earlier, was commonly felt among foreign-born recruits deployed in the eastern theater of operations where military defeat almost always encouraged Nativist denunciations of cultural nonconformity. Yet German soldiers in both theaters learned these hard lessons time and again. Whenever strategic progress had been stymied by superior Confederate generalship or by repeated Union blunders (especially in Virginia), eastern newspapers did not spare the "Dutchmen" who were denounced as incompetent, cowardly, and disloyal.[55]

Germans in America were not passive—and neither was Humke. Adopting a predominantly defensive posture was prudent, if not always effective. Impassioned rejoinders to scurrilous attacks were printed during wartime. But another common response—though not universally practiced—involved proudly identifying themselves as *Deutsch* in the broader cultural-linguistic sense. Enlisted men such as Corporal Humke participated in the prevailing trend—that is, openly acknowledging what amounted to a basic type of Germanic solidarity in private speech and public discourse.

Making explicit identifications with "Germanness" was already an acknowledged means by which to promote political agendas deemed compatible with high ideals derived from German philosophy. Beginning in the 1850s Carl Schurz, Emil Praetorius, Heinrich Börnstein, and many other *Forty-eighters* not only integrated liberal principles with their positions on slavery, they skillfully utilized the vibrant German-language press to reach a wider audience.[56]

Yet the purpose of referencing one's German background was never exclusively political. Nor was it always self-consciously achieved. Less formally educated immigrants lived their "Germanness" and, in doing so, reaffirmed loyalty to an entire array of traditions bound to family, religion, and ways of life.[57] Humke, for instance, wrote standard German even as he preferred to speak the *Plattdeutsch* dialect when around the regiment's Westphalians and Holsteiners (and after the war when raising his family and farming in Illinois). His closest friends were mostly fellow northerners, that is, former Prussian subjects. And he took special pride when learning about "the old *Forty-eighter*" Franz Sigel as well as the nationally known Samuel Kurtis (*sic*—Curtis), a competent general he wrongly assumed to be German. Typical was the humorous and yet boastful observation he offered about how "there were more Germans fighting at Shiloh than in the [Prussian] war against Denmark [1849]."[58] Nevertheless, Humke shared one political trait with many famous *Forty-eighters*—he remained a Republican after the war whereas most fellow immigrants voted Democratic.

Without question, domestic circumstances and not events abroad were mainly responsible for reinforcing Humke's willingness to identify with the cultural *Deutschtum* even as he sought to acquire American citizen status. Historian Stephen Engle has argued that a "wartime identity" took shape and mainly because of "the fear that Germans might lose their ethnic identity during the war."[59] Indeed, many of the anxieties fostered by the threatening rhetoric of the Know Nothing Party during the 1850s had persisted throughout the war years. And though political tensions subsided somewhat after 1865, they never entirely disappeared. This was a major reason leading German newspapers did not stop promoting a national perspective that at the same time vigorously encouraged political cooperation, promoted German-language instruction in schools, and opposed restrictive Sabbatarian "blue laws" pushed by the Temperance movement.[60]

German-born Americans of the middle and late nineteenth century, influenced as they were by political spokesmen and the examples set by such newspapers as Chicago's *Illinois Staatszeitung* and Saint Louis's *Anzeiger des Westens*, became less inclined to refer to themselves as Prussians, Hanoverians, Bavarians, or former subjects of other polities.[61] The observable tendency in writings and everyday speech was instead toward making direct identifications with presumed commonalities found in German culture and history. In this respect, Humke was not unlike other German Americans—for he, too, became less prone to cite specific regional and state origins. This practice, however, was not confined to two or three overlapping generations of Germans. It was an important manifestation of different ethnic kinship sentiments found elsewhere and may offer insights into the renewed eagerness of immigrants to acknowledge membership within larger groups. Making such identifications remained popular, too—and not just among Germans. Irish and Scandinavian immigrants were inclined to do the same.

As John Higham observed decades ago, open declarations of this sort offer evidence of a developing "made-in-America" ethnic consciousness that derived from the country's extreme competitiveness and grass-roots political life. Such conditions almost always encouraged first- and second-generation immigrants to seek satisfaction and even security through wider group identifications.[62] Ironically, the presumed solidarity among Germans (or, for that matter, Irish or Italians) never existed in the "old country" where the disparate peoples had remained internally divided by religion, class and custom, and dialect as well as by separate governments.

Whereas making general identifications clearly antedated both the Civil War and the struggle for German unification,[63] the practice gained wider support throughout the century as increasing numbers of Germans deliberately minimized particularism, which, in any event, meant little to English-speaking citizens ignorant of European political geography. Employment of *Deutsch* and *deutsch* (as noun and adjective) was also fully in keeping with the cultural solidarity German politicians and editors encouraged during and after the war. Furthermore, these verbal practices were commonsensical and deemed useful.

Generic word preferences, however, need not imply a strong desire on the part of speakers or authors to bolster self-confidence and resist becoming "Americanized."[64] Although difficult to quantify, Humke's writings, no less than the grammar and vocabulary used by other Germans in America, suggest instead a process of nuanced cultural amalgamation rather than outright assimilation. While the shift in word choices conformed to prevailing and practical trends in linguistic usage, such changes also indicated the presence of something more fundamental—namely, an underlying pragmatism that could preserve the older cultural inheritance, while facilitating basic identification with America, its legal protections, and its freedoms.

Typically, Humke's earliest descriptive references in the manuscript were specific and appropriately so—as when referencing different immigrants prior to the war as Westphalians or as residents of neighboring states. When recounting the war and life in Illinois, the preference was almost always to employ "German." His recollections—direct in vocabulary and sincere in tone—were also consistent with persistent efforts made by him after the war to succeed as a German-born farmer in Illinois and to become rather like other "Americans" who were responsible citizens honestly performing their civic duties.[65]

Nevertheless, it was the catastrophic war and not printed words of journalists, radical *Forty-eighters*, or anyone else that decisively influenced Humke's thinking about the country and his place in it.[66] Long after the war had ended, he emphasized military victory as being of foremost importance—and mainly because his own personal safety was at stake.[67] During the war years, his very existence had required dangerous military service and the rigorous dedication it demanded.[68] If resourcefulness and strength of character contributed to his survival, desperate military situations largely informed his practical patriotism, which was the opposite of blind obedience. Indeed, his three years of service was steeped in the sentiments he shared with other soldiers who fought alongside him. When describing his and other soldiers' exuberance after being mustered out of the army in November 1864, he wrote simply, "We were free."[69]

Fighting did not break Humke. Nor did the horrors of captivity. After he and over two hundred fellow Iowans of the Sixteenth and Fifteenth Regiments were overwhelmed by Confederate forces and captured on July 22, 1864, near Bald Hill north of Atlanta,[70] they were sent southward by rail to Andersonville where they suffered grievously.

Humke endured two months of imprisonment. His devotion to the Union and the army may not have constituted a patriotic "faith." Yet it doubtlessly contributed to hardening his grim determination to come out alive. Survival was a function of many factors and most obviously his strong physical constitution, friendships made with fellow prisoners of war, his quiet Protestant faith, and the keen interest he took in wanting to live long enough to witness the eventual hanging of commandant Henry Wirz and his "junge Bengels" ("young louts") who served as guards.[71] Vitally important, too, was his concealed money supply. He carefully related this wise decision before the Atlanta campaign to imitate others and hide army pay in clothing. As he recorded: "Every moment counted because the war was ever-present, always threatening to pull me back in again. For this reason, I made a seamless tear in my trousers, then wrapped my money in strong durable paper before carefully stitching it back into the pants. Two of my friends were told and I promised [to help] them: just in case [!]."[72]

The miseries within Andersonville's Camp Sumter resembled those found in concentration camps of the twentieth century. This infamous place, he wrote, was "Hell on Earth." The starving prisoners had little or no shelter. Infectious diseases were rampant. They were observed day and night by armed guards stationed in special watch platforms. They lacked adequate quantities of food and drinkable water.

There was not even enough firewood for cooking the meager rations of rice, corn meal, and rancid bacon. Dozens of men perished each day— "the corpses stacked on wagons hitched to mules" and driven by slaves to burial pits dug outside the camp's two stockade walls. Within a single year, fourteen thousand died.

Through good fortune Humke was selected to be part of a prisoner exchange hastily arranged between General Sherman and General *Hoot* [*sic*—John Bell Hood] two weeks after the fall of Atlanta on September 1. Humke "was one of the lucky few." On September 17, 1864, he joined seven hundred other emaciated soldiers still able to walk out of the Andersonville nightmare. Herded into rickety railway cars bound toward Atlanta, they were returned to Union lines. Two days later, 1100 other prisoners were similarly exchanged.[73]

Humke's health had been seriously impaired. But he and other exchanged prisoners were determined to carry on as best they could. They were determined to continue as soldiers: "Each of us decided we would rather fight and be shot to pieces than be captured again [!]." Chronically fatigued, Humke and other liberated men briefly served alongside other troops. But doctors judged them unfit to continue as front-line soldiers. They would not participate in Sherman's now famous "March to the Sea."

Corporal Humke's term of service soon ended.[74] He was discharged in mid-November and permitted to travel with other soldiers by rail to Chattanooga before returning to Saint Louis. Afterward he was reunited with his brother Conrad who had settled near Quincy, Illinois. Within two years he married Hannah Bödecker, purchased premium land with the generous assistance of his father-in-law, and began farming a few miles southeast of Warsaw near Sutter, an unincorporated hamlet.

Integration and Affirmation of Identity

In his maturity Carl Humke was German and American, Westphalian and midwestern. Military service had toughened his sensibilities and added depth to his determined character. Many of his affiliations and attachments proved complementary and consequential. The assimilative processes of *Anpassungen* (accommodations) were also continuous as new and old self-identifications persisted and tended to coalesce.[75]

Seemingly absent in his recollections was any serious conflict between his naturalized citizen status and his European origins. Revealing, too, was how he continued to speak *Plattdeutsch* even as he wrote in a fine standard German. Conversant in American English, he was sometimes listed in local records as Charles Humke. There is no evidence, however, that he self-consciously reflected on who he was or agonized about what kind of person he ought to be. Much like other rural and urban contemporaries residing in the upper Midwest, his sense of self was mostly intuitive. He lived his identity.

Throughout his long life Humke displayed a propensity toward self-reliance, thrift, and common sense. Moreover, he demonstrated a remarkable capacity to adapt to changing circumstances. Literally, and not just metaphorically, "blood and iron" were inseparable from his existence. While the struggle to preserve the Union severely challenged him in physical and psychological ways, his "Germanness" supplied a solid foundation that proved invaluable throughout his wartime service. The generally favorable circumstances he encountered afterward in the upper Midwest further sustained his self-confidence, giving rise to the positive, if cautious, outlook on life that infused his personal recollections.[76]

An avid church member, Humke shared much in common with German Protestants and Catholics. Like them, he never compartmentalized his devotional life. His family's involvement with the local Evangelical Church was always integral to their Protestant faith and quite inseparable from their German heritage, becoming, in fact, the nucleus of their social activities.[77] Humke participated in the congregation's communal services, made generous donations, and later personally contributed to the remodeling of the church. His own temperament was more traditional than pietistic. Acknowledging how a life "worthy and delightful" involved considerable "toil and labor,"[78] he faced the world and stoically accepted its inherent imperfections.

Humke did not ignore politics. Nor did he neglect civic duties. In contrast to German Americans who were inclined toward the Democratic Party, he consistently supported Republicans (notably Illinois' representative Benjamin Marsh, also a veteran of Shiloh and a resident of nearby Warsaw), and, beginning in 1877, served as a county tax collector and later local census enumerator (1880).[79] As an ex-soldier belonging to the Grand Army of the Republic and a voter who resided in the "Land of Lincoln," his political inclinations remained practical, businesslike, and profitable.

Postwar circumstances favored his eventual entrepreneurial and material success. Residing in Hancock County near Warsaw presented fewer obstacles to German-born citizens. Its demographic composition had never been ethnically homogeneous.[80] The German immigrant population, in fact, grew steadily and already approximated 20 percent of the total by the 1870s. His neighbors included fellow Westphalians. But other families residing nearby were old stock. Quite a few were Scots-Irish. Consequently, his business dealings and social interactions were never exclusively German as Humke reported in the recollections. The grain merchants and bankers in Warsaw, buyers and sellers of land, the farmhands he employed, and consumers of his dairy products in both Keokuk and Warsaw were a mix of English-speaking "Americans" and immigrants.

Humke's considerable success as a family farmer explains his expressions of personal contentment, which resonate in the recollections' final pages. Through many years of hard work and good fortune he successfully expanded and diversified his farming enterprise to the benefit of his wife Hannah and their sizable family. His written account fully detailed land purchases and sales; construction of houses, churches, and barns; and repeated efforts made by the entire family to increase production and seek improvements by using mechanical tools (such as reapers and mowers) and adopting more efficient farming techniques. By 1890 the family's property holdings were already considerable and their dairy farming had become a lucrative source of income.

The proud veteran remained devoted to his family. Friends and neighbors were also appreciated just as others' acts of generosity were frequently acknowledged by him. All the while, Humke's behavior combined individual resourcefulness and tenacity with a willingness to cooperate and even conform. These personal qualities were common and never exclusively German or Anglo-American. But they were characteristic of ethnically mixed communities—both rural and urban—and especially those heavily composed of Germans and Scandinavians residing in the great Midwest between the middle nineteenth and early twentieth centuries.

Not surprisingly, throughout the recollections Humke reaffirmed the importance of self-discipline and practicality, which were also never exclusively German traits. His willingness to exert himself (as when he became fluent in English) served him well as private soldier, prisoner, and farmer. Nor did success spoil him. Contrary to the popular meme repeated ad nauseam in modern fiction and often reiterated by today's journalists, his relative prosperity produced just the opposite effect. Postwar success and the immense satisfaction it brought invariably led him to reflect on the past. These were among the many reasons he came to believe his incredible experiences in one of the bloodiest wars in history deserved to be remembered and made available to his family but not to the public at large. Not unlike his German forebears, he remained protective of his privacy.

Humke's life as a family farmer deserves additional comment. Over the course of three decades he expanded and diversified his landed properties, purchased mowers and reapers, and became more like a commercial farmer who effectively combined the popular triad of corn, hog, and dairy farming into a more profitable enterprise. Owning six hundred acres of efficiently managed farmland by the early 1890s, his holdings were roughly twice the size of typical farms in the western counties of Illinois.[81] His successful farming, moreover, illustrates an interesting commingling of German and American behavioral traits detectable to this day in the Midwest.

As demonstrated by Kathleen Neils Conzen and Sonya Salamon, German family farmers exhibited older patrimonial practices, while English-speaking neighbors tended toward risk-taking ventures designed to bring immediate profits.[82] German born farmers were often hesitant to take risks in land purchases and profit-making enterprises. They usually did so when augmenting the size of their family farms—and done almost always with the next generation's welfare in mind. Old-stock farmers, in contrast, were more willing to move on and seek opportunities whenever and wherever they might arise. In most respects, Humke remained closer to traditional German practices. He expected his children to work on the farm and become farmers themselves. And this meant they remain anchored to the land.

Despite initial challenges posed by seasonal drought and flooding, Carl and Hannah adamantly refused to sell their land

and move on.⁸³ Unlike several of their old-stock neighbors (whose farmsteads they later purchased), the Humkes strongly resembled other Germans who possessed a very sincere, almost sacred reverence for their farmsteads. Yet the family was less averse than others when it came to taking risks. Carl improved upon the profitable practices adopted by others. He regularly took out needed loans, purchased more acreage, and systematically made his farmland more cost-effective through calculated investments in the latest reapers and mowers and by expanding his water resources by tapping deep wells through use of steam-powered drills. He stopped planting wheat and expanded corn production, all the while increasing the size of livestock. Hence, the Humke family energetically combined traditional German approaches toward family farming with contractual practices of small commercial enterprises.⁸⁴

Carl Humke gladly hired "Americans"—as he called farmhands who were native old stock. He remained sociable and maintained trustworthy business relations with non-German neighbors and local merchants in Warsaw and Keokuk. In fact, he significantly added to his annual income by regularly selling his dairy products (via written contract) to local businesses.⁸⁵ By the late 1880s he had paid off most of his debts. As early as 1890 his successive purchases of neighbors' farmland resulted in six hundred acres of mostly consolidated properties. Careful management of finances enabled him to distribute land and make generous cash allowances to each of his six sons and three daughters when they began marrying and establishing their own farms.⁸⁶

Yet Humke's farm enterprise remained familial and cooperative. In several respects, his land-owning practices resembled an expanding fiefdom that included a peculiar American form of subinfeudation practiced for the sake of distributing property to blood relations. However, in contrast to conditions faced in Prussia where the restrictive *Anerbenrecht* laws kept him from inheriting land, Humke, the strict and indefatigable patriarch, saw to it that his descendants (daughters included) and their own families were genuine beneficiaries of his not inconsiderable largesse. Like him, they never obsessed over profits, but they were genuinely shamed by debt.⁸⁷

Concluding Remarks

Writing in the first decade of the century, moreover, meant that this former Prussian subject's thinking was not yet affected by the First World War and the anti-German sentiments it unleashed. Whatever political disillusionment and personal doubts the global conflict engendered remain unclear.[88] What can be ascertained is how Humke, not unlike others who immigrated to the Unites States, willingly traded the Old World's authoritarianism and corporate social organization for the more open and egalitarian Midwest. Because he lived most of his life before the full emergence of centralized and regulatory government, his preferred existence as a fully bilingual German American residing in the country's heartland was made not only realizable but satisfying.[89] Indeed, this civil war veteran strongly affirmed his bicultural identity when writing the personal recollections.

Family, farm, religion—and not abstract principles—remained of overriding importance to him as they did to other Westphalian immigrants who settled in western Illinois, eastern Iowa, and parts of Missouri. Furthermore, his family's selective integration into American society reminds us of the many adaptive channels open to immigrants who inhabited a dynamic polyglot Midwest that was already becoming culturally pluralistic—and years before the concept was articulated and added to the popular lexicon.[90]

Carl Humke never expressed having any regrets about fundamental life choices. The absence of remorse, much like his satisfying coexistence with those who differed from him in speech and habit, suggests much about who he was and where he chose to settle: He immigrated at age sixteen, fought in the great war to preserve the Union, survived a terrible captivity, and went on to marry and live long and prosper. Humke may not have been typical of German Americans in the rural Midwest, but he shared much in common with them. His example was not unusual.

Notes

I wish to thank retired sociologist Gene Humke of Peoria, Illinois. The great-grandson of Carl Humke, Gene offered useful information, fresh insights, and strong support. Gratitude also is expressed to Professor Kurt Canow of Kansas City, Missouri, and CMSgt (Air Force, ret.) Paul Bishop of Peoria. Both offered valuable assistance when translating and interpreting the most difficult German passages contained within Humke's recollections.

1. Bismarck, *Reden 1847–1869*, W. Schüßler, ed., v. 10, *Bismarck: Die gesammelten Werke*, Hermann von Petersdorff, ed. (Berlin: Otto Stolberg, 1924–35), 139–40: the remarks (September 1862) as reported by others reads: "Preußen muß seine Kraft zusammenfassen und zusammenhalten auf den günstigen Augenblick, der schon einige Male verpaßt ist; Preußens Grenzen nach den Wiener Verträgen sind zu einem gesunden Staatsleben nicht günstig; *nicht durch Reden und Majoritätsbeschlüsse werden die großen Fragen der Zeit entschieden*—das ist der große Fehler von 1848 und 1849 gewesen—*sondern durch Eisen und Blut*" (my italics). Bismarck's reference to *Eisen und Blut* likely borrowed from Max von Schenkendorf (1783–1817) who wrote patriotic poems during the wars fought against Napoleonic France. Translators tend to reverse the order of the two words.

2. Of more than a half million immigrants who fought for the Union (24 percent of all northern troops), approximately 216,000 of them were Germans, most of them born abroad. Still useful is Ella Lonn, *Foreigners in the Union Army and Navy* (Baton Rouge: Louisiana State University Press, 1951). Perhaps 80,000 additional foreign-born soldiers and sailors also served; many were German-speaking and came from neighboring areas of central Europe. See Wolfgang Helbich, "Ethnic Legends in the Gray Zones of History: The Case of Germans in the American Civil War," *Central European Journal of Social Sciences and Humanities* 40, no. 1 (2014): 171–88.

3. Walter D. Kamphoefner and Wolfgang Helbich, eds., *Germans in the Civil War: The Letters They Wrote Home* (Chapel Hill: University of North Carolina Press, 2006; German ed., 2002). Consult also Helbich, "German-Born Union Soldiers: Motivation, Ethnicity and 'Americanization,'" in Helbich and Kamphoefner, eds., *German Immigration and Ethnicity in Comparative Perspective* (Madison, Wisconsin: Max Kade Institute, 2004), 295–325; and Christian B. Keller, *Chancellorsville and the Germans. Nativism, Ethnicity, and Civil War Memory* (New York: Fordham University Press, 2007),123–46, which described how German-born soldiers fighting in the east reacted to scapegoating by becoming "more German." Keller recognized how studies on German soldiers in the west discovered less negativity in Anglo-American press coverage.

4. Humke was born in 1841 near the village of Windheim. Today, Gorspen-Vahlsen is a township district of the municipality of Petershagen (within the federal state of North Rhine-Westphalia). See my detailed analysis of Humke's military service in "Assimilation and Adaptation in the Civil War: The Experiences of a German American Soldier," *Journal of the Illinois State Historical Society* 113, no. 1 (Spring 2020): 7–39.

5. The handwritten German manuscript titled *Errinerungen von Carl Diedrich Humke* continued to deteriorate after the 1920s (and may no longer exist).

However, a faithful line-by-line transcription survives (as does an abridged English version handwritten by Humke). On the last page of the surviving German text is written: "*Transcription made by Bertha Althide (youngest daughter of Carl Humke) in March 1962 at Quincy, Illinois.*" Bertha was born in 1887, making her seventy-five years of age when transcribing the MS. Today her 140-page handwritten copy (meticulously recorded in a 6" x 8" notebook) is preserved in the personal papers of Humke's great grandson R. Gene Humke, professor (retired) of sociology at Illinois Central College in East Peoria. Condition of original *Erinnerungen* document in 1962 is unclear. Bertha Althide's transcription of approximately 22,000 words was the second. She made her transcription in mostly Roman script because Humke's original was done in *Kurrentschrift* as was the first transcription made by a schoolteacher named Moeller (married to a member of the Lange family, a branch of the Humke family). Herr Moeller accurately transcribed the MS before its deteriorating condition made readability difficult. In either 1959 or 1960 he made available his transcription to Humke's descendants in Illinois.

6. Humke wrote his *Errinerungen* (hereafter cited as Humke, MS) over a span of several years and likely between 1900 and 1910. He completed its final section on family life and farming only in 1909–1910. According to the family, before and after 1900 Humke often discussed his wartime experiences with others.

7. Philip Gleason, "Identifying Identity: A Semantic History," in *Speaking of Diversity. Language and Ethnicity in Twentieth-Century America* (Baltimore: Johns Hopkins University Press, 1992), 123–49: on usages of *identity* as term and concept.

8. Data gathered from *U.S. Census Bureau* (Eighth, Ninth, Tenth, and Eleventh Censuses) indicate that by 1860 approximately 15 percent of the U.S. population (32 million) was foreign-born. Irish numbered 1.6 million, whereas Germans (of all origins) numbered 1.3 million on the eve of the war (of which 1.2 million resided in the north). While German immigration exceeded the Irish by the 1850s the wave of settlement slowed during the war, resuming afterward, overlapping with a third wave (c. 1870 to early 1890s) that mostly originated east of the Elbe.

9. Petra Dewitt, *Degrees of Allegiance: Harassment and Loyalty in Missouri's German-American Community during World War I* (Ohio University Press, 2012), 17: assimilation involved a "complex, multifaceted, and individual process of discarding old traditions, adopting new customs, and fusing several old and new traits into a new identity."

10. German settlement conformed to chain migration patterns. By the 1870s three out of five German Americans pursued farming or farm-related occupations in Iowa, parts of Illinois, Missouri, Minnesota, Wisconsin, and Michigan.

11. The German Triangle's boundaries were the Great Lakes, Ohio River, and Mississippi River, but German settlement extended into Missouri, Iowa, Kansas, Nebraska, and the Dakotas. The highest concentrations of first- and second-generation Germans resided in Wisconsin, Minnesota, Iowa, Michigan, and Illinois (composing from 10 to 30 percent of these state populations by the 1890s).
12. John Higham, "Integrating America: The Problem of Assimilation at the Turn of the Century," in Carl J. Guarneri, ed., *Hanging Together. Unity and Diversity in American Culture* (New Haven: Yale University Press, 2001), 85–99 (first appearing in the 1981 inaugural issue of the *Journal of American Ethnic History*). Higham emphasized how the decentralized American Republic was inclined to tolerate (and ignore) separate ethnic enclaves. This changed after c. 1890.
13. The distinction between "grays" and "greens" likely originated with the *Dreißiger* Friedrich Münch who settled in Missouri during the 1830s. Most Germans were "greens" who participated in the later (post-1848) second and third waves of migration. Only a minority were political refugees (the Forty-eighters).
14. Kathleen Neils Conzen, "German Americans and the Invention of Ethnicity," in Frank Trommler and Joseph McVeigh, eds., *America and the Germans* 1 (Philadelphia: University of Pennsylvania, 1985), 131–47. See Stephen D. Engle, "Yankee Dutchmen: Germans, the Union, and the Construction of a Wartime Identity," in Susannah J. Ural, ed., *Civil War Citizens. Race, Ethnicity and Identity in America's Bloodiest Conflict* (New York: New York University Press, 2010), 57–98; and Randi Julia Ramsden, "Shaping History. The History of German Language Newspapers in Wisconsin," *Wisconsin Magazine of History* 100, no. 1 (Autumn 2016): 28–43.
15. Inseparable from *Deutschtum* was the multilayered associational life. See Frederick C. Luebke, especially *Germans in the New World: Essays in the History of Immigration* (Urbana and Chicago: University of Illinois Press, 1990), 151, wherein he described assimilation as an "interactive process in which both the immigrant and the receiving societies are changed."
16. Humke, MS, 6: writing about illness. "Schuhe und Strümpfe waren freilich nicht zerissen, aber mein Gemüt um so mehr." In English the deceptively simple passage reads: "Shoes and stockings were obviously not torn—but my disposition all the more."
17. Humke completed the section on family life and farming in 1909–1910. An abridged English translation made by him exists. No personal letters are extant.
18. Reunited the following year with Conrad in Quincy, Illinois, Carl Humke bought land near Warsaw in Hancock County. In 1867 he married Hannah Louise Bödecker.

19. Urban dwellers enjoyed varied associational activities. Humke lived on the periphery of the new *Bürgertum*, which included professional middle classes, shopkeepers, and skilled workers residing in cities and smaller towns.
20. Humke, MS, 1–3. Protestant religious life in Westphalia was coordinated by the Prussian Union of Churches, a state-directed organization seeking to unite Lutheran and Reformed after the Napoleonic Wars. By the 1840s the Union officially became known as the Evangelical Church of Prussia.
21. "German" usually meant a German-language speaker. Most Germans lived in the nearly forty states (kingdoms, duchies, counties, and free cities) composing the German Confederation (1815–1867) and its successor, the German *Reich* (1871–1918). German Swiss and Austrians must not be ignored, nor the ethnic Germans residing in other provinces of the Austrian Empire and elsewhere.
22. Carl and Conrad Humke had an older brother. Prussia's strict inheritance laws (*Anerbenrecht*) resembled primogeniture in favoring the eldest son. Yet the Humkes owned land and were not tenants who sought to supplement their incomes through linen-weaving, a cottage industry already shrinking in importance during the 1840s. For more on this subject, see W. Kamphoefner, *The Westfalians. From Germany to Missouri* (Princeton: Princeton University Press, 1987), 12–39.
23. Humke MS, 2–3: "Not unlike others sowing their wild oats, I had committed my share of stupid but not truly wicked pranks and, like others my age, viewed the whole world as an object to be conquered. Therefore, I decided to make the trip." (All translations are my own.)
24. Humke, MS, 6: recurring fevers bothered him when working as a farmhand near Red Bud, Illinois (forty miles southeast of St. Louis). His recovery owed to care coming from a fellow northern German named Heinrich Gübert.
25. William John Petersen in *The Story of Iowa: The Progress of an American State* 3 (New York: Lewis Publ. Co., 1952), 569–70: included are descriptions of the Penningroths (who owned farmland near Lowden) and their descendants.
26. Humke, MS, 9–10: "I took advantage of this opportunity," he wrote, adding how "the children knew very good English. The oldest girl taught me and because I did so well, after only two lessons [reading primers] I could get through it all quite well." He reported acceptance among "Americans" who were old stock; that is, those descended from peoples of the British Isles: English, Scots, Scots-Irish, and Welsh. Although English-speaking, Irish Catholic immigrants were not included.
27. Humke, MS, 11–12: "The pay was 13 dollars and with 3 dollars 50 cents paid in the month of enlistment ... for those who at that moment needed money the cash allowance was made available through deductions made to the monthly pay of 13 dollars ... regular pay was increased by two dollars

per month with promise of an extra bounty of 100 dollars." Humke wrote: "to this day I receive 20 dollars a month or 240 dollars per year from the Veteran Soldier's pension." This amount tends to confirm he was writing c. 1900–1910.
28. Opposition to slavery developed over time. *Cf.* Chandra Manning, *Troubled Refuge: Struggling for Freedom in the Civil War* (New York: Vintage, 2016).
29. Ted Hinckley, "Davenport and the Civil War," *Annals of Iowa*, 34 (1958), 400–19: Davenport's population in 1861 was nearly 12,000 (20 percent German) and could boast five military installations.
30. Humke enlisted (for three years) 8 October 1861, joining the Sixteenth Regiment Iowa Volunteer Infantry, which was not predominantly German. But he served in Company B (typically about thirty-five soldiers), which was mostly German, and was promoted to corporal (1863–1864). Iowa produced forty-six infantry regiments and nine regiments of cavalry during the war. In proportion to its population in 1860 (slightly more than 600,000 residents), the number of Iowa volunteers was among the highest in the country. Unlike Humke, most German-born soldiers (perhaps three-fourths of them) did not serve the Union as members of largely German units.
31. See Miller, "Assimilation and Adaptation in the Civil War." Humke fought in pitched battles at Shiloh and Iuka and witnessed siege warfare at Corinth and Vicksburg; he was deployed in scouting operations that resembled small unit skirmishing and "fire fights" of later wars. Although never seriously wounded, the war left him physically drained. He repeatedly called attention to perpetual hunger, sickness, rainstorms and excessive heat, and the general confusion and fatigue. He retained a sense of humor: only once (MS, 112) did he suffer from "cannon-fever" and that after making acquaintance of "the young lady who would become my wife."
32. David L. Valuska and Christian B. Keller, *Damn Dutch: Pennsylvania Germans at Gettysburg* (Mechanicsburg, PA: Stackpole, 2004), and Keller, *Chancellorsville and the Germans, op. cit.* (2007), 123–46. See also Joseph R. Reinhart, ed., *Yankee Dutchmen under Fire: Civil War Letters from the 82nd Illinois Infantry* (Kent, Ohio: Kent State University, 2013).
33. Most old-stock soldiers in Iowa were Protestant as were most German recruits (coming as they did from north-central Germany). Iowa veterans were known for their gracious treatment of all those who served, including African American soldiers. See Robert Cook, "A War for Principle? Shifting Memories of the Union Cause in Iowa, 1865–1916," *Annals of Iowa* 74 (2015), 221–62, and Gary W. Gallagher, *The Union War* (Cambridge: Harvard University Press, 2011).
34. Humke humorously recorded in MS, 15, that his company had more Germans fighting at Shiloh than had fought in the brief war against Denmark in 1849. Only once (using phonetic spelling) did he reproduce

a few comments spoken in dialect: e.g., writing *Ik* for *Ich* and *nich* for *nicht* (MS, 34).

35. General Franz Sigel remained a personal favorite. But he respected the aforesaid McArthur, James McPherson ("a fine gentleman"), "unser Billi Shermann" [*sic*] and even gruff William "Old Rosy" Rosecrans for whom the Iowa troops showed special affection (MS, 38–40). Yet when recalling (MS, 66–67) the Meridian, Mississippi, expedition of early 1864, Humke excoriated vainglorious officers who sent men into harm's way.
36. Humke, MS, 60: *blaue Bohne*, slang for bullets.
37. Humke, MS, 76: on *"Jungen"* (boys) who were vulnerable.
38. The majority came from northern Germany and, like Humke, were born in villages where families toiled as small farmers and tenants.
39. According to great-grandson Gene Humke, Carl never stopped complaining to family members about the primogeniture laws in Prussia.
40. Humke, MS, 68–69*ff*. One episode involved a Mississippi planter who had to be restrained by the Iowans who immediately "trained their rifles" on the slaveholder who was "brandishing a whip."
41. Humke, MS, 69. When recounting marches through Mississippi in 1864, he admitted: "I believe the black people [following Union armies] might have done better for themselves had they stayed where they were residing—at least for the present.... There were so many, they could not move quickly enough [and keep up] and many suffered from extreme hunger. It was reported that 7000 black people may have followed us." *Cf.* descriptions in Manning, *Troubled Refuge*, op cit.
42. Humke, MS, 26–27: recalling an episode when lost in Mississippi prior to the battle of Iuka (September 1862).
43. Humke, MS, 26. 31, 50–51, 67, 89. He did not employ racial slurs. His use of *"Neger"* was the German equivalent of writing "Negro" or "Black."
44. Humke, MS, notably pages 18–20, 26–28, 33–36, 50–55*ff*. Humke frequently complained, as might be expected, about the damp climate (p. 104): "Our clothes never became dry the entire time. Just imagine dear reader how cozy was this predicament we found ourselves in [!]. After that we were [doing our part] plundering and even rounding up and shooting livestock."
45. Described in Miller, "Adaptation and Survival in the Civil War."
46. Susan-Mary Grant, *North Over South. Northern Nationalism and American Identity in the Antebellum Era* (Lawrence, Ks.: University of Kansas Press, 2000), 161–62. Grant in *North Over South* emphasized how army service engendered broader outlooks. Similar interpretations have been offered by James McPherson, Peter Parish, Gary W. Gallagher, and Robert Cook, *op cit*.
47. Reinhart, *Yankee Dutchmen*, 82–83: major English-language papers in the upper Midwest were not silent. The *Chicago Tribune* and *Milwaukee Sentinel*

not infrequently defended German soldiers against attacks of the *New York Herald*.
48. Humke, MS, 122–23: especially when chosen one of Hancock County's tax collectors (and later working as census-taker).
49. *Schmelztiegel* was not commonly used prior to 1900, but the term was known during the 1850s. See Conzen, "German Americans and the Invention of Ethnicity," in *America and the Germans* 1, 131–47.
50. Luebke, *Bonds of Loyalty. German Americans and World War One* (DeKalb: Northern Illinois University Press, 1974), 26–51: contrasting "stomach Germans" with "soul Germans." The latter were intellectuals and religious idealists, while the former pursued their Germanity through daily habits and folkways.
51. Humke, MS, 38–40: Rosecrans praised the Iowa regiments for their courage at Iuka, and later offered rousing words during the battle of Corinth. Humke described officers' expressions of respect as they advanced on Atlanta during summer, 1864.
52. Humke, MS, 34: suggested when reverting to Low German dialect and reproducing speech of soldiers. Elsewhere he referenced music and dance as well as visits in Memphis to taverns that resembled German beer gardens.
53. David M. Potter, "The Historian's Use of Nationalism and Vice Versa, *The South and the Sectional Crisis* (Baton Rouge: Louisiana State University Press, 1968), 34–83. *Cf.* Conzen, "German Americans and the Invention of Ethnicity," in *America and the Germans* 1, 131–47; and Liah Greenfeld, *Nationalism. Five Roads to Modernity* (Cambridge, MA: Harvard University Press, 1992), esp. "Afterword," 487–91.
54. Expressions of loyalty countered Nativist attacks and sought greater toleration of cultural differences. See Carl Frederick Wittke, *The German-Language Press in America* (University of Kentucky Press, 1957; Haskell Reprint, 1957), esp. Chapter eight; and Engle on wartime identity in "Yankee Dutchmen," in Ural, ed., *Civil War Citizens*, 57–98.
55. Valuska and Keller, *Damn Dutch* (2004); and Hecker's responses included in Reinhart, ed., *Yankee Dutchmen under Fire: Civil War* (2013).
56. Carl Frederick Wittke, *The German-Language Press in America* (1957; Haskell Reprint, 1973), esp. 127–68, *passim.*: articles about the new German *Reich* steadily declined in frequency and number. Domestic news predominated.
57. Humke, MS, 110–12, 134–35: on Protestant devotional life in Illinois.
58. Humke, MS, 15. Yet no mention was made of Peter Osterhaus or Hecker.
59. Engle, "Yankee Dutchmen," in Ural, ed., *Civil War Citizens*, 42; and Wittke, *The German Language Press in America*, 148–68, *passim.*
60. See R.J. Ramsden, "Shaping History," *Wisconsin Magazine of History*, 28–43, and Engle, "Yankee Dutchmen," in Ural, ed., *Civil War Citizens*, 57–98.
61. Frustrations over national identifications (during 1850s) are found in *An Immigrant Miller Picks Texas. The Letters of Carl Hilmar Guenther*, trans. by

Regina B. Hurst and Walter D. Kamphoefner (San Antonio: Maverick Publ. Co, 2001), 23.
62. Higham cited in William L. Burton, *Melting Pot Soldiers* (Ames: Iowa State University Press, 1988), 224–25: e.g., the melting pot operated in other ways—as when smaller groups tended to "melt" into larger groups.
63. Germans in America supported unification. But their enthusiasm mostly derived from the dislike for France and Louis-Napoleon Bonaparte (Napoleon III).
64. Gleason, "Identifying Identity: A Semantic History," in *Speaking of Diversity. Language and Ethnicity in Twentieth-Century America* (1992), 123–49; see also Higham's interpretation of a "melting pot" in reverse in "Integrating America: The Problem of Assimilation at the Turn of the Century," in Carl J. Guarneri, ed., *Hanging Together. Unity and Diversity in American Culture* (2001), 85–99.
65. Business and political contacts led to work as a Hancock County tax-collector (from 1877) and census-taker (1880). Carl was officially listed as Charles Humke. T. Gregg, *History of Hancock County, Illinois* (Chicago: Chapman, 1880), 571.
66. Compare Marcus M. Spiegel's letters in *A Jewish Colonel in the Civil War*, edited by Jean Powers Soman and Frank L. Byrne (Lincoln: University of Nebraska Press, 1995; reprint of 1985 edition), esp. 114–15.
67. Humke may not have been heavily influenced by German- or English-language newspapers during the war. Later, he did read newspapers and some books. In his MS he twice referenced "Dr. Zimmermann," who was Gustav Adolf Zimmermann (1850–1903), a Chicago-based pastor, journalist, and historian who published several works, including *Deutsch in Amerika* (1892) and the encyclopedic *Vierhundert Jahre amerikanische Geschichte*, published in Milwaukee by George Brumder (1893). German newspapers were available (by 1900 nearly eighty German dailies remained in the United States). Davenport published *Der tägliche Demokrat*, which was, despite its name, a Republican paper and therefore congenial to Humke's politics. Nearby Keokuk could boast the *Keokuk Anzeiger* (later *Anzeiger-Post* after a merger in the 1890s). Popular were Chicago's *Illinois Staats-Zeitung* and Saint Louis' *Westliche Post*.
68. Humke, MS, 56: a "cease fire" in June 1863 near Vicksburg. "There were occasions when both sides along the entrenchments sat together [trading food and tobacco and] talking." He admitted exchanges were "strictly forbidden" because "Grant said he wanted to starve them out. And yet we did give them food to eat."
69. Humke, MS, 104–05.
70. Humke's captivity is described at length in Miller, "Adaptation and Survival in the Civil War."
71. Humke wrote: "The murderous cruelties inflicted by the southerners are difficult to believe unless you had been there and seen it." In these passages

(MS, 83-95, *passim.*) he wrote about his and others' commitment to the Union. Consult the study by William Marvel, *Andersonville: The Last Depot* (Chapel Hill: North Carolina University Press, 1994).

72. Humke, MS, 71-72, 82-85. Money enabled purchase of additional rations, wood for cooking, blankets, and even tobacco at the camp's "Market Street." His closest friends were five German soldiers with whom he generously shared money as they huddled in their dugout. Concealing "greenbacks" (paper currency) in boots and trousers was common. *Cf.* memoir of William H. Allen of the Seventeenth Iowa: "One Hundred and Ninety Days in Rebel Prisons," *Annals of Iowa* 38 (1966), 222-38.

73. MS, 97-98: on his ability to walk. Unknown to Humke was how Sherman insisted in his communications with "General Hoot" (*sic*—Hood) that only men who were not yet incapacitated be exchanged.

74. Humke, MS, 97-101: his three-year enlistment came to an end in November; but he may not have reenlisted even had his health been better. Furthermore, the Sixteenth Iowa Regiment already suffered heavy casualties. Of 1441 men who served, 323 were fatalities (two-thirds victims of disease). See *Roster and Record of Iowa Soldiers in the War of the Rebellion* (9th-16th Regiments, Infantry), vol. II (Des Moines, 1908), 1122.

75. Potter, "The Historian's Use of Nationalism and Vice Versa, *The South and the Sectional Crisis*, 48-54*ff*. Potter's analysis of multiple loyalties drew upon the work of Merle Curti, Harold Guetzkow, and Morton Grodzins. Similar appreciations were made by Conzen, "German Americans and the Invention of Ethnicity," in *America and the Germans* 1, 131-47.

76. Although cautious optimism is detectable in others' writings, Humke uttered fewer grievances, reported no ill-treatment (except at Andersonville), and offered judicious assessments of enlisted men and officers.

77. Traditional cultural life was mediated through churches and parish schools (Catholic and Protestant). According to Gene Humke, his great-grandfather donated to new church construction and its parsonage outside Sutter in 1922 (becoming in 1957 the Bethlehem United Church of Christ). He is buried in the nearby cemetery. The epitaph reads "Charles Humke." His wartime service is inscribed.

78. Humke, MS, 134-35: these words amounted to a postscript to his memoir.

79. Humke, MS, 122-23, on his efficiency as tax collector and local census-enumerator (1880). *Cf.* listings in *History of Hancock County, Illinois* (1880), 571.

80. Warsaw was more like neighboring Keokuk, Iowa, than the smaller community of Hamilton to the immediate north. By 1900 Warsaw had about 2000 residents, several schools, a mostly Protestant religious life, small shops, a brewery, and manufacturing.

81. MS, 106-35: on agriculture and business transactions.

82. Kathleen Neils Conzen, "Peasant Pioneers. Generational Succession among German Farmers in Frontier Minnesota," in Steven Hahn and Jonathan

Prude, eds., *The Countryside in the Age of Capitalist Transformation* (Chapel Hill: University of North Carolina, 1985), 259–92; and Sonya Salamon, *Prairie Patrimony. Family, Farming, and Community in the Midwest* (Chapel Hill: University of North Carolina, 1992).

83. Humke, MS, 121: on Hannah's insistence they not sell the farm.
84. Humke, MS, 112–34, *passim*.: on making improvements to farm.
85. Humke, MS, 126: on contract with hotel (likely the Estes House) in Keokuk. See R.J. Bickel, "The Estes House," *Annals of Iowa* 40, no. 6 (Fall 1970), 427–44.
86. Short of cash in the 1880s, Humke assisted his oldest son Gottlieb in purchasing land. The others directly benefited from land distributions. His children also married Germans and farmed as did many of the next generation.
87. Humke, MS, 106–33: on land purchases and efforts to reduce debts.
88. Had Humke rewritten his recollections in 1920 (instead of 1900–1910) he likely would have injected a pessimistic tone. Yet during the war (owing to farm prices), the Humke family experienced increases in farm income.
89. Higham, *Hanging Together*: "melting pot" and "Americanization" became popular terms only in the twentieth century.
90. See Gleason, "The Odd Couple: Pluralism and Assimilation," *Speaking of Diversity*, 47–90.

Jason Stacy | **Popucrats**
Producerist Populism and the Formation of Midwestern Political Identity in the 1890s

There was renewed interest in the political identity of the Midwest when Hillary Clinton's "blue wall" crumbled in 2016. In his thorough review of election, Jon K. Lauck notes that the unexpected confluence of rural and blue-collar midwestern voters, "some of whom lived in rural areas, but many of whom would be more closely associated with Midwestern industrial areas," represented, in sociologist Michael McQuarrie's words, a "regional revolt" where rural and working-class whites became a potent voting bloc. Salena Zito and Brad Todd, in *The Great Revolt: Inside the Populist Coalition Reshaping American Politics* (2018), claim that if the coalition of rural and blue-collar voters built by Trump in 2016 held, it had "the potential to realign the American political construct and perhaps the country's commercial and cultural presumptions as well."[1] According to a Public Religion Research Institute survey for *The Atlantic*, 33 percent of voting-age Americans were working class in 2016, but 43 percent of Midwesterners were.[2] In the year after the 2016 election, public discourse about the "heartland" and "fly-over country" turned on the idea of a "forgotten America" that united rural and working-class interests into the nation's aggrieved political epicenter.[3]

This essay does not attempt to determine whether the election of 2016 was a replay of the election of 1896, where the People's Party and the Democrats sought to build a similar urban-rural coalition of the discontented. However, it recognizes a recurring perception of the Midwest as the place where a populist synthesis of working-class and rural resentment, based in a producerist ethos, naturally happens. From this angle, the election of 2016 inspires meditation on the election of 1896 since in both cases politicians and prognosticators saw the "fusion" of those who worked factory and farm as a potent political identity for their times. In this regard, Democrats who supported Bryan in 1896 depended upon the long-standing economic integration of agriculture and industry in the Midwest to forge, rhetorically at least, a voter who represented the interests of all producers. This chapter explores the midwestern origins of this political identity, which, in 1896, temporarily took over one party and sought to defeat the other.

Most historians recognize the significance of the Midwest to the fusion of Populist ideology, industrial activism, and the Democratic Party in 1896. For Robert Durden, the Populist nomination of Bryan was the culmination of agrarian politics in the second half of the nineteenth century, "consistent with their principles ... [and] essential if the party was to remain national in scope." For Durden, the nomination of Bryan represented the "climax of Populism" and "the time of its greatest significance in American history."[4] Lawrence Goodwyn takes a less sanguine approach to the election of 1896 and interprets the "fierce internal struggle within the People's Party" as "a contest between ... political office-seekers on the one hand and the Populist movement on the other."[5] While Goodwyn recognizes the significance of Midwesterners like Henry Demarest Lloyd and Clarence Darrow to the fusion of labor and agrarian politics before 1896, his emphasis is not on the way in which this fusion depended upon a newly formed political identity particular to the Midwest. And while Daniel Nelson, in *Farm and Factory: Workers in the Midwest, 1880–1990* (1995), gives two-thirds of his first chapter to both farmers and industrial workers, he has little to say about attempts at political integration between these two groups in the Midwest during the mid 1880s and 1890s.[6] Charles Postel makes the strongest case for the early admixture of industrial and agricultural reformers, especially in the Midwest and West.[7] Postel helpfully notes that the Populists always had a strong fusionist undercurrent, whether it was with "fusion agreements [between] Democrats and Republicans at the state and local levels," or laborers "of the Midwest and West, [who] ... overcame their reservations about farmers to make political agreements with the rural Populists."[8] It is in this spirit that this chapter explores a nineteenth-century attempt at the political integration of workers and farmers under the Populist-Democratic banner in 1896 and claims its particularly midwestern origins.

The fusion of urban and rural workers had roots in the political economics of "producerism," whose legacy traces back to the middle of the seventeenth century in England.[9] According to Robert Asher, producerism broadly underpinned a "sense of [laborers'] worth" in opposition to, variously, aristocrats, capitalists, bankers, and managers who were the "nonproducing predators whose wealth and power were amassed by robbing producers."[10] As Asher notes, producerism for steel and ironworkers in the late nineteenth century allowed for the political economics of unity with other industrial workers, while simultaneously eliding the divisions of race, gender, ethnicity, and class within the working class itself. This chapter extends Asher's characterization of producerism as a potent ideology for inter-class unity by analyzing the politics of fusion between farm and factory in the Midwest, where regional activists advanced reform policies for agricultural and industrial workers in the 1890s.

William Cronon's *Nature's Metropolis: Chicago and the Great West* (1991) also serves as a useful model for this argument. While Cronon is primarily interested in the integration of the burgeoning industrial hub Chicago, the agricultural hinterlands of Illinois, and the greater Midwest, his charge against historians who "see city and country as separate places" and "rarely reflect on how tightly bound together they really are" reminds us that Americans in the nineteenth century were acutely aware of the continuing integration of urban and rural economies. For Cronon, the transformation of the Midwest from frontier region to economic center forms a "unified narrative" where "city and country have a common history" whose "stories are best told together."[11]

Populist activists recognized the power of a farm-factory fusion one hundred years before Cronon. For example, in 1889, the "National Farmers' Alliance and Industrial Union" (a newly formed conglomerate of state-level southern alliances) and the "National Farmers' Alliance" (representing midwestern alliances) unsuccessfully sought national unity among agricultural, industrial, and regional constituencies.[12] Likewise, Indianan Herman Taubeneck, the first national chairman of the People's Party, built a strategy for the success of his newly formed third party on such a producerist fusion. According to Peter H. Argersinger, Taubeneck recognized that the advent of the People's Party in the early 1890s came amid the backdrop of rising labor and farmer activism and, by the 1880s, conceived a unity of factory and farm laborers as the germ of a new party.[13] By the 1890s, Taubeneck's vision for third-party success depended upon the dissatisfaction of members of mainstream parties, what Taubeneck called the "building material," for third-party success. This made populist victories in largely agricultural states like Iowa difficult, since both major parties appealed to farmers' interests. Likewise, in urban areas like Chicago, Democrats endorsed elements of labor ideology and thereby siphoned worker support for third-party alternatives. Therefore, to pull dissatisfied voters away from the major two parties, Taubeneck argued that a national third party needed to exploit dissatisfaction with government policies generally, and portray the major two parties as handmaidens of bad policy toward producers. With this strategy, Taubeneck sought to construct a crucible of farmer-worker grievances and form a coalition of ire aimed at the political establishment itself.[14] The Midwest in general, and Illinois in particular in the 1890s, with its farms and factories in relative proximity to each other, provided the ideal staging ground for Taubeneck's raid on self-identified producers in each party. Populist-leaning Democrats like Kansan David Overmyer had already melded the grievances of workers and farmers: "[we have] seen the independent, self-respecting mechanic pass away ... [and] the machine take the place of the *man,* and money take the place of *manhood*.... The land pirates have ... seized the great marts to which the farmers' produce must go, and thus ... they dismiss the bewildered farmer ... with the bland assurance that all things go by the great law of supply and demand."[15] While Taubeneck's Populists tried to nominate Overmyer to run on the People's Party ticket for Congress in 1892 to no avail, Overmyer's rhetorical positioning marked the political potential of Taubeneck's fusion of midwestern industrial and agricultural laborers under the banner of a single party.[16]

Midwestern activists like Clarence Darrow and Henry Demarest Lloyd found a fusion of farm-factory producerism appealing during the same period. Lloyd, though born in New York City, began his career at the *Chicago Tribune* in the 1870s and wrote an early muckraking analysis of the Standard Oil Company in 1881 where he exposed, among other things, the adverse effects of the company on the American farmer.[17] Darrow, born in Kinsman, Ohio, proved a contrarian from youth, traveling in 1880 the five hundred miles from Kinsman to Harvard,

Illinois, to hear a speech on evolution and its challenge to popular religion.[18] In 1887, Darrow moved permanently to Chicago and, inspired by Henry George's *Progress and Poverty* and John Peter Altgeld's *Our Penal Machinery and Its Victims*, joined George's Single Tax Club.[19] Under the patronage of Altgeld, Darrow, now a lawyer, took a position in the mayor's office as an assessment attorney and later assistant corporation counsel. By 1889, he had been promoted to corporation counsel, where he defended the city's interests on behalf of Mayor De Witt Cregier. After the Cregier administration was voted out of office, Darrow, again with Altgeld's assistance, accepted a position as a lawyer for the Chicago North Western Railroad in 1891.[20] Darrow, however, was never entirely settled in his role as corporate lawyer and wrote to Henry Demarest Lloyd upon hearing a speech Lloyd made against a police raid on a labor meeting, "your speech ... made me feel that I am a hypocrite & a slave and added to my resolution to make my time of servitude short."[21] Darrow resigned from the Chicago North Western Rail Road in 1893.

As early as 1892, Darrow was giving speeches on behalf of midwestern Democratic candidates that sought to meld working-class and agricultural grievances into a singular producer's identity. While the tariff debate had raged since the 1830s, the election of 1892 proved especially challenging to Democrats since the newly formed People's Party platform of the free coinage of silver threatened to pull votes from the party's traditional constituents and the McKinley Tariff of 1890 proved popular to voters in Illinois who perceived protectionism as a means to keep prices on foreign goods higher than on locally produced goods. In a speech on behalf of Democrats in Decatur, Illinois, Darrow argued for the common interests of farmers and laborers. Decatur was an ideal location for this argument since, by the early 1890s, the city had become an important transportation and industrial hub for central Illinois, as well as a center for agricultural distribution in the state.[22] According to Darrow, "to say that labor needs protection is an insult and to say that it ever had protection is a lie. All it needs is a place to work." And in his appeal to farmers, he said, "[The farmer] gets just what they will give there [in England] and he must take free trade money in payment. The United States does not allow him to buy there and bring back free trade goods.... Consequently, the farmer comes and pays $2 for what he should pay $1."[23] Foreshadowing William Jennings

Bryan's speech at Chicago four years later, Darrow argued, "This town is dependent on farmers. Take them away and Chicago would disappear as it did before the fire."[24] Though Darrow's defense of Eugene Debs after the Pullman Strike is popularly remembered as the beginning of his legacy as a defense attorney for producers against capital, by 1892 Darrow had already positioned himself to capitalize on the fusion of labor and farmer interests in the Midwest.[25]

After 1892, Lloyd and Darrow sought to build an agricultural-labor alliance in the Midwest within Taubeneck's People's Party. Lloyd ran for Congress on the People's Party ticket in 1894 while Darrow served as a delegate to a convention of Populists and labor advocates in Springfield, Illinois, in May 1894 to consolidate the political power of "urban industrialists and agriculturalists in one harmonious political party."[26] Representatives from the Farmers' Mutual Benefit Association, the Farmers' Alliance and Industrial Union, Industrial Legion, Knights of Labor, Social Labor Party, and the Federation of Labor attended the convention, and Lloyd and Darrow drafted a five-point program that "linked ... the political and economic desires of urban and rural workers" by urging members of the convention to "pledge themselves to the principle of collective ownership by the people of all such means of production and distribution as the people elect to operate for the commonwealth."[27] That same year Darrow campaigned for the People's Party in a series of speeches that took inspiration from Taubeneck's strategy of exposing the shortcomings of both major political parties:

> It is never too late for us to change our political associations.... Yet there are those so contented with themselves they close their eyes to the condition of their fellow-men. The two great political parties ... have deceived the people by false issues such as the currency and tariff.[28]

After the defeat of the People's Party in the 1894 midterm elections, Darrow and Lloyd fell out over the Illinois convention's advocacy of collective ownership of the means of production.[29] While Darrow admitted he was sympathetic to the argument that private property was the root of social injustice, he pinned the midterm defeats that year on the socialist proposals in the party platform: "I think it was done too much in the last campaign ... such was antagonistic to the large portion of the party."³⁰ Darrow perhaps realized that Lloyd's socialist rhetoric proved distasteful to Illinois farmers, many of whom were more prosperous than farmers on the Great Plains. After 1895, Darrow sought a reform position that more broadly tried to pull rural and agricultural midwestern voters to the Democrats.

The Populists' disappointing results in the midterm election of 1894 exposed the fissures between the more socialistic wing of the party who appealed to industrial-urban laborers, represented by Henry Lloyd, and the more traditional wing of the party, which represented agricultural-rural interests and sought redress through reform of the monetary system. In the aftermath of the Pullman strike and his conflict with the Cleveland administration, Democratic Governor Altgeld added Cleveland's support for sound money policies to his list of grievances with the president. At the People's Party convention in February 1895, Darrow sided with Altgeld in favor of the free coinage of silver and effectively left the People's Party in favor of Altgeld's fusion of Populist-infused Democratic politics. That same year, Governor Altgeld positioned Darrow to run as a Democrat for Congress representing a relatively safe district in Chicago, thereby sealing Darrow's shift back to the Democrats.³¹ According to Darrow biographer Andrew E. Kersten, Altgeld, in the aftermath of his controversial pardoning of three of the Haymarket Riot strikers and his lambasting of President Cleveland during the Pullman Strike, tried to draw Populist votes away from the People's Party to the Democratic ticket. In this regard, Altgeld used bi-metalism as a wedge to split Populists from socialist reformers and thereby overcome his liability among downstate voters for his seemingly radical positions in the aftermath of the Haymarket Affair and the Pullman Strike.

By the summer of 1896, Herman Taubeneck realized the shift of many midwestern Democrats toward the platform of bi-metalism threatened a core People's Party issue and argued against trusting either mainstream party: "the [People's] party cannot indorse [sic] a candidate for president who has not severed his affiliations with the old political parties."³² Pro-silver midwestern Democrats like Darrow and Altgeld first placed their hopes on the silverite Democratic Representative Richard "Silver Dick" Bland of Lebanon, Missouri.³³ However, when, at the party convention in Chicago in 1896, Williams Jennings Bryan swayed the delegates with his famous "Cross of Gold" speech from the convention rostrum, Darrow and Altgeld fell in with the will of the majority. According to Lawrence Goodwyn, in the aftermath of Bryan's nomination, Taubeneck's "fusion strategy came apart completely" as the attempt to pull reform-minded agriculturalists and workers from the mainstream sunk under the compelling weight of a major party adopting a core populist issue.[34] Taubeneck warned that Democrats would eschew other Populist goals for the sake of party unity and the Democratic Convention proved him correct by nominating Arthur Sewall, New England banker and transportation mogul (though a supporter of the free coinage of silver).[35] Nevertheless, Bryan's nomination at the 1896 Democratic convention proved a watershed for the party, where Democrats shifted from their post-war defensive crouch and the seemingly anti-labor stance of the Cleveland administration to an activist platform that took its cue from the fusionist rhetoric of the People's Party from four years previous. Bryan, himself an Illinoisan who settled in Nebraska, led the break with the policies of Democratic President Grover Cleveland.[36]

The Illinois poet Edgar Lee Masters's memory of the 1896 campaign proves illustrative of the excitement the fusion of midwestern producers inspired in some Democrats, and also the campaign's liabilities in appealing to Midwesterners generally. Masters had been raised by a Menard County state's attorney whose father had justified his support for the Democratic Party of Jackson as the inheritor of the Jeffersonian agrarian tradition, another legacy of a producerist ethos. At the Chicago convention, Masters and his father assured each other that Bryan "would sweep the country" and make it possible for regular Americans to take the country back from "banks and syndicates" who had controlled the country and "robbed the people." William Jennings Bryan, for Masters, was Andrew Jackson reborn and would smash eastern elites and save the country from economic exploitation.[37] In this regard, midwestern Democrats like Bryan, Altgeld, and Darrow used Taubeneck's political strategy of attacking mainstream politics as a means to unite a producerist movement but, in this case, grafted midwestern agricultural and labor interests onto a new Democratic political identity. Masters summed up the enthusiasm among Bryan's Democrats: "A new life had come ... to the Democracy."[38] Whereas Taubeneck imagined the gravity of aggrieved interests pulling from both the Democrats and Republicans to form a new political force, producerist Democrats in 1896 mastered the same strategy at the expense of the People's Party. Even Taubeneck's choice for the People's Party nominee, Henry M. Teller, came out in support of a populist fusion with the Democrats.[39] This created a dilemma for the People's Party in the summer of 1896. At their St. Louis convention in July that year, the delegates nominated Bryan but, in lieu of the silverite capitalist Arthur Sewall, nominated veteran Populist Tom Watson of Georgia for vice president.

But the producerist tickets of the Populists and the Democrats suffered from a latent antipathy among midwestern voters unforeseen by politicos as they negotiated the Bryan candidacy in Chicago and St. Louis that year: the reputation of radical politics left over from the 1894 campaign. This proved to be a convenient counterargument for the Republicans, who exploited the more radical positions of producerist Democrats like Altgeld and Darrow and countered Bryan's evangelistic style with support from the pulpit.[40] Chicago pastor Frank W. Gunsaulus summed up the moral counterargument to Bryan late in the summer of 1896:

> Let none suppose that Mr. Bryan's metaphors have exhausted the Bible.... The coin is a sacred emblem in which the moral ideal of people may be found. If you will open the book of Deuteronomy you will find more sound financial philosophy than ... the double-standard associations.... "Thou shalt not have in thy bag different weights, a great and a small..." The people spoke at [the Republican National Convention in] St. Louis ... [and] simply registered the will of the mine and the work bench, the manufactory and the counting room, the farm and the village, the patriotism and hope of the republic, and nominated William McKinley for president.[41]

Likewise, Reverend Thomas Dixon titled an anti-silver sermon "Thou Shall Not Steal" and Reverend A.J.F. Behrends argued "such a doctrine leads on the trail of anarchy." Reverend Cortland Myers went so far as to claim that "Altgeld and his comrades were the stenographers of his Satanic Majesty."[42] The Republican press echoed these arguments. The *McHenry Plaindealer,* of McHenry, Illinois, claimed, "No laboring man who has a true conception of his own interests will vote the Bryan-Altgeld-Anarchist ticket."[43] Bryan defended himself against these attacks by accusing his critics of similarly nefarious ends: "When I hear a man talking about sound money without telling you what he means by it ... I am afraid it is because his deeds are evil."[44] Nevertheless, when Edgar Lee Masters went home to Petersburg, Illinois, to campaign for Bryan, he found his hometown antagonistic toward Bryan. After he gave a speech in favor of the Democrat, his grandfather told him that he planned to vote for the Prohibitionist ticket instead. His uncle called Bryan an "anarchist" for his support from Illinois Governor Altgeld who was "no better than a murderer." Even a hired hand that worked for Masters's grandfather dismissed Bryan on the argument that the free coinage of silver would cheapen the few dollars he made. Masters returned to Chicago "considerably dispirited."[45]

Richard Jensen claims that the key to Republican success in the Midwest that year was McKinley's (and his campaign impresario, Mark Hanna's) "offering pluralism to the American people."

> Every occupation, every religion, every industry, every section would receive fair treatment with the protective tariff serving as the umbrella for all. Cooperation and compromise, within the framework of sound economics, would be McKinley's principles.[46]

Jensen's statistical analysis bears out the scope of McKinley's victory, if not his explanation. The Republican Party saw gains throughout Illinois, for example, of between 5.6 and 14.7 percentage points in medium-sized cities between 1892 and 1896.[47] Republicans saw similar gains in midwestern coal-mining towns during the same period.[48] Likewise, among the six ethnic groups in Chicago Jensen analyzed, only the Irish did not vote overwhelmingly for McKinley that year.[49] From Norwegian settlements in Wisconsin to residents of Michigan's Upper Peninsula, from industrialized Milwaukee to predominantly German counties in rural Iowa, the Republicans carried election day in 1896.[50] Jensen's argument for the political potency of McKinley's "pluralism" is appealing considering the broad swath McKinley cut across the Midwest's economic, geographic, and ethnic lines. Indeed, McKinley's later promise of a "full dinner pail" for every American drew from the producerist image of the common voter. R. Hal Williams agrees with Jensen's appraisal and notes that McKinley undermined Bryan's overture to factory and farm in the Midwest by highlighting the underlying class warfare and sectional divisiveness that shaped Populist-Democratic rhetoric in the campaign. Instead, McKinley offered

> broad, positive programs in which everyone could share. United, the nation could turn with renewed vigor to the critical tasks at hand, a process in which farmers, laborers, and manufacturers—city and country, East and West, natives and foreign-born—all had vital roles to play.[51]

According to Richard Jensen, McKinley's victory

> quickly set the tone for ... midwestern politics ... [that favored] pragmatic solutions, based on the wisdom of many groups [and] facilitated the entry of new groups into American politics, [finally leading] to the ... triumph of pluralism in the New Deal [where] Franklin Roosevelt perfected McKinley's strategy of inclusive pluralism by giving practically every major economic, ethnic, cultural, and regional interest group ... recognition.[52]

In this light, the ultimate fusion of farm and factory was achieved not by producerist populism in 1896, but by pro-business Republicans. In hindsight, the Populist strategy to fuse rural and urban Midwesterners through producerist arguments lay dormant until the late twentieth century. While states like Illinois increasingly divided politically between industrial, rural, and later, suburban regions, often splitting along party lines in the twentieth century, the descendants of Jensen's "new groups" gradually positioned themselves within a revised midwestern producerist identity, beginning with "Reagan Democrats," a term coined by Stanley Greenburg in his research on Macomb County, Michigan, after the election of 1984.[53] This new fusion of rural and working-class voters was leavened not with the rhetoric of pluralism, as Jensen would have it, but with the language of ethnic grievance and an antipathy toward government welfare. In this regard, Reagan Democrats united Masters's grandfather's suspicion of radical politics with the older grievances of producerism to form a potent political identity that continues to shape American politics. Not so unlike the Democrats in 1896, the Republican Party in 2016 appealed to Midwesterners to create a revived identity of so-called forgotten Americans, but with much greater success and for very different ends.

Notes

1. Jon K. Lauck, "Trump and the Midwest: Avenues of Midwestern Historiography," *Studies in Midwestern History* 3, no. 1 (January 2017): 10; Michael McQuarrie, "How the Rust Belt Delivered Trump the Presidency: A Deep Dive," *Newsweek*, 19 November 2016, quoted in Lauck, 11; Salena Zito, Brad Todd, *The Great Revolt: Inside the Populist Coalition Reshaping American Politics* (New York: Crown Forum, 2018), 3.
2. The survey defined white working-class adults as white, non-Hispanic, "with less than a 4-year college degree," and "an occupation that pays hourly or by the job and is not salaried." Robert P. Jones and Daniel Cox, "Beyond Guns and God: Understanding the Complexity of the White Working Class in America." PRRI. 2012. http://www.prri.org/research/race-class-culture-survey-2012/; Robert P. Jones, Daniel Cox, and Rachel Lienesch, "Beyond Economics: Fears of Cultural Displacement Pushed the White Working Class to Trump | PRRI/*The Atlantic* Report." PRRI. 2017 [accessed 25 October 2018].
3. Nelson D. Schwartz and Julie Creswell, "A Global Chill in Commodity Hits America's Heartland," *New York Times*, 23 October 2015 [accessed 25 October 2018]; Silvia Ascarelli, "These 'flyover states' boast some of America's Best Downtowns," *MarketWatch*, 6 March 2015 [accessed 25 October 2018]; Peter Bella, "Forgotten American elected Donald Trump," *Interesting Chicago*, 14 November 2016, [accessed 25 October 2018].
4. Robert F. Durden, *The Climax of Populism: The Election of 1896* (Westport, Connecticut: Greenwood Press, 1965), ix.
5. Lawrence Goodwyn, *Democratic Promise: The Populist Movement in America* (New York: Oxford University Press, 1976), 426–27.
6. Daniel Nelson, *Farm and Factory: Workers in the Midwest, 1880–1990* (Bloomington: Indiana University Press, 1995), 3–47.
7. Charles Postel, *The Populist Vision* (Oxford: Oxford University Press, 2007), 207.
8. Postel, *The Populist Vision*, 272, 206.

9. Robert Asher, "Producerism is Consciousness of Class: Ironworkers' and Steelworkers' Views on Political Economy, 1894–1920, in Kevin Boyle, ed., *Organized Labor and American Politics, 1894–1994* (Albany: State University of New York Press, 1998), 51.
10. Ibid.
11. William Cronon, *Nature's Metropolis: Chicago and the Great West* (New York: W.W. Norton & Company, 1991), xvi.
12. Herman Clarence Nixon, "The Cleavage Within the Farmers' Alliance Movement," *The Mississippi Valley Historical Review* 15, no. 1 (June 1928), 22; Andrew E. Kersten, *Clarence Darrow: American Iconoclast* (New York: Hill and Wang, 2011), 78.
13. Peter H. Argersinger, "Taubeneck's Laws: Third Parties in American Politics in the Late Nineteenth-Century," *American Nineteenth Century History* 3, no. 2 (Summer 2002). Also see Chester McArthur Destler, "Consummation of a Labor-Populist Alliance in Illinois, 1894," *The Mississippi Valley Historical Review* 27, no. 4 (March 1941): 594.
14. Argersinger, "Taubeneck's Laws," 93–98.
15. David Overmyer, "The Future of the Democratic Party: A Reply," *The Arena* 18, no. 94 (September 1894): 302–03.
16. For Overmyer's refusal to caucus with the People's Party, see the *Kansas State Journal*, 18 June 1892, and "Overmyer Solid as a Rock," *The Kansas Democrat*, 18 July 1892, 2.
17. Henry Demarest Lloyd, "The Story of the Great Monopoly," *The Atlantic*, March 1881.
18. Andrew E. Kersten, *Clarence Darrow: American Iconoclast* (New York: Hill and Wang, 2011), 22.
19. Ibid., 28–32, 42.
20. Ibid., *Clarence Darrow*, 44.
21. Clarence Darrow, "To Henry Demarest Lloyd, Chicago, Monday, 28 December 1891," Randall Tietjen, ed., *In the Clutches of the Law, Clarence Darrow's Letters* (Berkeley: University of California Press), 65.
22. *History of Decatur, Illinois* (Cleveland, OH: Wiggins and Co.), 11, 14.
23. *Decatur Daily Republican*, 24 October 1892, 2.
24. "Scott and Darrow. Democrats Meet Last Night," *The Decatur Herald and Review*, 23 October 1892, 6.
25. Altgeld had supported labor rights from within the Democratic Party since the 1880s, advocating for labor reform, defending the accused strikers in the Haymarket riot, and, later, lambasting President Grover Cleveland for breaking up the Pullman strike by force. See *"Eagle Forgotten": The Life of John Peter Altgeld* (Indianapolis: Bobbs-Merrill Co., 1938).
26. Chester McArthur Destler, *American Radicalism, 1865–1901, Essays and Documents* (New London, CT: Connecticut College, 1946), 169.

27. Kersten, *Clarence Darrow*, 79; "Populists Plan to Enlist All Third Party Organizations," *Chicago Tribune*, 29 May 1894, 2; Willis J. Abbot, "The Chicago Populist Campaign," *The Arena* 11, no. 63 (February 1895): 331.
28. "Pops Out in Force," *Chicago Tribune*, 20 October 1894, 2.
29. Kersten, *Clarence Darrow*, 81.
30. Clarence Darrow, "To Henry Demarest Lloyd, Chicago, Monday, 24 November 1894," Randall Tietjen, ed., *In the Clutches of the Law, Clarence Darrow's Letters* (Berkeley: University of California Press), 73.
31. Kersten, *Clarence Darrow*, 82–84.
32. Herman Taubeneck, "Populists Demand Teller," *New York Tribune*, 8 July 1896, 3.
33. For sympathetic memorials of Bland's life, see *Memorial Addresses on the Life and Character of Richard P. Bland (Late a Representative from Missouri), Delivered in the House of Representatives and Senate*, Washington, 1900.
34. Goodwyn, *Democratic Promise*, 470.
35. Taubeneck, *New York Tribune*, 8 July 1896, 3; Goodwyn, *Democratic Promise*, 477.
36. Michael Kazin, *A Godly Hero: The Life of William Jennings Bryan* (New York: Anchor Books, 2007), 55.
37. Edgar Lee Masters, *Across Spoon River* (New York: The MacMillan Company, 1921), 209–12.
38. Ibid., 209.
39. Durden, *The Climax of Populism*, 24.
40. Richard Jensen, *Winning the Midwest: Social and Political Conflict, 1888–1896* (Chicago: The University of Chicago Press, 1971), 284.
41. Frank W. Gunsaulus, "Dr. Gunsaulus Urges Republicanism at Plymouth, Begins with Gospel, Says the Bible Supports the McKinley Standard," *The Inter Ocean*, 21 August 1896, 10.
42. "Ministers Denounce Silverites," *Lebanon Semi-Weekly News* (Lebanon, PA), 21 September 1896, 2.
43. *The McHenry Plaindealer*, 28 October 1896, 4.
44. "Crowd Fears a Panic," *Chicago Tribune*, 30 August 1896, 4.
45. Masters, *Across Spoon River*, 212.
46. Jensen, *Winning the Midwest*, 291.
47. Ibid., 302.
48. Ibid., 257.
49. "Old stock," Germans, Irish, Scandinavian, British, "Other," Jensen, *Winning the Midwest*, 298.
50. Jensen, *Winning the Midwest*, 144, 228, 128, 97.
51. R. Hal Williams, *Realigning America: McKinley, Bryan, and the Remarkable Election of 1896* (Lawrence, KS: University Press of Kansas, 2010), 145.
52. Jensen, *Winning the Midwest*, 308.
53. David A. Schultz, Rafael Jacob, *Presidential Swing States* (Lanham, MD: Lexington Books), 253.

Contributors

Christa Adams, PhD, is Assistant Professor of History at Bard Early College in Cleveland, Ohio, where she teaches courses in modern United States and East Asian history. Her work examines the methods of acquisition adopted by curatorial staff at the Cleveland Museum of Art, and at other midwestern art museums, in the early twentieth century. Current research interests include evaluating changing popular perceptions of East Asian art in early-twentieth-century America and analyzing processes of collection and presentation of East Asian art objects and antiquities in both private and public collections in the United States.

Brie Swenson Arnold is Whipple Associate Professor of History at Coe College, where she teaches early American, Civil War, African American, and women's history. She received a BA from Concordia College (MN) and MA and PhD degrees from the University of Minnesota. She has presented at the annual meetings of the Organization of American Historians, Western History Association, Northern Great Plains History Conference, and National Council on Public History and authored award-winning articles on antebellum political culture and postbellum black migration to the Midwest. She is an active public historian, collaborating with museums, community organizations, and state agencies on exhibits and historical markers.

Terry A. Barnhart is Professor Emeritus of History at Eastern Illinois University in Charleston. Barnhart's research and teaching interests include nineteenth-century U.S. intellectual and cultural history, American regionalism, research methods in American local history, historical interpretation for public audiences, and public history. He joined the faculty at EIU in 1994 and retired in 2018. Barnhart previously worked as an associate curator of history and director of special projects at the Ohio Historical Society in Columbus from 1983 to 1994 (today the Ohio History Connection). He received the doctorate in history from Miami University in Oxford, Ohio, in 1989.

Michael Leonard Cox is Associate Professor of History at San Diego Mesa College. He earned his PhD in Native American History at the University of California–Riverside, where his dissertation focused on the history of the Wyandot community of Northwestern Ohio from 1795 to 1843 in the context of cultural change, religious identities, and Indian removal. His research focuses on the intersections of race, religion, and identity in Native America in the eighteenth and nineteenth centuries.

Wayne Duerkes received his PhD from Iowa State University and continues to study midwestern rural societies in the antebellum period.

Sara Egge is the Claude D. Pottinger Professor of History at Centre College. She is the author of *Woman Suffrage and Citizenship in the Midwest, 1870–1920* (2018). It won the Benjamin F. Shambaugh Award for best book in Iowa history and the Gita Chaudhuri Prize for the best book on rural women's history. Among her recent publications is a chapter in *Equality at the Ballot Box: Votes for Women on the Northern Great Plains* (2019) and two articles in the *Middle West Review*. She received her PhD from Iowa State University and undergraduate degrees from North Dakota State University.

Nicole Etcheson is Alexander M. Bracken Professor of History at Ball State University. She is the author of *A Generation at War: The Civil War Era in a Northern Community* (which won the 2012 Avery O. Craven Award from the Organization of American Historians); *Bleeding Kansas* (2004); and *The Emerging Midwest* (1996). She is currently working on a project about suffrage in the post–Civil War era.

Edward O. Frantz is Professor of History at the University of Indianapolis. He is the author of *The Door of Hope: Republican Presidents and the First Southern Strategy, 1877–1933* and co-author, with John Mutz, of *An Examined Life: The John Mutz Story*. He teaches classes on midwestern history, civil rights history, and a variety of post–Civil War topics.

Contributors 397

Jacob K. Friefeld is the Illinois and Midwest studies research historian at the Abraham Lincoln Presidential Library and Museum. He earned his PhD at the University of Nebraska–Lincoln. He is the author (with coauthors) of *Homesteading the Plains: Toward a New History* (University of Nebraska Press, 2017). He is also the author or coauthor of several other articles, essays, and book reviews dealing with midwestern history.

A. James Fuller is Professor of History at the University of Indianapolis. He is a scholar of nineteenth-century America, especially the Civil War era. Among his many publications are seven books, including *Chaplain to the Confederacy: Basil Manly and Baptist Life in the Old South* (2000); *The Election of 1860 Reconsidered* (2012); *Oliver P. Morton and the Politics of the Civil War and Reconstruction* (2017), and *Morton, Marshall, McNutt, and Mitch: Four Governors Who Shaped Indiana and the Midwest* (forthcoming). Currently, he is writing a biography of Richard Yates, the Civil War governor and Reconstruction senator of Illinois.

Kenyon Gradert is a Postdoctoral Fellow in the Department of English at Auburn University.

Born and raised in Frankfort, Ohio, **Joshua Jeffers** received his PhD in history from Purdue University in 2014 where he specialized in Native American history and U.S. settler colonialism. His current book project, "From *Ohi'yo* to Ohio: Conceptual Landscapes and the Transformation of Ohio Country, 1729–1847," examines how beliefs about the Ohio landscape have shaped its history. He is also working on a chapter exploring the Blood Run mound complex and its relationship to the Great Pipestone Quarry for a forthcoming volume in the Rediscovering the American Midwest series. He currently teaches early American history at California State University–Dominguez Hills.

A native Hoosier, **Jason Lantzer** holds three degrees, all from Indiana University. His research and writing interests center on the intersection of religion, politics, and law in American history. He serves as the assistant director of the Butler University Honors Program and is the author of five books and numerous book chapters and articles, most of which center on the Midwest.

Contributors

Jon K. Lauck is the editor-in-chief of *Middle West Review*, based at the University of South Dakota. He is the author of several books, including *The Lost Region: Toward a Revival of Midwestern History* (University of Iowa Press) and *From Warm Center to Ragged Edge: The Erosion of Midwestern Literary and Historical Regionalism, 1920–1965* (University of Iowa Press).

A graduate of the University of California–Riverside, **David C. Miller** received his MA and PhD in History at the University of Kansas. Wanting to devote more time to research, Miller retired early from teaching full-time at Kansas City, Missouri's Longview College (of the Metropolitan Community College system). He has published in *The Catholic Historical Review* and *Catholic Library World*. He transcribed and translated Union veteran Carl Humke's unpublished recollections (*Erinnerungen*), which inspired the essay presented here. His article, "Adaptation and Survival in the Civil War," recently appeared in the *Journal of the Illinois State Historical Society* (Spring 2020).

Marcia Noe is Professor of English and Director of Women, Gender, and Sexuality Studies at The University of Tennessee at Chattanooga. She is the editor of *MidAmerica*, published by The Society for the Study of Midwestern Literature, and the author of *Susan Glaspell: Voice from the Heartland* and over twenty other publications on Pulitzer Prize–winning playwright Susan Glaspell.

C.A. Norling is a PhD student in historical musicology at the University of Iowa, where he studies a broad range of topics related to operatic dissemination, consumption, and reception. He is currently conducting dissertation research regarding the civic density of operatic cultures in interwar Chicago and maintains additional research interests in midwestern musical institutions. Norling received the National Opera Association's Leland Fox Scholarly Paper Award in 2016 for his work on indigenous depictions in Puccini's *La fanciulla del West*. In addition to recent talks for the Opera as Popular Culture and Society for American Music conferences, he was a guest speaker for the Des Moines Symphony's 2019/2020 season.

Contributors

Lisa Payne Ossian is Emerita Professor at Des Moines Area Community College and earned her women's studies master's at Eastern Michigan University and history doctorate at Iowa State University. Ossian has received grants from the Hoover Institution at Stanford, Truman Presidential Library, and Hoover Presidential Foundation. She edited *American Women's War Writings: A Near Century of Violence, 1852–1945*, and published three books with the University of Missouri Press: *The Home Fronts of Iowa, 1939–1945*; *The Forgotten Generation: American Children and World War II*; and *The Depression Dilemmas of Rural Iowa, 1929–1933*. She has presented papers at national and international conferences.

Barton E. Price holds a PhD in Religion from Florida State University, where he completed his dissertation "Evangelical Periodicals and the Making of the American Heartland, 1789–1900." He is a currently Lecturer at Purdue University Fort Wayne.

Eric Michael Rhodes is a fellow at Lamar University's Center for History and Culture of Southeast Texas and the Upper Gulf Coast and a researcher for the Deindustrialization and the Politics of Our Time project. After earning his MA from Miami University, Rhodes taught urban history at the University of Angers in France. His work has appeared in publications such as *The Middle West Review*, *New Jersey Studies*, and *Belt Magazine*. Rhodes is a book review editor at *The Metropole: The Official Blog of the Urban History Association*.

Gregory S. Rose is Dean and Director of The Ohio State University at Marion and Associate Professor of Geography. His bachelor's degrees in geography and history are from Valparaiso University in Indiana, his master's and doctorate degrees in geography from Michigan State University. His research area is the nineteenth-century Midwest. He has researched and published on birthplace origins and previous residences of immigrant populations using Census nativity data and genealogical records, their cultural impacts on the Midwest, the region's historical economic development, and definitions of the Midwest according to cultural elements, vernacular perceptions, agricultural areas, and the environment.

Michael J. Sherfy was born and raised in Southern Illinois. After graduating from Illinois State University, he earned his PhD in History and his master's in Library and Information Science from the University of Illinois in Urbana-Champaign, where he wrote his dissertation on historical memory and the Black Hawk War. He has worked for the University of Illinois, Ohio State University, Western Illinois University, the Newark Earthworks Center, and other institutions. He currently resides in Central Ohio, works at a public library, and teaches at North Central State College.

Jason Stacy is Professor of History and Social Science Pedagogy at Southern Illinois University–Edwardsville. His interests are in nineteenth-century U.S. history, with an emphasis on print culture, journalism, and literature. Stacy's authored and edited books include *Walt Whitman's Multitudes: Labor Reform and Persona in Whitman's Journalism and First Leaves of Grass* (2008), *Leaves of Grass, 1860: The 150th Anniversary Edition* (2010), and *Walt Whitman's Selected Journalism* (2015). His current book project, *Spoon River America: Edgar Lee Masters and the Myth of the American Small Town* (2021) is in production with University of Illinois Press.

www.ingramcontent.com/pod-product-compliance
Lightning Source LLC
Chambersburg PA
CBHW071950110526
44592CB00012B/1048